For the *SPSS Survival Manual* website, go to
www.mheducation.co.uk/SPSS

**This is what readers from around the world say about
the *SPSS Survival Manual*:**

'Whenever a student asks my advice on what textbook to use to help them with SPSS and statistical testing, it is always Julie Pallant's text that I pull off the shelf for them. This text is ideal for getting to the point of the test. What students find most useful are the sections providing examples of how to report the results. Personally, I am never without a copy of Pallant on my bookshelf: one at home and one at the office.' — **Dr Hazel Brown, Senior Lecturer, University of Winchester, UK**

'Julie Pallant is a saint and responsible for the successful graduation of hundreds and hundreds of students, including myself.' — **Kopitzee Parra-Thornton, PhD, St Joseph Health, US**

'Best book ever written. My ability to work the maze of statistics and my sanity has been SAVED by this book.' — **Natasha Davison, Doctorate of Health Psychology, Deakin University, Australia**

'One of the greatest advantages with the *SPSS Survival Manual* is the thought-through structure; it is therefore easy to apply, both for our teacher students writing their master theses and for PhD students and researchers more experienced with statistics.' — **Karolina Broman, Department of Science and Mathematics Education (NMD), Umeå University, Sweden**

'. . . highly recommended for both beginners and experienced SPSS users . . . an invaluable resource . . . SPSS is a powerful tool for data management and statistical analysis and this user-friendly book makes it very accessible.' — **Dr Polly Yeung, Aotearoa New Zealand Social Work**

'I just wanted to say how much I value Julie Pallant's *SPSS Survival Manual*. It's quite the best text on SPSS I've encountered and I recommend it to anyone who's listening!' — **Professor Carolyn Hicks, Health Sciences, Birmingham University, UK**

'. . . not everyone would greet the appearance of a book with the word "SPSS" in the title with a glad cry . . . [but] my experience with using earlier editions of this book has been very positive . . . Pallant's book would be an excellent investment for you.' — **Felicity Allen, Psychotherapy and Counselling Journal of Australia**

'This book was responsible for an A on our educational research project. This is the perfect book for people who are baffled by statistical analysis, but still have to understand and accomplish it.' — **Becky, Houston, Texas, US**

'This most recent edition of Julie Pallant's SPSS bible continues to combine a number of essential elements: clear explanations of different use cases for SPSS; guides on interpreting the (often voluminous and poorly labelled) output; and example data files (from real studies) to practice on . . . If I had PhD students, this would be their welcome gift on their first day. Essential.' — *Dr P.J.A. Wicks, Research Psychologist, London, UK*

'Having perceived myself as one who was not confident in anything statistical, I worked my way through the book and with each turn of the page gained more and more confidence until I was running off analyses with (almost) glee. I now enjoy using SPSS and this book is the reason for that.' — *Dr Marina Harvey, Centre for Professional Development, Macquarie University, Australia*

'This book really lives up to its name . . . I highly recommend this book to any MBA student carrying out a dissertation project, or anyone who needs some basic help with using SPSS and data analysis techniques.' — *Business student, UK*

'I wouldn't have survived my senior research project and class without this book! There's a reason they have a life preserver on the front cover.' — *Manda, goodreads.com*

'I must say how much I value the *SPSS Survival Manual.* It is so clearly written and helpful. I find myself using it constantly and also ask any students doing a thesis or dissertation to obtain a copy.' — *Associate Professor Sheri Bauman, Department of Educational Psychology, University of Arizona, US*

'This book is simple to understand, easy to read and very concise. Those who have a general fear or dislike for statistics or statistics and computers should enjoy reading this book.' — *Lloyd G. Waller PhD, Jamaica*

'There are several SPSS manuals published and this one really does "do what it says on the tin" . . . Whether you are a beginner doing your BSc or struggling with your PhD research (or beyond!), I wholeheartedly recommend this book.' — *British Journal of Occupational Therapy, UK*

'I love the *SPSS Survival Manual* . . . I can't imagine teaching without it. After seeing my copy and hearing me talk about it many of my other colleagues are also utilising it.' — *Wendy Close PhD, Psychology Department, Wisconsin Lutheran College, US*

'This book is a "must have" introduction to SPSS. Brilliant and highly recommended.' — *Dr Joe, South Africa*

'I didn't think it was possible for me to love SPSS but with the help of this book I do! The step-by-step guide is everything I need to use this difficult software. I would recommend it to anyone!' — *Alissa Johnston, Occupational Therapy student*

'I love this book! I haven't touched stats or SPSS in nearly fifteen years. This book told me everything I needed to know to do my job better with clear, concise language. It's like she knew what all my questions were before I asked them!' — *T. James, Australia*

'Pallant's excellent book has all the ingredients to take interested students, including the statistically naïve and the algebraically challenged, to a new level of skill and understanding.' — *Geoffrey N. Molloy, Behaviour Change journal*

'Not buying this manual would have been the biggest mistake of my academic experience.' — *Israel Katura James, Amazon.com*

'I have four SPSS manuals and have found that this is the only manual that explains the issues clearly and is easy to follow. SPSS is evil and anything that makes it less so is fabulous.' — *Helen Scott, Psychology Honours student, University of Queensland, Australia*

'To any students who have found themselves faced with the horror of SPSS when they had signed up for a degree in psychology—this is a godsend.' — *Psychology student, Ireland*

'This is the best SPSS manual I've had. It's comprehensive and easy to follow. I really enjoy it.' — *Norshidah Mohamed, Kuala Lumpur, Malaysia*

'I am now getting an A in my course, due in no small part to this book.' — *L.E. Eastman, doctoral statistcs student, US*

'As a PhD student, my biggest problem with SPSS (and statistics in general) was deciding which analytical technique would be suitable for my objective and type of data. I found all the answers I was looking for within 12 hours of owning this book!' — *P. Raf-D, Amazon.co.uk*

'Simply the best book on introductory SPSS that exists. I know nothing about the author but having bought this book in the middle of a statistics open assignment I can confidently say that I love her and want to marry her. There must be dozens of books that claim to be beginners' guides to SPSS. This one actually does what it says.' — *J. Sutherland, Amazon.co.uk*

JULIE PALLANT

SPSS

SURVIVAL MANUAL

A STEP BY STEP GUIDE TO DATA ANALYSIS USING IBM SPSS

7th
EDITION

Open University Press

Open University Press
McGraw-Hill Education
8th Floor, 338 Euston Road
London
England
NW1 3BH

and 1325 Avenue of the Americas, 5th Floor, New York, NY 10019, USA

First published 2001
Second edition published 2004
Third edition published 2007
Fourth edition published 2010
Fifth edition published 2013
Sixth edition published 2016
Seventh Edition Published 2020

Copyright © Julie Pallant, 2020
First published in Australia by Allen & Unwin in 2020.

Set in 11/13.5 pt Minion by Midland Typesetters, Australia

A catalogue record of this book is available from the British Library

ISBN-13: 9780335249497
ISBN-10: 0335249493
eISBN: 9780335249503

Library of Congress Cataloging-in-Publication Data
CIP data applied for

Typeset by Transforma Pvt. Ltd., Chennai, India

Contents

Preface

For many students, the thought of completing a statistics subject, or using statistics in their research, is a major source of stress and frustration. The aim of the original *SPSS Survival Manual* (published in 2000) was to provide a simple step-by-step guide to the process of data analysis using IBM SPSS Statistics. Unlike other statistical titles, it did not focus on the mathematical underpinnings of the techniques, but rather on the appropriate use of the program as a tool. Since the publication of the first *SPSS Survival Manual,* I have received many hundreds of emails from students who have been grateful for the helping hand (or lifeline).

The same simple approach has been incorporated in this seventh edition. Over the last decade SPSS has undergone many changes—including a brief period when it changed name. During 2009, Version 18 of the program was renamed **PASW Statistics** (Predictive Analytics Software). The name was changed again in 2010 to **IBM SPSS**, and the program is now referred to as **IBM SPSS Statistics**. Every year or two IBM makes changes to the program, the procedures and the output. All chapters in this current edition have been updated to match Version 26 of the IBM SPSS Statistics package (although most of the material is also suitable for users of earlier versions). Where possible, I have also incorporated suggested changes and improvements—a big thankyou to those of you who have sent me feedback. Special thanks to David Gow, a colleague from the Australian Consortium for Social and Political Research, for his thorough review and recommendations.

In this seventh edition I have:

- ➤ updated the output in all chapters to match that provided by IBM SPSS Statistics Version 26
- ➤ made changes to the interpretation of some of the output and presentation of results obtained from Multiple Regression (Chapter 13) and Logistic Regression (Chapter 14)
- ➤ changed the procedures used to calculate Wilcoxon Signed Rank Test and Friedman Test (Chapter 16)
- ➤ updated the procedure used for Analysis of Covariance (Chapter 22)

➤ added additional examples of how to display the results in table format for Multiple Regression (Chapter 13), T-tests (Chapter 17) and Analysis of Variance (Chapter 18).

I have resisted urges from students, instructors and reviewers to add too many extra topics, but instead have upgraded and expanded the existing material. This book is not intended to cover all possible statistical procedures available in IBM SPSS Statistics, or to answer all questions researchers might have about statistics. Instead, it is designed to get you started with your research and to help you gain confidence in the use of the program to analyse your data. There are many other excellent statistical texts available that you should refer to—suggestions are made throughout each chapter and in the Recommended Reading section at the end of the book. Keep an eye out for statistics texts written for your discipline area. Additional material is also available on the book's website (details in the next section).

Data files and website

Throughout this book, you will see examples of research that are taken from data files included on its accompanying website: **www.mheducation.co.uk/SPSS**. If you are an instructor, please email **enquiries@mheducation.com** and request the password for the instructor resources section. All other sections of the website are free to access. From this site you can download the data files to your hard drive or memory stick by following the instructions on screen. These files can only be opened in IBM SPSS Statistics.

The **survey.sav** data file is a 'real' data file, based on a research project that was conducted by one of my graduate diploma classes. So that you can get a feel for the research process from start to finish, I have also included in the Appendix a copy of part of the questionnaire that was used to generate these data and the codebook used to code the data. This will allow you to follow along with the analyses that are presented in the book, and to experiment further using other variables. The full questionnaire can be downloaded from the website.

The second data file, **error.sav**, is the same file as the **survey.sav**, but I have deliberately added some errors to give you practice in Chapter 5 at screening and cleaning your data file.

The third data file (**experim.sav**) is a manufactured (fake) data file, constructed and manipulated to illustrate the use of techniques covered in Part Five of the book (e.g. paired-samples t-test, repeated measures ANOVA). This file also includes additional variables that allow you to practise the skills learnt throughout the book. Just don't get too excited about the results you obtain and attempt to replicate them in your own research!

The fourth file (**manipulate.sav**) contains data extracted from hospital records which allows you to try using some of the IBM SPSS Statistics data manipulation procedures covered in Chapter 8, Manipulating the Data. This includes converting text data (Male, Female) to numbers (1, 2) that can be used in statistical analyses and manipulating dates to create new variables (e.g. length of time between two dates).

The fifth file used in the examples in the book is **depress.sav**. This is used in Chapter 16, on non-parametric techniques, to illustrate some techniques used in health and medical research.

Two other data files have been included, giving you the opportunity to complete some additional activities with data from different discipline areas. The **sleep.sav** file is a real data file from a study conducted to explore the prevalence and impact of sleep problems on aspects of people's lives. The **staffsurvey.sav** file comes from a Staff Satisfaction Survey conducted for a large national educational institution.

See the Appendix for further details of these files (and associated materials). Apart from the data files, the *SPSS Survival Manual* website also contains useful items for students and instructors, including:

➢ guidelines for preparing a research report
➢ practice exercises
➢ updates on changes to IBM SPSS Statistics as new versions are released
➢ useful links to other websites
➢ additional reading
➢ an instructor's guide.

Introduction and overview

This book is designed for students completing research design and statistics courses and for those involved in planning and executing research of their own. Hopefully, this guide will give you the confidence to tackle statistical analyses calmly and sensibly, or at least without too much stress!

Many of the problems that students experience with statistical analysis are due to anxiety and confusion from dealing with strange jargon, complex underlying theories and too many choices. Unfortunately, most statistics courses and textbooks encourage both of these sensations! In this book I try to translate statistics into a language that can be more easily understood and digested.

The *SPSS Survival Manual* is presented in a structured format, setting out step by step what you need to do to prepare and analyse your data. Think of your data as the raw ingredients in a recipe. You can choose to cook your ingredients in different ways—a first course, main course, dessert. Depending on what ingredients you have available, different options may, or may not, be suitable. (There is no point planning to make beef stroganoff if all you have available is chicken.) Planning and preparation are important parts of the process (both in cooking and in data analysis). Some things you need to consider are:

➢ Do you have the correct ingredients in the right amounts?
➢ What preparation is needed to get the ingredients ready to cook?
➢ What type of cooking approach will you use (boil, bake, stir-fry)?
➢ Do you have a picture in your mind of how the end result (e.g. chocolate cake) is supposed to look?
➢ How can you tell when it is cooked?
➢ Once it is cooked, how should you serve it so that it looks appetising?

The same questions apply equally well to the process of analysing your data. You must plan your experiment or survey so that it provides the information you need, in the correct format. You must prepare your data file properly and enter your data carefully. You should have a clear idea of your research questions and how you might go about addressing them. You need to know what statistical techniques are available, what sorts of variables are suitable and what are not. You must be able to perform your chosen statistical technique (e.g. t-test) correctly and interpret the output. Finally, you need to relate this output back to your original research question and know how to present this in your report (or, in cooking terms, should you serve your chocolate cake with cream or ice-cream, or perhaps some berries and a sprinkle of icing sugar on top?).

In both cooking and data analysis, you can't just throw all your ingredients in together, shove them in the oven (or IBM SPSS Statistics, as the case may be) and hope for the best. Hopefully, this book will help you understand the data analysis process a little better and give you the confidence and skills to be a better 'cook'.

STRUCTURE OF THIS BOOK

This *SPSS Survival Manual* consists of 22 chapters, covering the research process from designing a study through to the analysis of the data and presentation of the results. It is broken into five main parts. Part One (Getting Started) covers the preliminaries: designing a study, preparing a codebook and becoming familiar with IBM SPSS Statistics. In Part Two (Preparing the Data File) you are shown how to prepare a data file, enter your data and check for errors. Preliminary analyses are covered in Part Three, which includes chapters on the use of descriptive statistics and graphs, the manipulation of data and the procedures for checking the reliability of scales. You are also guided, step by step, through the sometimes difficult task of choosing which statistical technique is suitable for your data.

In Part Four the major statistical techniques that can be used to explore relationships are presented (i.e. correlation, partial correlation, multiple regression, logistic regression and factor analysis). These chapters summarise the purpose of each technique, the underlying assumptions, how to obtain results, how to interpret the output and how to present these results in your thesis or report.

Part Five discusses the statistical techniques that can be used to compare groups. These are non-parametric techniques, t-tests, analysis of variance, multivariate analysis of variance and analysis of covariance.

USING THIS BOOK

To use this book effectively as a guide to IBM SPSS Statistics, you need some basic computer skills. In the instructions and examples provided throughout the text I assume that you are already familiar with using a computer, particularly the Windows functions. You need to be able to open, save, rename and move files; create folders; use the left and right buttons on the mouse; and move between programs.

This book is not designed to stand alone. It is assumed that you have been exposed to the fundamentals of statistics and have access to a statistics text. It is important that you understand some of what goes on below the surface when using IBM SPSS Statistics. It is an extremely powerful data analysis package that can handle very complex statistical procedures. This manual does not attempt to cover all the different statistical techniques available in the program. Only the most commonly used statistics are covered. It is designed to get you started and to develop your confidence in using the program.

Depending on your research questions and your data, it may be necessary to tackle some of the more complex analyses available in IBM SPSS Statistics. There are many good books available covering the various statistical techniques in more detail. Read as widely as you can. Browse the shelves in your library, look for books that explain statistics in a language that you understand (well, at least some of it, anyway!). Collect this material together to form a resource to be used throughout your statistics classes and your research project. It is also useful to collect examples of journal articles where statistical analyses are explained and results presented. You can use these as models for your final write-up.

The *SPSS Survival Manual* is suitable for use both as an in-class text, where you have an instructor taking you through the various aspects of the research process, and as a self-instruction book for those conducting an individual research project. If you are teaching yourself, be sure to practise using IBM SPSS Statistics by analysing the data files that are included on the website accompanying this book (see p. ix for details). The best way to learn is by actually doing, rather than just reading. Play with the data files from which the examples in the book are taken before you start using your own data file. This will improve your confidence and also allow you to check that you are performing the analyses correctly.

Sometimes, you may find that the output you obtain is different from that presented in the book. This is likely to occur if you are using a different version of IBM SPSS Statistics from that used throughout this book (Version 26). IBM SPSS Statistics regularly updates its products, which is great in terms of improving the program, but it can lead to confusion for students who find that what is on the screen differs from what is in the book. Usually, the difference is not too dramatic, so stay calm and play detective. The information may be there but just in a different form. For information on changes to the IBM SPSS Statistics products you may like to go to the IBM SPSS Statistics website (www.spss.com).

RESEARCH TIPS

If you are using this book to guide you through your own research project, there are a few additional tips I would like to recommend.

➢ *Plan your project carefully.* Draw on existing theories and research to guide the design of your project. Know what you are trying to achieve and why.

➢ *Think ahead.* Anticipate potential problems and hiccups—every project has them! Know what statistics you intend to employ and use this information to guide the formulation of data collection materials. Make sure that you have the right sorts of data to use when you are ready to do your statistical analyses.

➢ *Get organised.* Keep careful notes of all relevant research, references etc. Work out an effective filing system for the mountain of journal articles you will acquire and, later on, the output from IBM SPSS Statistics. It is easy to become disorganised, overwhelmed and confused.

➢ *Keep good records.* When using IBM SPSS Statistics to conduct your analyses, keep careful records of what you do. I recommend to all my students that they keep a record of every session they spend on IBM SPSS Statistics. You should record the date, new variables you create, all analyses you perform and the names of the files where you have saved the output. If you have a problem or something goes horribly wrong with your data file, this information can be used by your supervisor to help rescue you!

➢ *Stay calm!* If this is your first exposure to IBM SPSS Statistics and data analysis, there may be times when you feel yourself becoming overwhelmed. Take some deep breaths and use some positive self-talk. Just take things step by step—give yourself permission to make mistakes and become confused sometimes. If it all gets too much then stop, take a walk and clear your head before you tackle it again. Most students find IBM SPSS Statistics quite easy to use once they get the hang of it. Like learning any new skill, you just need to get past that first feeling of confusion and lack of confidence.

➢ *Give yourself plenty of time.* The research process, particularly the data entry and data analysis stages, always takes longer than expected, so allow plenty of time for this.

➢ *Work with a friend.* Make use of other students for emotional and practical support during the data analysis process. Social support is a great buffer against stress!

PART ONE
Getting started

Data analysis is only one part of the research process. Before you can use IBM SPSS Statistics to analyse your data, there are several things that need to happen. First, you must design your study and choose appropriate data collection instruments. Once you have conducted your study, the information obtained needs to be prepared for entry into IBM SPSS Statistics using something called a 'codebook'. To enter the data you must understand how the program works and how to talk to it appropriately. Each of these steps is discussed in Part One.

Chapter 1 provides some tips and suggestions for designing a study, with the aim of obtaining good-quality data. Chapter 2 covers the preparation of a codebook to translate the information obtained from your study into a format suitable for IBM SPSS Statistics. Chapter 3 takes you on a guided tour of the program, and some of the basic skills that you need are discussed. If this is your first time using the program, it is important that you read the material presented in Chapter 3 before attempting any of the analyses presented later in the book.

PART ONE
Getting started

1
Designing a study

Although it might seem a bit strange to discuss research design in a book on IBM SPSS Statistics, it is an essential part of the research process that has implications for the quality of the data collected and analysed. The data you enter must come from somewhere—responses to a questionnaire, information collected from interviews, coded observations of behaviour or objective measurements of output or performance. The data are only as good as the instrument that you used to collect them and the research framework that guided their collection.

In this chapter various aspects of the research process are discussed that have an impact on the potential quality of the data. First, the overall design of the study is considered; this is followed by a discussion of some of the issues to consider when choosing scales and measures; and finally, some guidelines for preparing a questionnaire are presented.

PLANNING THE STUDY

Good research depends on the careful planning and execution of the study. There are many excellent books written on the topic of research design to help you with this process—from a review of the literature to formulation of hypotheses, choice of study design, selection and allocation of participants, recording of observations and collection of data. Decisions made at each of these stages can affect the quality of the data you have to analyse and the way you address your research questions. In designing your own study, I would recommend that you take your time working through the design process to make it the best study that you can produce. Reading a variety of texts on the topic will help. A few good, easy-to-follow titles are listed in the Recommended Reading section at the back of the book.

To get you started, consider these tips when designing your study:

➢ Consider what type of research design (e.g. experiment, survey, observation) is the best way to address your research question. There are advantages and disadvantages to all types of research approaches; choose the most appropriate approach for your particular research question. Have a good understanding of the research that has already been conducted in your topic area.

➢ If you choose to use an experiment, decide whether a between-groups design (different cases in each experimental condition) or a repeated measures design (same cases tested under all conditions) is the more appropriate for your research question. There are advantages and disadvantages to each approach, so weigh up each approach carefully.

➢ In experimental studies, make sure you include enough levels in your independent variable. Using only two levels (or groups) means fewer participants are required, but it limits the conclusions that you can draw. Is a control group necessary or desirable? Will the lack of control group limit the conclusions that you can draw?

➢ Always select more participants than you need, particularly if you are using a sample of humans. People are notoriously unreliable—they don't turn up when they are supposed to, and they get sick, drop out and don't fill out questionnaires properly! So plan accordingly. Err on the side of pessimism rather than optimism.

➢ In experimental studies, check that you have enough participants in each of your groups (and try to keep them equal when possible). With small groups, it is difficult to detect statistically significant differences between groups (an issue of power, discussed in the introduction to Part Five). There are calculations you can perform to determine the sample size that you need. See, e.g. Stangor (2006).

➢ Wherever possible, randomly assign participants to each of your experimental conditions, rather than using existing groups. This reduces the problem associated with non-equivalent groups in between-groups designs. Also worth considering is taking additional measurements of the groups to ensure that they don't differ substantially from one another. You may be able to statistically control for differences that you identify (e.g. using analysis of covariance).

➢ Choose appropriate dependent variables that are valid and reliable (see discussion on this point later in this chapter). It is a good idea to include a variety of measures—some measures are more sensitive than others. Don't put all your eggs in one basket.

➢ Try to anticipate the possible influence of extraneous or confounding variables. These are variables that could provide an alternative explanation for your results. Sometimes, they are hard to spot when you are immersed in designing the study yourself. Always have someone else (e.g. supervisor, fellow researcher) check over your design before conducting the study. Do whatever you can to control for these potential confounding variables. Knowing your topic area well can also help you identify possible confounding variables. If there are additional variables that you cannot control, can you measure them? By measuring them, you may be able to control for them statistically (e.g. using analysis of covariance).

➤ If you are distributing a survey, pilot-test it first to ensure that the instructions, questions and scale items are clear. Wherever possible, pilot-test on the same types of people who will be used in the main study (e.g. adolescents, unemployed youth, prison inmates). You need to ensure that your respondents can understand the survey or questionnaire items and respond appropriately. Pilot-testing should also pick up any questions or items that may offend potential respondents.

➤ If you are conducting an experiment, it is a good idea to have a full dress rehearsal and to pilot-test both the experimental manipulation and the dependent measures you intend to use. If you are using equipment, make sure it works properly. If you are using different experimenters or interviewers, make sure they are properly trained and know what to do. If different observers are required to rate behaviours, make sure they know how to appropriately code what they see. Have a practice run and check for inter-rater reliability (i.e. how consistent scores are from different raters). Pilot-testing of the procedures and measures helps you identify anything that might go wrong on the day and any additional contaminating factors that might influence the results. Some of these you may not be able to predict (e.g. workers doing noisy construction work just outside the lab's window), but try to control those factors that you can.

CHOOSING APPROPRIATE SCALES AND MEASURES

There are many different ways of collecting data, depending on the nature of your research. This might involve measuring output or performance on some objective criteria, or rating behaviour according to a set of specified criteria. It might also involve the use of scales that have been designed to operationalise some underlying construct or attribute that is not directly measurable (e.g. self-esteem). There are many thousands of validated scales that can be used in research. Finding the right one for your purpose is sometimes difficult. A thorough review of the literature in your topic area is the first place to start. What measures have been used by other researchers in the area? Sometimes, the actual items that make up the scales are included in the appendix to a journal article; otherwise, you may need to trace back to the original article describing the design and validation of the scale you are interested in. Some scales have been copyrighted, meaning that to use them you need to purchase official copies from the publisher. Other scales, which have been published in their entirety in journal articles, are considered to be 'in the public domain', meaning that they can be used by researchers without charge. It is very important, however, to properly acknowledge each of the scales you use, giving full reference details.

In choosing appropriate scales there are two characteristics that you need to be aware of: reliability and validity. Both of these factors can influence the quality of the data you obtain. When reviewing possible scales to use, you should collect information on the reliability and validity of each of the scales. You need this information for the Method section of your research report. No matter how good the reports are concerning the reliability and validity of your scales, it is important to pilot-test them with your intended sample. Sometimes, scales are reliable with some groups (e.g. adults with an English-speaking background) but are totally unreliable when used with other groups (e.g. children from non-English-speaking backgrounds).

Reliability

The reliability of a scale indicates how free it is from random error. Two frequently used indicators of a scale's reliability are test-retest reliability (also referred to as 'temporal stability') and internal consistency. The test-retest reliability of a scale is assessed by administering it to the same people on two different occasions and calculating the correlation between the two scores obtained. High test-retest correlations indicate a more reliable scale. You need to take into account the nature of the construct that the scale is measuring when considering this type of reliability. A scale designed to measure current mood states is not likely to remain stable over a period of a few weeks. The test-retest reliability of a mood scale, therefore, is likely to be low. You would, however, hope that measures of stable personality characteristics would stay much the same, showing quite high test-retest correlations.

The second aspect of reliability that can be assessed is internal consistency. This is the degree to which the items that make up the scale are all measuring the same underlying attribute (i.e. the extent to which the items 'hang together'). Internal consistency can be measured in several different ways. The most commonly used statistic is Cronbach's coefficient alpha (available using IBM SPSS Statistics; see Chapter 9). This statistic provides an indication of the average correlation among all of the items that make up the scale. Values range from 0 to 1, with higher values indicating greater reliability.

While different levels of reliability are required, depending on the nature and purpose of the scale, Nunnally (1978) recommends a minimum level of .7. Cronbach alpha values are dependent on the number of items in the scale. When there are a small number of items in the scale (fewer than 10), Cronbach alpha values can be quite small. In this situation it may be better to calculate and report the mean inter-item correlation for the items. Optimal mean inter-item correlation values range from .2 to .4 (as recommended by Briggs & Cheek 1986).

Validity

The validity of a scale refers to the degree to which it measures what it is supposed to measure. Unfortunately, there is no one clear-cut indicator of a scale's validity. The validation of a scale involves the collection of empirical evidence concerning its use. The main types of validity you will see discussed in the literature are content validity, criterion validity and construct validity.

Content validity refers to the adequacy with which a measure or scale has sampled from the intended universe or domain of content. *Criterion validity* concerns the relationship between scale scores and some specified, measurable criterion. *Construct validity* involves testing a scale not against a single criterion but in terms of theoretically derived hypotheses concerning the nature of the underlying variable or construct. The construct validity is explored by investigating its relationship with other constructs, both related (convergent validity) and unrelated (discriminant validity). An easy-to-follow summary of the various types of validity is provided in Streiner and Norman (2015).

If you intend to use scales in your research, it would be a good idea to read further on this topic: see Kline (2005) for information on psychological tests, and Streiner and Norman (2015) for health measurement scales. Bowling also has some great books on health and medical scales.

PREPARING A QUESTIONNAIRE

In many studies it is necessary to collect information from your participants or respondents. This may involve obtaining demographic information from participants prior to exposing them to some experimental manipulation. Alternatively, it may involve the design of an extensive survey to be distributed to a selected sample of the population. A poorly planned and designed questionnaire will not give good data with which to address your research questions. In preparing a questionnaire, you must consider how you intend to use the information; you must know what statistics you intend to use. Depending on the statistical technique you have in mind, you may need to ask the question in a particular way or provide different response formats. Some of the factors you need to consider in the design and construction of a questionnaire are outlined in the sections that follow.

This section only briefly skims the surface of questionnaire design, so I would suggest that you read further on the topic if you are designing your own study. A really great book for this purpose is De Vaus (2014).

Question types

Most questions can be classified into two groups: closed and open-ended. A closed question involves offering respondents a set of defined response choices. They are asked to mark their response using a tick, cross, circle and so on. The choices may be a simple 'yes' or 'no', 'male' or 'female', or may involve a range of different choices. For example:

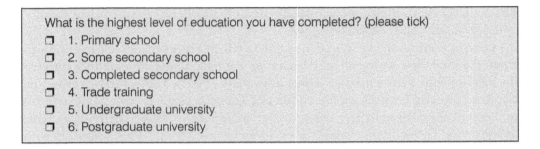

What is the highest level of education you have completed? (please tick)
- ❑ 1. Primary school
- ❑ 2. Some secondary school
- ❑ 3. Completed secondary school
- ❑ 4. Trade training
- ❑ 5. Undergraduate university
- ❑ 6. Postgraduate university

Closed questions are usually quite easy to convert to the numerical format required for IBM SPSS Statistics. For example, no can be coded as a 0, yes can be coded as a 1; males as 1, females as 2. In the education question shown above, the number corresponding to the response ticked by the respondent would be entered. For example, if the respondent ticked 'undergraduate university', this would be coded as a 5. Numbering each of the possible responses helps with the coding process. For data entry purposes, decide on a convention for the numbering (e.g. in order across the page, and then down), and stick with it throughout the questionnaire.

Sometimes, you cannot guess all the possible responses that respondents might make—it is therefore necessary to use open-ended questions. The advantage here is that respondents have the freedom to respond in their own way and are not restricted to the choices provided by the researcher. For example:

What is the major source of stress in your life at the moment?

_____

_____

Responses to open-ended questions can be summarised into different categories for entry into IBM SPSS Statistics. These categories are usually identified after scanning through the range of responses received from the respondents. Some possibilities could also be raised from an understanding of previous research in the area. Each of these response categories is assigned a value (e.g. work = 1, finances = 2, relationships = 3), and this number is entered into IBM SPSS Statistics. More details on this are provided in the section on preparing a codebook in Chapter 2.

Sometimes, a combination of both closed and open-ended questions works best. This involves providing respondents with a set of defined responses and an additional category ('other') that they can tick if the response they wish to give is not listed. A line or two are provided so that they can write the response they wish to give. This combination of closed and open-ended questions is particularly useful in the early stages of research in an area, as it gives an indication of whether the defined response categories adequately cover all the responses that respondents wish to give.

Response format

In asking respondents a question, you also need to decide on a response format. The type of response format you choose can have implications when you come to do your statistical analysis. Some analyses (e.g. correlation) require scores that are continuous, from low through to high, with a wide range of scores. If you had asked respondents to indicate their age by giving them a category to tick (e.g. less than 30, between 31 and 50, and over 50), these data would not be suitable to use in a correlational analysis. So, if you intend to explore the correlation between age and, say, self-esteem, you need to ensure that you ask respondents for their actual age in years. Be warned, though: some people don't like giving their exact age (e.g. women over 30!).

Try to provide as wide a choice of responses to your questions as possible. You can always condense (or 'collapse') things later if you need to (see Chapter 8). Don't just ask respondents whether they agree or disagree with a statement—use a Likert-type scale, which can range from strongly disagree to strongly agree:

strongly disagree	1	2	3	4	5	6	strongly agree

This type of response scale gives you a wider range of possible scores and increases the statistical analyses that are available to you. You need to make a decision concerning the number of response steps (e.g. 1 to 6) that you use. DeVellis (2012) has a good discussion concerning the advantages and disadvantages of different response scales. Whatever type of response format you choose, you must provide clear instructions. Do you want your respondents to tick a box, circle a number, make a mark on a line? For some respondents, this may be the first questionnaire that they have completed. Don't assume they know how to respond appropriately. Give clear instructions, provide an example if appropriate, and always pilot-test on the types of people that will make up your sample. Iron out any sources of confusion before distributing hundreds of your questionnaires. In designing your questions, always consider how a respondent might interpret the question and all the possible responses a person might want to make. For example, you may want to know whether people smoke or not. You might ask the question:

Do you smoke? (please tick)	❐ Yes	❐ No

In pilot-testing this questionnaire, your respondent might ask whether you mean cigarettes, cigars or marijuana. Is knowing whether they smoke enough? Should you also find out how much they smoke (two or three cigarettes, versus two or three packs) and/or how often they smoke (every day or only on social occasions)? The message here is to consider each of your questions, what information they will give you and what information might be missing.

Wording the questions

There is a real art to designing clear, well-written questionnaire items. Although there are no clear-cut rules that can guide this process, there are some things you can do to improve the quality of your questions, and therefore your data. Try to avoid:

- ➢ long, complex questions
- ➢ double negatives
- ➢ double-barrelled questions
- ➢ jargon or abbreviations
- ➢ culture-specific terms
- ➢ words with double meanings
- ➢ leading questions
- ➢ emotionally loaded words.

When appropriate, you should consider including a response category for 'don't know' or 'not applicable'. For further suggestions on writing questions, see De Vaus (2014) and Kline (2005).

2

Preparing a codebook

Before you can enter the information from your questionnaire, interviews or experiment into IBM SPSS Statistics, it is necessary to prepare a codebook. This is a summary of the instructions you will use to convert the information obtained from each subject or case into a format that the program can understand. The steps involved are demonstrated in this chapter using a data file that was developed by a group of my graduate diploma students. A copy of the questionnaire, and the codebook that was developed for this questionnaire, can be found in the Appendix. The data file is provided on the website that accompanies this book. The provision of this material allows you to see the whole process, from questionnaire development through to the creation of the final data file ready for analysis. Although I have used a questionnaire to illustrate the steps involved in the development of a codebook, a similar process is also necessary in experimental studies or when retrieving information from existing records (e.g. hospital medical records).

Preparing the codebook involves deciding (and documenting) how you will go about:

➢ defining and labelling each of the variables
➢ assigning numbers to each of the possible responses.

All this information should be recorded in a book or computer file. Keep this somewhere safe; there is nothing worse than coming back to a data file that you haven't used for a while and wondering what the abbreviations and numbers refer to.

In your codebook you should list all of the variables in your questionnaire, the abbreviated variable names that you will use in IBM SPSS Statistics and the way in which you will code the responses. In this chapter simplified examples are given to illustrate the various steps. In the first column in the codebook (see Table 2.1) you write the abbreviated name for that variable that will appear in the data file (see conventions below), and in the second column you can describe this variable in more detail so you can identify it later.

	SPSS name	Variable	Coding instructions	Measurement Scale
Table 2.1	ID	Identification number	Number assigned to each survey	Scale
Example of a	Sex	Sex	1 = Males 2 = Females	Nominal
codebook	Age	Age	Age in years	Scale
	Marital	Marital status	1 = single, 2 = steady relationship, 3 = married for the first time, 4 = remarried, 5 = divorced/ separated, 6 = widowed	Nominal
	Educ	Highest level of education completed	1=primary, 2=some secondary, 3=completed high school, 4=some additional training, 5=completed undergraduate, 6=completed postgraduate	Ordinal

In the third column you detail how you will code each of the responses obtained. The fourth column identifies the level of measurement of the variable, which you need to specify when setting up the data file. There are three choices: *nominal* (categories without any particular order), *ordinal* (categories that are ordered, representing different levels of a variable) and *scale* (continuous scores with lots of values). You will see I have identified sex as a nominal variable as the numbers assigned are arbitrary and don't represent levels. I have identified education as ordinal because numbers represent increasing levels of education completed. Age has been nominated as scale as it is a continuous variable, with each person specifying their exact age. If I had used age categories (e.g. 18–30, 31–50, 51+) then the variable would be identified as ordinal.

Variable names

Each question or item in your questionnaire must have a unique variable name. Some of these names will clearly identify the information (e.g. sex, age). Other questions, such as the items that make up a scale, may be identified using an abbreviation (e.g. op1, op2, op3 are used to identify the items that make up the Optimism Scale).

There is a set of conventions you must follow in assigning names to your variables in IBM SPSS Statistics. These are set out in the 'Rules for naming of variables' box. Try to keep your variable names as brief as possible as very long names can make the output hard to read.

The first variable in any data set should be ID—that is, a unique number that identifies each case. Before beginning the data entry process, go through and assign a number to each of the questionnaires or data records. Write the number clearly on the front cover. Later, if you find an error in the data set, having the questionnaires or data records numbered allows you to check back and find where the error occurred.

Rules for naming of variables

Variable names:

➢ must be unique (i.e. each variable in a data set must have a different name)

➢ must begin with a letter (not a number)

➢ cannot include full stops, spaces or symbols (! , ? * ")

➢ cannot include words used as commands by SPSS (all, ne, eq, to, le, lt, by, or, gt, and, not, ge, with)

➢ cannot exceed 64 characters.

CODING RESPONSES

Each response must be assigned a numerical code before it can be entered into IBM SPSS Statistics. Some of the information will already be in this format (e.g. age in years); other variables such as sex will need to be converted to numbers (e.g. 1 = males, 2 = females). If you have used numbers in your questions to label your responses (see, for example, the education question in Chapter 1), this is relatively straightforward. If not, decide on a convention and stick to it. For example, code the first listed response as 1, the second as 2 and so on across the page.

What is your current marital status? (please tick)

❏ single   ❏ in a relationship   ❏ married   ❏ divorced

To code responses to the question above: if a person ticked 'single', they would be coded as 1; if 'in a relationship', they would be coded 2; if 'married', 3; and if 'divorced', 4.

CODING OPEN-ENDED QUESTIONS

For open-ended questions (where respondents can provide their own answers), coding is slightly more complicated. Take, for example, the question 'What is the major source of stress in your life at the moment?' To code responses to this, you will need to scan through the questionnaires and identify common themes. You might notice a lot of respondents listing their source of stress as related to work, finances, relationships, health or lack of time. In your codebook you list these major groups of responses under the variable name stress and assign a number to each (work = 1, spouse/partner = 2 etc.). You also need to add another numerical code for responses that did not fall into these listed categories (other = 99). When entering the data for each respondent, you compare their response with those listed in the codebook and enter the appropriate number into the data set under the variable stress.

Once you have drawn up your codebook, you are almost ready to enter your data. First, you need to get to know IBM SPSS Statistics (Chapter 3), and then you need to set up a data file and enter your data (Chapter 4).

3

Getting to know
IBM SPSS Statistics

IBM SPSS Statistics operates using different screens, or windows, designed to do different things. Before you can access these windows, you need to either open an existing data file or create one of your own. So, in this chapter we will cover how to open and exit the program, how to open and close existing data files and how to create a data file from scratch. We will then go on to explore the different windows IBM SPSS Statistics uses.

STARTING IBM SPSS STATISTICS

There are several different ways to start the program:

➢ The simplest way is to search for an IBM SPSS Statistics icon on your desktop or taskbar and double-click.
➢ You can also start the program by clicking on **Start**, and then scanning the list of programs available. See if you have a folder labelled IBM SPSS Statistics which should contain the option **IBM SPSS Statistics 26**. This may vary depending on your computer and the version and licence that you have.
➢ The program will also start up if you double-click on an IBM SPSS Statistics data file listed in Windows Explorer—these files have a '.sav' extension.

When you open the program, you may encounter a front cover screen asking 'What would you like to do?' I suggest that you close this screen (click on the cross in the top right-hand corner) and use the menus.

OPENING AN EXISTING DATA FILE

If you wish to open an existing data file (e.g. **survey.sav**, one of the files included on the website that accompanies this book—see p. ix), click on **File** from the menu across the top of the screen, and then choose **Open**, and then slide across to **Data**. The **Open File** dialogue box will allow you to search through the various directories on your computer to find where your data file is stored.

You should always open data files from the hard drive of your computer. If you have data on a memory stick or flash drive, transfer them to a folder on the hard drive of your computer before opening it. Find the file you wish to use and click on **Open**. Remember, all IBM SPSS Statistics data files have a '.sav' extension. The data file will open in front of you in what is labelled the **Data Editor** window (more on this window later).

WORKING WITH DATA FILES

In IBM SPSS Statistics, you must keep at least one data file open at all times. If you close a data file, the program will ask if you would like to save the file before closing. If you don't save it, you will lose any data you may have entered and any recoding or computing of new variables that you may have done since the file was opened. While you can have more than one data file open at any one time, it can be confusing, so I suggest you avoid it and close files when you have finished the analysis.

Saving a data file

When you first create a data file or make changes to an existing one (e.g. creating new variables), you must remember to save your data file. This does not happen automatically. If you don't save regularly and there is a power blackout or you accidentally press the wrong key (it does happen!), you will lose all of your work. So, save yourself the heartache and save regularly.

To save a file you are working on, go to the **File** menu (top left-hand corner) and choose **Save**. Or, if you prefer, you can also click on the icon that looks like a floppy disk, which appears on the toolbar at the top left of your screen. This will save your file to whichever drive you are currently working on. This should always be the hard drive—working from a flash drive is a recipe for disaster! I have had many students come to me in tears after corrupting their data file by working from an external drive rather than from the hard drive. This also applies to files stored online (e.g. Dropbox, OneDrive) or on network drives—transfer them to the hard drive before conducting analyses.

When you first save a new data file, you will be asked to specify a name for the file and to indicate a directory and a folder in which it will be stored. Choose the directory and then type in a file name. IBM SPSS Statistics will automatically give all data file names the extension '.sav'. This is so that it can recognise it as a data file. Don't change this extension; otherwise, the program won't be able to find the file when you ask for it again later.

Opening a different data file

If you finish working on a data file and wish to open another one, click on **File**, select **Open**, and then slide across to **Data**. Find the directory where your second file is stored. Click on the desired file and then click the **Open** button. This will open the second data file, while still leaving the first data file open in a separate window. It is a good idea to close files that you are not currently working on—it can get very confusing having multiple files open.

Starting a new data file

Starting a new data file is easy. Click on **File**, then, from the drop-down menu, click on **New** and then **Data**. From here you can start defining your variables and entering your data. Before you can do this, however, you need to understand a little about the windows and dialogue boxes that the program uses. These are discussed in the next section.

WINDOWS

The main windows you will use in IBM SPSS Statistics are the **Data Editor**, the **Viewer**, the **Pivot Table Editor**, the **Chart Editor** and the **Syntax Editor**. These windows are summarised here but are discussed in more detail in later sections of this book.

When you begin to analyse your data, you will have several of these windows open at the same time. Some students find this idea very confusing. Once you get the hang of it, it is really quite simple. You will always have the **Data Editor** open because this contains the data file that you are analysing. Once you start to do some analyses, you will have the **Viewer** window open because this is where the results of all your analyses are displayed, listed in the order in which you performed them.

The different windows are like pieces of paper on your desk—you can shuffle them around, so that sometimes one is on top and at other times another. Each of the windows you have open will be listed along the bottom of your screen. To change windows, just click on whichever window you would like to have on top. You can also click on **Window** on the top menu bar. This will list all the open windows and allow you to choose which you would like to display on the screen.

Sometimes, the windows that IBM SPSS Statistics displays do not initially fill the screen. It is much easier to have the **Viewer** window (where your results are displayed) enlarged on top, filling the entire screen. To do this, look on the top right-hand area of your screen. There should be three little buttons or icons. Click on the middle button to maximise that window (i.e. to make your current window fill the screen). If you wish to shrink it again, just click on this middle button.

Data Editor window

The **Data Editor** window displays the contents of your data file, and in this window you can open, save and close existing data files, create a new data file, enter data, make changes to the existing data file and run statistical analyses (see Figure 3.1).

Figure 3.1
Example of a Data Editor window

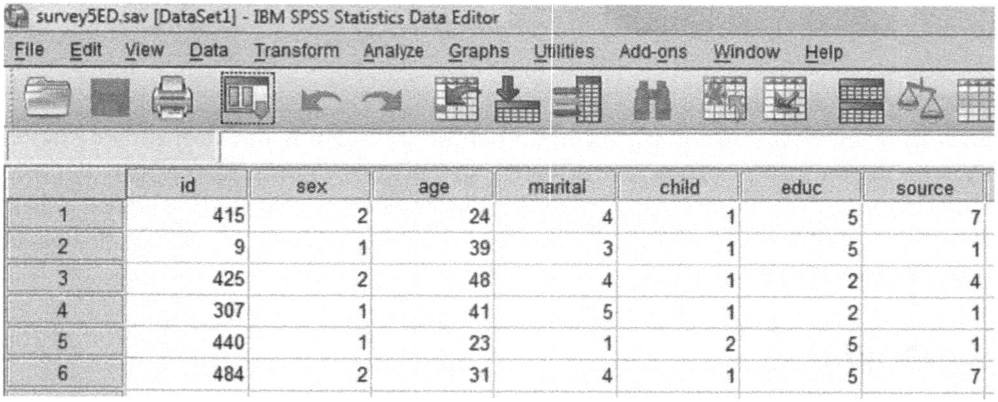

	id	sex	age	marital	child	educ	source
1	415	2	24	4	1	5	7
2	9	1	39	3	1	5	1
3	425	2	48	4	1	2	4
4	307	1	41	5	1	2	1
5	440	1	23	1	2	5	1
6	484	2	31	4	1	5	7

Viewer window

When you start to do analyses, the **Viewer** window should open automatically (see Figure 3.2). If it does not open automatically, click on **Window** from the menu and this should be listed. This window displays the results of the analyses you have conducted, including tables and graphs (also referrred to as charts). In this window you can modify the output, delete it, copy it, save it, or even transfer it into a Word document.

The **Viewer** window consists of two parts. On the left is an outline, or navigation pane, which gives you a full list of all the analyses you have conducted. You can use this side to quickly navigate your way around your output (which can become very long). Just click on the section you want to move to and it will appear on the right-hand side of the screen. On the right-hand side of the **Viewer** window are the results of your analyses, which can include tables and graphs (also referred to as charts).

Saving output

When you save the output from IBM SPSS Statistics, it is saved in a separate file with a '.spv' extension, to distinguish it from data files, which have a '.sav' extension.

To save the results of your analyses, you must have the **Viewer** window open on the screen in front of you. Click on **File** from the menu at the top of the screen. Click on **Save**. Choose the directory and folder in which you wish to save your output, and then type in a file name that uniquely identifies your output. Click on **Save**.

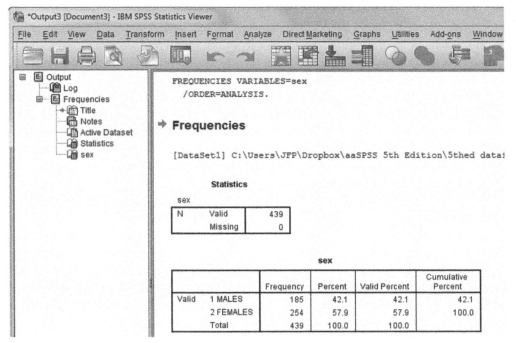

Figure 3.2
Example of a Viewer
window

To name my files, I use an abbreviation that indicates the data file I am working on and the date I conducted the analyses. For example, the file 'survey8may2019.spv' would contain the analyses I conducted on 8 May 2019 using the survey data file. I keep a log book that contains a list of all my file names, along with details of the analyses that were performed. This makes it much easier for me to retrieve the results of specific analyses. When you begin your own research, you will find that you can very quickly accumulate a lot of different files containing the results of many different analyses. To prevent confusion and frustration, get organised and keep good records of the analyses you have done and of where you have saved the results.

It is important to note that the output file (with a '.spv' extension) can only be opened in IBM SPSS Statistics. This can be a problem if you, or someone who needs to read the output, does not have the program. To get around this problem, you may choose to export your output. If you wish to save the entire output, select **File** from the menu and then choose **Export**. You can choose the format type that you would like to use (e.g. pdf, Word/rtf). Saving as a Word/rtf file means that you will be able to modify the tables in Word. Use the **Browse** button to identify the folder you wish to save the file into, specify a suitable name in the **Save File** pop-up box that appears, then click on **Save** and then OK.

If you don't want to save the whole file, you can select specific parts of the output to export. Select these in the **Viewer** window using the left-hand navigation pane. With the selections highlighted, select **File** from the menu and choose **Export**. In the **Export Output** dialog box you will need to tick the box at the top labelled **Selected** and then select the format of the file and the location you wish to save to.

Another option is to cut and paste the results from the IBM SPSS Statistics output into a Word document. In the navigation panel on the left-hand side click on the results that you want, right click and choose **Copy** from the pop-up menu. Move across to an open document in Word and right click and choose **Paste** (or press the (Ctrl) key and the V key together). Putting the output into Word allows you to add comments, notes, interpretations and so on.

Printing output

You can use the navigation pane (left-hand side) of the **Viewer** window to select particular sections of your results to print out. To do this, you need to highlight the sections that you want. Click on the first section you want, hold down the Ctrl key on your keyboard and then just click on any other sections you want. To print these sections, click on the **File** menu (from the top of your screen) and choose **Print**. The program will ask whether you want to print your selected output or the whole output.

Pivot Table Editor

The tables you see in the **Viewer** window (which IBM SPSS Statistics calls 'pivot tables') can be modified to suit your needs. To modify a table you need to double-click on it. You will see some dotted lines around your pivot table indicating that you are now in editing mode. You can use this editor to change the appearance of your table, its size, the fonts used and the dimensions of the columns—you can even swap the presentation of variables around (transpose rows and columns). To get out of editing mode just click somewhere on the screen away from the pivot table.

If you click the right mouse button on a table in the **Viewer** window, a pop-up menu of options that are specific to that table will appear. If you double-click on a table and then click on your right mouse button even more options appear, including the option to **Create Graph** using these results. You may need to highlight the part of the table that you want to graph by holding down the Ctrl key while you select the parts of the table you want to display.

Chart Editor window

When you ask IBM SPSS Statistics to produce a histogram, bar graph or scatterplot, it initially displays these in the **Viewer** window. If you wish to make changes to the type or presentation of the chart, you need to activate the **Chart Editor** window by double-clicking on your chart. In this window you can modify the appearance and format of your graph and change the fonts, colours, patterns and line markers (see Figure 3.3). The procedure to generate charts and to use the **Chart Editor** is discussed further in Chapter 7.

Figure 3.3
Example of a Chart
Editor window

Syntax Editor window

In the good old days, all IBM SPSS Statistics commands were given using a special command language or syntax. The program still creates these sets of commands, but all you usually see are the Windows menus that 'write' the commands for you. Although the options available through the menus are usually all that most undergraduate students need to use, there are some situations when it is useful to go behind the scenes and to take more control over the analyses that you wish to conduct.

Syntax is a good way of keeping a record of what commands you have used, particularly when you need to do a lot of recoding of variables or computing new variables (demonstrated in Chapter 8). It is also useful when you need to repeat a lot of analyses or generate a set of similar graphs.

You can use the normal IBM SPSS Statistics menus to set up the basic commands of a statistical technique and then paste these to the **Syntax Editor** using the **Paste** button provided with each procedure (see Figure 3.4). It allows you to copy and paste commands, and to make modifications to the commands generated by the program. Quite complex commands can also be written to allow more sophisticated recoding and manipulation of the data. IBM SPSS Statistics has a **Command Syntax Reference** under the **Help** menu if you would like additional information. (*Warning*: This is not for beginners—it is quite complex to follow.)

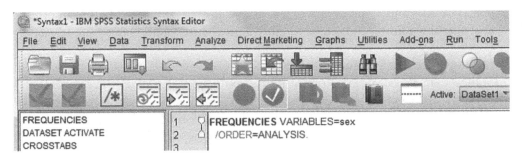

Figure 3.4
Example of a Syntax
Editor window

The commands pasted to the **Syntax Editor** are not executed until you choose to run them. To run the command, highlight the specific command (making sure you include the final full stop), or select it from the left-hand side of the screen, and then click on the **Run** menu option or the arrow icon from the menu. Extra comments can be added to the syntax file by starting them with an asterisk.

Syntax is stored in a separate text file with a '.sps' extension. Make sure you have the **Syntax Editor** open in front of you and then select **File** from the menu. Select the **Save** option from the drop-down menu, choose the location you wish to save the file to and then type in a suitable file name. Click on the **Save** button.

The syntax file (with the extension '.sps') can only be opened using IBM SPSS Statistics. Sometimes, it may be useful to copy and paste the syntax text from the **Syntax Editor** into a Word document so that you (or others) can view it even if the program is not available. To do this, hold down the left mouse button and drag the cursor over the syntax you wish to save. Choose **Edit** from the menu and then select **Copy** from the drop-down menu. Open a Word document and paste this material using the **Edit, Paste** option or hold the Ctrl key down and press V on the keyboard.

MENUS

Within each of the windows described above, IBM SPSS Statistics provides you with quite a bewildering array of menu choices. These choices are displayed in drop-down menus across the top of the screen, and also as icons. Try not to become overwhelmed; initially, just learn the key ones, and as you get a bit more confident you can experiment with others.

DIALOGUE BOXES

Once you select a menu option, you will usually be asked for further information. This is done in a dialogue box. Figure 3.5 shows the dialogue box that appears when you use the **Frequencies** procedure to get some descriptive statistics. To see this, click on **Analyze** from the menu at the top of the screen, select **Descriptive Statistics** and then slide across and select **Frequencies**. The dialogue box will ask you to nominate which variables you want to use (see Figure 3.5).

Selecting variables in a dialogue box

To indicate which variables you want to use you need to highlight the selected variables in the list provided (by clicking on them), then click on the arrow button in the centre of the screen to move them into the empty box labelled **Variable(s)**. You can select variables one at a time, clicking on the arrow each time, or you can select a group of variables. If the variables you want to select are all listed together, just click

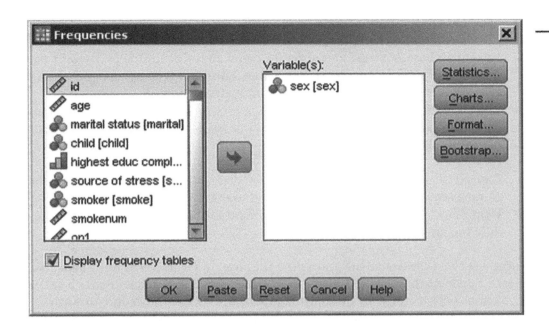

Figure 3.5
Example of a
Frequencies
dialogue box

on the first one, hold down the Shift key on your keyboard and press the down arrow key until you have highlighted all the desired variables. Click on the arrow button and all of the selected variables will move across into the **Variable(s)** box.

If the variables you want to select are spread throughout the variables list, you should click on the first variable you want, hold down the Ctrl key, move the cursor down to the next variable you want and then click on it, and so on. Once you have all the desired variables highlighted, click on the arrow button. They will move into the box.

To assist in finding the variables you can right click on one of the variables in the list and select **Sort Alphabetically**. This right click menu also allows you to choose between **Display Variable Names** (the short SPSS name) and **Display Variable Labels** (the extended label you might have provided for the variable).

To remove a variable from the **Variable(s)** box, you just reverse the process used to select them. Click on the variable that you wish to remove, click on the arrow button, and it shifts the variable back into the original list. You will notice the direction of the arrow button changes, depending on whether you are moving variables into or out of the **Variable(s)** box.

Dialogue box buttons

In most dialogue boxes you will notice a set of standard buttons: **OK**, **Paste**, **Reset**, **Cancel** and **Help** (see Figure 3.5). The uses of each of these buttons are:

> **OK:** Click on this button when you have selected your variables and are ready to run the analysis or procedure.
> **Paste:** This button is used to transfer the commands that IBM SPSS Statistics has generated in this dialogue box to the **Syntax Editor**. This is useful if you wish to keep a record of the command or repeat an analysis a number of times.
> **Reset:** This button is used to clear the dialogue box of all the previous commands you might have given when you last used this particular statistical technique or procedure. It gives you a clean slate to perform a new analysis, with different variables.
> **Cancel:** Clicking on this button closes the dialogue box and cancels all of the commands you may have given in relation to that technique or procedure.
> **Help:** Click on this button to obtain information about the technique or procedure you are about to perform.

Although I have illustrated the use of dialogue boxes in Figure 3.5 by using **Frequencies**, all dialogue boxes work on the same basic principle. Each will have a series of buttons with a choice of options relating to the specific procedure or analysis. These buttons will open subdialogue boxes that allow you to specify which analyses you wish to conduct or which statistics you would like displayed.

CLOSING IBM SPSS STATISTICS

When you have finished your session and wish to close the program down, click on the **File** menu at the top left of the screen. Click on **Exit**. IBM SPSS Statistics will prompt you to save your data file and a file that contains your output. You should not rely on the fact that the program will prompt you to save when closing the program. It is important that you save both your output and your data file regularly throughout your session. Unlike programs such as Microsoft Word, IBM SPSS Statistics does not save automatically throughout a session. If the program crashes (a reasonably common occurrence!) or there is a power cut, you will lose all your work.

GETTING HELP

If you need help while using IBM SPSS Statistics or don't know what some of the options refer to, you can use the in-built **Help** menu. Under the **Help** menu click on **Documentation in PDF format** and scroll down to access a range of manuals covering different statistical procedures. Within each of the major dialogue boxes there is an additional **Help** menu that will assist you with the procedure you have selected. You will need to be online to access the Help material.

PART TWO
Preparing the data file

Preparation of the data file for analysis involves several steps. These include creating the data file and entering the information obtained from your study in a format defined by your codebook (covered in Chapter 2). The data file then needs to be checked for errors, and these errors corrected. Part Two of this book covers these two steps. In Chapter 4, the procedures required to create a data file and enter the data are discussed. In Chapter 5, the process of screening and cleaning the data file is covered.

4

Creating a data file and entering data

The flow chart of data analysis process shown on the next page outlines the main steps that are needed to set up your data file and analyse the data.

To prepare a data file, there are three key steps, which are covered in this chapter:

> *Step 1:* Check and modify, where necessary, the options that IBM SPSS Statistics uses to display the data and the output that is produced.
> *Step 2:* Set up the structure of the data file by defining the variables.
> *Step 3:* Enter the data—i.e. the values obtained from each participant or respondent for each variable.

To illustrate these procedures I have used the data file **survey.sav**, which is described in the Appendix. The codebook used to generate these data is also provided in the Appendix.

Data files can also be imported from other spreadsheet-type programs (e.g. Excel). This can make the data entry process much more convenient, particularly for students who don't have IBM SPSS Statistics on their home computers. You can set up a basic data file on Excel and enter the data at home. When it is complete, you can then import the file into IBM SPSS Statistics and proceed with the data manipulation and data analysis stages. The instructions for using Excel to enter the data are provided later in this chapter.

CHANGING THE IBM SPSS STATISTICS OPTIONS

Before you set up your data file, it is a good idea to check the IBM SPSS Statistics options that govern the way your data and output are displayed. The options allow you to define how your variables will be displayed, the types of tables that will be

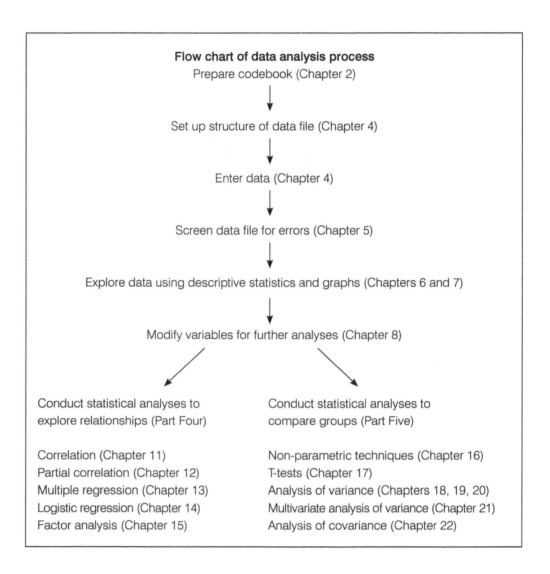

Flow chart of data analysis process

Prepare codebook (Chapter 2)

Set up structure of data file (Chapter 4)

Enter data (Chapter 4)

Screen data file for errors (Chapter 5)

Explore data using descriptive statistics and graphs (Chapters 6 and 7)

Modify variables for further analyses (Chapter 8)

Conduct statistical analyses to explore relationships (Part Four)

Correlation (Chapter 11)
Partial correlation (Chapter 12)
Multiple regression (Chapter 13)
Logistic regression (Chapter 14)
Factor analysis (Chapter 15)

Conduct statistical analyses to compare groups (Part Five)

Non-parametric techniques (Chapter 16)
T-tests (Chapter 17)
Analysis of variance (Chapters 18, 19, 20)
Multivariate analysis of variance (Chapter 21)
Analysis of covariance (Chapter 22)

displayed in the output and many other aspects of the program. Some of this will seem confusing at first, but once you have used the program to enter data and run some analyses you may want to refer back to this section.

If you are sharing a computer with other people (e.g. in a computer lab), it is worth being aware of these options. Sometimes, other students will change these options, which can influence how the program appears. It is useful to know how to change things back to the way you want them.

To open the **Options** screen, click on **Edit** from the menu at the top of the screen and then choose **Options**. The screen shown in Figure 4.1 should appear. There are a lot of choices listed, many of which you won't need to change. I have described the key ones below, organised by the tab they appear under. To move between the various tabs, just click on the one you want. Don't click on **OK** until you have finished all the changes you want to make, across all the tabs.

General tab

When you come to do your analyses, you can ask for your variables to be listed in alphabetical order or by the order in which they appear in the file. I always use the file order, because this is consistent with the order of the questionnaire items and the codebook. To keep the variables in file order, just make sure the option **File** in the **Variable Lists** section is selected.

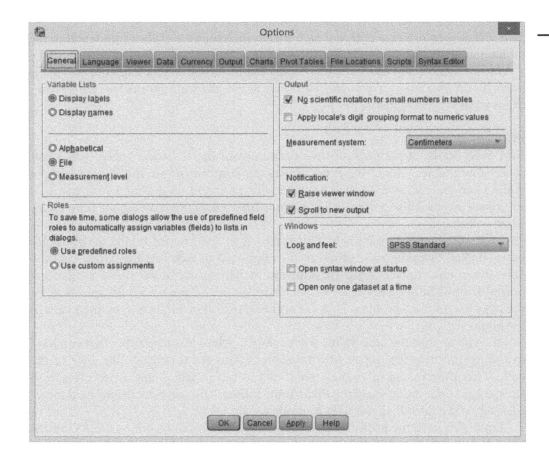

Figure 4.1

Example of an Options screen

In the **Output** section on the right-hand side, place a tick in the box **No scientific notation for small numbers in tables**. This will stop you getting some very strange numbers in your output for the statistical analyses.

Data tab

Click on the **Data** tab to make changes to the way that your data file is displayed. If your variables do not involve values with decimal places, you may like to change the display format for all your variables. In the section labelled **Display Format for New Numeric Variables**, change the **Decimal Places** value to 0. This means that all new variables will not display any decimal places. This reduces the size of your data file and simplifies its appearance.

Output tab

The options in this section allow you to customise how you want the variable names and value labels displayed in your output. In the very bottom section under **Variable values in labels are shown as:** choose **Values and Labels** from the drop-down options. This will allow you to see both the numerical values and the explanatory labels in the tables that are generated in the **Viewer** window.

In the section labelled **Output Display** choose **Pivot tables and charts**. This is particularly important if you are intending to use the non-parametric tests procedures in IBM SPSS Statistics.

Pivot Tables tab

IBM SPSS Statistics presents most of the results of the statistical analyses in tables called 'pivot tables'. Under the **Pivot Tables** tab you can choose the format of these tables from an extensive list. It is a matter of experimenting to find a style that best suits your needs. I use a style called **CompactBoxed** as this saves space (and paper when printing).

One other option you might find useful is at the bottom of the **Pivot Tables** tab—labelled **Copying wide tables to the clipboard in rich text form**. Click on the drop-down box and select **Shrink width to fit**. This is useful when you are pasting output from IBM SPSS Statistics to Microsoft Word and the results are too wide for the page (a common problem in some of the statistical procedures presented later in the book).

You can change the table styles as often as you like—just remember that you have to change the style *before* you run the analysis. You cannot change the style of the tables after they appear in your output, but you can modify many aspects (e.g. font sizes, column width) by using the **Pivot Table Editor**. This can be activated by double-clicking on the table that you wish to modify.

Once you have made all the changes you wish to make on the various **Options** tabs, click on **OK**. You can then proceed to define your variables and enter your data.

DEFINING THE VARIABLES

Before you can enter your data, you need to tell IBM SPSS Statistics about your variable names and coding instructions. This is called 'defining the variables'. You will do this in the **Data Editor** window (see Figure 4.2). The **Data Editor** window consists of two different views: **Data View** and **Variable View**. You can move between these two views using the little tabs at the bottom left-hand side of the screen.

You will notice that in the **Data View** window each of the columns is labelled **var** (see Figure 4.2). These will be replaced with the variable names that you listed in your codebook. Down the side you will see the numbers **1, 2, 3** and so on. These are the case numbers that IBM SPSS Statistics assigns to each of your lines of data. These are *not* the same as your ID numbers, and these case numbers change if you sort or split your file to analyse subsets of your data.

Procedure

To define each of the variables that make up your data file, you first need to click on the **Variable View** tab at the bottom left of your screen. In this view (see Figure 4.3) the variables are listed down the side, with their characteristics listed along the top (**Name, Type, Width, Decimals, Label, Values** and **Missing**).

Your job now is to define each of your variables by specifying the required information for each variable listed in your codebook. Some of the information you will need to provide yourself (e.g. name); other bits are provided automatically using default values. These default values can be changed if necessary. The key pieces of information that are needed are described below. The headings I have used correspond to the column headings displayed in the **Variable View**. I have provided the simple step-by-step

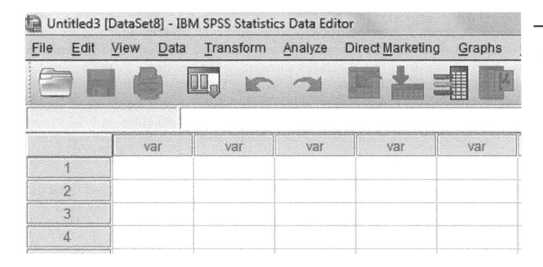

Figure 4.2

Example of a Data Editor window

Figure 4.3

Example of a
Variable View

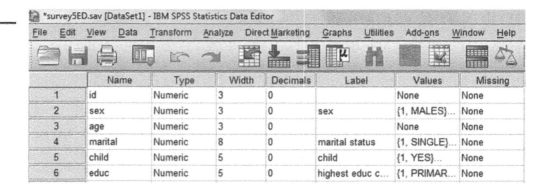

procedures below; however, there are several shortcuts that you can use once you are comfortable with the process. These are listed later, in the section headed Optional Shortcuts. You should become familiar with the basic techniques first.

Name

In this column, type in the short variable name that will be used to identify each of the variables in the data file (listed in your codebook). Keep these variable names as short as possible, not exceeding 64 characters. They must follow the naming conventions specified by IBM SPSS Statistics (listed in Chapter 2). Each variable name must be unique, must start with a letter and cannot contain spaces or symbols. For ideas on how to label your variables, have a look at the codebooks provided in the Appendix. These list the variable names used in data files that accompany this book (see p. ix for details of these files).

Type

The default value for **Type** that will appear automatically as you enter your first variable name is **Numeric**. For most purposes, this is all you will need to use. There are some circumstances where other options may be appropriate. For example, if you need to enter text information (e.g. a person's surname or their response to an open-ended question), you need to change the type to **String**. A **Date** option is also available if your data include dates (e.g. date of admission). To change the variable type, click in the cell and a box with three dots should appear giving you the options available. You can also use this window to adjust the width of the variable and the number of decimal places.

Width

The default value for **Width** is 8 characters (unless this has been changed using the **Options** instructions presented earlier in this chapter). This is usually sufficient for most data. If your variable has very large values, or you have requested a string variable, you may need to change this default value; otherwise, leave it as is.

Decimals

The default value for **Decimals** is usually 2 (however, this can be changed using the **Options** facility described earlier in this chapter). If your variable has decimal places, adjust this to suit your needs.

Label

The **Label** column allows you to provide a longer description for your variable than used in the **Name** column. This will be used in the output generated from the analyses. For example, you may wish to give the label 'Total Optimism' to your variable TOPTIM.

Values

In the **Values** column you can define the meaning of the values you have used to code your variables. I demonstrate this process for the variable sex below.

1. Click in the cell under the heading **Values** for the variable you wish to specify (sex). A box with three dots should appear on the right-hand side of the cell. This opens the **Value Labels** dialogue box.
2. Click in the box marked **Value**. Type in 1.
3. Click in the box marked **Label**. Type in Male.
4. Click on **Add**. You will then see in the summary box: 1=Male.
5. Repeat for females: **Value**: enter 2, **Label**: enter Female. **Add**.
6. When you have finished defining all the possible values (as listed in your codebook), click on **OK**.

Missing

Sometimes, researchers assign specific values to indicate missing values for their data. This is not necessary—IBM SPSS Statistics will recognise any blank cell as missing data. So, if you intend to leave a blank when a piece of information is not available, it is not necessary to do anything with this **Variable View** column.

If you do intend to use specific missing value codes (e.g. 99 = not applicable), you *must* specify this value in the **Missing** section; otherwise, the program will use the value as a legitimate value in any statistical analyses (with potentially disastrous consequences!). Click in the cell and then on the shaded box with three dots that appears. Choose the option **Discrete missing values** and type the value (e.g. 99) in the space provided. Up to three values can be specified this way. Click on **OK**. If you are using these special codes, it is also a good idea to go back and label these values in the **Values** column.

Columns

The default column width is usually set at 8, which is sufficient for most purposes. Change it only if necessary to accommodate your values or long variable names.

Align

The alignment of the columns is usually set at right alignment. There is no need to change this.

Measure

The column heading **Measure** refers to the level of measurement of each of your variables. The default is **Scale**, which refers to continuous data measured at interval or ratio level of measurement. If your variable consists of categories (e.g. sex), click in the cell and then on the arrow key that appears. Choose **Nominal** for categorical data and **Ordinal** if your data involve rankings or ordered values (e.g. level of education completed). It is important that you set the measurement levels of your variables correctly; otherwise, the program may stop you using some of the procedures (e.g. creating graphs).

Role

There is no need to make any changes to this section. Just leave as the default, **Input.**

Optional shortcuts

The process described above can be rather tedious if you have a large number of variables in your data file. There are shortcuts you can use to speed up the process. If you have a several variables that have the same attributes (e.g. type, width, decimals), you can set the first variable up correctly and then copy these attributes to one or more other variables.

Copying variable definition attributes to one other variable

1. In **Variable View**, click on the cell that has the attribute you wish to copy (e.g. **Width**).
2. From the menu, click on **Edit** and then **Copy** or you can right click in the cell and select **Copy** from the pop-up menu that appears.
3. Click on the same attribute cell for the variable you wish to apply this to.
4. From the menu, click on **Edit** and then **Paste** or right click in the cell and select **Paste** from the pop-up menu.

Copying variable definition attributes to other variables

1. In **Variable View**, click on the cell that has the attribute you wish to copy (e.g. **Width**).
2. From the menu, click on **Edit** and then **Copy**, or you can right click in the cell and select **Copy** from the pop-up menu that appears.
3. Click on the same attribute cell for the first variable you wish to copy to and then, holding your left mouse button down, drag the cursor down the column to highlight all the variables you wish to copy to.
4. From the menu, click on **Edit** and then **Paste**, or right click in the cell and select **Paste** from the pop-up menu.

Setting up a series of new variables all with the same attributes

If your data consist of scales made up of a set of items, you can create the new variables and define the attributes of all of these items in one go. The procedure is detailed below, using the six items of the Optimism Scale as an example (optim1 to optim6).

1. In **Variable View**, define the attributes of the first variable (optim1) following the instructions provided earlier. This involves defining the value labels 1 = strongly disagree, 2 = disagree, 3 = neutral, 4 = agree, 5 = strongly agree.
2. With the **Variable View** selected, click on the row number of this variable (this should highlight the whole row).
3. From the menu, select **Edit** and then **Copy**, or you can right click in the cell and select **Copy** from the pop-up menu that appears.
4. Click on the row number of the next empty row.
5. From the menu, select **Edit** and then **Paste Variables**, or right click in the cell and select **Paste** from the pop-up menu.
6. In the dialogue box that appears, enter the number of additional variables you want to add (in this case, 5). Enter the prefix you wish to use (optim) and the number you wish the new variables to start on (in this case, 2). Click on **OK**.

This will give you five new variables (optim2, optim3, optim4, optim5 and optim6).

To set up the items in other scales, just repeat the process detailed above (e.g. sest1 to sest10 for the items in the Self-esteem Scale). Remember, this procedure is suitable only for items that have all the same attributes. It is not appropriate if the items have different response scales (e.g. if some are categorical and others continuous) or if the values are coded differently.

ENTERING DATA

Once you have defined each of your variable names and given them value labels (where appropriate), you are ready to enter your data. Make sure you have your codebook ready.

Procedure for entering data

1. To enter data, you need to have the **Data View** active. Click on the **Data View** tab at the bottom left-hand side of the screen of the **Data Editor** window. A spreadsheet should appear with your newly defined variable names listed across the top.
2. Click on the first cell of the data set (first column, first row).
3. Type in the number (if this variable is ID, this should be 1).
4. Press the right arrow key on your keyboard; this will move the cursor into the second cell, ready to enter your second piece of information for case number 1.
5. Move across the row, entering all the information for Case 1, making sure that the values are entered in the correct columns.
6. To move back to the start of the data file, press the Home key on your keyboard (on some computers you may need to hold the Ctrl key or the Function (Fn) key down and then press the Home key). Press the down arrow to move to the second row, and enter the data for Case 2.
7. If you make a mistake and wish to change a value, click in the cell that contains the error. Type in the correct value and then press the right arrow key.

After you have defined your variables and entered your data, your **Data Editor** window should look something like that shown previously in Figure 3.1.

If you have entered value labels for some of your variables (e.g. sex: 1 = male, 2 = female), you can choose to have these labels displayed in the **Data Editor** window instead of just the numbers. To do this, click on **View** from the menu and select the option **Value Labels**. This option can also be activated during the data entry process so that you can choose an option from a drop-down menu, rather than typing a number in each cell. This is slower but does ensure that only valid numbers are entered. To turn this option off, go to **View** and click on **Value Labels** again to remove the tick.

MODIFYING THE DATA FILE

After you have created a data file, you may need to make changes to it (e.g. to add, delete or move variables, or to add or delete cases). Make sure you have the **Data Editor** window open on the screen, showing **Data View**.

Delete a case

Move down to the case (row) you wish to delete. Position your cursor in the shaded section on the left-hand side that displays the case number. Click once to highlight the row. Press the Delete button on your computer keyboard. You can also click on the **Edit** menu and click on **Clear**.

Insert a case between existing cases

Move your cursor to a cell in the case (row) immediately below where you would like the new case to appear. Click on the **Edit** menu and choose **Insert Cases**. An empty row will appear in which you can enter the data of the new case.

Delete a variable

Position your cursor in the shaded section (which contains the variable name) above the column you wish to delete. Click once to highlight the whole column. Press the Delete button on your keyboard. You can also click on the **Edit** menu and click on **Clear**.

Insert a variable between existing variables

Position your cursor in a cell in the column (variable) to the right of where you would like the new variable to appear. Click on the **Edit** menu and choose **Insert Variable**. An empty column will appear in which you can enter the data of the new variable.

Move an existing variable(s)

In the **Data Editor** window, have the **Variable View** showing. Highlight the variable you wish to move by clicking in the left-hand margin. Click and hold your left mouse button and then drag the variable to the new position (a red line will appear as you drag). Release the left mouse button when you get to the desired spot.

DATA ENTRY USING EXCEL

Data files can be prepared in the Microsoft Excel program and then imported into IBM SPSS Statistics for analysis. This is great for students who don't have access to the program at home. Excel usually comes as part of the Microsoft Office package. The procedure for creating a data file in Excel and then importing it into IBM SPSS Statistics is described below. If you intend to use this option you should have at least a basic understanding of Excel, as this will not be covered here.

Step 1: Set up the variable names

> Set up an Excel spreadsheet with the variable names in the first row across the page. The variable names must conform to the rules for naming variables (see Chapter 2).

Step 2: Enter the data

> 1. Enter the information for the first case on one row across the page, using the appropriate columns for each variable.
> 2. Repeat for each of the remaining cases. Don't use any formulas or other Excel functions. Remember to save your file regularly.
> 3. Click on **File**, **Save**. In the section marked **Save as Type**, make sure **Microsoft Excel Workbook** is selected. Type in an appropriate file name.

Step 3: Convert to IBM SPSS Statistics

> 1. After you have entered the data, save and close your file.
> 2. Start IBM SPSS Statistics and select **File**, **Open**, **Data** from the menu at the top of the screen.
> 3. In the section labelled **Files of type**, choose **Excel**. Excel files have a '.xls' or '.xlsx' extension. Find the file that contains your data. Click on it so that it appears in the **File name** section.
> 4. Click on the **Open** button. A screen will appear labelled **Opening Excel Data Source**. Make sure there is a tick in the box **Read variable names from the first row of data**. Click on **OK**.

The data will appear on the screen with the variable names listed across the top. You will then need to save this new data file.

Step 4: Save as an IBM SPSS Statistics file

1. Choose **File**, and then **Save As** from the menu at the top of the screen.
2. Type in a suitable file name. Make sure that the **Save as Type** is set at **SPSS Statistics (*.sav)**. Click on **Save**.
3. In the **Data Editor**, **Variable view**, you will now need to define the **Label**, **Values** and **Measure** information (see instructions presented earlier). You may also want to reduce the width of the columns as they often come in from Excel with a width of 11 or 12.

When you wish to open this file later to analyse your data using IBM SPSS Statistics, make sure you choose the file that has a '.sav' extension (not your original Excel file, which has a '.xlsx' extension).

USEFUL IBM SPSS STATISTICS FEATURES

There are many useful features of IBM SPSS Statistics that can be used to help with analyses, and to save you time and effort. I have highlighted a few of the main ones in the following sections.

Sort the data file

You can ask IBM SPSS Statistics to sort your data file according to values on one of your variables (e.g. sex, age).

1. Click on the **Data** menu, choose **Sort Cases** and specify which variable will be used to sort by. Choose either **Ascending** or **Descending**. Click on **OK**.
2. Alternatively, you can click on the name of the variable in the **Data View** tab to highlight it, right click, and select **Sort Ascending** or **Sort Descending** from the pop-up menu.
3. If you need to return your file to its original order, repeat the process, asking IBM SPSS Statistics to sort the file by ID.

Split the data file

Sometimes, it is necessary to split your file and to repeat analyses for groups (e.g. males and females) separately. This procedure does not permanently alter your file; it is an option you can turn on and off as it suits your purposes. The order in which the cases are displayed in the data file will change, however. You can return the data file to its original order (by ID) by using the **Sort Cases** command described above.

> 1. Click on the **Data** menu and choose the **Split File** option.
> 2. Click on **Compare groups** and select the grouping variable (e.g. sex) from the left-hand box and move it into the box labelled **Groups Based on**. Click on **OK**.

For the analyses that you perform after this split file procedure, the two groups (in this case, males and females) will be analysed separately.

Important: When you have finished the analyses, you need to go back and turn the **Split File** option off.

> 1. Click on the **Data** menu and choose the **Split File** option.
> 2. Click on the first dot (**Analyze all cases, do not create groups**). Click on **OK**.

Select cases

For some analyses, you may wish to select a subset of your sample (e.g. only males).

> 1. Click on the **Data** menu and choose the **Select Cases** option.
> 2. Click on the **If condition is satisfied** button.
> 3. Click on the button labelled **If**.
> 4. Choose the variable that defines the group that you are interested in (e.g. sex).
> 5. Click on the arrow button to move the variable name into the box.
> 6. Click on the = key from the keypad displayed on the screen or on your own keyboard.
> 7. Type in the value that corresponds to the group you are interested in (check with your codebook). For example, males in this sample are coded 1; therefore, you would type in 1. The command line should read: sex = 1.
> 8. Click on **Continue** and then **OK**.

For the analyses (e.g. correlation) that you perform after this **Select Cases** procedure, only the group that you selected (e.g. males) will be included.

Important: When you have finished the analyses, you need to go back and turn the **Select Cases** option off; otherwise, it will apply to all analyses conducted.

> 1. Click on the **Data** menu and choose **Select Cases** option.
> 2. Click on the first **All cases** option. Click on **OK**.

MERGING FILES

There are times when it is necessary to merge different data files. IBM SPSS Statistics allows you to merge files by adding additional cases at the end of your file, or to add variables for each of the cases in an existing data file (e.g. merge Time 1 and Time 2 data). This second option is also useful when you have Excel files with information spread across different spreadsheets that need to be merged by ID.

To merge files by adding cases

This procedure will allow you to merge files that have the same variables but different cases—for example, where the same information is recorded at two different sites (e.g. clinic settings) or entered into separate files by two different people. The two files should have exactly the same variable names and properties (e.g. width, type, decimals) for the data you wish to merge.

If the ID numbers used in each file are the same (starting at ID = 1, 2, 3), you will need to change the ID numbers in one of the files before merging so that each case is still uniquely identified. You cannot have two different cases with the same ID.

---

1. Choose **Transform** from the menu, and then **Compute Variable**.
2. Type ID in the **Target Variable** box, and then ID + 1000 in the **Numeric Expression** box (or some number that is bigger than the number of cases in the file).
3. Click on the **OK** button, and then on **OK** in the dialogue box that asks if you wish to change the variable. This will create new ID numbers for this file starting at 1001,1002 etc. Note this in your codebook for future reference.

Then you are ready to merge the files.

1. Open the first file that you wish to merge.
2. Go to the **Data** menu, choose **Merge Files** and then **Add Cases**.
3. In the dialogue box, click on **An external SPSS data file** and choose the file that you wish to merge with. (If your second file is already open it will be listed in the top box, **An open dataset**.)
4. Click on **Continue** and then on **OK**.
5. Save the new data file using a different name by using **File**, **Save As**.

To merge files by adding variables

This option is useful when adding additional information for each case by merging a second file containing additional variables. Each file must start with an ID variable which has identical properties (e.g. width, type, decimals).

1. Sort each file in ascending order by ID by clicking on the **Data** menu, choose **Sort Cases** and choose **ID** and then click **OK**. Alternatively, click on the variable name in the **Data View** tab, right click in the column and select **Sort Ascending**.

2. Go to the **Data** menu, choose **Merge files** and then **Add Variables**.

3. In the dialogue box, click on **An external SPSS data file** and choose the file that you wish to merge with. If your second file is already open it will be listed in the top box, **An open dataset**.

4. Click on **Continue**.

5. Click on the **Variables** tab at the top of the screen. Make sure that the ID variable is listed in the **Key Variables** box. SPSS has selected this for you as it is the only variable that occurs in both data files.

6. Choose the second option: **One-to-one based on key values**. This allows you to specify ID to ensure the files merge correctly.

7. In the **Key variables** section towards the bottom of the screen make sure that the ID variable is listed. This means that all information will be matched by ID. Click on **OK**.

8. Save your merged file under a different name (**File**, **Save As**).

USING SETS

With large data files, it can be a pain to have to scroll through lots of variable names in the dialogue boxes to reach the ones that you want to analyse. IBM SPSS Statistics allows you to define and use sets of variables. This is particularly useful in the **survey. sav** data file, where there are lots of individual items that are added to give total scores, located at the end of the file. In the following example, I establish a set that includes only the demographic variables and the scale totals.

1. Click on **Utilities** from the menu and choose **Define Variable Sets**.

2. Choose the variables you want in your set from the list. Include ID, the demographic variables (sex through to smoke number) and then all the totals at the end of the data file from Total Optimism onwards. Move these into the **Variables in Set** box.

3. In the box **Set Name**, type an appropriate name for your set (e.g. Totals).

4. Click on the **Add Set** button and then on **Close**.

To use the sets you have created, you need to activate them.

1. Click on **Utilities** and on **Use Variable Sets**.
2. In the list of variable sets, tick the set you have created (Totals) and then go up and untick the **ALLVARIABLES** option, as this would display all variables. Leave **NEWVARIABLES** ticked. Click on **OK**.

With the sets activated, only the selected variables will be displayed in the data file and in the dialogue boxes used to conduct statistical analyses.

To turn the Sets option off

1. Click on **Utilities** and on **Use Variable Sets**.
2. Tick the **ALLVARIABLES** option and click **OK**.

Data file comments

Under the **Utilities** menu, IBM SPSS Statistics provides you with the chance to save descriptive comments with a data file.

1. Select **Utilities** and **Data File Comments**.
2. Type in your comments, and if you would like them recorded in the output file, click on the option **Display comments in output**. Comments are saved with the date they were made.

Display value labels in data file

When the data file is displayed in the **Data Editor** window, the numerical values for all variables are usually shown. If you would like the value labels (e.g. male, female) displayed instead, go to the **View** menu and choose **Value Labels**. To turn this option off, go to the **View** menu and click on **Value Labels** again to remove the tick.

5

Screening and cleaning the data

Before you start to analyse your data, it is essential that you check your data set for errors. It is very easy to make mistakes when entering data, and unfortunately some errors can completely mess up your analyses. For example, entering 35 when you mean to enter 3 can distort the results of a correlation analysis. Some analyses are very sensitive to outliers—that is, values that are well below or well above the other scores. So, it is important to spend the time checking for mistakes initially, rather than trying to repair the damage later. Although boring, and a threat to your eyesight if you have large data sets, this process is essential and will save you a lot of heartache later!

The data screening process involves two steps:

> *Step 1: Check for errors:* Check each of your variables for scores that are out of range (i.e. not within the range of possible scores).
> *Step 2: Find and correct the error in the data file:* Find where in the data file this error occurred (i.e. which case is involved) and correct or delete the value.

To give you the chance to practise these steps, I have created a modified data file (**error.sav**) that is provided on the website accompanying this book (this is based on the main file **survey.sav**—see details on p. ix and in the Appendix). To follow along, you will need to start IBM SPSS Statistics and open the **error.sav** file. In working through each of the steps on the computer you will become more familiar with the use of menus, interpreting the output and manipulating your data file. For each of the procedures, I have included the IBM SPSS Statistics syntax, the commands that the program uses behind the scenes. For more information on the use of the **Syntax Editor** for recording and saving the IBM SPSS Statistics commands, see Chapter 3.

Important: Before you start, you should go to the **Edit** menu and choose **Options**. Under the **Output** tab, go down to the final box (**Variable values in labels shown as:**) and choose **Values and Labels**. This will allow you to display both the values and the labels used for each of your categorical variables—making identification of errors easier.

STEP 1: CHECK FOR ERRORS

When checking for errors, you are trying to identify values that fall outside the range of possible values for a variable. For example, if sex is coded 1 = male, 2 = female, you should not find any scores other than 1 or 2 for this variable. Scores that fall outside the possible range can distort your statistical analyses—so it is very important that all these errors are corrected before you start. To check for errors, you will need to inspect the frequencies for *each* of your variables. This includes all of the individual items that make up the scales. Errors must be corrected before total scores for these scales are calculated. It is a good idea to keep a log book in which you record any errors that you detect and any changes that you make to your data file.

There are several ways to check for errors using IBM SPSS Statistics. I illustrate two different ways below, one that is more suitable for categorical variables (e.g. sex) and the other for continuous variables (e.g. age).

Checking categorical variables

In the example shown below, I use the **error.sav** data file (included on the website accompanying this book—see p. ix), checking for errors on the categorical variables sex, marital and educ. Some deliberate errors have been introduced in the **error.sav** data file so that you can get practice spotting them.

Procedure for checking categorical variables
1. From the main menu at the top of the screen, click on **Analyze**, then click on **Descriptive Statistics**, then **Frequencies**.
2. Choose the variables that you wish to check (e.g. sex, marital, educ).
   To assist in finding the variables you want you can right click on the list of variables and select **Sort Alphabetically**, or to show **Variable Names** or **Variable Labels**.
3. Click on the arrow button to move these into the **Variable** box.
4. Click on the **Statistics** button. Tick **Minimum** and **Maximum** in the **Dispersion** section.
5. Click on **Continue** and then on **OK** (or on **Paste** to save to **Syntax Editor**).

The syntax generated from this procedure is:

```
FREQUENCIES
  VARIABLES=sex marital educ
  /STATISTICS=MINIMUM MAXIMUM
  /ORDER= ANALYSIS .
```

Selected output generated using this procedure is displayed as follows.

Statistics

		sex sex	marital marital status	educ highest educ completed
N	Valid	439	439	439
	Missing	0	0	0
Minimum		1	1	1
Maximum		3	8	22

sex sex

		Frequency	Percent	Valid Percent	Cumulative Percent
Valid	1 MALES	185	42.1	42.1	42.1
	2 FEMALES	253	57.6	57.6	99.8
	3	1	.2	.2	100.0
	Total	439	100.0	100.0	

marital marital status

		Frequency	Percent	Valid Percent	Cumulative Percent
Valid	1 SINGLE	105	23.9	23.9	23.9
	2 STEADY RELATIONSHIP	37	8.4	8.4	32.3
	3 LIVING WITH PARTNER	37	8.4	8.4	40.8
	4 MARRIED FIRST TIME	189	43.1	43.1	83.8
	5 REMARRIED	30	6.8	6.8	90.7
	6 SEPARATED	10	2.3	2.3	92.9
	7 DIVORCED	24	5.5	5.5	98.4
	8 WIDOWED	7	1.6	1.6	100.0
	Total	439	100.0	100.0	

educ highest educ completed

		Frequency	Percent	Valid Percent	Cumulative Percent
Valid	1 PRIMARY	2	.5	.5	.5
	2 SOME SECONDARY	52	11.8	11.8	12.3
	3 COMPLETED HIGHSCHOOL	85	19.4	19.4	31.7
	4 SOME ADDITIONAL TRAINING	120	27.3	27.3	59.0
	5 COMPLETED UNDERGRADUATE	123	28.0	28.0	87.0
	6 POSTGRADUATE COMPLETED	56	12.8	12.8	99.8
	22	1	.2	.2	100.0
	Total	439	100.0	100.0	

There are two parts to the output. The first table provides a summary of each of the variables you requested. The remaining tables give you a breakdown, for each variable, of the range of responses. (These are listed using the value label and the code number that were used if you changed the **Options** as suggested earlier in this chapter.)

➢ Check your **Minimum** and **Maximum** values. Do they make sense? Are they within the range of possible scores on that variable? You can see from the first table (labelled **Statistics**) that, for the variable sex, the minimum value is 1 and the maximum is 3. This value is incorrect, as the maximum value should only be 2 according to the codebook in the Appendix. For marital status, the scores are within the appropriate range of 1 to 8. The maximum value for highest level of education is 22, indicating an error, as the maximum value should only be 6.

➢ Check the number of **Valid** and **Missing** cases. If there are a lot of missing cases, you need to ask why. Have you made errors in entering the data (e.g. put the data in the wrong columns)? Sometimes, extra cases appear at the bottom of the data file, where you may have moved your cursor too far down and accidentally created some empty cases. If this occurs, open your **Data Editor** window, move down to the empty case row, click in the shaded area where the case number appears and press **Delete** on your keyboard. Rerun the **Frequencies** procedure again to get the correct values.

➢ Other tables are also presented in the output, corresponding to each of the variables. In these tables, you can see how many cases fell into each of the legitimate categories. They also show how many cases have out-of-range values. There is one case with a value of 3 for sex, and one person with a value of 22 for education. We will need to find out where these errors occurred, but first I demonstrate how to check for errors in some of the continuous (Scale) variables in the data file.

Checking continuous variables

Procedure for checking continuous variables
1. From the menu at the top of the screen, click on **Analyze**, then click on **Descriptive statistics**, then **Descriptives**.
2. Click on the variables that you wish to check (e.g. age). Click on the arrow button to move them into the **Variables** box.
3. Click on the **Options** button. You can ask for a range of statistics. The main ones at this stage are mean, standard deviation, minimum and maximum. Click on the statistics you wish to generate.
4. Click on **Continue**, and then on **OK** (or on **Paste** to save to **Syntax Editor**).

The syntax generated from this procedure is:

```
DESCRIPTIVES
   VARIABLES=age
   /STATISTICS=MEAN STDDEV MIN MAX .
```

The output generated from this procedure is shown as follows.

Descriptive Statistics

	N	Minimum	Maximum	Mean	Std. Deviation
age	439	2	82	37.39	13.293
Valid N (listwise)	439				

➢ Check the **Minimum** and **Maximum** values. Do these make sense? In this case, the ages range from 2 to 82. The minimum value suggests an error (given this was an adult-only sample).
➢ Does the **Mean** score make sense? If there is an out-of-range value in the data file, this will distort the mean value. If the variable is the total score on a scale, is the mean value what you expected from previous research on this scale?

STEP 2: FIND AND CORRECT THE ERROR IN THE DATA FILE

So, what do we do if we find some out-of-range responses (e.g. a value of 3 for sex)? First, we need to find the error in the data file. Don't try to scan through your entire data set looking for the error—there are more efficient ways to find an error in a data file.

Finding the error

1. Click on the **Data** menu and choose **Sort Cases**.

2. In the dialogue box that pops up, click on the variable that you know has an error (e.g. sex) and then on the arrow to move it into the **Sort By** box. Click on either **Ascending** or **Descending** (depending on whether you want the higher values at the top or the bottom). For sex, we want to find the person with the value of 3, so we would choose **Descending**. Click on **OK**.

    Alternatively, you can click on the variable's column in the **Data View** tab, right click in the column and choose **Sort Ascending** in the pop-up menu that appears.

In the **Data Editor** window, make sure that you have selected the **Data View** tab so that you can see your data values. The case with the error for your selected variable (e.g. sex) should now be located at the top of your data file. Look across to the variable column for sex. In this example, you will see that the first case listed (ID = 103) has a value of 3 for sex. If these were your data, you would need to access the original questionnaires and check whether the person with an identification number of 103 was male or female. You would then delete the value of 3 and type in the correct value. Record this information in your log book. If you don't have access to the original data, you should delete the incorrect value and let the program replace it with the system missing code (it will show as a full stop—this happens automatically; don't type a full stop).

When you find an error in your data file, it is important that you check for other errors in the surrounding columns. In this example, notice that the inappropriate value of 2 for age is also for person ID = 103.

After you have corrected your errors, it is essential to repeat **Frequencies** to double-check. Sometimes, in correcting one error you may have accidentally caused another error. Although this process is tedious, it is very important that you start with a clean, error-free data set. The success of your research depends on it. Don't cut corners!

CASE SUMMARIES

One other aspect of IBM SPSS Statistics that may be useful in this data screening process is **Summarize Cases**. This allows you to select and display specific pieces of information for each case.

1. Click on **Analyze**, go to **Reports** and choose **Case Summaries**.
2. Choose the ID variable and other variables you are interested in (e.g. sex, child, smoker).
3. Remove the tick from the **Limit cases to first 100**.
4. Click on the **Statistics** button and remove **Number of cases** from the **Cell Statistics** box. Click on **Continue**.
5. Click on the **Options** button and remove the tick from **Subheadings for totals**.
6. Click on **Continue** and then on **OK** (or on **Paste** to save to **Syntax Editor**).

The syntax from this procedure is:

```
SUMMARIZE
  /TABLES=id sex child smoke
  /FORMAT=VALIDLIST NOCASENUM NOTOTAL
  /TITLE='Case Summaries'
  /MISSING=VARIABLE
  /CELLS=NONE.
```

Part of the output is shown below.

Case Summaries

	id	sex sex	child child	smoke smoker
1	1	1 MALES	1 YES	2 NO
2	2	2 FEMALES	2 NO	2 NO
3	3	2 FEMALES	1 YES	2 NO
4	4	2 FEMALES	1 YES	2 NO

In this chapter, we have checked for errors in only a few of the variables in the data file to illustrate the process. For your own research, you would obviously check every variable in the data file. If you would like some more practice finding errors, repeat the procedures described above for all the variables in the **error.sav** data file. I have deliberately included a few errors to make the process more meaningful. Refer to the codebook in the Appendix for **survey.sav** to find out what the legitimate values for each variable should be.

For additional information on the screening and cleaning process, I would strongly recommend you read Chapter 4 in Tabachnick and Fidell (2013).

PART THREE
Preliminary analyses

Once you have a clean data file, you can begin the process of inspecting your data file and exploring the nature of your variables. This is in readiness for conducting specific statistical techniques to address your research questions. There are five chapters that make up Part Three of this book. In Chapter 6, the procedures required to obtain descriptive statistics for both categorical and continuous variables are presented. This chapter also covers checking the distribution of scores on continuous variables in terms of normality and possible outliers. Graphs can be useful tools when getting to know your data. Some of the more commonly used graphs available through IBM SPSS Statistics are presented in Chapter 7. Sometimes, manipulation of the data file is needed to make it suitable for specific analyses. This may involve calculating the total score on a scale, by adding up the scores obtained on each of the individual items. It may also involve collapsing a continuous variable into a smaller number of categories. These data manipulation techniques are covered in Chapter 8. In Chapter 9, the procedure used to check the reliability (internal consistency) of a scale is presented. This is particularly important in survey research, or in studies that involve the use of scales to measure personality characteristics, attitudes, beliefs and so on. In Chapter 10, you are provided with an overview of some of the statistical techniques available in IBM SPSS Statistics and led step by step through the process of deciding which one would suit your needs. Important aspects that you need to consider (e.g. types of question, data types, characteristics of the variables) are highlighted.

6

Descriptive statistics

Once you are sure there are no errors in the data file (or at least no out-of-range values on any of the variables), you can begin the descriptive phase of your data analysis. Descriptive statistics are used to:

➤ describe the characteristics of your sample in the Method section of your report
➤ check your variables for any violation of the assumptions underlying the statistical techniques that you will use to address your research questions
➤ address specific research questions.

The two procedures outlined in Chapter 5 for checking the data will also give you information for describing your sample in the Method section of your report. In studies involving human participants, it is useful to collect information on the number of people or cases in the sample, the number and percentage of males and females in the sample, the range and mean of ages, education level, and any other relevant background information. Prior to doing many of the statistical analyses (e.g. t-test, ANOVA, correlation), it is important to check that you are not violating any of the assumptions made by the individual tests. (These are covered in detail in Part Four and Part Five of this book.)

Testing of assumptions usually involves obtaining descriptive statistics on your variables. These descriptive statistics include the mean, standard deviation, range of scores, skewness and kurtosis. In IBM SPSS Statistics there are several ways to obtain descriptive statistics. If all you want is a quick summary of the characteristics of the variables in your data file, you can use **Codebook**. To follow along with the examples in this chapter, open the **survey.sav** file.

Procedure for obtaining Codebook

1. Click on **Analyze**, go to **Reports** and choose **Codebook**.
2. Select the variables you want (e.g. sex, age) and move them into the **Codebook Variables** box.
3. Click on the **Output** tab and untick (by clicking on the box with a tick) all the **Options** except **Label**, **Value Labels** and **Missing Values**.
4. Click on the **Statistics** tab and make sure that all the options in both sections are ticked.
5. Click on **OK** (or on **Paste** to save to **Syntax Editor**).

The syntax generated from this procedure is:

```
CODEBOOK sex [n] age [s]
  /VARINFO LABEL VALUELABELS MISSING
  /OPTIONS VARORDER=VARLIST SORT=ASCENDING MAXCATS=200
  /STATISTICS COUNT PERCENT MEAN STDDEV QUARTILES.
```

The output is shown below.

sex

		Value	Count	Percent
Standard Attributes	Label	sex		
Valid Values	1	MALES	185	42.1%
	2	FEMALES	254	57.9%

age

		Value
Standard Attributes	Label	<none>
N	Valid	439
	Missing	0
Central Tendency and Dispersion	Mean	37.44
	Standard Deviation	13.202
	Percentile 25	26.00
	Percentile 50	36.00
	Percentile 75	47.00

The output from the procedure shown above gives you a quick summary of the cases in your data file. If you need more detailed information this can be obtained using the **Frequencies**, **Descriptives** or **Explore** procedures. These are all procedures listed under the **Analyze, Descriptive Statistics** drop-down menu. There are, however, different procedures depending on whether you have a categorical or continuous variable. Some of the statistics (e.g. mean, standard deviation) are not appropriate if you have a categorical variable. The different approaches to be used with categorical and continuous variables are presented in the following two sections. If you would like to follow along with the examples in this chapter, open the **survey.sav** file.

CATEGORICAL VARIABLES

To obtain descriptive statistics for categorical variables, you should use **Frequencies**. This will tell you how many people gave each response (e.g. how many males, how many females). It doesn't make any sense asking for means, standard deviations and so on for categorical variables, such as sex or marital status.

Procedure for obtaining descriptive statistics for categorical variables
1. From the menu click on **Analyze**, then click on **Descriptive Statistics**, then **Frequencies**.
2. Choose and highlight the categorical variables you are interested in (e.g. sex). Move these into the **Variables** box.
3. Click on **OK** (or on **Paste** to save to **Syntax Editor**).

The syntax generated from this procedure is:

```
FREQUENCIES
  VARIABLES=sex
  /ORDER= ANALYSIS .
```

The output is shown below.

sex sex

		Frequency	Percent	Valid Percent	Cumulative Percent
Valid	1 MALES	185	42.1	42.1	42.1
	2 FEMALES	254	57.9	57.9	100.0
	Total	439	100.0	100.0	

Interpretation of output from Frequencies

From the output shown above, we know that there are 185 males (42.1%) and 254 females (57.9%) in the sample, giving a total of 439 respondents. It is important to take note of the number of respondents you have in different subgroups in your sample. If you have very unequal group sizes, particularly if the group sizes are small, it may be inappropriate to run some of the parametric analyses (e.g. ANOVA).

CONTINUOUS VARIABLES

For continuous variables (e.g. age) it is easier to use **Descriptives**, which will provide you with the basic summary statistics such as mean, median and standard deviation. In some disciplines (e.g. medicine) you may be asked to provide a confidence interval around the mean. If you need this you should use **Explore** (this is explained later in this chapter).

You can collect the descriptive information on all your continuous variables in one go using **Descriptives**; it is not necessary to do it variable by variable. Just transfer all the variables you are interested in into the box labelled **Variables**. If you have a lot of variables, however, your output will be extremely long. Sometimes, it is easier to do them in chunks and tick off each group of variables as you do them.

Procedure for obtaining descriptive statistics for continuous variables
1. From the menu click on **Analyze**, then select **Descriptive Statistics**, then **Descriptives**.
2. Click on all the continuous variables that you wish to obtain descriptive statistics for. Click on the arrow button to move them into the **Variables** box (e.g. age, Total perceived stress: tpstress).
3. Click on the **Options** button. Make sure **mean**, **standard deviation**, **minimum**, **maximum** are ticked and then click on **skewness**, **kurtosis**.
4. Click on **Continue**, and then **OK** (or on **Paste** to save to **Syntax Editor**).

The syntax generated from this procedure is:

```
DESCRIPTIVES
 VARIABLES=age tpstress
 /STATISTICS=MEAN STDDEV MIN MAX KURTOSIS SKEWNESS .
```

The output generated from this procedure is shown below.

Descriptive Statistics

	N	Minimum	Maximum	Mean	Std. Deviation	Skewness		Kurtosis	
	Statistic	Statistic	Statistic	Statistic	Statistic	Statistic	Std. Error	Statistic	Std. Error
age	439	18	82	37.44	13.202	.606	.117	- 203	.233
tpstress Total perceived stress	433	12	46	26.73	5.848	.245	.117	182	.234
Valid N (listwise)	433								

Interpretation of output from Descriptives

In the output presented above, the information we requested for each of the variables is summarised. For the variable age we have information from 439 respondents, ranging in age from 18 to 82 years, with a mean of 37.44 and standard deviation of 13.202. This information may be needed for the Method section of a report to describe the characteristics of the sample. When reported in a thesis or journal article these values are usually rounded to two decimal places.

Descriptives also provides some information concerning the distribution of scores on continuous variables (skewness and kurtosis). This information may be needed if these variables are to be used in parametric statistical techniques (e.g. t-tests, analysis of variance). The **Skewness** value provides an indication of the symmetry of the distribution. **Kurtosis**, on the other hand, provides information about the 'peakedness' of the distribution. If the distribution is perfectly normal, you would obtain a skewness and kurtosis value of 0 (rather an uncommon occurrence in the social sciences).

Positive skewness values suggest that scores are clustered to the left at the low values. Negative skewness values indicate a clustering of scores at the high end (right-hand side of a graph). Positive kurtosis values indicate that the distribution is rather peaked (clustered in the centre), with long, thin tails. Kurtosis values below 0 indicate a distribution that is relatively flat (too many cases in the extremes). With reasonably large samples, skewness will not 'make a substantive difference in the analysis' (Tabachnick & Fidell 2013, p. 80). Kurtosis can result in an underestimate of the variance, but this risk is also reduced with a large sample (200+ cases; see Tabachnick & Fidell 2013, p. 80).

While there are tests that you can use to evaluate skewness and kurtosis values, these are too sensitive with large samples. Tabachnick and Fidell (2013, p. 81) recommend inspecting the shape of the distribution (e.g. using a histogram). The procedure for further assessing the normality of the distribution of scores is provided later in this chapter.

When you have skewed data you should report non-parametric descriptive statistics which do not assume a normal distribution (discussed in more detail later in this chapter). The **mean** (a parametric statistic) can be distorted when you have very skewed data, and it is generally recommended that you present the **median** instead (a non-parametric statistic). The median is the value that cuts the distribution of scores in half—50 per cent fall above and below this point.

Whenever you present a median value you should also provide an indication of the spread, or dispersion, of your scores. The non-parametric statistic appropriate here is the *interquartile range* (IQR), which represents the 25th percentile and the 75th percentile values. The easiest way to get these values is to use the **Codebook** procedure outlined earlier in this chapter. These results show as 'Percentile 25', 'Percentile 50' (this is actually the median) and 'Percentile 75'. You can also obtain the same values from the **Frequencies** procedure by requesting **Quartiles** under the **Statistics** button.

Using the example of age presented earlier in this chapter, you would present the information shown in the output in a thesis or article as *Md* = 36 (*IQR*: 26, 47).

MISSING DATA

When you are doing research, particularly with human beings, it is rare that you will obtain complete data from every case. It is important that you inspect your data file for missing data. Run **Descriptives** and find out what percentage of values is missing for each of your variables. If you find a variable with a lot of unexpected missing data, you need to ask yourself why. You should also consider whether your missing values occur randomly, or whether there is some systematic pattern (e.g. lots of women over 30 years of age failing to answer the question about their age!).

You also need to consider how you will deal with missing values when you come to do your statistical analyses. The **Options** button in many of the IBM SPSS Statistics statistical procedures offers you choices for how you want to deal with missing data. It is important that you choose carefully, as it can have dramatic effects on your results. This is particularly important if you are including a list of variables and repeating the same analysis for all variables (e.g. correlations among a group of variables, t-tests for a series of dependent variables).

➤ The **Exclude cases listwise** option will include cases in the analysis only if they have full data on *all of the variables* listed in your **Variables** box for that case. A case will be totally excluded from all the analyses if it is missing even one piece of information. This can severely, and unnecessarily, limit your sample size.
➤ The **Exclude cases pairwise** option excludes the case (person) only if they are missing the data required for the specific analysis. They will still be included in any of the analyses for which they have the necessary information.
➤ The **Replace with mean** option, which is available in some IBM SPSS Statistics statistical procedures (e.g. multiple regression), calculates the mean value for the variable

and gives every missing case this value. This option should *never* be used, as it can severely distort the results of your analysis, particularly if you have a lot of missing values.

Always press the **Options** button for any statistical procedure you conduct, and check which of these options is ticked (the default option varies across procedures). I would suggest that you use pairwise exclusion of missing data, unless you have a pressing reason to do otherwise. The only situation where you might need to use listwise exclusion is when you want to refer only to a subset of cases that provided a full set of results.

For more experienced researchers, there are more advanced options available in IBM SPSS Statistics for estimating missing values (e.g. imputation). These are included in the **Missing Value Analysis** procedure. This can also be used to detect patterns within missing data. I recommend you read Chapter 4 in Tabachnick and Fidell (2013) for more detailed coverage of missing data.

ASSESSING NORMALITY

Many of the statistical techniques presented in Part Four and Part Five of this book assume that the distribution of scores on the dependent variable is normal. *Normal* is used to describe a symmetrical, bell-shaped curve, which has the greatest frequency of scores in the middle with smaller frequencies towards the extremes. Normality can be assessed to some extent by obtaining skewness and kurtosis values (as described earlier in this chapter). However, other techniques are also available in IBM SPSS Statistics using the **Explore** option of the **Descriptive Statistics** menu. This procedure is detailed below. In this example, I assess the normality of the distribution of scores for the Total perceived stress variable. You also have the option of doing this separately for different groups in your sample by specifying an additional categorical variable (e.g. sex) in the **Factor List** option that is available in the **Explore** dialogue box.

Procedure for assessing normality using Explore

1. From the menu at the top of the screen click on **Analyze**, then select **Descriptive Statistics**, then **Explore**.
2. Click on all the variables you are interested in (e.g. Total perceived stress: tpstress). Click on the arrow button to move them into the **Dependent List** box.
3. In the **Label Cases by** box, put your ID variable.
4. In the **Display** section, make sure that **Both** is selected.
5. Click on the **Statistics** button and click on **Descriptives** and **Outliers**. Click on **Continue**.
6. Click on the **Plots** button. Under **Descriptive**, click on **Histogram** to select it. Click on **Stem-and-leaf** to unselect it. Click on **Normality plots with tests**. Click on **Continue**.
7. Click on the **Options** button. In the **Missing Values** section, click on **Exclude cases pairwise**. Click on **Continue** and then **OK** (or on **Paste** to save to **Syntax Editor**).

The syntax generated is:

```
EXAMINE VARIABLES=tpstress
 /ID=id
 /PLOT BOXPLOT HISTOGRAM NPPLOT
 /COMPARE GROUPS
 /STATISTICS DESCRIPTIVES EXTREME
 /CINTERVAL 95
 /MISSING PAIRWISE
 /NOTOTAL.
```

Selected output generated from this procedure is shown below.

Descriptives

			Statistic	Std. Error
tpstress Total perceived stress	Mean		26.73	.281
	95% Confidence Interval for Mean	Lower Bound	26.18	
		Upper Bound	27.28	
	5% Trimmed Mean		26.64	
	Median		26.00	
	Variance		34.194	
	Std. Deviation		5.848	
	Minimum		12	
	Maximum		46	
	Range		34	
	Interquartile Range		8	
	Skewness		.245	.117
	Kurtosis		.182	.234

Extreme Values

			Case Number	id	Value
tpstress Total perceived stress	Highest	1	7	24	46
		2	262	157	44
		3	216	61	43
		4	190	6	42
		5	257	144	42[a]
	Lowest	1	366	404	12
		2	189	5	12
		3	247	127	13
		4	244	119	13
		5	98	301	13

a. Only a partial list of cases with the value 42 are shown in the table of upper extremes.

Tests of Normality

	Kolmogorov-Smirnov[a]			Shapiro-Wilk		
	Statistic	df	Sig.	Statistic	df	Sig.
tpstress Total perceived stress	.069	433	.000	.992	433	.021

a. Lilliefors Significance Correction

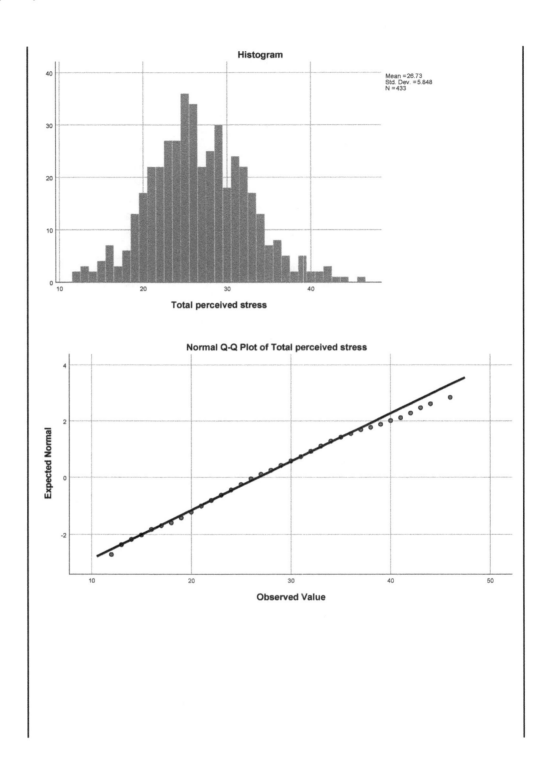

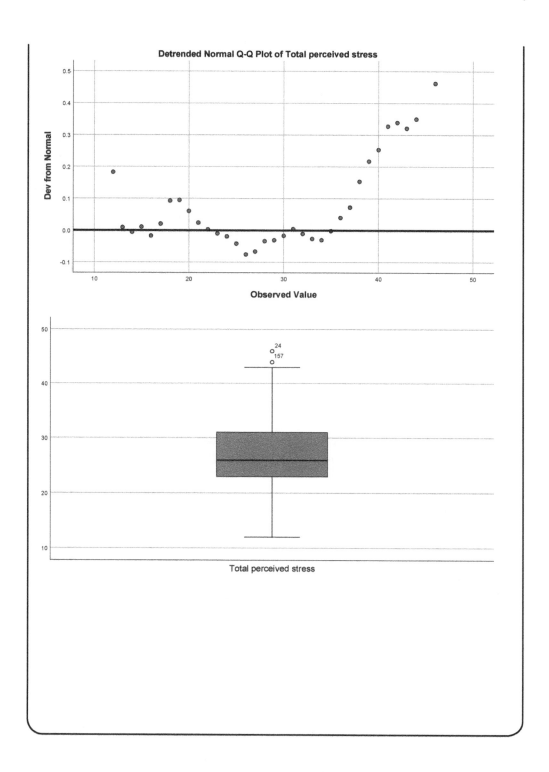

Interpretation of output from Explore

Quite a lot of information is generated as part of this output. I take you through it step by step below.

➤ In the table labelled **Descriptives**, you are provided with descriptive statistics and other information concerning your variables. If you specified a grouping variable in the **Factor List**, this information will be provided separately for each group, rather than for the sample as a whole. Some of this information you may recognise (mean, median, standard deviation, minimum, maximum etc.). This output also shows the 95 per cent confidence interval surrounding the mean. We can be 95 per cent confident that the true mean value in the population falls within this range.

One statistic you may not know is the **5% Trimmed Mean**. To obtain this value, IBM SPSS Statistics removes the top and bottom 5 per cent of your cases and calculates a new mean value. If you compare the original mean (26.73) and this new trimmed mean (26.64), you can see whether your extreme scores are having a strong influence on the mean. If these two mean values are very different, you may need to investigate these data points further. The ID values of the most extreme cases are shown in the **Extreme Values** table.

➤ **Skewness** and **kurtosis** values are also provided as part of this output, giving information about the distribution of scores for the two groups (see discussion of the meaning of these values earlier in this chapter).

➤ In the table labelled **Tests of Normality**, you are given the results of the **Kolmogorov-Smirnov** statistic. This assesses the normality of the distribution of scores. A non-significant result (**Sig.** value of more than .05) indicates normality. In this case, the Sig. value is .000, suggesting violation of the assumption of normality. This is quite common in larger samples. Tabachnick and Fidell (2013) recommend using the histograms instead to judge normality.

➤ The actual shape of the distribution for each group can be seen in the **Histograms**. In this example, scores appear to be reasonably normally distributed. This is also supported by an inspection of the normal probability plots (labelled **Normal Q-Q Plot**). In this plot, the observed value for each score is plotted against the expected value from the normal distribution. A reasonably straight line suggests a normal distribution.

➤ The **Detrended Normal Q-Q Plots** are obtained by plotting the deviation of the scores from the straight line. There should be no real clustering of points, with most collecting around the zero line.

➤ The final plot that is provided in the output is a **boxplot** of the distribution of scores for the two groups. The rectangle represents 50 per cent of the cases, with the whiskers (the lines protruding from the box) going out to the smallest and largest values. Sometimes, you will see additional circles outside this range—these are classified by IBM SPSS Statistics as outliers. The line inside the rectangle is the median value. Boxplots are discussed further in the next section, on detecting outliers.

In the example given above, the distribution of scores was reasonably normal. Often, this is not the case. Many scales and measures used in the social sciences have scores that are skewed, either positively or negatively. This does not necessarily indicate a problem with the scale but rather reflects the underlying nature of the construct being measured. Life satisfaction measures, for example, are often negatively skewed, with most people being reasonably happy with their life. Clinical measures of anxiety or depression are often positively skewed in the general population, with most people recording relatively few symptoms of these disorders. Some authors in this area recommend that with skewed data the scores be transformed statistically. This issue is discussed further in Chapter 8.

CHECKING FOR OUTLIERS

Many of the statistical techniques covered in this book are sensitive to outliers (cases with values well above or well below the majority of other cases). The techniques described in the previous section can also be used to check for outliers.

➤ Inspect the **Histogram**. Check the tails of the distribution. Are there data points sitting on their own, out on the extremes? If so, these are potential outliers. If the scores drop away in a reasonably even slope, there is probably not too much to worry about.

➤ Inspect the **Boxplot**. Any scores that IBM SPSS Statistics considers are outliers appear as little circles with a number attached (this is the ID number of the case). IBM SPSS Statistics defines points as outliers if they extend more than 1.5 box-lengths from the edge of the box. Extreme points (indicated with an asterisk) are those that extend more than 3 box-lengths from the edge of the box. In the example above there are no extreme points, but there are two outliers: ID numbers 24 and 157. If you find points like this, you need to decide what to do with them.

➤ It is important to check that an outlier's score is genuine and not an error. Check the score and see whether it is within the range of possible scores for that variable. Check back with the questionnaire or data record to see if there was a mistake in entering the data. If it is an error, correct it, and repeat the boxplot. If it turns out to be a genuine score, you then need to decide what you will do about it. Some statistics writers suggest removing all extreme outliers from the data file. Others suggest changing the value to a less extreme value, thus including the case in the analysis but not allowing the score to distort the statistics (for more advice on this, see Chapter 4 in Tabachnick & Fidell 2013).

> ➤ The information in the **Descriptives** table can give you an indication of how much of a problem these outlying cases are likely to be. The value you are interested in is the **5% Trimmed Mean**. If the trimmed mean and mean values are very different, you may need to investigate these data points further. In the example above, the two mean values (26.73 and 26.64) are very similar. Given this, and the fact that the values are not too different from the remaining distribution, I would retain these cases in the data file.

> ➤ If you wish to change or remove values in your file, go to the **Data Editor** window, sort the data file in descending order to find the cases with the highest values or in ascending order if you are concerned about cases with very low values. The cases you need to investigate in more detail are then at the top of the data file. Move across to the column representing that variable and modify or delete the value of concern. Always record changes to your data file in a log book.

ADDITIONAL EXERCISES

Business

Data file: **staffsurvey.sav**. See Appendix for details of the data file.

1. Follow the procedures covered in this chapter to generate *appropriate* descriptive statistics to answer the following questions.
   (a) What percentage of the staff in this organisation are permanent employees? (Use the variable *employstatus*.)
   (b) What is the average length of service for staff in the organisation? (Use the variable *service*.)
   (c) What percentage of respondents would recommend the organisation to others as a good place to work? (Use the variable *recommend*.)
2. Assess the distribution of scores on the Total Staff Satisfaction Scale (*totsatis*) for employees who are permanent versus casual (*employstatus*).
   (a) Are there any outliers on this scale that you would be concerned about?
   (b) Are scores normally distributed for each group?

Health

Data file: **sleep.sav**. See Appendix for details of the data file.

1. Follow the procedures covered in this chapter to generate *appropriate* descriptive statistics to answer the following questions.
   (a) What percentage of respondents are female (*gender*)?
   (b) What is the average age of the sample?
   (c) What percentage of the sample indicated that they had a problem with their sleep (*probsleeprec*)?
   (d) What is the median number of hours sleep per weeknight (*hourweeknight*)?
2. Assess the distribution of scores on the Sleepiness and Associated Sensations Scale (*totSAS*) for people who feel that they do/don't have a sleep problem (*probsleeprec*).
   (a) Are there any outliers on this scale that you would be concerned about?
   (b) Are scores normally distributed for each group?

7

Using graphs to describe and explore the data

While the numerical values obtained in Chapter 6 provide useful information concerning your sample and your variables, some aspects are better explored visually. IBM SPSS Statistics provides a variety of graphs (also referred to as charts). In this chapter, I cover the basic procedures to obtain histograms, bar graphs, line graphs, scatterplots and boxplots.

In IBM SPSS Statistics there are different ways of generating graphs, using the **Graph** menu option. These include **Chart Builder**, **Graphboard Template Chooser** and **Legacy Dialogs**. In this chapter I demonstrate the graphs using **Chart Builder**. Spend some time playing with each of the different graphs and exploring their possibilities. In this chapter only a brief overview is given to get you started. To illustrate the various graphs I use the **survey.sav** data file, which is included on the website accompanying this book (see p. ix and the Appendix for details). If you wish to follow along with the procedures described in this chapter, you will need to start IBM SPSS Statistics and open the file labelled **survey.sav**.

At the end of this chapter, instructions are also given on how to edit a graph to better suit your needs. This may be useful if you intend to use the graph in your research paper or thesis. The procedure for importing graphs directly into Microsoft Word is also detailed. For additional hints and tips on presenting graphs I suggest you see Nicol and Pexman (2010a).

Before you begin any of the graphs procedures it is important that you have defined the measurement properties of each of your variables in the **Data Editor** window (see Chapter 4, in the Defining the Variables section). Each variable needs to be correctly identified as **Nominal** (categories involving no order), **Ordinal** (categories which are ordered), and **Scale** (continuous with lots of values).

HISTOGRAMS

Histograms are used to display the distribution of a single continuous variable (e.g. age, perceived stress scores).

Procedure for creating a histogram

1. From the menu click on **Graphs**, then select **Chart Builder**. Click **OK**.
2. To choose the type of graph that you want, click on the **Gallery** tab, and choose **Histogram**.
3. Click on the first image shown (**Simple Histogram**) and drag it up to the **Chart Preview** area, holding your left mouse button down.
4. Choose your continuous variable from the list of **Variables** (e.g. tpstress) and drag it across to the area on the **Chart preview** screen labelled **X-Axis** holding your left mouse button down. This will only work if you have identified your variable as scale in the **Data Editor** window (the icon next to the variable should be a ruler).
5. If you would like to generate separate graphs for different groups (e.g. males/females) you can click on the **Groups/Point ID** tab and choose the **Column Panels variable** option. This will produce separate graphs next to each other; if you would prefer them to be on top of one another choose the **Rows panel variable**.
6. Choose your categorical grouping variable (e.g. sex) and drag it across to the section labelled **Panel** in the **Chart Preview** area.
7. Click on the **Options** tab on the right-hand side of the screen and select **Exclude variable-by-variable**.
8. Click on **OK** (or on **Paste** to save to **Syntax Editor**).

The syntax generated from this procedure is:

```
GRAPH
 /GRAPHDATASET NAME="graphdataset" VARIABLES=tpstress sex
MISSING=VARIABLEWISE REPORTMISSING=NO
 /GRAPHSPEC SOURCE=INLINE.
BEGIN GPL
  SOURCE: s=userSource(id("graphdataset"))
  DATA: tpstress=col(source(s), name("tpstress"))
  DATA: sex=col(source(s), name("sex"), unit.category())
  GUIDE: axis(dim(1), label("Total perceived stress"))
  GUIDE: axis(dim(2), label("Frequency"))
  GUIDE: axis(dim(3), label("sex"), opposite())
  GUIDE: text.title(label("Simple Histogram of Total perceived stress by sex"))
  SCALE: cat(dim(3), include("1", "2"))
  ELEMENT: interval(position(summary.count(bin.rect(tpstress*1*sex))), shape.
  interior(shape.square))
END GPL.
```

The output generated from this procedure is shown below.

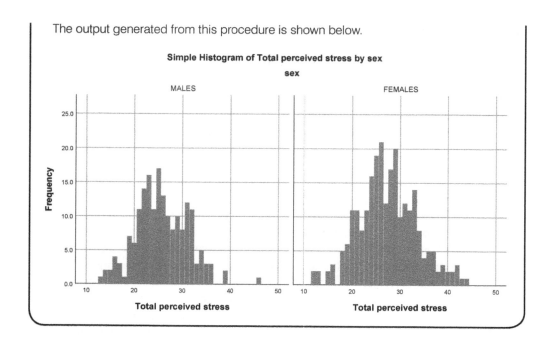

Simple Histogram of Total perceived stress by sex

Interpretation of output from Histogram

Inspection of the shape of the histogram provides information about the distribution of scores on the continuous variable. Many of the statistics discussed in this manual assume that the scores on each of the variables are normally distributed (i.e. follow the shape of the normal curve). In this example the scores are reasonably normally distributed, with most scores occurring in the centre and the rest tapering out towards the extremes. It is quite common in the social sciences, however, to find that variables are not normally distributed. Scores may be skewed to the left or right or, alternatively, arranged in a rectangular shape. For further discussion of the assessment of the normality of variables see Chapter 6.

BAR GRAPHS

Bar graphs can be simple or very complex, depending on how many variables you wish to include. A bar graph can show the number of cases in specific categories, or it can show the score on a continuous variable for different categories. Basically, you need two main variables—one categorical and one continuous. You can also break this down further with another categorical variable if you wish.

Procedure for creating a bar graph

1. From the menu at the top of the screen, click on **Graphs**, then select **Chart Builder** and click **OK**. Click on the **Gallery** tab and select **Bar** from the bottom left-hand menu. Click on the second graph displayed (**Clustered Bar**). Holding your left mouse button down, drag this graph to the **Chart Preview** area.

2. Select the **Element Properties** tab from the right-hand side of the screen. Click on **Display error bars**.

3. From the list of **Variables** drag one of your grouping variables (e.g. sex) to the section on the **Chart Preview** screen labelled **Cluster on X: set colour**. Click and drag your other categorical variable (e.g. agegp3) to the section labelled **X-Axis** at the bottom of the graph. Click and drag your continuous variable (Total Perceived Stress: tpstress) to the remaining blue section, the **Y-axis**.

4. Click on **OK** (or on **Paste** to save to **Syntax Editor**).

The syntax generated from this procedure is:

```
GGRAPH
 /GRAPHDATASET NAME="graphdataset" VARIABLES=agegp3 MEANCI(tpstress,
 95)[name="MEAN_tpstress"
  LOW="MEAN_tpstress_LOW" HIGH="MEAN_tpstress_HIGH"] sex
  MISSING=VARIABLEWISE REPORTMISSING=NO
 /GRAPHSPEC SOURCE=INLINE.
BEGIN GPL
 SOURCE: s=userSource(id("graphdataset"))
 DATA: agegp3=col(source(s), name("agegp3"), unit.category())
 DATA: MEAN_tpstress=col(source(s), name("MEAN_tpstress"))
 DATA: sex=col(source(s), name("sex"), unit.category())
 DATA: LOW=col(source(s), name("MEAN_tpstress_LOW"))
 DATA: HIGH=col(source(s), name("MEAN_tpstress_HIGH"))
 COORD: rect(dim(1,2), cluster(3,0))
 GUIDE: axis(dim(3), label("age 3 groups"))
 GUIDE: axis(dim(2), label("Mean Total perceived stress"))
 GUIDE: legend(aesthetic(aesthetic.color.interior), label("sex"))
 GUIDE: text.title(label("Clustered Bar Mean of Total perceived stress by age
 3 groups by sex"))
 GUIDE: text.footnote(label("Error Bars: 95% CI"))
 SCALE: cat(dim(3), include("1", "2", "3"))
 SCALE: linear(dim(2), include(0))
```

```
SCALE: cat(aesthetic(aesthetic.color.interior), include("1", "2"),
aestheticMissing(color.black))
SCALE: cat(dim(1), include("1", "2"))
ELEMENT: interval(position(sex*MEAN_tpstress*agegp3), color.interior(sex),
   shape.interior(shape.square))
ELEMENT: interval(position(region.spread.range(sex*(LOW+HIGH)*agegp3)),
   shape.interior(shape.ibeam))
END GPL.
```

The output generated from this procedure is shown below.

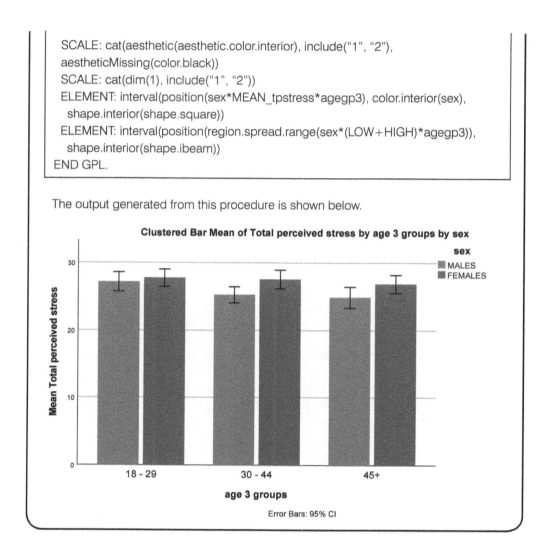

Interpretation of output from Bar Graph

The output from this procedure gives you a quick summary of the distribution of scores for the groups that you have requested (in this case, males and females from the different age groups). The graph presented above suggests that females had higher perceived stress scores than males, and that this difference was more pronounced among the two older age groups. Among the 18 to 29 age group, the difference in scores between males and females is very small.

Care should be taken when interpreting the output from **Bar Graph**. You should always check the scale used on the Y (vertical) axis. Sometimes, what appears to be a dramatic difference is really only a few scale points and, therefore, probably of little importance. This is clearly evident in the bar graph displayed above. You will see that the difference between the groups is quite small when you consider the scale used to display the graph. The difference between the smallest score (males aged 45 or more) and the highest score (females aged 18 to 29) is only about 3 points.

To assess the significance of any difference you might find between groups, it is necessary to conduct further statistical analyses. In this case, a two-way between-groups analysis of variance (see Chapter 19) would be conducted to find out if the differences are statistically significant.

LINE GRAPHS

A line graph allows you to inspect the mean scores of a continuous variable across different values of a categorical variable (e.g. age groups: 18–29, 30–44, 45+). They are also useful for graphically exploring the results of a one- or two-way analysis of variance. Line graphs are provided as an optional extra in the output of analysis of variance (see Chapters 18 and 19).

Procedure for creating a line graph
1. From the menu at the top of the screen, select **Graphs**, then **Chart Builder**, and then **OK**.
2. Click on the **Gallery** tab and select **Line** from the bottom left-hand list. Click on the second graph shown (**Multiple Line**) and drag this to the **Chart preview** area holding your left mouse button down.
3. From the **Variables** list drag your continuous variable (Total perceived stress: tpstress) to the **Y-axis**. Drag one of your categorical variables (e.g. sex) to the section labelled **Set color** and drag the other categorical variable (agegp5) to the **X-Axis**.
4. Click on **OK** (or on **Paste** to save to **Syntax Editor**).

The syntax generated from this procedure is:

```
GRAPH
 /GRAPHDATASET NAME="graphdataset" VARIABLES=agegp5 MEAN(tpstress)
 [name="MEAN_tpstress"] sex
   MISSING=VARIABLEWISE REPORTMISSING=NO
 /GRAPHSPEC SOURCE=INLINE.
BEGIN GPL
```

```
SOURCE: s=userSource(id("graphdataset"))
DATA: agegp5=col(source(s), name("agegp5"), unit.category())
DATA: MEAN_tpstress=col(source(s), name("MEAN_tpstress"))
DATA: sex=col(source(s), name("sex"), unit.category())
GUIDE: axis(dim(1), label("age 5 groups"))
GUIDE: axis(dim(2), label("Mean Total perceived stress"))
GUIDE: legend(aesthetic(aesthetic.color.interior), label("sex"))
GUIDE: text.title(label("Multiple Line Mean of Total perceived stress by age
5 groups by sex"))
GUIDE: text.footnote(label("Error Bars: 95% CI"))
SCALE: cat(dim(1), include("1", "2", "3", "4", "5"))
SCALE: linear(dim(2), include(0))
SCALE: cat(aesthetic(aesthetic.color.interior), include("1", "2"),
aestheticMissing(color.black))
ELEMENT: line(position(agegp5*MEAN_tpstress), color.interior(sex), missing.
wings())
END GPL.
```

The output from the procedure is shown below. For display purposes I have modified the output graph so that the line for females is shown as dashed, and I have also reduced the scale of the Y-axis to start at a score of 24. The procedure for modifying graphs is provided later in this chapter.

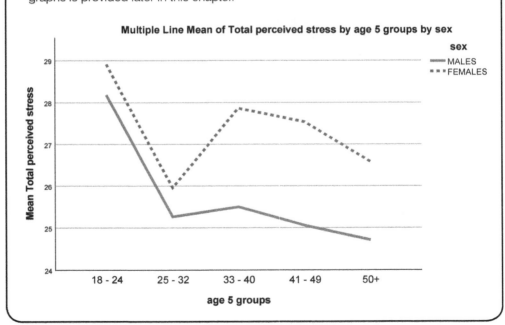

Interpretation of output from Line Graph

➤ First, you can examine the impact of age on perceived stress for each of the sexes separately. Younger males appear to have higher levels of perceived stress than either middle-aged or older males. For females, the difference across the age groups is not quite so pronounced. The older females are only slightly less stressed than the younger group.

➤ You can also consider the differences between males and females. Overall, males appear to have lower levels of perceived stress than females. Although the difference for the younger group is only small, there appears to be a discrepancy for the older age groups. Whether or not these differences reach statistical significance can be determined only by performing a two-way analysis of variance (see Chapter 19).

The results presented above suggest that, to understand the impact of age on perceived stress, you must consider the respondents' gender. This sort of relationship is referred to as an 'interaction effect'. While the use of a line graph does not tell you whether this relationship is statistically significant, it certainly gives you a lot of information and raises a lot of additional questions.

Sometimes, in interpreting the output, it is useful to consider other research questions. In this case, the results suggest that it may be worthwhile to explore in more depth the relationship between age and perceived stress for the two groups (males and females) separately, rather than assuming that the impact of age is similar for both groups.

SCATTERPLOTS

Scatterplots are typically used to explore the relationship between two continuous variables (e.g. age and self-esteem). It is a good idea to generate a scatterplot *before* calculating correlations (see Chapter 11). The scatterplot will give you an indication of whether your variables are related in a linear (straight-line) or curvilinear fashion. Only linear relationships are suitable for the correlation analyses described in this book.

The scatterplot will also indicate whether your variables are positively related (high scores on one variable are associated with high scores on the other) or negatively related (high scores on one are associated with low scores on the other). For positive correlations, the points form a line pointing upwards to the right (i.e. they start low on the left-hand side and move higher on the right). For negative correlations, the line starts high on the left and moves down on the right (see an example of this in the output below).

The scatterplot also provides a general indication of the strength of the relationship between your two variables. If the relationship is weak the points will be all over the place, in a blob-type arrangement. For a strong relationship the points will form a vague cigar shape, with a definite clumping of scores around an imaginary straight line.

In the example that follows, I request a scatterplot of scores on two of the scales in the survey: the Total perceived stress and the Total Perceived Control of Internal States Scale (PCOISS). I ask for two groups in my sample (males and females) to be represented separately on the one scatterplot (using different symbols). This not only provides me with information concerning my sample as a whole but also gives additional information on the distribution of scores for males and females.

Procedure for creating a scatterplot

1. From the menu at the top of the screen, click on **Graphs**, then **Chart Builder**, and then **OK**.
2. Click on the **Gallery** tab and select **Scatter/Dot**. Click on the third graph (**Grouped Scatter**) and drag this to the **Chart Preview** area by holding your left mouse button down.
3. Click and drag your continuous, independent variable (Total PCOISS: tpcoiss) to the **X-Axis**, and click and drag your dependent variable (Total perceived stress: tpstress) to the **Y-Axis**. Both variables need to be nominated as Scale variables. If you want to show groups (e.g. males, females) separately choose your categorical grouping variable (e.g. sex) and drag to the **Set Colour** box.
4. Choose the **Groups/Point ID** tab. Tick **Point ID** label. Click on the ID variable and drag to the **Point ID** box on the graph.
5. Click on **OK** (or on **Paste** to save to **Syntax Editor**).

The syntax generated from this procedure is:

```
GRAPH
 /GRAPHDATASET NAME="graphdataset" VARIABLES=tpcoiss tpstress sex
 MISSING=VARIABLEWISE
  REPORTMISSING=NO
 /GRAPHSPEC SOURCE=INLINE
 /FITLINE TOTAL=NO SUBGROUP=NO.
BEGIN GPL
  SOURCE: s=userSource(id("graphdataset"))
  DATA: tpcoiss=col(source(s), name("tpcoiss"))
  DATA: tpstress=col(source(s), name("tpstress"))
  DATA: sex=col(source(s), name("sex"), unit.category())
  GUIDE: axis(dim(1), label("Total PCOISS"))
  GUIDE: axis(dim(2), label("Total perceived stress"))
 GUIDE: legend(aesthetic(aesthetic.color.interior), label("sex"))
```

```
UIDE: text.title(label("Grouped Scatter of Total perceived stress by Total PCOISS by
sex"))
SCALE: cat(aesthetic(aesthetic.color.interior), include("1", "2"),
aestheticMissing(color.black))
ELEMENT: point(position(tpcoiss*tpstress), color.interior(sex))
END GPL.
```

The output generated from this procedure, modified slightly for display purposes, is
shown below. Instructions for modifying graphs are provided later in this chapter.

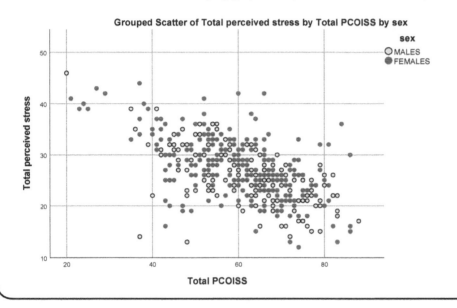

Interpretation of output from Scatterplot

From the output above, there appears to be a moderate negative correlation between
the two variables (Perceived Stress and PCOISS). Respondents with high levels of
perceived control (shown on the X, or horizontal, axis) experience lower levels of
perceived stress (shown on the Y, or vertical, axis). On the other hand, people with low
levels of perceived control have much greater perceived stress.

Remember, the scatterplot does not give you definitive answers; you need to
follow it up with the calculation of the appropriate statistic. There is no indication of
a curvilinear relationship, so it would be appropriate to calculate a Pearson product-
moment correlation for these two variables (see Chapter 11) if the distributions are
roughly normal (check the histograms for these two variables).

In the example above, I explored the relationship between only two variables. It is also possible to generate a matrix of scatterplots between a whole group of variables. This is useful as preliminary assumption testing for analyses such as MANOVA.

Procedure to generate a matrix of scatterplots
1. From the menu at the top of the screen, click on **Graphs**, then **Chart Builder**, then **OK**.
2. Click on the **Gallery** tab and choose **Scatter/Dot** and then select the eighth option (**Scatterplot Matrix**). Drag this to the **Chart Preview** area holding your left mouse button down.
3. From the **Variables** list choose the first of the continuous variables that you wish to display (e.g. tposaff) and drag this to the **Scattermatrix** box. Choose and drag each of the other variables in turn (tnegaff, tpstress).
4. Click on the **Options** button on the top right of the screen and choose how you would like to deal with missing data. In this example I have chosen **Exclude variable-by-variable** to maximise the use of data. Click on **OK** (or on **Paste** to save to **Syntax Editor**).

The syntax generated from this procedure is:

```
GGRAPH
 /GRAPHDATASET NAME="graphdataset" VARIABLES=tposaff tnegaff tpstress
 MISSING=VARIABLEWISE
  REPORTMISSING=NO
 /GRAPHSPEC SOURCE=INLINE
 /FITLINE TOTAL=NO.
BEGIN GPL
 SOURCE: s=userSource(id("graphdataset"))
 DATA: tposaff=col(source(s), name("tposaff"))
 DATA: tnegaff=col(source(s), name("tnegaff"))
 DATA: tpstress=col(source(s), name("tpstress"))
 GUIDE: axis(dim(1.1), ticks(null()))
 GUIDE: axis(dim(2.1), ticks(null()))
 GUIDE: axis(dim(1), gap(0px))
 GUIDE: axis(dim(2), gap(0px))
 GUIDE: text.title(label("Scatterplot Matrix Total positive affect,Total negative
 affect,Total ",
   "perceived stress"))
 TRANS: tposaff_label = eval("Total positive affect")
```

```
TRANS: tnegaff_label = eval("Total negative affect")
TRANS: tpstress_label = eval("Total perceived stress")
ELEMENT: point(position((tposaff/tposaff_label+tnegaff/tnegaff_label+tpstress/
tpstress_label)*
  (tposaff/tposaff_label+tnegaff/tnegaff_label+tpstress/tpstress_label)))
END GPL.
```

The output generated from this procedure is shown below.

Scatterplot Matrix Total positive affect,Total negative affect,Total perceived stress

BOXPLOTS

Boxplots are useful when you wish to compare the distribution of scores on variables. You can use them to explore the distribution of one continuous variable for the whole sample or, alternatively, you can ask for scores to be broken down for different groups. In the example below, I explore the distribution of scores on the Positive Affect Scale for males and females.

Procedure for creating a boxplot

1. From the menu at the top of the screen, click on **Graphs**, then select **Chart Builder**, and click **OK**.
2. Click on the **Gallery** tab and choose **Boxplot**. Click on the first option (**Simple Boxplot**) and drag it up to the **Chart Preview** area, holding your left mouse button down.
3. From the **Variables** box choose your categorical variable (e.g. sex) and drag it to the **X-axis** box on the **Chart Preview** area. Drag your continuous variable (Total Positive Affect: tposaff) to the **Y-axis**.
4. Click on the **Groups/Point ID** tab and select **Point ID label.**
5. Select the ID variable from the list and drag it to the **Point ID** box on the graph.
6. Click on **OK** (or on **Paste** to save to **Syntax Editor**).

The syntax generated from this procedure is:

```
GGRAPH
 /GRAPHDATASET NAME="graphdataset" VARIABLES=sex tposaff id
 MISSING=VARIABLEWISE REPORTMISSING=NO
 /GRAPHSPEC SOURCE=INLINE.
BEGIN GPL
 SOURCE: s=userSource(id("graphdataset"))
 DATA: sex=col(source(s), name("sex"), unit.category())
 DATA: tposaff=col(source(s), name("tposaff"))
 DATA: id=col(source(s), name("id"))
 GUIDE: axis(dim(1), label("sex"))
 GUIDE: axis(dim(2), label("Total positive affect"))
 GUIDE: text.title(label("Simple Boxplot of Total positive affect by sex"))
 SCALE: cat(dim(1), include("1", "2"))
 SCALE: linear(dim(2), include(0))
 ELEMENT: schema(position(bin.quantile.letter(sex*tposaff)), label(id))
END GPL.
```

The output generated from this procedure is shown as follows.

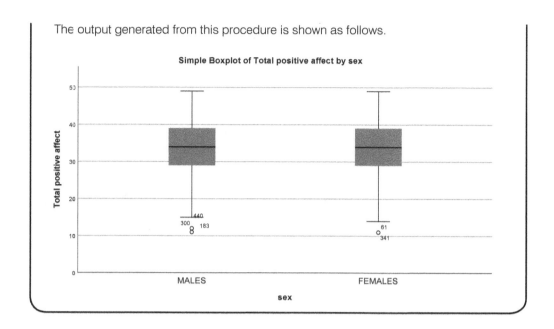

Simple Boxplot of Total positive affect by sex

Interpretation of output from Boxplot

The output from **Boxplot** gives you a lot of information about the distribution of your continuous variable and the possible influence of your other, categorical, variable (and cluster variable if used).

➤ Each distribution of scores is represented by a box and protruding lines (called whiskers). The length of the box is the variable's interquartile range and contains 50 per cent of cases. The line across the inside of the box represents the median value. The whiskers protruding from the box go out to the variable's smallest and largest values.

➤ Any scores that IBM SPSS Statistics considers to be outliers appear as little circles with a number attached (this is the ID number of the case). Outliers are cases with scores that are quite different from the remainder of the sample, either much higher or much lower. IBM SPSS Statistics defines points as outliers if they extend more than 1.5 box-lengths from the edge of the box. Extreme points (indicated with an asterisk) are those that extend more than 3 box-lengths from the edge of the box. For more information on outliers, see Chapter 6. In the example above, there are several outliers at the low values for Positive Affect for both males and females.

➤ In addition to providing information on outliers, a boxplot allows you to inspect the pattern of scores for your various groups. It provides an indication of the variability in scores within each group and allows a visual inspection of the differences between groups. In the example presented above, the distribution of scores on Positive Affect for males and females is very similar.

EDITING A GRAPH

Sometimes, modifications need to be made to the titles, labels, markers and so on of a graph before you can print it or use it in your report. I have edited some of the graphs displayed in this chapter to make them clearer (e.g. changing the patterns in the bar graph, thickening the lines used in the line graph).

To edit a chart or graph, you need to open the **Chart Editor** window. To do this, place your cursor on the graph that you wish to modify. Double-click and a new window will appear showing your graph, complete with additional menu options and icons (see Figure 7.1).

You should see a smaller **Properties** window pop up, which allows you to make changes to your graphs. If this does not appear, click on the **Edit** menu and select **Properties**.

There are various changes you can make while in **Chart Editor**:

➤ To change the words used in a label, click once on the label to highlight it (a gold-coloured box should appear around the text). Click once again to edit the text (a red cursor should appear). Modify the text and then press Enter on your keyboard when you have finished.

➤ To change the position of the X and Y axis labels (e.g. to centre them), *double-click* on the title you wish to change. In the **Properties** box, click on the **Text Layout** tab. In the section labelled **Justify**, choose the position you want (the dot means centred, the left arrow moves it to the left, and the right arrow moves it to the right).

➤ To change the characteristics of the text, lines, markers, colours, patterns and scale used in the chart, click *once* on the aspect of the graph that you wish to change. The **Properties** window will adjust its options depending on the aspect you click on. The various tabs in this box will allow you to change aspects of the graph. If you want to change one of the lines of a multiple-line graph (or markers for a group), you will need to highlight the specific category in the legend (rather than on the graph itself). This is useful for changing one of the lines to dashes so that it is more clearly distinguishable when printed out in black and white.

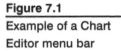

Figure 7.1

Example of a Chart Editor menu bar

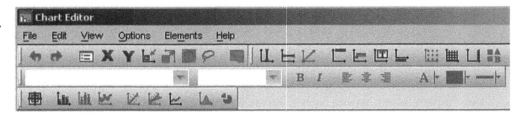

The best way to learn how to use these options is to experiment—so go ahead and play!

IMPORTING GRAPHS INTO WORD DOCUMENTS

IBM SPSS Statistics allows you to copy charts directly into your word processor (e.g. Microsoft Word). This is useful when you are preparing the final version of your report and want to present some of your results in the form of a graph. Sometimes, a graph will present your results more simply and clearly than numbers in a box. Don't go overboard—use only for special effect. Make sure you modify the graph in IBM SPSS Statistics to make it as clear as possible before transferring it to Word.

Procedure for importing a chart into a Word document

1. Start Microsoft Word and open the file in which you would like the graph to appear. Click on the IBM SPSS Statistics icon on the taskbar at the bottom of your screen to return to IBM SPSS Statistics.
2. In IBM SPSS Statistics make sure you have the **Output** (**Viewer**) window on the screen in front of you.
3. Click once on the graph that you would like to copy. A border should appear around the graph.
4. Click on **Edit** (from the menu at the top of the page) and then choose **Copy**. This saves the graph to the clipboard (you won't be able to see it, however). Alternatively, you can right click on the graph and select **Copy** from the pop-up menu.
5. From the list of minimised programs at the bottom of your screen, click on your Word document.
6. In the Word document, place your cursor where you wish to insert the graph.
7. Click on **Edit** from the Word menu and choose **Paste**. Or just click on the **Paste** icon on the top menu bar (it looks like a clipboard). The keyboard shortcut, pressing Ctrl and V, can also be used.
8. Click on **File** and then **Save** to save your Word document, or use the keyboard shortcut Ctrl and S.
9. To move back to IBM SPSS Statistics to continue with your analyses, click on the IBM SPSS Statistics icon, which should be listed at the bottom of your screen. With both programs open you can just jump backwards and forwards between the two programs, copying graphs, tables etc. There is no need to close either of the programs until you have finished completely. Just remember to save as you go along.

ADDITIONAL EXERCISES

Business

Data file: **staffsurvey.sav**. See Appendix for details of the data file.

1. Generate a **histogram** to explore the distribution of scores on the Staff Satisfaction Scale (*totsatis*).
2. Generate a **bar graph** to assess the staff satisfaction levels for permanent versus casual staff employed for less than or equal to 2 years, 3 to 5 years and 6 or more years. The variables you will need are *totsatis*, *employstatus* and *servicegp3*.
3. Generate a **scatterplot** to explore the relationship between years of service and staff satisfaction. Try first using the *service* variable (which is very skewed) and then try again with the variable towards the bottom of the list of variables (*logservice*). This new variable is a mathematical transformation (log 10) of the original variable (*service*), designed to adjust for the severe skewness. This procedure is covered in Chapter 8.
4. Generate a **boxplot** to explore the distribution of scores on the Staff Satisfaction Scale (*totsatis*) for the different age groups (*age*).
5. Generate a **line graph** to compare staff satisfaction for the different age groups (use the *agerecode* variable) for permanent and casual staff.

Health

Data file: **sleep.sav**. See Appendix for details of the data file.

1. Generate a **histogram** to explore the distribution of scores on the Epworth Sleepiness Scale (*ess*).
2. Generate a **bar graph** to compare scores on the Sleepiness and Associated Sensations Scale (*totSAS*) across three age groups (*agegp3*) for males and females (*gender*).
3. Generate a **scatterplot** to explore the relationship between scores on the Epworth Sleepiness Scale (*ess*) and the Sleepiness and Associated Sensations Scale (*totSAS*). Ask for different markers for males and females (*gender*).
4. Generate a **boxplot** to explore the distribution of scores on the Sleepiness and Associated Sensations Scale (*totSAS*) for people who report that they do/don't have a problem with their sleep (*probsleeprec*).
5. Generate a **line graph** to compare scores on the Sleepiness and Associated Sensations Scale (*totSAS*) across the different age groups (use the *agegp3* variable) for males and females (*gender*).

8

Manipulating the data

Once you have entered the data and the data file has been checked for accuracy, the next step involves manipulating the raw data into a form that you can use to conduct analyses and to test your hypotheses. This usually involves creating an additional variable, keeping your original data intact. Depending on the data file, your variables of interest and the types of research questions that you wish to address, this process may include:

> adding up the scores from the items that make up each scale to give an overall score for scales such as self-esteem, optimism, perceived stress etc. IBM SPSS Statistics does this quickly, easily and accurately—don't even think about doing this by hand for each separate case
> collapsing a continuous variable (e.g. age) into a categorical variable (e.g. young, middle-aged and old) by creating a new variable (e.g. agegp3) to use in techniques such as analysis of variance
> reducing or collapsing the number of categories of a categorical variable (e.g. collapsing marital status into just two categories representing people 'in a relationship'/'not in a relationship'). This creates an extra variable in your data file that can be used to address specific research questions
> recoding data entered as text (e.g. male, female) to numeric data (e.g. 1, 2) that can be used in statistical analyses
> calculating with dates (e.g. determining how many days there are between two dates in the data file)
> transforming skewed variables for analyses that require normally distributed scores.

When you make changes to the variables in your data file or create new modified variables, it is important that you note this in your codebook. The **Paste to Syntax** option available in all of the procedures in IBM SPSS Statistics is a useful tool for keeping a record of any changes made to the data file. I describe this process first before demonstrating how to recode and transform your variables.

Using Syntax to record procedures

As discussed previously, in Chapter 3, IBM SPSS Statistics has a **Syntax Editor** window that can be used to record the commands generated using the menus for each procedure. To access the syntax, follow the instructions shown in the procedure sections to come, but stop before clicking the final **OK** button. Instead, click on the **Paste** button. This will open a new window, the **Syntax Editor**, showing the commands you have selected. Figure 8.1 shows part of the **Syntax Editor** window that was used to recode items and compute the total scores used in **survey.sav**. The complete syntax file (**surveysyntax.sps**) can be downloaded from the *SPSS Survival Manual* website.

Figure 8.1

Example of a Syntax Editor window

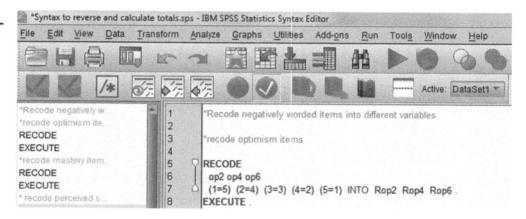

The commands pasted to the **Syntax Editor** are not executed until you choose to run them. To run the command, highlight the specific command (making sure you include the final full stop) and then click on the **Run** menu option or the arrow icon from the menu bar.

Extra comments can be added to the syntax file by starting them with an asterisk. If you add comments, make sure you leave at least one line of space both before and after syntax commands. For each of the procedures described in the remainder of the *SPSS Survival Manual*, the syntax will also be shown.

CALCULATING TOTAL SCALE SCORES

Before you can perform statistical analyses on your data set, you need to calculate total scale scores for any scales used in your study. This involves two steps:

> *Step 1:* Reverse any negatively worded items.
> *Step 2:* Add together scores from all the items that make up the subscale or scale.

It is important that you understand the scales and measures that you are using for your research. You should check with the scale's manual or the journal article it was published in to find out which items, if any, need to be reversed and how to go about calculating a total score. Some scales consist of subscales that either can or, alternatively, should not be added together to give an overall score. It is important that you do this correctly, and it is much easier to do it right the first time than to have to repeat analyses later.

Important: You should do this only when you have a complete data file, as IBM SPSS Statistics does not update these commands when you add extra data.

Step 1: Reverse negatively worded items

In some scales the wording of particular items has been reversed to help prevent response bias. This is evident in the Optimism Scale used in the survey (see Appendix). Item 1 is worded in a positive direction (high scores indicate *high* optimism): 'In uncertain times I usually expect the best.' Item 2, however, is negatively worded (high scores indicate *low* optimism): 'If something can go wrong for me it will.' Items 4 and 6 are also negatively worded. The negatively worded items need to be reversed before a total score can be calculated for this scale. We need to ensure that all items are scored so that high scores indicate high levels of optimism.

The procedure for reversing Items 2, 4 and 6 of the Optimism Scale is shown below. A 5-point Likert-type scale was used for the Optimism Scale; therefore, scores for each item can range from 1 (strongly disagree) to 5 (strongly agree).

Although the procedure illustrated here shows how to reverse score scale items, the same procedure can be used on single questionnaire items to ensure that high scores represent high levels of the characteristic being measured (e.g. satisfaction).

While it is possible to rescore variables into the same variable name, we will ask IBM SPSS Statistics to create new variables rather than overwrite the existing data. This is a much safer option, and it retains our original data.

If you wish to follow along with the instructions shown below, you should open **survey.sav**.

1. From the menu at the top of the screen, click on **Transform**, then click on **Recode Into Different Variables**.
2. Select the items you want to reverse (op2, op4, op6). Move these into the **Input Variable—Output Variable** box.

3. Click on the first variable (op2) and type a new name in the **Output Variable** section on the right-hand side of the screen and then click the **Change** button. I have used Rop2 in the existing data file. If you wish to create your own (rather than overwrite the ones already in the data file), use another name (e.g. revop2). Repeat for each of the other variables you wish to reverse (op4 and op6).

4. Click on the **Old and New Values** button.
   In the **Old Value** section, type 1 in the **Value** box.
   In the **New Value** section, type 5 in the **Value** box (this will change all scores that were originally scored as 1 to a 5).

5. Click on **Add**. This will place the instruction (1 → 5) in the box labelled **Old > New**.

6. Repeat the same procedure for the remaining scores. E.g.:
   Old Value—type in 2. **New Value**—type in 4. **Add**.
   Old Value—type in 3. **New Value**—type in 3. **Add**.
   Old Value—type in 4. **New Value**—type in 2. **Add**.
   Old Value—type in 5. **New Value**—type in 1. **Add**.
   Always double-check the item numbers that you specify for recoding and the old and new values that you enter. Not all scales use 5 points; some have 4 possible responses, some 6, and some 7. Check that you have reversed all the possible values for your particular scale.

7. Click on **Continue** and then **OK** (or on **Paste** to save to **Syntax Editor**. To execute after pasting to the **Syntax Editor**, highlight the command and select **Run** from the menu.)

The syntax generated for this command is:

```
RECODE
 op2 op4 op6
 (1=5) (2=4) (3=3) (4=2) (5=1) INTO Rop2 Rop4 Rop6 .
EXECUTE .
```

The new variables with reversed scores can be found at the end of the data file. Check this in your **Data Editor** window, choose the **Variable View** tab and go down to the bottom of the list of variables. In the **survey.sav** file you will see a whole series of variables with an 'R' at the front of the variable name. These are the items that I have reversed. If you follow the instructions shown above using a 'rev' prefix, you should see yours at the very bottom with 'rev' at the start of each. It is important to check your recoded variables to see what effect the recode had on the values. For the first few cases in your data set, take note of the scores on the original variables and then check the corresponding reversed variables to ensure that it worked properly.

Step 2: Add up the total scores for the scale

After you have reversed the negatively worded items in the scale, you will be ready to calculate total scores for each case.

Important: You should do this only when you have a complete data file, as IBM SPSS Statistics does not update this command when you add extra data.

Procedure for calculating total scale scores

1. From the menu at the top of the screen, click on **Transform**, then click on **Compute Variable**.
2. In the **Target Variable** box, type in the new name you wish to give to the total scale scores. (It is useful to use a 'T' prefix to indicate total scores, as this makes them easier to find in the list of variables when you are doing your analyses.)

   Important: Make sure you do not accidentally use a variable name that has already been used in the data set. If you do, you will lose all the original data (potential disaster), so check your codebook. The variable name cannot contain spaces, symbols or other punctuation—just letters and numbers. (See 'Rules for naming of variables' on p. 12.)
3. Click on the **Type and Label** button. Click in the **Label** box and type in a description of the scale (e.g. total optimism). Click on **Continue**.
4. From the list of variables on the left-hand side, click on the first item in the scale (op1).
5. Click on the arrow button to move it into the **Numeric Expression** box.
6. Click on + on the calculator.
7. Repeat the process until all scale items appear in the box. In this example we would select the unreversed items first (op3, op5) and then the reversed items (obtained in the previous procedure), which are located at the bottom of the list of variables (Rop2, Rop4, Rop6).
8. The complete numeric expression should read as follows:
   op1+op3+op5+Rop2+Rop4+Rop6.
9. Double-check that all items are correct and that there are + signs in the right places. Click **OK** (or on **Paste** to save to **Syntax Editor**. To execute after pasting to the **Syntax Editor**, highlight the command and select **Run** from the menu.).

The syntax for this command is:

```
COMPUTE toptim = op1+op3+op5+Rop2+Rop4+Rop6 .
EXECUTE.
```

This will create a new variable at the end of your data set called Toptim. Scores for each person will consist of the addition of scores on each of the items op1 to op6 (with recoded items where necessary). If any items had missing data, the overall score will also be missing. This is indicated by a full stop, instead of a score, in the data file. You will notice in the literature that some researchers go a step further and divide the total scale score by the number of items in the scale. This can make it a little easier to interpret the scores of the total scale because it is back in the original scale used for each of the items (e.g. from 1 to 5 representing strongly disagree to strongly agree). To do this, you also use the **Transform**, **Compute** menu of IBM SPSS Statistics. This time you will need to specify a new variable name and then type in a suitable formula (e.g. Toptim/6).

Always record in your codebook details of any new variables that you create. Specify the new variable's name, what it represents and full details of what was done to calculate it. If any items were reversed, this should be specified, along with details of which items were added to create the score. It is also a good idea to include the possible range of scores for the new variable in the codebook (see the Appendix). This gives you a clear guide when checking for any out-of-range values.

After creating a new variable, it is important to run **Descriptives** on this new scale to check that the values are appropriate (see Chapter 6). It also helps you get a feel for the distribution of scores on your new variable.

➤ Check back with the questionnaire—what is the possible range of scores that could be recorded? For a 10-item scale using a response scale from 1 to 4, the minimum total value would be 10 and the maximum total value would be 40. If a person answered 1 to every item, their overall score would be $10 \times 1 = 10$. If a person answered 4 to each item, their score would be $10 \times 4 = 40$.
➤ Check the output from **Descriptives** to ensure that there are no out-of-range cases (see Chapter 5)—i.e. values that exceed your minimum and maximum values.
➤ Compare the mean score on the scale with values reported in the literature. Is your value similar to that obtained in previous studies? If not, why not? Have you done something wrong in the recoding? Or is your sample different from that used in other studies?

You should also run other analyses to check the distribution of scores on your new total scale variable:

➤ Check the distribution of scores using skewness and kurtosis (see Chapter 6).
➤ Obtain a histogram of the scores and inspect the spread of scores. Are they normally distributed? If not, you may need to consider transforming the scores for some analyses (this is discussed later in this chapter).

COLLAPSING A CONTINUOUS VARIABLE INTO GROUPS

For some analyses, or when you have very skewed distributions, you may wish to divide the sample into equal groups according to respondents' scores on some variable (e.g. to give low, medium and high scoring groups). To illustrate this process, I use the **survey.sav** file that is included on the website that accompanies this book (see p. ix and the Appendix for details). I use **Visual Binning** to identify suitable cut-off points to break the continuous variable age into three approximately equal groups. The same technique could be used to create a median split—that is, to divide the sample into two groups, using the median as the cut-off point. Once the cut-off points are identified, **Visual Binning** will create a new categorical variable that has only three values—corresponding to the three age ranges chosen. This technique leaves the original variable age, measured as a continuous variable, intact so that you can use it for other analyses.

Procedure for collapsing a continuous variable into groups

1. From the menu at the top of the screen, click on **Transform** and choose **Visual Binning**.
2. Select the continuous variable that you want to use (e.g. age). Transfer it into the **Variables to Bin** box. Click on the **Continue** button.
3. In the **Visual Binning** window, a histogram showing the distribution of age scores should appear.
4. In the section at the top labelled **Binned Variable**, type the name for the new categorical variable that you will create (e.g. agegp3). You can also change the suggested label that is shown (e.g. age in 3 groups).
5. Click on the button labelled **Make Cutpoints**. In the dialogue box that appears, click on the option **Equal Percentiles Based on Scanned Cases**. In the box **Number of Cutpoints**, specify a number one less than the number of groups that you want (e.g. if you want three groups, type in 2 for cutpoints). In the **Width (%)** section below, you will then see 33.33 appear. This means that IBM SPSS Statistics will try to put 33.3% of the sample in each group. Click on the **Apply** button.
6. Click on the **Make Labels** button back in the main dialogue box. This will automatically generate value labels for each of the new groups created.
7. Click on **OK** (or on **Paste** to save to **Syntax Editor**. To execute after pasting to the **Syntax Editor**, highlight the command and select **Run** from the menu.).

The syntax generated by this command is:

```
RECODE age
  ( MISSING = COPY )
  ( LO THRU 29 =1 )
  ( LO THRU 44 =2 )
  ( LO THRU HI = 3 )
  ( ELSE = SYSMIS ) INTO agegp3.
VARIABLE LABELS agegp3 'age in 3 groups'.
FORMAT agegp3 (F5.0).
VALUE LABELS agegp3
  1 '<= 29'
  2 '30—44'
  3 '45+'.
MISSING VALUES agegp3 ( ).
VARIABLE LEVEL agegp3 ( ORDINAL ).
EXECUTE.
```

A new variable (agegp3) should appear at the end of your data file. Go back to your **Data Editor** window, choose the **Variable View** tab, and it should be at the bottom. To check the number of cases in each of the categories of your newly created variable (agegp3), go to **Analyze** and select **Descriptives**, then **Frequencies**.

COLLAPSING THE NUMBER OF CATEGORIES OF A CATEGORICAL VARIABLE

There are some situations where you may want to reduce or collapse the number of categories of a categorical variable. You may want to do this for research or theoretical reasons (e.g. collapsing marital status into just two categories representing people 'in a relationship'/'not in a relationship'), or you may make the decision after evaluating the nature of the data. For example, after running **Descriptive Statistics** you may find you have only a few people in your sample who fall into a particular category (e.g. for our education variable, we only have two people in our first category, 'primary school'). As it stands, this education variable could not appropriately be used in many of the statistical analyses covered later in the book. We could decide just to remove these people from the sample, or we could recode them to combine them with the next category ('some secondary school'). We would have to relabel the variable so that it represented people who did not complete secondary school.

The procedure for recoding a categorical variable is shown below. It is very important to note that here we are creating a new, additional variable (so that we keep our original data intact).

Procedure for recoding a categorical variable

1. From the menu at the top of the screen, click on **Transform**, then on **Recode into Different Variables**. (Make sure you select 'different variables', as this retains the original variable for other analyses.)
2. Select the variable you wish to recode (e.g. educ). In the **Name** box, type a name for the new variable that will be created (e.g. educrec). Type in an extended label if you wish in the **Label** section. Click on the button labelled **Change**.
3. Click on the button labelled **Old and New Values**.
4. In the section **Old Value**, you will see a box labelled **Value**. Type in the first code or value of your current variable (e.g. 1). In the **New Value** section, type in the new value that will be used (or if the same one is to be used, type that in). In this case I recode to the same value, so type 1 in both the **Old Value** and **New Value** sections. Click on the **Add** button.
5. For the second value, I type 2 in **Old Value** but 1 in **New Value**. This will recode all the values of both 1 and 2 from the original coding into one group in the new variable to be created with a value of 1.
6. For the third value of the original variable, I type 3 in **Old Value** and 2 in **New Value**. This is just to keep the values in the new variable in sequence. Click on **Add**. Repeat for all the remaining values of the original values. In the table **Old > New**, you should see the following codes for this example: 1→1, 2→1, 3→2, 4→3, 5→4, 6→5.
7. Click on **Continue** and then on **OK** (or on **Paste** to save to **Syntax Editor**. To execute after pasting to the **Syntax Editor**, highlight the command and select **Run** from the menu.).
8. Go to your **Data Editor** window and choose the **Variable View** tab. Type in appropriate value labels to represent the new values (1 = did not complete high school, 2 = completed high school, 3 = some additional training, 4 = completed undergrad uni, 5 = completed postgrad uni). Remember, these will be different from the codes used for the original variable, and it is important that you don't mix them up.

The syntax generated by this command is:

```
RECODE  educ
  (1=1) (2=1) (3=2) (4=3) (5=4) (6=5) INTO educrec .
  EXECUTE.
```

When you recode a variable, make sure you run **Frequencies** on both the old variable (educ) and the newly created variable (educrec, which appears at the end of your data file). Check that the frequencies reported for the new variable are correct. For example, for the newly created educrec variable, you should now have 2 + 53 = 55 in the first group. This represents the two people who ticked 1 on the original variable ('primary school') and the 53 people who ticked 2 ('some secondary school').

The **Recode** procedure demonstrated here could be used for a variety of purposes. You may find later, when you come to do your statistical analyses, that you will need to recode the values used for a variable. For example, in Chapter 14 (Logistic Regression) you may need to recode variables originally coded 1 = yes, 2 = no to a new coding system, 1 = yes, 0 = no. This can be achieved in the same way as described in the previous procedure section. Just be very clear before you start on what your original values are and what you want the new values to be.

USING AUTOMATIC RECODE TO CONVERT TEXT TO NUMERIC VALUES

When analysing data that have been extracted from existing databases (e.g. Microsoft Access) it is common to see data entered as text, rather than as numbers (e.g. M for males and F for females). To use these variables in some statistical analyses it is necessary to convert these text entries to numbers. This can easily be done using the **Automatic Recode** feature in IBM SPSS Statistics.

Procedure for automatic recode

If you wish to follow along with this example you will need to open the file **manipulate.sav.**

1. Click on **Transform** and then select **Automatic Recode**.
2. Select your text variable (e.g. Sex) and move this into the **Variable-New Name** box.
3. Type the name you would like to give the recoded variable in the **New name** box (e.g. SexNum). Click on the **Add New Name** button (or on **Paste** to save to **Syntax Editor**).
4. Click on **OK**.

The syntax generated by this command is:

```
AUTORECODE VARIABLES=Sex
  /INTO SexNum
  /PRINT.
```

In your output you should see a summary of the old text values and the new numeric values that have been assigned. The new variable that has been created will appear at the end of your data file. If you wish to move it click on the variable name in **Variable View** and, holding the left mouse button down, drag it to the position you wish.

CALCULATING USING DATES

IBM SPSS Statistics has a **Date and Time Wizard** which allows you to calculate using any date or time variables in your data file (e.g. how many days/years occur between two dates). In the example below I demonstrate how to use this to determine how long each patient stayed in hospital using the **manipulate.sav** data file.

1. Click on **Transform** from the menu at the top of the screen and choose **Date and Time Wizard**.
2. Click on **Calculate with dates and times** and then click on **Next**.
3. Select the option **Calculate the number of time units between two dates**. Click on **Next**.
4. Select your first date variable (this is usually the most recent; in this example I used DischargeDate) and move it into the box labelled **Date1**.
5. Select your second date variable (e.g. ArrivalDate) and move it into the box labelled **minus Date2**.
6. Select the unit of time that you want (e.g. days) from the drop-down list provided next to **Unit**. Select how you want to deal with leftovers—whether you want to **Truncate to integer** or **Round to integer** or **Retain fractional part**. In this example involving days I have chosen **Round to integer**.
7. Click on **Next**.
8. In the box labelled **Result Variable** type in a name for the variable (e.g. LengthofStay), and a more detailed label if you wish.
9. In the **Execution** section select whether you want to create the variable now, or, alternatively, you can choose to **Paste** the syntax into the syntax window.
10. Click on **Finish**.

The syntax generated by this command is:

```
COMPUTE LOS=RND((DischargeDate - ArrivalDate) / time.days(1)).
 VARIABLE LABELS LengthofStay.
 VARIABLE LEVEL LengthofStay (SCALE).
 FORMATS LOS (F5.0).
 VARIABLE WIDTH LOS(5).
 EXECUTE.
```

A new variable should appear at the end of your data file. This new numeric variable can now be used for statistical analyses.

TRANSFORMING VARIABLES

Often, when you check the distribution of scores on a scale or measure (e.g. self-esteem, anxiety), you will find (to your dismay!) that the scores do not fall in a nice, normally distributed curve. Sometimes, scores will be positively skewed, where most of the respondents record low scores on the scale (e.g. depression). Sometimes, you will find a negatively skewed distribution, where most scores are at the high end (e.g. self-esteem). Given that many of the parametric statistical tests assume or require normally distributed scores, what do you do about these skewed distributions? Your decision will depend on the degree of skewness involved, the statistical technique you would like to use and the discipline area that you are working in.

One of the choices you have is to abandon the use of parametric statistics (those that require normal distributions—(e.g. Pearson correlation, analysis of variance) and instead choose to use non-parametric alternatives (e.g. Spearman's *rho*, Kruskal-Wallis Test). IBM SPSS Statistics Test includes a set of useful non-parametric techniques in its package. These are discussed in Chapter 16.

Alternatively, you could choose to collapse a skewed continuous variable into a number of discrete categories and use an alternative statistical technique suitable for categorical variables. I often have to do this when using depression scales, which yield very skewed distributions, with most cases recording low values. In this situation I would create a new categorical variable, cutting the sample at the published clinical cut-points for the scale, which identify people with 'normal' versus 'clinical' levels of depression. Be warned—if you choose to use this approach, you will lose information by collapsing a continuous variable down into a small number of categories. The procedure for collapsing a continuous variable into discrete categories is presented earlier in this chapter.

Another alternative when you have a non-normal distribution is to transform your variables. This involves mathematically modifying the scores until the distribution looks more normal. There is considerable controversy in the literature concerning this approach, with some authors strongly supporting, and others arguing against, transforming variables to better meet the assumptions of the various parametric techniques. This also varies across different disciplines, so check articles in your topic area. For a discussion of the issues and the approaches to transformation, you should read Chapter 4 in Tabachnick and Fidell (2013).

If you decide you want to transform your variables to achieve a less skewed distribution of scores there are two approaches you can choose from. You can either use the **IBM SPSS Statistics Rank Cases** procedure to generate normal scores or select specific mathematical transformations depending on the distribution of your scores. These two approaches are described in the sections that follow.

Generating Normal Scores

Procedure for generating normal scores
1. From the menu at the top of the screen click on **Transform** and then click on **Rank Cases**.
2. Select all the variables that you wish to transform (e.g. Total Mastery: tmast) and move them into the **Variable(s)** box.
3. Click on the **Rank Types** button.
4. Tick the option **Normal scores** and choose **Blom** in the section labelled **Proportion Estimation Formula**. Remove the tick in the option **Rank**.
5. Click on **Continue**.
6. Click on **OK** (or on **Paste** to save to **Syntax Editor**).

The syntax from this procedure is:

```
RANK VARIABLES=tmast (A)
  /NORMAL
  /PRINT=YES
  /TIES=MEAN
  /FRACTION=BLOM.
```

In your output, you should see a table labelled **Created Variables**, which tells you that a new variable has been created and added to the end of your data file. The new variable will have the prefix 'N' before the name of the original variable (in this case Ntmast). Before using this variable in other statistical analyses you should run **Descriptive Statistics** and generate a histogram (see Chapter 6) to check what impact the conversion to normal scores has had on your variable.

Applying mathematical transformations to scores

In some literature areas you may see researchers referring to the specific mathematical transformations that they used to reduce the skew in their variables (e.g. square root). In this section I describe how this is done.

There are different types of transformations, depending on the shape of your distribution. In Figure 8.2 some of the more common problems are represented, along with the type of transformation recommended by Tabachnick and Fidell (2013, p. 87).

Figure 8.2

Distribution
of scores and
suggested
transformations

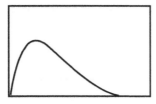

Square root
Formula: new variable = SQRT (old variable)

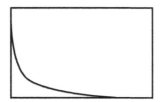

Logarithm
Formula: new variable = LG10 (old variable)

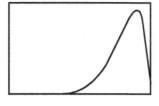

Inverse
Formula: new variable = 1 / (old variable)

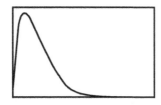

Reflect and square root
Formula: new variable = SQRT (K – old variable) where
K = largest possible value +1

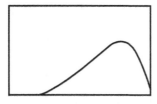

Reflect and logarithm
Formula: new variable = LG10 (K – old variable) where
K = largest possible value +1

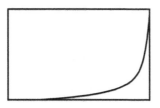

Reflect and inverse
Formula: new variable = 1 / (K – old variable) where
K = largest possible value +1

You should compare your distribution with those shown in Figure 8.2, and decide which picture it most closely resembles. I have also given the formula beside each of the suggested transformations. Don't let this throw you—these are just formulas that IBM SPSS Statistics will use on your data, giving you a new, hopefully normally distributed variable to use in your analyses. In the procedures section to follow, you are shown the IBM SPSS Statistics procedure for this. Before attempting any of these transformations, however, it is important that you read Tabachnick and Fidell (2013, Chapter 4), or a similar text, thoroughly.

Procedure for transforming variables

1. From the menu at the top of the screen, click on **Transform**, then click on **Compute Variable**.

2. **Target Variable**. In this box, type in a new name for the variable. Try to include an indication of the type of transformation and the original name of the variable. For example, for a variable called tnegaff I would make this new variable sqtnegaff if I had performed a square root. Be consistent in the abbreviations that you use for each of your transformations.

3. **Functions**. Listed are a wide range of possible actions you can use. You need to choose the most appropriate transformation for your variable. Look at the shape of your distribution; compare it with those in Figure 8.2. Take note of the formula listed next to the picture that matches your distribution. This is the one that you will use.

4. **Transformations involving square root or logarithm**. In the **Function group** box, click on **Arithmetic**, and scan down the list that shows up in the bottom box until you find the formula you need (e.g. SQRT or LG10). Highlight the one you want and click on the up arrow. This moves the formula into the **Numeric Expression** box. You will need to tell it which variable you want to recalculate. Find it in the list of variables and click on the arrow to move it into the **Numeric Expression** box. If you prefer, you can just type the formula in yourself without using the **Functions** or **Variables** list. Just make sure you spell everything correctly.

5. **Transformations involving Reflect**. You need to find the value K for your variable. This is the largest value that your variable can have (see your codebook) + 1. Type this number in the **Numeric Expression** box. Complete the remainder of the formula using the **Functions** box, or, alternatively, type it in yourself.

6. **Transformations involving Inverse**. To calculate the inverse, you need to divide your scores into 1. So, in the **Numeric Expression** box type in 1, then type / and then your variable or the rest of your formula (e.g. 1/tslfest).

7. Check the final formula in the **Numeric Expression** box. Write this down in your codebook next to the name of the new variable you created.

8. Click on the button **Type and Label**. Under **Label**, type in a brief description of the new variable (or you may choose to use the actual formula).

9. Check in the **Target Variable** box that you have given your new variable a new name, not the original one. If you accidentally put the old variable name, you will lose all your original scores. So, always double-check.
10. Click on **OK** (or on **Paste** to save to **Syntax Editor**. To execute after pasting to the **Syntax Editor**, highlight the command and select **Run** from the menu.). A new variable will be created and will appear at the end of your data file.
11. Run **Analyze, Frequencies** to check the skewness and kurtosis values for your old and new variables. Have they improved?
12. Under **Frequencies**, click on the **Charts** button and select **Histogram** to inspect the distribution of scores on your new variable. Has the distribution improved? If not, you may need to consider a different type of transformation.

After undertaking any transformation of your data, it is important that you run **Descriptive Statistics** and generate a histogram to see what impact the transformation has had on the distribution of scores.

ADDITIONAL EXERCISES

Business
Data file: **staffsurvey.sav**. See Appendix for details of the data file.

1. Practise the procedures described in this chapter to add up the total scores for a scale using the items that make up the Staff Satisfaction Survey. You will need to add together the items that assess agreement with each item in the scale (i.e. Q1a + Q2a + Q3a . . . to Q10a). Name your new variable *staffsatis*.
2. Check the descriptive statistics for your new total score (*staffsatis*) and compare this with the descriptives for the variable *totsatis*, which is already in your data file. This is the total score that I have already calculated for you.
3. What are the minimum possible and maximum possible scores for this new variable? *Tip:* Check the number of items in the scale and the number of response points on each item (see Appendix).
4. Check the distribution of the variable *service* by generating a histogram. You will see that it is very skewed, with most people clustered down the low end (with less than 2 years' service) and a few people stretched up at the very high end (with more than 30 years' service). Check the shape of the distribution against those displayed in Figure 8.2 and try a few different transformations. Remember to check the distribution of the new transformed variables you create. Are any of the new variables more normally distributed?

5. Collapse the years of service variable (*service*) into three groups using the **Visual Binning** procedure from the **Transform** menu. Use the **Make Cutpoints** button and ask for **Equal Percentiles**. In the section labelled **Number of Cutpoints**, specify 2. Call your new variable *gp3service* to distinguish it from the variable I have already created in the data file using this procedure (*service3gp*). Run **Frequencies** on your newly created variable to check how many cases are in each group.

Health

Data file: **sleep.sav**. See Appendix for details of the data file.

1. Practise the procedures described in this chapter to add up the total scores for a scale using the items that make up the Sleepiness and Associated Sensations Scale. You will need to add together the items *fatigue, lethargy, tired, sleepy* and *energy*. Call your new variable *sleeptot*. Please note: none of these items needs to be reversed before being added.
2. Check the descriptive statistics for your new total score (*sleeptot*) and compare them with the descriptives for the variable *totSAS*, which is already in your data file. This is the total score that I have already calculated for you.
3. What are the minimum possible and maximum possible scores for this new variable? *Tip:* Check the number of items in the scale and the number of response points on each item (see Appendix).
4. Check the distribution (using a histogram) of the variable that measures the number of cigarettes smoked per day by the smokers in the sample (*smokenum*). You will see that it is very skewed, with most people clustered down the low end (with fewer than 10 per day) and a few people stretched up at the very high end (with more than 70 per day). Check the shape of the distribution against those displayed in Figure 8.2 and try a few different transformations. Remember to check the distribution of the new transformed variables you create. Are any of the new transformed variables more normally distributed?
5. Collapse the age variable (*age*) into three groups using the **Visual Binning** procedure from the **Transform** menu. Use the **Make Cutpoints** button and ask for **Equal Percentiles**. In the section labelled **Number of Cutpoints**, specify 2. Call your new variable *gp3age* to distinguish it from the variable I have already created in the data file using this procedure (*age3gp*). Run **Frequencies** on your newly created variable to check how many cases are in each group.

9

Checking the reliability of a scale

When you are selecting scales to include in your study, it is important that they are reliable. There are different types of reliability to be considered (see discussion of this in Chapter 1). One of the main issues concerns the scale's internal consistency. This refers to the degree to which the items that make up the scale hang together. Are they all measuring the same underlying construct? One of the most commonly used indicators of internal consistency is Cronbach's alpha coefficient. Ideally, the Cronbach alpha coefficient of a scale should be above .7 (DeVellis 2012). Cronbach alpha values are, however, quite sensitive to the number of items in the scale. With short scales (e.g. fewer than 10 items) it is common to find quite low Cronbach values (e.g. .5). In this case, it may be more appropriate to report the mean inter-item correlation for the items. Briggs and Cheek (1986) recommend an optimal range for the inter-item correlation of .2 to .4.

The reliability of a scale can vary depending on the sample. It is therefore necessary to check that each of your scales is reliable with your particular sample. This information is usually reported in the Method section of your research paper or thesis. If your scale contains some items that are negatively worded (common in psychological measures), these need to be reversed *before* checking reliability. Instructions on how to do this are provided in Chapter 8.

Make sure that you check with the scale's manual (or the journal article in which it is reported) for instructions concerning the need to reverse items and for information on any subscales. Sometimes, scales contain subscales that may, or may not, be combined to form a total scale score. If necessary, the reliability of each of the subscales and the total scale will need to be calculated.

If you are developing your own scale for use in your study, make sure you read widely on the principles and procedures of scale development. There are some good, easy-to-read books on the topic, including Streiner and Norman (2015), DeVellis (2012) and Kline (2005).

DETAILS OF EXAMPLE

To demonstrate this technique, I use the **survey.sav** data file included on the website accompanying this book (see p. ix for details). Full details of the study, the questionnaire and the scales used are provided in the Appendix. If you wish to follow along with the steps described in this chapter, you should start IBM SPSS Statistics and open the file **survey.sav**. In the procedure described below, I explore the internal consistency of one of the scales from the questionnaire. This is the Satisfaction With Life Scale (Pavot, Diener, Colvin & Sandvik 1991), which is made up of five items. In the data file these items are labelled as lifsat1, lifsat2, lifsat3, lifsat4 and lifsat5.

Procedure for checking the reliability of a scale

Important: Before starting, you should check that all negatively worded items in your scale have been reversed (see Chapter 8). If you don't do this, you will find that you have very low (and incorrect) Cronbach alpha values. In this example none of the items needs to be rescored.

1. From the menu at the top of the screen, click on **Analyze**, select **Scale**, then **Reliability Analysis**.
2. Click on all of the individual items that make up the scale (e.g. lifsat1, lifsat2, lifsat3, lifsat4, lifsat5). Move these into the box marked **Items**.
3. In the **Model** section, make sure **Alpha** is selected.
4. In the **Scale label** box, type in the name of the scale or subscale (Life Satisfaction).
5. Click on the **Statistics** button. In the **Descriptives for** section, select **Item**, **Scale** and **Scale if item deleted**. In the **Inter-Item** section, click on **Correlations**. In the **Summaries** section, click on **Correlations**.
6. Click on **Continue** and then **OK** (or on **Paste** to save to **Syntax Editor**).

The syntax from this procedure is:

```
RELIABILITY
  /VARIABLES=lifsat1 lifsat2 lifsat3 lifsat4 lifsat5
  /SCALE('Life Satisfaction') ALL
  /MODEL=ALPHA
  /STATISTICS=DESCRIPTIVE SCALE CORR
  /SUMMARY=TOTAL CORR.
```

The output generated from this procedure is shown below.

Case Processing Summary

		N	%
Cases	Valid	436	99.3
	Excluded[a]	3	.7
	Total	439	100.0

a. Listwise deletion based on all variables in the procedure.

Reliability Statistics

Cronbach's Alpha	Cronbach's Alpha Based on Standardized Items	N of Items
.890	.895	5

Item Statistics

	Mean	Std. Deviation	N
lifsat1	4.37	1.528	436
lifsat2	4.57	1.554	436
lifsat3	4.69	1.519	436
lifsat4	4.75	1.641	436
lifsat5	3.99	1.855	436

Inter-Item Correlation Matrix

	lifsat1	lifsat2	lifsat3	lifsat4	lifsat5
lifsat1	1.000	.763	.720	.573	.526
lifsat2	.763	1.000	.727	.606	.481
lifsat3	.720	.727	1.000	.721	.587
lifsat4	.573	.606	.721	1.000	.594
lifsat5	.526	.481	.587	.594	1.000

Summary Item Statistics

	Mean	Minimum	Maximum	Range	Maximum / Minimum	Variance	N of Items
Inter-Item Correlations	.630	.481	.763	.282	1.587	.009	5

Item-Total Statistics

	Scale Mean if Item Deleted	Scale Variance if Item Deleted	Corrected Item-Total Correlation	Squared Multiple Correlation	Cronbach's Alpha if Item Deleted
lifsat1	18.00	30.667	.758	.649	.861
lifsat2	17.81	30.496	.752	.654	.862
lifsat3	17.69	29.852	.824	.695	.847
lifsat4	17.63	29.954	.734	.574	.866
lifsat5	18.39	29.704	.627	.421	.896

Scale Statistics

Mean	Variance	Std. Deviation	N of Items
22.38	45.827	6.770	5

INTERPRETATION OF OUTPUT FROM RELIABILITY

➢ Check that the number of cases is correct (in the **Case Processing Summary** table) and that the number of items is correct (in the **Reliability Statistics** table).

➢ Check the **Inter-Item Correlation Matrix** for negative values. All values should be positive, indicating that the items are measuring the same underlying characteristic. The presence of negative values could indicate that some of the items have not been correctly reverse scored. Incorrect scoring would also show up in the **Item-Total Statistics** table with negative values for the **Corrected Item–Total Correlation** values. These should be checked carefully if you obtain a lower than expected Cronbach alpha value.

➢ Check the **Cronbach's Alpha** value shown in the **Reliability Statistics** table. In this example the value is .89, suggesting very good internal consistency reliability for the scale with this sample. Values above .7 are considered acceptable; however, values above .8 are preferable.

➢ The **Corrected Item–Total Correlation** values shown in the **Item-Total Statistics** table give you an indication of the degree to which each item correlates with the total score. Low values (less than .3) here indicate that the item is measuring something different from the scale as a whole. If your scale's overall Cronbach alpha is too low (i.e. less than .7) and you have checked for incorrectly scored items, you may need to consider removing items with low item-total correlations.

➢ In the column headed **Cronbach's Alpha if Item Deleted**, in the Item–Total Statistics table, the impact of removing each item from the scale is given. Compare these values with the final alpha value obtained. If any of the values in this column are higher than the final alpha value for the scale as a whole, you may want to consider removing this item from the scale. This is useful if you are developing a scale, but if you are using established, validated scales, removal of items means that you could not compare your results with other studies using the scale. Always compare your results against other studies reported in the literature.

➤ For scales with a small number of items (e.g. fewer than 10), it is sometimes difficult to get a decent Cronbach alpha value. In this situation you may wish to consider reporting the mean inter-item correlation value, which is shown in the **Summary Item Statistics** table. In this case the mean inter-item correlation is .63, with values ranging from .48 to .76. This suggests quite a strong relationship among the items. For many scales, this is not the case.

PRESENTING THE RESULTS FROM RELIABILITY

You would normally report the internal consistency of the scales that you are using in your research in the Method section of your report, under the heading Measures, or Materials. Check for how it is done in your literature area. After describing the scale (number of items, response scale used, history of use), you should include a summary of reliability information reported by the scale developer and other researchers, and then a sentence to indicate the results for your sample. For example:

According to Pavot, Diener, Colvin and Sandvik (1991), the Satisfaction With Life Scale has good internal consistency, with a Cronbach alpha coefficient reported of .85. In the current study, the Cronbach alpha coefficient was .89.

ADDITIONAL EXERCISES

Business

Data file: **staffsurvey.sav**. See Appendix for details of the data file.

1. Check the reliability of the Staff Satisfaction Survey, which is made up of the agreement items in the data file: Q1a to Q10a. None of the items of this scale needs to be reversed.

Health

Data file: **sleep.sav**. See Appendix for details of the data file.

1. Check the reliability of the Sleepiness and Associated Sensations Scale, which is made up of the items *fatigue*, *lethargy*, *tired*, *sleepy* and *energy*. None of the items of this scale needs to be reversed.

10

Choosing the right statistic

One of the most difficult (and potentially fear-inducing) parts of the research process for most research students is choosing the correct statistical technique to analyse their data. Although most statistics courses teach you how to calculate a correlation co-efficient or perform a t-test, they typically do not spend much time helping students learn how to choose which approach is appropriate to address particular research questions. In most research projects it is likely that you will use quite a variety of statistical techniques, depending on the question you are addressing and the nature of the data that you have. It is therefore important that you have at least a basic understanding of the different statistics, the types of questions they address and their underlying assumptions and requirements.

So, dig out your statistics texts and review the basic techniques and the principles underlying them. You should also read journal articles on your topic and identify the statistical techniques used in these studies. Different topic areas may make use of different statistical approaches, so it is important that you find out what other researchers have done in terms of data analysis. Look for long, detailed journal articles that clearly spell out the statistics that were used. Collect these together in a folder for handy reference. You might also find them useful later when considering how to present the results of your own analyses.

In this chapter I review the various statistical techniques that are available and take you step by step through the decision-making process. If the whole statistical process sends you into a panic, just think of it as choosing which recipe you will use to cook dinner tonight. What ingredients do you have in the refrigerator, what type of meal do you feel like (soup, roast, stir-fry, stew), and what steps do you have to follow? In statistical terms, we need to consider the types of research questions you have, which variables you want to analyse and the nature of the data themselves. If you take this process step by step, you will find the final decision is often surprisingly simple. Once you have determined what you have and what you want to do, there often is only one choice. The most important part of this whole process is clearly spelling out what you have and what you want to do with it.

OVERVIEW OF THE DIFFERENT STATISTICAL TECHNIQUES

This section is broken into two main parts. First, we will look at the techniques used to explore the *relationship among variables* (e.g. between age and optimism), and second, we will consider the techniques you can use when you want to assess *differences between groups* (e.g. sex differences in optimism scores). I have separated the techniques into these two sections, as this is consistent with the way most basic statistics texts are structured and how the majority of students will have been taught statistics. This tends to somewhat artificially emphasise the difference between these two groups of techniques. There are, in fact, many underlying similarities between the various statistical techniques, which is perhaps not evident on initial inspection. A full discussion of this point is beyond the scope of this book. If you would like to know more, I would suggest you start by reading Chapter 17 of Tabachnick and Fidell (2013). That chapter provides an overview of the General Linear Model, under which many of the statistical techniques can be considered.

I have deliberately kept the summaries of the different techniques brief and simple, to aid initial understanding. This chapter certainly does not cover all the different techniques available, but it does give you the basics to get you started and to build your confidence.

Exploring relationships

Often, in survey research, you will be interested in the strength of the relationship between variables. There are several different techniques that you can use to calculate this.

Correlation

Pearson correlation or Spearman correlation is used when you want to explore the strength of the relationship between two continuous variables. This gives you an indication of both the direction (positive or negative) and the strength of the relationship. A positive correlation indicates that as one variable increases, so does the other. A negative correlation indicates that as one variable increases, the other decreases. This topic is covered in Chapter 11.

Partial correlation

Partial correlation is an extension of Pearson correlation—it allows you to control for the possible effects of another confounding variable. Partial correlation removes the effect of the confounding variable (e.g. socially desirable responding), allowing you to get a more accurate picture of the relationship between your two variables of interest. Partial correlation is covered in Chapter 12.

Multiple regression

Multiple regression is a more sophisticated extension of correlation and is used when you want to explore the predictive ability of a set of independent variables on one *continuous*, dependent measure. Different types of multiple regression allow you to compare the predictive ability of particular independent variables and to find the best set of variables to predict a dependent variable. See Chapter 13.

Factor analysis

Factor analysis allows you to condense a large set of variables or scale items down to a smaller, more manageable number of dimensions or factors. It does this by summarising the underlying patterns of correlation and identifying 'clumps' or groups of closely related items. This technique is often used to determine the underlying structure when developing scales and measures. See Chapter 15.

Additional techniques

All of the analyses described above involve exploration of the relationship between continuous variables. If you have only categorical variables, you can use the Chi-Square Test for Relatedness or Independence to explore their relationship (e.g. if you wanted to see whether gender influenced clients' dropout rates from a treatment program). In this situation, you are interested in the number of people in each category (males and females who drop out of/complete the program) rather than their score on a scale. Some additional techniques you should know about but which are not covered in this text are described below. For more information on these, see Tabachnick and Fidell (2013).

➤ *Discriminant function analysis* is used when you want to explore the predictive ability of a set of independent variables on one *categorical*, dependent measure. That is, you want to know which variables best predict group membership. The dependent variable in this case is usually some clear criterion (passed/failed, dropped out of/continued with treatment). See Chapter 9 in Tabachnick and Fidell (2013).

➤ *Canonical correlation* is used when you wish to analyse the relationship between two *sets* of variables. For example, a researcher might be interested in how a range of demographic variables relate to measures of wellbeing and adjustment. See Chapter 12 in Tabachnick and Fidell (2013).

➤ *Structural equation modelling* is a relatively new, and quite sophisticated, technique that allows you to test various models concerning the interrelationships among a set of variables. Based on multiple regression and factor analytic techniques, it allows you to evaluate the importance of each of the independent variables in the model and to test the overall fit of the model to your data. It also allows you to compare alternative models. IBM SPSS Statistics does not have a structural equation modelling module, but it does support an add on called AMOS. See Chapter 14 in Tabachnick and Fidell (2013).

Exploring differences between groups

There is another family of statistics that can be used when you want to find out whether there is a statistically significant difference between groups. The parametric versions of these tests, which are suitable when you have interval-scaled data with normal distribution of scores, are presented below, along with the non-parametric alternatives.

T-tests

T-tests are used when you have *two* groups (e.g. males and females) or two sets of data (before and after) and you wish to compare the mean score on some continuous variable. There are two main types of t-tests. *Paired-samples* t-*tests* (also called 'repeated measures') are used when you are interested in changes in scores for participants tested at Time 1, and then again at Time 2 (often after some intervention or event). The samples are related because they are the *same* people tested each time. *Independent-samples* t-*tests* are used when you have two different (independent) groups of people (males and females) and you are interested in comparing their scores. In this case, you collect information on only one occasion but from two different sets of people. T-tests are covered in Chapter 17. The non-parametric alternatives, Mann-Whitney *U* Test and Wilcoxon Signed Rank Test, are presented in Chapter 16.

One-way analysis of variance

One-way analysis of variance is similar to a t-test but is used when you have *two or more groups* and you wish to compare their mean scores on a continuous variable. It is called 'one-way' because you are evaluating the impact of only one independent variable on your dependent variable. A one-way analysis of variance (ANOVA) will let you know whether your groups differ, but it won't tell you where the significant difference is (e.g. between Groups 1, and 3 or between Groups 2 and 3). You can conduct post-hoc comparisons to find out which groups are significantly different from one another. You could also choose to test differences between specific groups, rather than comparing all the groups, by using planned comparisons. Similar to t-tests, there are two types of one-way ANOVAs: repeated measures ANOVA (same people on more than two occasions) and between-groups (or independent-samples) ANOVA, where you are comparing the mean scores of two or more different groups of people. One-way ANOVA is covered in Chapter 18, while the non-parametric alternatives (Kruskal-Wallis Test and Friedman Test) are presented in Chapter 16.

Two-way analysis of variance

Two-way analysis of variance allows you to test the impact of two independent variables on one dependent variable. The advantage of using a two-way ANOVA is that it allows you to test for an interaction effect—that is, when the effect of one independent variable is influenced by another. An example of this is when you suspect that optimism increases with age, but only for males.

It also tests for main effects—that is, the overall effect of each independent variable (e.g. sex, age). There are two different two-way ANOVAs: between-groups ANOVA (when the groups are different) and repeated measures ANOVA (when the same people are tested on more than one occasion). Some research designs combine both between-groups and repeated measures in the one study. These are referred to as 'Mixed Between-Within Designs', or 'Split Plot'. Two-way ANOVA is covered in Chapter 19. Mixed between-within designs are covered in Chapter 20.

Multivariate analysis of variance

Multivariate analysis of variance (MANOVA) is used when you want to compare your groups on a set of different, but *related*, dependent variables—for example, comparing the effects of different treatments on a variety of outcome measures (such as anxiety or depression). Multivariate ANOVA can be used with one-way, two-way and higher factorial designs involving one, two or more independent variables. MANOVA is covered in Chapter 21.

Analysis of covariance

Analysis of covariance (ANCOVA) is used when you want to statistically control for the possible effects of an additional confounding variable (covariate). This is useful when you suspect that your groups differ on some variable that may influence the effect that your independent variables have on your dependent variable. To be sure that it is the independent variable that is doing the influencing, ANCOVA statistically removes the effect of the covariate. Analysis of covariance can be used as part of a one-way, two-way or multivariate design. ANCOVA is covered in Chapter 22.

THE DECISION-MAKING PROCESS

Having explored the variety of choices available, it is time to choose which techniques are suitable for your needs. In choosing the right statistic, you will need to consider several different factors. These include consideration of the type of question you wish to address, the types of items and scales that were included in your questionnaire, the nature of the data you have available for each of your variables and the assumptions that must be met for each of the different statistical techniques. I have specified below some steps that you can use to navigate your way through the decision-making process.

Step 1: Decide what questions you want to address

Write yourself a full list of all the questions you would like to answer from your research. You might find that some questions could be asked in a variety of ways. You will use these alternatives when considering the different statistical approaches you might use. For example, you might be interested in the effect of age on optimism. There are two ways you could ask the question:

> ➢ Is there a relationship between age and level of optimism?
> ➢ Are older people more optimistic than younger people?

These two questions require different statistical techniques. The question of which is more suitable may depend on the nature of the data you have collected. So, for each area of interest, detail a set of different questions.

Step 2: Find the questionnaire items and scales that you will use to address these questions

The types of items and scales that were included in your study will play a large part in determining which statistical techniques are suitable to address your research questions. That is why it is so important to consider the analyses that you intend to use when first designing your study. For example, the way in which you collected information about respondents' age (see example in Step 1) will determine which statistics are available for you to use. If you asked people to tick one of two options (under 35/35 or over), your choice of statistics would be very limited, because there are only two possible values for your variable age. If, on the other hand, you asked people to give their age in years, your choices are broadened, because you can have scores varying across a wide range of values, from 18 to 80+. In this situation, you may choose to collapse the range of ages down into a smaller number of categories for some analyses (ANOVA), but the full range of scores is also available for other analyses (e.g. correlation).

If you administered a questionnaire or survey for your study, go back to the specific questionnaire items and your codebook and find each of the individual questions (e.g. age) and total scale scores (e.g. optimism) that you will use in your analyses. Identify each variable, how it was measured, how many response options there were and the possible range of scores.

If your study involved an experiment, check how each of your dependent and independent variables was measured. Did the scores on the variable consist of the number of correct responses, an observer's rating of a specific behaviour or the length of time a subject spent on a specific activity? Whatever the nature of the study, just be clear that you know how each of your variables was measured.

Step 3: Identify the nature of each of your variables

The next step is to identify the nature of each of your variables. In particular, you need to determine whether each variable is an independent variable or a dependent variable. This information comes not from your data but from your understanding of the topic area, relevant theories and previous research. It is essential that you are clear in your own mind (and in your research questions) concerning the relationship between your variables—which ones are doing the influencing (independent) and which ones are being affected (dependent). There are some analyses (e.g. correlation) where it is not necessary to specify which variables are independent and dependent. For other analyses, such as ANOVA, it is important that you have this clear. Drawing a model of how you see your variables relating is often useful here (see Step 4, discussed next).

It is also important that you know the level of measurement for each of your variables. Different statistics are required for variables that are categorical and continuous, so it is important to know what you are working with. Are your variables:

➢ categorical, with no order—e.g. sex: male/females (referred to as 'nominal level data')?
➢ categorical, but ordered by the level of the characteristic—e.g. age group: young, middle-aged, old (referred to as 'ordinal level data')?
➢ continuous—e.g. age in years or scores on the Optimism Scale (also referred to as 'interval level data')? These variables are labelled 'Scale' in IBM SPSS Statistics.

There are some occasions when you might want to change the level of measurement for particular variables. You can collapse continuous variable responses down into a smaller number of categories (see Chapter 8). For example, age can be broken down into different categories (e.g. under 35/35 or over). This can be useful if you want to conduct an ANOVA. It can also be used if your continuous variables do not meet some of the assumptions for particular analyses (e.g. very skewed distributions). Summarising the data does have some disadvantages, however, as you lose information. By lumping people together, you can sometimes miss important differences. You need to weigh up the benefits and disadvantages carefully.

Additional information required for continuous and categorical variables

For *continuous* variables, you should collect information on the distribution of scores. Are they normally distributed, or are they badly skewed? What is the range of scores? (See Chapter 6 for the procedures to do this.) If your variable involves *categories* (e.g. Group 1/Group 2, males/females), find out how many people fall into each category. Are the groups equal, or very unbalanced? Are some of the possible categories empty? (See Chapter 6.) All of this information that you gather about your variables will be used later to narrow down the choice of statistics to use.

Step 4: Draw a diagram for each of your research questions

I often find that students are at a loss for words when trying to explain what they are researching. Sometimes, it is easier, and clearer, to summarise the key points in a diagram. The idea is to pull together some of the information you have collected in Steps 1 and 2 above in a simple format that will help you choose the correct statistical technique to use or choose from a set of different options.

One of the key issues you should consider is: am I interested in the *relationship* between two variables, or am I interested in *comparing* two groups of participants? Summarising the information that you have, and drawing a diagram for each question, may help clarify this for you. I demonstrate by setting out the information and drawing diagrams for different research questions.

Question 1: Is there a relationship between age and level of optimism?

Variables:
➤ age: Continuous—age in years from 18 to 80
➤ optimism: Continuous—scores on the Optimism Scale, ranging from 6 to 30.

From your literature review you hypothesise that older people are more optimistic than younger people. This relationship between two continuous variables could be illustrated as follows:

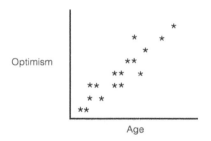

If you expected optimism scores to increase with age, you would place the points starting low on the left and moving up towards the right. If you predicted that optimism would decrease with age, then your points would start high on the left-hand side and would fall as you moved towards the right.

Question 2: Are males more optimistic than females?

Variables:
➤ sex: Independent, categorical (two groups)—males/females
➤ optimism: Dependent, continuous—scores on the Optimism Scale, ranging from 6 to 30.

The results from this question, with one categorical variable (with only two groups) and one continuous variable, could be summarised as follows:

	Males	Females
Mean optimism score		

Question 3: Is the effect of age on optimism different for males and females?

If you wished to investigate the joint effects of age and gender on optimism scores, you might decide to break your sample into three age groups (30 or under, 31–49 and 50+).

Variables:
➢ sex: Independent, categorical—males/females
➢ age: Independent, categorical—participants divided into three equal groups
➢ optimism: Dependent, continuous—scores on the Optimism Scale, ranging from 6 to 30.

The diagram might look like this:

		Age (years)		
		30 or under	31–49	50 and over
Mean optimism score	Males			
	Females			

Question 4: How much of the variance in life satisfaction can be explained by a set of personality factors (self-esteem, optimism, perceived control)?

Perhaps you are interested in comparing the predictive ability of a set of independent variables on a continuous, dependent measure. You are also interested in how much variance in your dependent variable is explained by the set of independent variables.

Variables:
➢ self-esteem: Independent, continuous
➢ optimism: Independent, continuous
➢ perceived control: Independent, continuous
➢ life satisfaction: Dependent, continuous.

Your diagram might look like this:

Step 5: Decide whether a parametric or a non-parametric statistical technique is appropriate

The wide variety of statistical techniques that are available can be classified into two main groups: parametric and non-parametric. Parametric statistics are more powerful, but they do have more strings attached; that is, they make assumptions about the data that are more stringent. For example, they assume that the underlying distribution of scores in the population from which you have drawn your sample is normal.

Each of the different parametric techniques (such as t-tests, ANOVA, Pearson correlation) has other additional assumptions. It is important that you check these *before* you conduct your analyses. The specific assumptions are listed for each of the techniques covered in the remaining chapters of this book.

What if you don't meet the assumptions for the statistical technique that you want to use? Unfortunately, in social science research this is a common situation. Many of the attributes we want to measure are in fact not normally distributed. Some are strongly skewed, with most scores falling at the low end of the scale (e.g. depression); others are skewed so that most of the scores fall at the high end (e.g. self-esteem).

If you don't meet the assumptions of the statistic you wish to use you have several different choices, and these are detailed below.

Option 1

You can use the parametric technique anyway and hope that it does not seriously invalidate your findings. Some statistics writers argue that most of the approaches are fairly robust; that is, they will tolerate minor violations of assumptions, particularly if you have a good-size sample. If you decide to go ahead with the analysis anyway you will need to justify this in your write-up, so collect together useful quotes from statistics writers, previous researchers and so on to support your decision. Check journal articles on your topic area, particularly those that have used the same scales. Do they mention similar problems? If so, what have these other authors done? For a simple, easy-to-follow review of the robustness of different tests, see Cone and Foster (2006).

Option 2

You may be able to manipulate your data so that the assumptions of the statistical test (e.g. normal distribution) are met. Some authors suggest transforming your variables if their distribution is not normal (see Chapter 8). There is some controversy concerning this approach, so make sure you read up on this so that you can justify what you have done (see Tabachnick & Fidell 2013).

Option 3

The other alternative when you don't meet parametric assumptions is to use a non-parametric technique instead. For some of the commonly used parametric techniques, there is a corresponding non-parametric alternative. These still come with some assumptions, but less stringent ones. These non-parametric alternatives (e.g. Kruskal-Wallis, Mann-Whitney U, chi-square) tend to be not as powerful; that is, they may be less sensitive in detecting a relationship or a difference among groups. Some of the more commonly used non-parametric techniques are covered in Chapter 16.

Step 6: Make the final decision

Once you have collected the necessary information concerning your research questions, the level of measurement for each of your variables and the characteristics of the data you have available, you are finally in a position to consider your options. In the text below, I have summarised the key elements of some of the major statistical approaches you are likely to encounter. Scan down the list, find an example of the type of research question you want to address and check that you have all the necessary ingredients. Also consider whether there might be other ways you could ask your question and use a different statistical approach. I have included a summary table at the end of this chapter to help with the decision-making process.

Seek out additional information on the techniques you choose to use to ensure that you have a good understanding of their underlying principles and their assumptions. It is a good idea to use a variety of sources for this process: different authors have different opinions. You should have an understanding of the controversial issues—you may even need to justify the use of a particular statistic in your situation—so make sure you have read widely.

KEY FEATURES OF THE MAJOR STATISTICAL TECHNIQUES

This section is divided into two subsections:
1. Techniques used to explore relationships among variables (covered in Part Four of this book)
2. Techniques used to explore differences among groups (covered in Part Five of this book).

Exploring relationships among variables
Chi-Square Test for Independence
Example of research question: What is the relationship between gender and dropout rates from therapy?

What you need:
➤ one categorical, independent variable (e.g. sex: males/females)
➤ one categorical, dependent variable (e.g. dropout: yes/no).

You are interested in the *number* of people in each category (not scores on a scale).

Diagram:

		Males	Females
Dropout	Yes		
	No		.

Correlation

Examples of research questions: Is there a relationship between age and optimism scores? Does optimism increase with age?

What you need: Two continuous variables (e.g. age, optimism scores).

Diagram:

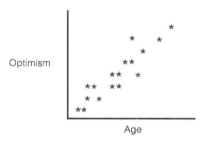

Non-parametric alternative: Spearman's Rank Order Correlation.

Partial correlation

Example of research question: After controlling for the effects of socially desirable responding, is there still a significant relationship between optimism and life satisfaction scores?

What you need: Three continuous variables (e.g. optimism, life satisfaction, socially desirable responding).

Non-parametric alternative: None.

Multiple regression

Examples of research questions: How much of the variance in life satisfaction scores can be explained by the following set of variables: self-esteem, optimism and perceived control? Which of these variables is a better predictor of life satisfaction?

What you need:
➢ one continuous, dependent variable (e.g. life satisfaction)
➢ two or more continuous, independent variables (e.g. self-esteem, optimism, perceived control).

Diagram:

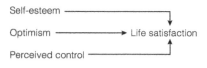

Non-parametric alternative: None.

Exploring differences between groups

Independent-samples t-test

Example of research question: Are males more optimistic than females?

What you need:
➢ one categorical, independent variable with only *two* groups (e.g. sex: males/females)
➢ one continuous, dependent variable (e.g. optimism score).

Participants can belong to only *one group.*

Diagram:

	Males	**Females**
Mean optimism score		

Non-parametric alternative: Mann-Whitney *U* Test.

Paired-samples t-test (repeated measures)

Examples of research questions: Does 10 weeks of meditation training result in a decrease in participants' level of anxiety? Is there a change in anxiety levels from Time 1 (pre-intervention) to Time 2 (post-intervention)?

What you need:
➢ one categorical, independent variable (e.g. Time 1/Time 2)
➢ one continuous, dependent variable (e.g. anxiety score measured on two different occasions).

The *same participants* are tested on *two* separate occasions: Time 1 (before intervention) and Time 2 (after intervention).

Diagram:

	Time 1	Time 2
Mean anxiety score		

Non-parametric alternative: Wilcoxon Signed Rank Test.

One-way between-groups analysis of variance

Example of research question: Is there a difference in optimism scores for people who are aged 30 and under, between 31 and 49, and 50 and over?

What you need:
➢ one categorical, independent variable with two or more groups (e.g. age: 30 and under, 31–49, 50+)
➢ one continuous, dependent variable (e.g. optimism score).

Diagram:

	Age (years)		
	30 or under	31–49	50 and over
Mean optimism score			

Non-parametric alternative: Kruskal-Wallis Test.

Two-way between-groups analysis of variance

Example of research question: What is the effect of age on optimism scores for males and females?

What you need:
➢ two categorical, independent variables (e.g. sex: males/female, age group: 30 and under, 31–49, 50+)
➢ one continuous, dependent variable (e.g. optimism score).

Diagram:

		Age (years)		
		30 or under	31–49	50 and over
Mean optimism score	Males			
	Females			

Non-parametric alternative: None.

Note: Analysis of variance can also be extended to include three or more independent variables (usually referred to as 'Factorial Analysis of Variance').

Mixed between-within analysis of variance

Example of research question: Which intervention (maths skills/confidence building) is more effective in reducing participants' fear of statistics, measured across three periods (pre-intervention, post-intervention, 3-month follow-up)?

What you need:

➢ one between-groups, independent variable (e.g. type of intervention)
➢ one within-groups, independent variable (e.g. Time 1, Time 2, Time 3)
➢ one continuous, dependent variable (e.g. scores on Fear of Statistics Test).

Diagram:

		Time		
		1	2	3
Mean score on Fear of Statistics Test	Maths skills intervention			
	Confidence-building intervention			

Non-parametric alternative: None.

Multivariate analysis of variance

Example of research question: Are males better adjusted than females in terms of their psychological health (e.g. anxiety, depression and perceived stress)?

What you need:

➢ one categorical, independent variable (e.g. sex: males/females)
➢ two or more continuous, dependent variables (e.g. anxiety, depression, perceived stress).

Diagram:

	Males	Females
Anxiety		
Depression		
Perceived stress		

Non-parametric alternative: None.

Note: Multivariate analysis of variance can be used with one-way (one independent variable), two-way (two independent variables) and higher-order factorial designs. Covariates can also be included.

Analysis of covariance

Example of research question: Is there a significant difference in the Fear of Statistics Test scores for participants in the maths skills group and for those in the confidence-building group, while controlling for their pre-intervention scores on this test?

What you need:

➤ one categorical, independent variable (e.g. type of intervention)
➤ one continuous, dependent variable (e.g. Fear of Statistics Test scores at Time 2)
➤ one or more continuous covariates (e.g. Fear of Statistics Test scores at Time 1).

Non-parametric alternative: None.

Note: Analysis of covariance can be used with one-way (one independent variable), two-way (two independent variables) and higher-order factorial designs, and with multivariate designs (two or more dependent variables).

FURTHER READINGS

The statistical techniques discussed in this chapter are only a small sample of all the different approaches that you can take to data analysis. It is important that you are aware of the existence, and potential uses, of a wide variety of techniques in order to choose the most suitable one for your situation. Read as widely as you can.

For a coverage of the basic techniques (t-test, analysis of variance, correlation) go back to your basic statistics texts—for example, Cooper and Schindler (2013); Gravetter and Wallnau (2012); Peat (2001); Norman and Streiner (2014). If you would like more detailed information, particularly on multivariate statistics, see Hair, Black, Babin, Anderson and Tatham (2009) or Tabachnick and Fidell (2013).

Summary table of the characteristics of the main statistical techniques

Purpose	Example of question	Parametric statistic	Non-parametric alternative	Independent variable	Dependent variable	Essential features
Exploring relationships	What is the relationship between gender and dropout rates from therapy?	None	Chi-square Chapter 16	One categorical variable *Sex: M/F*	One categorical variable *Dropout/complete therapy: yes/no*	The number of cases in each category is considered, not scores
	Is there a relationship between age and optimism scores?	Pearson product-moment correlation coefficient (r) Chapter 11	Spearman's Rank Order Correlation (*rho*) Chapter 11	Two continuous variables *Age, optimism scores*		One sample with scores on two different measures, or same measure at Time 1 and Time 2
	After controlling for the effects of socially desirable responding bias, is there still a relationship between optimism and life satisfaction?	Partial correlation Chapter 12	None	Two continuous variables and one continuous variable that you wish to control for *Optimism, life satisfaction, scores on a social desirability scale*		One sample with scores on two different measures, or same measure at Time 1 and Time 2
	How much of the variance in life satisfaction scores can be explained by self-esteem, perceived control and optimism? Which of these variables is the best predictor?	Multiple regression Chapter 13	None	Set of two or more continuous, independent variables *Self-esteem, perceived control, optimism*	One continuous, dependent variable *Life satisfaction*	One sample with scores on all measures
	What is the underlying structure of the items that make up the Positive and Negative Affect Scale? How many factors are involved?	Factor analysis Chapter 15	None	Set of related continuous variables *Items of the Positive and Negative Affect Scale*		One sample, multiple measures

Purpose	Example of question	Parametric statistic	Non-parametric alternative	Independent variable	Dependent variable	Essential features
Comparing groups	Are males more likely to drop out of therapy than females?	None	Chi-square Chapter 16	One categorical independent variable *Sex*	One categorical, dependent variable *Dropout/complete therapy*	You are interested in the *number of people* in each category, not scores on a scale
	Is there a difference in optimism scores for males and females?	Independent-sample, t-test Chapter 17	Mann-Whitney U Test Chapter 16	One categorical independent variable (two levels) *Sex*	One continuous, dependent variable *Optimism score*	Two groups, different people in each group
	Is there a change in participants' anxiety scores from Time 1 to Time 2?	Paired-samples t-test Chapter 17	Wilcoxon Signed Rank Test Chapter 16	One categorical independent variable (two levels) *Time 1/Time 2*	One continuous, dependent variable *Anxiety score*	Same people on two different occasions
	Is there a difference in optimism scores for people who are aged 35 and under, 36–49 and 50+?	One-way between-groups ANOVA Chapter 18	Kruskal-Wallis Test Chapter 16	One categorical independent variable (three or more levels) *Age group*	One continuous, dependent variable *Optimism score*	Three or more groups: different people in each group
	Is there a change in participants' anxiety scores from Time 1 to Time 2 and Time 3?	One-way repeated measures ANOVA Chapter 18	Friedman Test Chapter 16	One categorical independent variable (three or more levels) *Time 1/Time 2/Time 3*	One continuous, dependent variable *Anxiety score*	Three or more groups: same people on two different occasions
	Is there a difference in the optimism scores for males and females, who are aged 35 and under, 36–49 and 50+?	Two-way between-groups ANOVA Chapter 19	None	Two categorical independent variables (two or more levels) *Age group, sex*	One continuous, dependent variable *Optimism score*	Two or more groups for each independent variable: different people in each group

Purpose	Example of question	Parametric statistic	Non-parametric alternative	Independent variable	Dependent variable	Essential features
	Which intervention (maths skills/confidence building) is more effective in reducing participants' fear of statistics, measured across three time periods?	Mixed between-within ANOVA Chapter 20	None	One between-groups, independent variable (two or more levels), one within-groups, independent variable (two or more levels) *Type of intervention, time*	One continuous, dependent variable *Fear of Statistics Test scores*	Two or more groups with different people in each group, each measured on two or more occasions
	Is there a difference between males and females, across three different age groups, in terms of their scores on a variety of adjustment measures (anxiety, depression and perceived stress)?	Multivariate ANOVA (MANOVA) Chapter 21	None	One or more categorical, independent variables (two or more levels) *Age group, sex*	Two or more related continuous, dependent variables *Anxiety, depression and perceived stress scores?*	
	Is there a significant difference in the Fear of Statistics Test scores for participants in the maths skills group and the confidence-building group, while controlling for their scores on this test at Time 1?	Analysis of covariance (ANCOVA) Chapter 22	None	One or more categorical, independent variables (two or more levels), one continuous, covariate variable *Type of intervention, Fear of Statistics Test scores at Time 1*	One continuous, dependent variable *Fear of Statistics Test scores at Time 2*	

PART FOUR
Statistical techniques to explore relationships among variables

In the chapters included in this section, we examine some of the techniques available in IBM SPSS Statistics for exploring relationships among variables. In this section, our focus is on detecting and describing relationships among variables. All of the techniques covered here are based on correlation. Correlational techniques are often used by researchers engaged in non-experimental research designs. Unlike in experimental designs, variables are not deliberately manipulated or controlled—variables are described as they exist naturally. These techniques can be used to:

➤ explore the association between pairs of variables (correlation)
➤ predict scores on one variable from scores on another variable (bivariate regression)
➤ predict scores on a dependent variable from scores of a set of independent variables (multiple regression)
➤ identify the structure underlying a group of related variables (factor analysis).

This family of techniques is used to test models and theories, predict outcomes and assess reliability and validity of scales.

TECHNIQUES COVERED IN PART FOUR

There is a range of techniques available in IBM SPSS Statistics to explore relationships. These vary according to the type of research question that needs to be addressed and the types of data available. In this book, however, only the most commonly used techniques are covered.

Correlation (Chapter 11) is used when you wish to describe the strength and direction of the relationship between two variables. The variables are usually continuous, but correlation can also be used when one of the variables is dichotomous—that is, it has only two values (e.g. sex: males/females). The statistic obtained is Pearson's product-moment correlation (r). The statistical significance of r is also provided. The non-parametric alternative, Spearman correlation (rho), is also described in Chapter 11 for use in situations where your data do not meet the assumptions required by Pearson correlation.

Partial correlation (Chapter 12) is used when you wish to explore the relationship between two variables while statistically controlling for a third variable. This is useful when you suspect that the relationship between your two variables of interest may be influenced, or confounded, by the impact of a third variable. Partial correlation statistically removes the influence of the third variable, giving a clearer picture of the actual relationship between your two variables.

Multiple regression (Chapter 13) allows prediction of a single dependent, continuous variable from a group of independent variables. It can be used to test the predictive power of a set of variables and to assess the relative contribution of each individual variable.

Logistic regression (Chapter 14) is performed, instead of multiple regression, when your dependent variable is categorical. It can be used to test the predictive power of a set of variables and to assess the relative contribution of each individual variable.

Factor analysis (Chapter 15) is conducted when you have a large number of related variables (e.g. the items that make up a scale) and you wish to explore the underlying structure of this set of variables. It is useful in reducing a large number of related variables to a smaller, more manageable number of dimensions or components. In the remainder of this introduction to Part Four I review some of the basic principles of correlation that are common to all the techniques covered in Part Four. This material should be reviewed before you attempt to use any of the procedures covered in this section.

REVISION OF THE BASICS

Correlation coefficients (e.g. Pearson product-moment correlation) provide a numerical summary of the direction and the strength of the linear relationship between two variables. Pearson correlation coefficients (r) can range from −1 to +1. The sign in front indicates whether there is a positive correlation (as one variable increases, so too does the other) or a negative correlation (as one variable increases, the other decreases). The size of the absolute value (ignoring the sign) provides information on the strength of the relationship. A perfect correlation of 1 or −1 indicates that the value of one variable can be determined exactly by knowing the value of the other variable. On the other hand, a correlation of 0 indicates no relationship between the two variables. Knowing the value of one of the variables provides no assistance in predicting the value of the second variable.

The relationship between variables can be inspected visually by generating a scatterplot. This is a plot of each pair of scores obtained from the participants in the sample. Scores on the first variable are plotted along the X (horizontal) axis, and the corresponding scores on the second variable are plotted on the Y (vertical) axis. An inspection of the scatterplot provides information on both the direction of the relationship (positive or negative) and the strength of the relationship (this is demonstrated in more detail in Chapter 11). A scatterplot of a perfect correlation ($r = 1$ or −1) would show a straight line. A scatterplot when $r = 0$, however, would show a blob of points, with no pattern evident.

Factors to consider when interpreting a correlation coefficient

There are several things you need to be careful of when interpreting the results of a correlation analysis or other techniques based on correlation. Some of the key issues are outlined below, but I would suggest you go back to your statistics books and review this material.

Non-linear relationship

The correlation coefficient (e.g. Pearson r) provides an indication of the linear (straight-line) relationship between variables. In situations where the two variables are related in non-linear fashion (e.g. curvilinear), Pearson r will seriously underestimate the strength of the relationship. Always check the scatterplot, particularly if you obtain low values of r.

Outliers

Outliers (values that are substantially lower or higher than the other values in the data set) can have a dramatic effect on the correlation coefficient, particularly in small samples. In some circumstances outliers can make the r value much higher than it should be, and in other circumstances they can result in an underestimate of the true relationship. A scatterplot can be used to check for outliers—scan for values that are sitting out on their own. These could be due to a data entry error (typing 11, instead of 1) or a careless answer from a respondent, or it could be a true value from a rather strange individual! If you find an outlier, you should check for errors and correct if appropriate. You may also need to consider removing or recoding the offending value to reduce the effect it is having on the *r* value (see Chapter 6 for a discussion on outliers).

Restricted range of scores

You should always be careful interpreting correlation coefficients when they come from only a small subsection of the possible range of scores (e.g. using university students to study IQ). Correlation coefficients from studies using a restricted range of cases are often different from studies where the full range of possible scores is sampled. In order to provide an accurate and reliable indicator of the strength of the relationship between two variables, there should be as wide a range of scores on each of the two variables as possible. If you are involved in studying extreme groups (e.g. clients with high levels of anxiety), you should not try to generalise any correlation beyond the range of the variable used in the sample.

Correlation versus causality

Correlation provides an indication that there is a relationship between two variables; it does not, however, indicate that one variable *causes* the other. The correlation between two variables (A and B) could be due to the fact that A causes B, that B causes A or (just to complicate matters) that an additional variable (C) causes both A and B. The possibility of a third variable that influences both of your observed variables should always be considered. To illustrate this point, there is the famous story of the strong correlation that one researcher found between ice-cream consumption and the number of homicides reported in New York City. Does eating ice-cream cause people to become violent? No. Both variables (ice-cream consumption and crime rate) were influenced by the weather. During the very hot spells, both the ice-cream consumption and the crime rate increased. Despite the positive correlation obtained, this did not prove that eating ice-cream causes homicidal behaviour. Just as well—the ice-cream manufacturers would very quickly be out of business!

The warning here is clear—watch out for the possible influence of a third, confounding variable when designing your own study. If you suspect the possibility of other variables that might influence your result, see if you can measure these at the same time. By using partial correlation (described in Chapter 12) you can statistically control for these additional variables and therefore gain a clearer, and less contaminated, indication of the relationship between your two variables of interest.

Statistical versus practical significance

Don't get too excited if your correlation coefficients are significant. With large samples, even quite small correlation coefficients (e.g. $r = .2$) can reach statistical significance. Although statistically significant, the practical significance of a correlation of .2 is very limited. You should focus on the actual size of Pearson's r and the amount of shared variance between the two variables. The amount of shared variance can be calculated by squaring the value of the correlation coefficient (e.g. $.2 \times .2 = .04 = 4\%$ shared variance).

To interpret the strength of your correlation coefficient, you should also take into account other research that has been conducted in your particular topic area. If other researchers in your area have been able to predict only 9 per cent of the variance ($r = .3$) in a particular outcome (e.g. anxiety), then your study that explains 25 per cent ($r = .5$) would be impressive in comparison. In other topic areas, 25 per cent of the variance explained may seem small and irrelevant.

Assumptions

There is a set of assumptions common to all the techniques covered in Part Four. These are discussed below. You will need to refer back to these assumptions when performing any of the analyses covered in Chapters 11, 12, 13, 14 and 15.

Level of measurement

When choosing a statistical technique one of the important considerations is the level of measurement of the variables to be used in the analysis. The measurement levels for the variables for most of the techniques covered in Part Four should be interval or ratio (continuous). One exception to this is if you have one dichotomous, independent variable (with only two values—e.g. sex) and one continuous, dependent variable. You should, however, have roughly the same number of people or cases in each category of the dichotomous variable.

Spearman's *rho*, which is a correlation coefficient suitable for ordinal or ranked data, is discussed in Chapter 11, along with the parametric alternative Pearson correlation coefficient. *Rho* is commonly used in the health and medical literature and is also increasingly being used in psychology research as researchers become more aware of the potential problems of assuming that ordinal level ratings (e.g. Likert scales) approximate interval level scaling.

Related pairs

Each subject must provide a score on both variable X and variable Y (related pairs). Both pieces of information must be from the same subject.

Independence of observations

The observations that make up your data must be independent of one another. That is, each observation or measurement must not be influenced by any other observation or measurement. Violation of this assumption, according to Stevens (1996, p. 238), is very serious. There are various research situations that may violate this assumption of independence. Examples of some such studies are described below (these are drawn from Stevens 1996, p. 239; and Gravetter & Wallnau 2004, p. 251):

➤ *Studying the performance of students working in pairs or small groups:* The behaviour of each member of the group influences all other group members, thereby violating the assumption of independence.

➤ *Studying the TV-watching habits and preferences of children drawn from the same family:* The behaviour of one child in the family (e.g. watching Program A) is likely to affect all children in that family; therefore, the observations are not independent.

➤ *Studying teaching methods within a classroom and examining the impact on students' behaviour and performance:* In this situation, all students could be influenced by the presence of a small number of trouble-makers; therefore, individual behavioural or performance measurements are not independent.

Any situation where the observations or measurements are collected in a group setting, or participants are involved in some form of interaction with one another, should be considered suspect. In designing your study, you should try to ensure that all observations are independent. If you suspect some violation of this assumption, Stevens (1996, p. 241) recommends that you set a more stringent alpha value (e.g. $p < .01$).

There are more complex statistical techniques that can be used for data that involve non-independent samples (e.g. children within different classrooms, within different schools). This approach involves multilevel modelling, which is beyond the scope of this book (see Chapter 15 in Tabachnick & Fidell 2013).

Normality

Ideally, scores on each variable should be normally distributed. This can be checked by inspecting the histograms of scores on each variable (see Chapter 6 for instructions).

Linearity

The relationship between the two variables should be linear. When you inspect a scatterplot of scores you should see a straight line (roughly), not a curve.

Homoscedasticity

The variability in scores for variable X should be similar at all values of variable Y. Check the scatterplot (see Chapter 7 for instructions). It should show a fairly even cigar shape along its length.

Missing data

When you are doing research, particularly with human beings, it is very rare that you will obtain complete data from every case. It is important that you inspect your data file for missing data. Run **Descriptives** and find out what percentage of values is missing for each of your variables. If you find a variable with a lot of unexpected missing data, you need to ask yourself why. You should also consider whether your missing values are happening randomly, or whether there is some systematic pattern (e.g. lots of women failing to answer the question about their age). IBM SPSS Statistics has a **Missing Value Analysis** procedure that may help find patterns in your missing values.

You also need to consider how you will deal with missing values in each of the IBM SPSS Statistics procedures. The **Options** button in many of the dialogue boxes offers you choices for how you want the program to deal with missing data. It is important that you choose carefully, as it can have dramatic effects on your results. This is particularly important if you are including a list of variables and repeating the same analysis for all variables (e.g. correlations among a group of variables, t-tests for a series of dependent variables).

> The **Exclude cases listwise** option will include cases (persons) in the analysis only if it has full data on *all of the variables* listed in your **Variables** box for that case. A case will be totally excluded from all the analyses if it is missing even one piece of information. This can severely, and unnecessarily, limit your sample size.
> The **Exclude cases pairwise** option, however, excludes the cases only if they are missing the data required for the specific analysis. They will still be included in any of the analyses for which they have the necessary information.
> The **Replace with mean** option, which is available in some IBM SPSS Statistics statistical procedures (e.g. multiple regression), calculates the mean value for the variable and gives every missing case this value. This option should *never* be used as it can severely distort the results of your analysis, particularly if you have a lot of missing values.

Always press the **Options** button for any statistical procedure you conduct and check which of these options is ticked (the default option varies across procedures). I would strongly recommend that you use **pairwise** exclusion of missing data, unless you have a pressing reason to do otherwise. The only situation where you might need to use **listwise** exclusion is when you want to refer only to a subset of cases that provided a full set of results.

Strange-looking numbers

In your output, you may come across some strange-looking numbers that take the form '1.24E-02'. These small values are presented in scientific notation. To prevent this happening, choose **Edit** from the main menu bar, select **Options**, and make sure there is a tick in the box **No scientific notation for small numbers in tables** on the **General** tab.

11

Correlation

Correlation analysis is used to describe the strength and direction of the linear relationship between two variables. There are several different statistics available from IBM SPSS Statistics, depending on the level of measurement and the nature of your data. In this chapter, the procedure for obtaining and interpreting a Pearson product-moment correlation coefficient (r) is presented, along with Spearman Rank Order Correlation (rho). Pearson r is designed for interval level (continuous) variables. It can also be used if you have one continuous variable (e.g. scores on a measure of self-esteem) and one dichotomous variable (e.g. sex: male/female). Spearman rho is designed for use with ordinal level, or ranked, data and is particularly useful when your data do not meet the criteria for Pearson correlation.

IBM SPSS Statistics can calculate two types of correlation for you. First, it can give you a simple bivariate correlation (which just means between two variables), also known as 'zero-order correlation'. It will also allow you to explore the relationship between two variables while controlling for another variable. This is known as 'partial correlation'. The procedure to obtain a bivariate Pearson r and non-parametric Spearman rho is presented here in Chapter 11. Partial correlation is covered in Chapter 12.

Pearson correlation coefficients (r) can only take on values from -1 to $+1$. The sign out the front indicates whether there is a positive correlation (as one variable increases, so too does the other) or a negative correlation (as one variable increases, the other decreases). The size of the absolute value (ignoring the sign) provides an indication of the strength of the relationship. A perfect correlation of 1 or -1 indicates that the value of one variable can be determined exactly by knowing the value on the other variable. A scatterplot of this relationship would show a straight line. On the other hand, a correlation of 0 indicates no relationship between the two variables. Knowing the value on one of the variables provides no assistance in predicting the value on the second variable. A scatterplot would show a circle of points, with no pattern evident.

There are several issues associated with the use of correlation that you need to consider. These include the effect of non-linear relationships, outliers, restriction of range, correlation versus causality and statistical versus practical significance. These topics are discussed in the introduction to Part Four of this book. I would strongly recommend that you read through that material before proceeding with the remainder of this chapter.

DETAILS OF EXAMPLE

To demonstrate the use of correlation, I explore the interrelationships among some of the variables included in the **survey.sav** data file provided on the website accompanying this book. The survey was designed to explore the factors that affect respondents' psychological adjustment and wellbeing (see the Appendix for a full description of the study). In this example, I am interested in assessing the correlation between respondents' feelings of control and their level of perceived stress. If you wish to follow along with this example, you should start IBM SPSS Statistics and open the **survey.sav** file.

Example of research question: Is there a relationship between the amount of control people have over their internal states and their levels of perceived stress? Do people with high levels of perceived control experience lower levels of perceived stress?

What you need: Two variables: both continuous, or one continuous and the other dichotomous (two values).

What it does: Correlation describes the relationship between two continuous variables, in terms of both the strength of the relationship and the direction.

Assumptions: See the introduction to Part Four.

Non-parametric alternative: Spearman Rank Order Correlation (*rho*).

PRELIMINARY ANALYSES FOR CORRELATION

Before performing a correlation analysis, it is a good idea to generate a scatterplot. This enables you to check for outliers and for violation of the assumptions of linearity (see introduction to Part Four). Inspection of the scatterplots also gives you a better idea of the nature of the relationship between your variables.

> To generate a scatterplot between your independent variable (Total PCOISS) and dependent variable (Total perceived stress) follow the instructions detailed in Chapter 7. The output generated from this procedure is shown below.

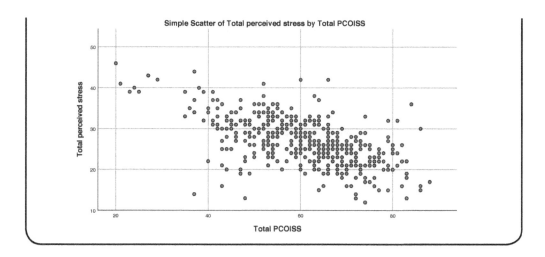

Simple Scatter of Total perceived stress by Total PCOISS

Interpretation of output from Scatterplot

The scatterplot can be used to check several aspects of the distribution of these two variables.

Step 1: Check for outliers

Check your scatterplot for outliers—that is, data points that are out on their own, either very high or very low, or away from the main cluster of points. Extreme outliers are worth checking: Was the information entered correctly? Could these values be errors? Outliers can seriously influence some analyses, so this is worth investigating. Some statistical texts recommend removing extreme outliers from the data set. Others suggest recoding them down to a value that is not so extreme (see Chapter 6).

If you identify an outlier and want to find out the ID number of the case, you can use the **Data Label Mode** icon in the **Chart Editor**. Double-click on the chart to activate the **Chart Editor** window. Click on the icon that looks a bit like a bullseye (or choose **Data Label Mode** from the **Elements** menu) and move your cursor to the point on the graph you wish to identify. Click on it once and a number will appear—this is the ID number if you selected ID in Step 4 of the Scatterplot instructions in Chapter 7; otherwise, the case number assigned by IBM SPSS Statistics will be displayed. To turn the numbering off, just click on the icon again.

Step 2: Inspect the distribution of data points

The distribution of data points can tell you various things about your data:

➤ Are the data points spread all over the place? This suggests a very low correlation.
➤ Are all the points neatly arranged in a narrow cigar shape? This suggests quite a strong correlation.

> ➤ Could you draw a straight line through the main cluster of points, or would a curved line better represent the points? If a curved line is evident (suggesting a curvilinear relationship) Pearson correlation should not be used, as it assumes a linear relationship.

Step 3: Determine the direction of the relationship between the variables

The scatterplot can tell you whether the relationship between your two variables is positive or negative. If a line were drawn through the points, what direction would it point—from left to right, upward or downward? An upward trend indicates a positive relationship; high scores on the X axis are associated with high scores on the Y axis. A downward line suggests a negative correlation; low scores on the X axis are associated with high scores on the Y axis. In this example, we appear to have a negative correlation of moderate strength.

Once you have explored the distribution of scores on the scatterplot and established that the relationship between the variables is roughly linear and that the scores are evenly spread in a cigar shape, you can proceed with calculating Pearson or Spearman correlation coefficients.

Before you start the following procedure, choose **Edit** from the menu, select **Options,** and on the **General** tab make sure there is a tick in the box **No scientific notation for small numbers in tables** in the **Output** section.

Procedure for requesting Pearson *r* or Spearman *rho*

1. From the menu at the top of the screen, click on **Analyze**, then select **Correlate**, then **Bivariate**.
2. Select your two variables and move them into the box marked **Variables** (e.g. Total perceived stress: tpstress, Total PCOISS: tpcoiss). If you wish you can list a whole range of variables here, not just two. In the resulting matrix, the correlation between all possible pairs of variables will be listed. This can be quite large if you list more than just a few variables.
3. In the **Correlation Coefficients** section, the **Pearson** box is the default option. If you wish to request the **Spearman** *rho* (the non-parametric alternative), tick the **Spearman** box instead (or as well).
4. Click on the **Options** button. For **Missing Values**, click on the **Exclude cases pairwise** box. Under **Options**, you can also obtain means and standard deviations if you wish.
5. Click on **Continue** and then on **OK** (or on **Paste** to save to **Syntax Editor**).

The syntax generated from this procedure is:

```
CORRELATIONS
 /VARIABLES=tpstress tpcoiss
 /PRINT=TWOTAIL NOSIG
 /MISSING=PAIRWISE.
NONPAR CORR
 /VARIABLES=tpstress tpcoiss
 /PRINT=SPEARMAN TWOTAIL NOSIG
 /MISSING=PAIRWISE.
```

The output generated from this procedure (showing both Pearson and Spearman results) is presented below.

Correlations

		tpstress Total perceived stress	tpcoiss Total PCOISS
tpstress Total perceived stress	Pearson Correlation	1	-.581**
	Sig. (2-tailed)		.000
	N	433	426
tpcoiss Total PCOISS	Pearson Correlation	-.581**	1
	Sig. (2-tailed)	.000	
	N	426	430

**. Correlation is significant at the 0.01 level (2-tailed).

Nonparametric Correlations

			tpstress Total perceived stress	tpcoiss Total PCOISS
Spearman's rho	tpstress Total perceived stress	Correlation Coefficient	1.000	-.556**
		Sig. (2-tailed)	.	.000
		N	433	426
	tpcoiss Total PCOISS	Correlation Coefficient	-.556**	1.000
		Sig. (2-tailed)	.000	.
		N	426	430

**. Correlation is significant at the 0.01 level (2-tailed).

INTERPRETATION OF OUTPUT FROM CORRELATION

For both Pearson and Spearman results, IBM SPSS Statistics provides you with a table giving the correlation coefficients between each pair of variables listed, the significance level and the number of cases. The results for Pearson correlation are shown in the section headed **Correlation**. If you requested Spearman *rho*, these results are shown in the section labelled **Nonparametric Correlations**. You interpret the output from the parametric and non-parametric approaches in the same way.

Step 1: Check the information about the sample

The first thing to inspect is the table labelled **Correlations** is the *N* (number of cases). Is this correct? If there are a lot of missing data, you need to find out why. Did you forget to tick the **Exclude cases pairwise** box in the missing data option? Using listwise deletion (the other option) means any case with missing data on any of the variables will be removed from the analysis. This can sometimes severely restrict your *N*. In the above example we have 426 cases that had scores on both of the scales used in this analysis. If a case was missing information on either of these variables, it would have been excluded from the analysis.

Step 2: Determine the direction of the relationship

The second thing to consider is the direction of the relationship between the variables. Is there a negative sign in front of the correlation coefficient value? This would suggest a negative (inverse) correlation between the two variables (i.e. high scores on one are associated with low scores on the other). The interpretation of this depends on the way the variables are scored. Always check with your questionnaire, and remember that for many scales some items are negatively worded and therefore are reversed before scoring. What do high values really mean? This is one of the major areas of confusion for students, so make sure you get this clear in your mind before you interpret the correlation output.

In the example given here, the Pearson correlation coefficient ($r = -.58$) and Spearman value ($rho = -.56$) are negative, indicating a negative correlation between perceived control and stress. The *more* control people feel they have, the *less* stress they experience.

Step 3: Determine the strength of the relationship

The third thing to consider in the output is the size of the correlation coefficient. This can range from -1 to $+1$. This value will indicate the strength of the relationship between your two variables. A correlation of 0 indicates no relationship at all, a correlation of 1 indicates a perfect positive correlation, and a value of -1 indicates a perfect negative correlation.

How do you interpret values between 0 and 1? Different authors suggest different interpretations; however, Cohen (1988, pp. 79–81) suggests the following guidelines:

small	$r = .10$ to $.29$
medium	$r = .30$ to $.49$
large	$r = .50$ to 1.00

These guidelines apply whether or not there is a negative sign out the front of your *r* value. Remember, the negative sign refers only to the direction of the relationship, not the strength. The *strength* of correlation of $r = .5$ and $r = -.5$ is the same. It is only in a different *direction*.

In the example presented above, there is a large correlation between the two variables (above .5), suggesting quite a strong relationship between perceived control and stress.

Step 4: Calculate the coefficient of determination

To get an idea of how much variance your two variables share, you can also calculate what is referred to as the 'coefficient of determination'. Sounds impressive, but all you need to do is square your *r* value (multiply it by itself). To convert this to percentage of variance, just multiply by 100 (shift the decimal place two columns to the right). For example, two variables that correlate $r = .2$ share only $.2 \times .2 = .04 = 4\%$ of their variance. There is not much overlap between the two variables. A correlation of $r = .5$, however, means 25 per cent shared variance $(.5 \times .5 = .25)$.

In our example the Pearson correlation is .581, which, when squared, indicates 33.76 per cent shared variance. Perceived control helps to explain nearly 34 per cent of the variance in respondents' scores on the Perceived Stress Scale. This is quite a respectable amount of variance explained when compared with a lot of the research conducted in the social sciences.

Step 5: Assess the significance level

The next thing to consider is the significance level (listed as **Sig. 2 tailed**). This is a frequently misinterpreted area, so care should be exercised here. The level of statistical significance does not indicate how strongly the two variables are associated (this is given by *r* or *rho*), but instead it indicates how much confidence we should have in the results obtained. The significance of *r* or *rho* is strongly influenced by the size of the sample. In a small sample (e.g. $n = 30$), you may have moderate correlations that do not reach statistical significance at the traditional $p < .05$ level. In large samples $(N = 100+)$, however, very small correlations (e.g. $r = .2$) may reach statistical significance. While you need to report statistical significance, you should focus on the strength of the relationship and the amount of shared variance (see Step 4).

When publishing in some literature areas (particularly health and medical) you may be asked to provide confidence intervals for your correlation coefficients—that is, the range of values in which we are 95 per cent confident the true value lies (if we actually could measure it!). Unfortunately, IBM SPSS Statistics does not provide these; however, there are some websites that provide online calculators for you. If you need to obtain these values I suggest that you go to the website http://vassarstats.net/rho.html. All you need to provide is the *r* and *n* values that are available in your SPSS output. You might like to check out the whole VassarStats website, which provides a range of tools for performing statistical computation (http://vassarstats.net/).

PRESENTING THE RESULTS FROM CORRELATION

The results of the above example using Pearson correlation could be presented in a research report as follows. If you need to report the results for Spearman's Correlation, just replace the *r* value with the *rho* value shown in the output. Typically, the value of *r* is presented using two decimal places (rather the three decimal places provided in the SPSS output), but check with the conventions used in the journals in your literature area. For correct APA style the statistics are presented in italics (r, n, p).

> The relationship between perceived control of internal states (as measured by the PCOISS) and perceived stress (as measured by the Perceived Stress Scale) was investigated using a Pearson product-moment correlation coefficient. Preliminary analyses were performed to ensure no violation of the assumptions of normality and linearity. There was a strong negative correlation between the two variables, $r = -.58$, $n = 426$, $p < .001$, with high levels of perceived control associated with lower levels of perceived stress.

Correlation is often used to explore the relationship among a group of variables, rather than just two as described above. In this case, it would be awkward to report all the individual correlation coefficients in a paragraph; it would be better to present them in a table. One way this could be done is shown below.

Table 1

Pearson Product-Moment Correlations Between Measures of Perceived Control and Wellbeing

Scale	1	2	3	4	5
1. Total PCOISS	–				
2. Total perceived stress	–.58 **	–			
3. Total negative affect	–.48 **	.67 **	–		
4. Total positive affect	.46**	–.44 **	–.29 **	–	
5. Total life satisfaction	.37 **	–.49 **	–.32 **	.42 **	–

Note. PCOISS = Perceived Control of Internal States Scale.
** $p < .001$ (2-tailed).

For other examples of how to present the results of correlation see Chapter 7 in Nicol and Pexman (2010b).

OBTAINING CORRELATION COEFFICIENTS BETWEEN GROUPS OF VARIABLES

In the previous procedures section, I showed you how to obtain correlation coefficients between two continuous variables. If you have a group of variables and you wish to explore the interrelationships among all of them, you can ask IBM SPSS Statistics to do this in one procedure. Just include all the variables in the **Variables** box. This can, however, result in an enormous correlation matrix that can be difficult to read and interpret.

Sometimes, you want to explore only a subset of all these possible relationships. For example, you might want to assess the relationship between control measures (Mastery, PCOISS) and a set of adjustment and wellbeing measures (positive affect, negative affect, life satisfaction). You don't want a full correlation matrix, because this would give you correlation coefficients among all the variables, including between each of the various pairs of adjustment measures. There is a way that you can limit the correlation coefficients that are displayed. This involves using **Syntax Editor** (described in Chapter 3) to limit the correlation coefficients that are produced by IBM SPSS Statistics.

Procedure for obtaining correlation coefficients between two groups of variables

1. From the menu at the top of the screen, click on **Analyze**, then select **Correlate**, then **Bivariate**.
2. Move the variables of interest into the **Variables** box. Select the first group of variables (e.g. Total Positive Affect: tposaff, total negative affect: tnegaff, total life satisfaction: tlifesat), followed by the second group (e.g. Total PCOISS: tpcoiss, Total Mastery: tmast). In the output that is generated, the first group of variables will appear down the side of the table as rows and the second group will appear across the table as columns. Put your longer list first; this stops your table being too wide to appear on one page.
3. Click on **Paste**. This opens the **Syntax Editor** window.
4. Put your cursor between the first group of variables (e.g. tposaff, tnegaff, tlifesat) and the other variables (e.g. tpcoiss and tmast). Type in the word **WITH** (tposaff tnegaff tlifesat **with** tpcoiss tmast). This will ask IBM SPSS Statistics to calculate correlation coefficients between tmast and tpcoiss and each of the other variables listed.

The final syntax should be:

```
CORRELATIONS
 /VARIABLES=tposaff tnegaff tlifesat with tpcoiss tmast
 /PRINT=TWOTAIL NOSIG
 /MISSING=PAIRWISE.
```

5. To run this new syntax, you need to highlight the text from CORRELATIONS down to and including the full stop at the end. It is very important that you include the full stop in the highlighted section.

6. With this text highlighted, click on the green triangle or arrow-shaped icon, or, alternatively, click on **Run** from the **Menu**, and then **Selection** from the drop-down menu that appears.

The output generated from this procedure is shown as follows.

		tpcoiss Total PCOISS	tmast Total Mastery
tposaff Total positive affect	Pearson Correlation	.456**	.432**
	Sig. (2-tailed)	.000	.000
	N	429	436
tnegaff Total negative affect	Pearson Correlation	-.484**	-.464**
	Sig. (2-tailed)	.000	.000
	N	428	435
tlifesat Total life satisfaction	Pearson Correlation	.373**	.444**
	Sig. (2-tailed)	.000	.000
	N	429	436

**. Correlation is significant at the 0.01 level (2-tailed).

Presented in this manner, it is easy to compare the relative strength of the correlations for my two control scales (Total PCOISS, Total Mastery) with each of the adjustment measures.

COMPARING THE CORRELATION COEFFICIENTS FOR TWO GROUPS

Sometimes, when doing correlational research, you may want to compare the strength of the correlation coefficients for two separate groups. For example, you may want to explore the relationship between optimism and negative affect for males and females separately. One way that you can do this is described below.

Procedure for comparing correlation coefficients for two groups of participants

Step 1: Split the sample

1. From the menu at the top of the screen, click on **Data**, then select **Split File**.
2. Click on **Compare Groups**.
3. Move the grouping variable (e.g. sex) into the box labelled **Groups based on**. Click on **OK** (or on **Paste** to save to **Syntax Editor**). If you use Syntax, remember to run the procedure by highlighting the command and clicking on **Run**.
4. This will split the sample by sex and repeat any analyses that follow for these two groups separately.

The syntax for this command is:

```
SORT CASES  BY sex.
SPLIT FILE LAYERED BY sex.
```

Step 2: Run correlation

Follow the steps in the earlier section of this chapter to request the correlation between your two variables of interest (e.g. Total optimism: toptim, Total negative affect: tnegaff). The results will be reported separately for the two groups.

The syntax for this command is:

```
CORRELATIONS
 /VARIABLES=toptim tnegaff
 /PRINT=TWOTAIL NOSIG
 /M SSING=PAIRWISE .
```

Important: The **Split File** operation stays in place until you turn it off. Therefore, when you have finished examining males and females separately you will need to turn the **Split File** option off. To do this, click on **Data**, **Split File** and select the first button: **Analyze all cases, do not create groups**.

The output generated from the correlation procedure is shown below.

sex sex			toptim Total Optimism	tnegaff Total negative affect
1 MALES	toptim Total Optimism	Pearson Correlation	1	-.220**
		Sig. (2-tailed)		.003
		N	184	184
	tnegaff Total negative affect	Pearson Correlation	-.220**	1
		Sig. (2-tailed)	.003	
		N	184	185
2 FEMALES	toptim Total Optimism	Pearson Correlation	1	-.394**
		Sig. (2-tailed)		.000
		N	251	250
	tnegaff Total negative affect	Pearson Correlation	-.394**	1
		Sig. (2-tailed)	.000	
		N	250	250

Correlation is significant at the 0.01 level (2-tailed).

Interpretation of output from correlation for two groups

From the output given above, the correlation between Total optimism and Total negative affect for males was $r = -.22$, while for females it was slightly higher, $r = -.39$. Although these two values seem different, is this difference big enough to be considered significant? Detailed in the next section is one way that you can test the statistical significance of the difference between these two correlation coefficients. It is important to note that this process is different from testing the statistical significance of the correlation coefficients reported in the output table above. The significance levels reported above (for males: $p = .003$, for females: $p = .000$) provide a test of the null hypothesis that the correlation coefficient in the population is 0. The significance test described below, however, assesses the probability that the *difference* in the correlations observed for the two groups (males and females) would occur as a function of a sampling error, when in fact there was no real difference in the strength of the relationship for males and females.

TESTING THE STATISTICAL SIGNIFICANCE OF THE DIFFERENCE BETWEEN CORRELATION COEFFICIENTS

In this section, I describe a procedure that can be used to find out whether the correlations for the two groups (males/females) are significantly different. IBM SPSS Statistics does not provide this information. The quickest way to check this is to use an online calculator.

One of the easiest ones I have found to use is available at http://vassarstats.net/rdiff.html.

Assumptions

As always, there are assumptions to check first. It is assumed that the *r* values for the two groups were obtained from random samples and that the two groups of cases are independent (not the same participants tested twice). The distribution of scores for the two groups is assumed to be normal (see histograms for the two groups). It is also necessary to have at least 20 cases in each of the groups.

Procedure for using the online calculator

From the IBM SPSS Statistics Correlation output, find the *r* value and *n* for Group 1 (males) and Group 2 (females).

Males:	$r_a = .22$	Females: $r_b = .394$
	$n_a = 184$	$n_b = 250$

In the online calculator (http://vassarstats.net/rdiff.html) enter this information into the boxes provided for **Sample A** (males) and **Sample B** (females) and press the **Calculate** button.

The result of the procedure will appear in the boxes labelled **z**, **p (one-tailed)** and **p (two-tailed)**. In this example the *z* value is −1.97 and the *p* (two-tailed) is .0488. Given that the *p* value is less than .05 the result is statistically significant. We can conclude that there is a statistically significant difference in the strength of the correlation between optimism and negative affect for males and females. Optimism explains significantly more of the variance in negative affect for females than for males.

ADDITIONAL EXERCISES

Health

Data file: **sleep.sav**. See Appendix for details of the data file.

1. Check the strength of the correlation between scores on the Sleepiness and Associated Sensations Scale (*totSAS*) and the Epworth Sleepiness Scale (*ess*).
2. Use Syntax to assess the correlations between the Epworth Sleepiness Scale (*ess*) and each of the individual items that make up the Sleepiness and Associated Sensations Scale (*fatigue, lethargy, tired, sleepy, energy*).

12

Partial correlation

Partial correlation is similar to Pearson product-moment correlation (described in Chapter 11), except that it allows you to control for an additional variable. This is usually a variable that you suspect might be influencing your two variables of interest. By statistically removing the influence of this confounding variable, you can get a clearer and more accurate indication of the relationship between your two variables.

In the introduction to Part Four, the influence of contaminating or confounding variables was discussed (see the section on correlation versus causality). This occurs when the relationship between two variables (A and B) is influenced, at least to some extent, by a third variable (C). This can serve to artificially inflate the size of the correlation coefficient obtained. This relationship can be represented graphically as:

In this case, A and B may appear to be related, but in fact their apparent relationship is due to the influence of C. If you were to statistically control for the variable C then the correlation between A and B is likely to be reduced, resulting in a smaller correlation coefficient.

DETAILS OF EXAMPLE

To illustrate the use of partial correlation, I use the same example as described in Chapter 11 but extend the analysis further to control for an additional variable. This time I am interested in exploring the relationship between scores on the Perceived Control of Internal States Scale (PCOISS) and scores on the Perceived Stress Scale, while controlling for what is known as 'socially desirable responding bias'. This variable refers to people's tendency to present themselves in a positive, or socially desirable, way (also known as 'faking good') when completing questionnaires. This tendency is measured by the Marlowe-Crowne Social Desirability Scale (Crowne & Marlowe 1960). A short version of this scale (Strahan & Gerbasi 1972) was included in the questionnaire used to measure the other two variables.

If you would like to follow along with the example presented below, you should start IBM SPSS Statistics and open the file labelled **survey.sav**, which is included on the website accompanying this book.

Example of research question: After controlling for participants' tendency to present themselves in a positive light on self-report scales, is there still a significant relationship between perceived control of internal states (PCOISS) and levels of perceived stress?

What you need:
➢ two continuous variables that you wish to explore the relationship between (e.g. Total PCOISS, Total perceived stress)
➢ one continuous variable that you wish to control for (e.g. total social desirability: tmarlow).

What it does: Partial correlation allows you to examine the relationship between two variables while statistically controlling for (getting rid of) the effect of another variable that you think might be contaminating or influencing the relationship.

Assumptions: For full details of the assumptions for correlation, see the introduction to Part Four.

Before you start the following procedure, choose **Edit** from the menu, select **Options**, and make sure there is a tick in the box **No scientific notation for small numbers in tables**.

Procedure for partial correlation
1. From the menu at the top of the screen, click on **Analyze**, then select **Correlate**, then **Partial**.
2. Click on the two continuous variables that you want to correlate (e.g. Total PCOISS: tpcoiss, Total perceived stress: tpstress). Click on the arrow to move these into the **Variables** box.
3. Click on the variable that you wish to control for (e.g. Total social desirability: tmarlow) and move it into the **Controlling for** box.

4. Click on **Options**.
   ➢ In the Missing Values section, click on Exclude cases pairwise.
   ➢ In the Statistics section, click on Zero order correlations.
5. Click on **Continue** and then **OK** (or on **Paste** to save to **Syntax Editor**).

The syntax from this procedure is:

```
PARTIAL CORR
/VARIABLES= tpcoiss tpstress BY tmarlow
/SIGNIFICANCE=TWOTAIL
/STATISTICS=CORR
/MISSING=ANALYSIS .
```

The output generated from this procedure is shown below.

Control Variables			tpcoiss Total PCOISS	tpstress Total perceived stress	tmarlow Total social desirability
-none-[a]	tpcoiss Total PCOISS	Correlation	1.000	-.581	.295
		Significance (2-tailed)	.	.000	.000
		df	0	424	425
	tpstress Total perceived stress	Correlation	-.581	1.000	-.228
		Significance (2-tailed)	.000	.	.000
		df	424	0	426
	tmarlow Total social desirability	Correlation	.295	-.228	1.000
		Significance (2-tailed)	.000	.000	.
		df	425	426	0
tmarlow Total social desirability	tpcoiss Total PCOISS	Correlation	1.000	-.552	
		Significance (2-tailed)	.	.000	
		df	0	423	
	tpstress Total perceived stress	Correlation	-.552	1.000	
		Significance (2-tailed)	.000	.	
		df	423	0	

a. Cells contain zero-order (Pearson) correlations.

INTERPRETATION OF OUTPUT FROM PARTIAL CORRELATION

The output provides you with a table made up of two sections:

1. In the top half of the table is the Pearson product-moment correlation matrix between your two variables of interest (e.g. perceived control and perceived stress), *not* controlling for your other variable. In this case, the correlation is −.581. The word 'none' in the left-hand column indicates that no control variable is in operation. This is often referred to as the 'zero-order correlation coefficient'.
2. The bottom half of the table repeats the same set of correlation analyses, but this time controlling for (removing) the effects of your control variable (e.g. social desirability). In this case, the new partial correlation is −.552. You should compare these two sets of correlation coefficients to see whether controlling for the additional variable had any impact on the relationship between your two variables of interest. In this example, there was only a small decrease in the strength of the correlation (from −.581 to −.552). This suggests that the observed relationship between perceived control and perceived stress is not due merely to the influence of socially desirable responding.

PRESENTING THE RESULTS FROM PARTIAL CORRELATION

Although IBM SPSS Statistics provides the correlation coefficients using three decimal places, they are usually reported in journal articles as two decimals (see APA *Publication Manual* for details).

The results of this analysis could be presented as:

> Partial correlation was used to explore the relationship between perceived control of internal states (as measured by the PCOISS) and perceived stress (measured by the Perceived Stress Scale) while controlling for scores on the Marlowe-Crowne Social Desirability Scale. Preliminary assessments were performed to ensure no violation of the assumptions of normality and linearity. There was a strong, negative partial correlation between perceived control of internal states and perceived stress, controlling for social desirability, $r = -.55$, $n = 425$, $p < .001$, with high levels of perceived control being associated with lower levels of perceived stress. An inspection of the zero-order correlation coefficient ($r = -.58$) suggested that controlling for socially desirable responding had very little effect on the strength of the relationship between these two variables.

ADDITIONAL EXERCISE

Health

Data file: **sleep.sav**. See Appendix for details of the data file.

1. Check the strength of the correlation between scores on the Sleepiness and Associated Sensations Scale (*totSAS*) and the impact of sleep problems on overall wellbeing (*impact6*) while controlling for *age*. Compare the zero-order correlation (Pearson correlation) and the partial correlation coefficient. Does controlling for *age* make a difference?

13

Multiple regression

In this chapter I briefly outline how to use IBM SPSS Statistics to run multiple regression analyses. This is a *very* simplified outline. It is important that you do more reading on multiple regression before using it in your own research. A good reference is Chapter 5 in Tabachnick and Fidell (2013), which covers the underlying theory, the different types of multiple regression analyses and the assumptions that you need to check.

Multiple regression is a family of techniques that can be used to explore the relationship between one continuous, dependent variable and a set of independent variables. The dependent variable (the thing you are trying to explain or predict) needs to be a continuous variable with reasonably normally distributed scores. The independent (or predictor) variables can be continuous or dichotomous (two categories).

Multiple regression is based on correlation (covered in Chapter 11) but allows a more sophisticated exploration of the interrelationship within a set of variables. This makes it ideal for the investigation of complex real-life, rather than laboratory-based, research questions. However, you cannot just throw variables into a multiple regression and hope that, magically, answers will appear. You should have a sound theoretical or conceptual reason for the analysis and the order of variables entering the model. Don't use multiple regression as a fishing expedition.

Multiple regression can be used to address a variety of research questions. It can tell you how well a set of variables is able to predict a particular outcome. For example, you may be interested in exploring how well a set of subscales on an intelligence test is able to predict performance on a specific task. Multiple regression will provide you with information about the model as a whole (all subscales) and the relative contribution of each of the variables that make up the model (individual subscales). As an extension of this, multiple regression will allow you to test whether adding a variable (e.g. motivation) contributes to the predictive ability of the model over and above those variables already included in the model. Multiple regression can also be used to statistically control for an additional variable (or variables) when exploring the predictive ability of the model. Some of the main types of research questions that multiple regression can be used to address are:

➢ how well a *set of variables* is able to predict a particular outcome
➢ *which variable* in a set of variables is the best predictor of an outcome
➢ whether a predictor variable is still able to predict an outcome when the effects of another variable are *controlled for* (e.g. socially desirable responding).

MAJOR TYPES OF MULTIPLE REGRESSION

There are three main types of multiple regression analyses:

➢ standard or simultaneous
➢ hierarchical or sequential
➢ stepwise.

Typical of the statistical literature, you will find different authors using different terms when describing these three main types of multiple regression—very confusing for an experienced researcher, let alone a beginner to the area!

Standard multiple regression

In standard multiple regression, all the independent (or predictor) variables are entered into the model simultaneously. Each independent variable is evaluated in terms of its predictive power, over and above that offered by all the other independent variables. This is the most commonly used multiple regression analysis. You would use this approach if you had a set of variables (e.g. various personality scales) and wanted to know how much variance in a dependent variable (e.g. anxiety) they were able to explain as a group or block. This approach would also tell you how much unique variance in the dependent variable each of the independent variables explained.

Hierarchical multiple regression

In hierarchical multiple regression (also called sequential regression), the independent variables are entered into the model in the order specified by the researcher, based on theoretical grounds. Variables, or sets of variables, are entered in steps (or blocks), with each independent variable being assessed in terms of what it adds to the prediction of the dependent variable after the previous variables have been controlled for. For example, if you wanted to know how well optimism predicts life satisfaction, after the effect of age is controlled for, you would enter age in Block 1 and total optimism in Block 2. Once all sets of variables are entered, the overall model is assessed in terms of its ability to predict the dependent measure. The relative contribution of each block of variables is also reported.

Stepwise multiple regression

In stepwise regression, the researcher provides a list of independent variables and then allows the program to select which variables it will enter and in which order they go into the equation, based on a set of statistical criteria. There are many problems with stepwise regression, and it is not accepted in journals published in many discipline areas. I would strongly recommend *against* using this approach. For further reading on the criticisms of stepwise regression see Antonakis & Dietz (2011), Harrell (2001) and Thompson (1989, 1995, 2001).

ASSUMPTIONS

Multiple regression is one of the fussier of the statistical techniques. It makes assumptions about the data, and it is not all that forgiving if they are violated. It is not the technique to use on small samples, where the distribution of scores is very skewed! The following summary of the major assumptions is taken from Chapter 5, Tabachnick and Fidell (2013). It would be a good idea to read this chapter before proceeding with your analysis.

You should also review the material covered in the introduction to Part Four of this book, which covers the basics of correlation, and see the list of recommended references at the back of the book. The IBM SPSS Statistics procedures for testing these assumptions are discussed in more detail in the examples provided later in this chapter.

Sample size

If you use multiple regression with small samples you may obtain a result that does not generalise (cannot be repeated) to other samples. If your results do not generalise to other samples, they are of little scientific value. So, how many cases or participants do you need? Different authors give different guidelines concerning the number of cases required for multiple regression. Stevens (1996, p. 72) recommends that 'for social science research, about 15 participants per predictor are needed for a reliable equation'. Tabachnick and Fidell (2013, p. 123) give a formula for calculating sample size requirements, taking into account the number of independent variables that you wish to use: $N > 50 + 8m$ (where m = number of independent variables). If you have five independent variables, you will need at least 90 cases. More cases are needed if the dependent variable is skewed.

Multicollinearity and singularity

This refers to the relationship among the independent (predictor) variables, which you can check by generating a correlation matrix (see Chapter 11). Multicollinearity exists when the independent variables are highly correlated ($r = .7$ and above). Singularity occurs when one independent variable is a combination of other independent variables (e.g. when both subscale scores and the total score of a scale are included). If you include highly intercorrelated variables in the model, multiple regression has difficulty separating the unique contribution of each predictor and may report them as not statistically significant. Always check for these problems before you start, and make a careful selection of the variables to include in the model. The output from the multiple regression procedure also provides some useful statistics (referred to as 'collinearity diagnostics') to help you identify any multicollinearity issues in your model. These are described in the Interpretation of Output From Standard Multiple Regression section later in this chapter.

Outliers

There are two types of outliers that might affect the results of a multiple regression analysis: univariate outliers and multivariate outliers.

Univariate outliers can occur when a person or case has an unusual score on one of the predictor variables in the model (e.g. a very high income). Checking for these extreme scores should be part of the initial data screening process (see Chapters 5, 6 and 7). You should do this for all the variables, both dependent and independent, that you will be using in your regression analysis. Outlying scores or cases can be deleted or, alternatively, assigned a score that is high but not too different from the remaining cluster of scores.

Multivariate outliers occur when the person or case has an unusual combination of scores on the dependent and independent variables (e.g. a young person who reports a high income). They may not necessarily be an outlier on the individual age or income variables, but the combination is unexpected and likely to deviate from the model generated by multiple regression. These unusual cases have the potential to unduly impact the results of the analysis and are known as 'influential cases'. Statistical and graphical methods for detecting outliers are also included in the IBM SPSS Statistics multiple regression procedure and are described in the Interpretation of Output From Standard Multiple Regression section later in this chapter.

Normality, linearity, homoscedasticity, independence of residuals

These assumptions all refer to various aspects of the distribution of scores and the nature of the underlying relationship between the variables. They can be checked from the *residuals* scatterplots which are generated as part of the multiple regression procedure. Residuals are the differences between the obtained and the predicted dependent variable scores. The residuals scatterplots allow you to check:

➤ *normality:* The residuals should be normally distributed about the predicted dependent variable scores
➤ *linearity:* The residuals should have a straight-line relationship with predicted dependent variable scores
➤ *homoscedasticity:* The variance of the residuals around predicted dependent variable scores should be the same for all predicted scores.

The interpretation of the residuals scatterplots generated by IBM SPSS Statistics is presented later in this chapter; however, for a more detailed discussion of this rather complex topic, see Chapter 5 in Tabachnick and Fidell (2013).

DETAILS OF EXAMPLE

To illustrate the use of multiple regression, I use examples taken from the **survey.sav** data file included on the website with this book (see p. ix). The survey was designed to explore the factors that affect respondents' psychological adjustment and wellbeing (see the Appendix for full details of the study). For the multiple regression example detailed below, I explore the impact of respondents' perceptions of control on their levels of perceived stress. The literature in this area suggests that if people feel that they are in control of their lives, they are less likely to experience stress. In the questionnaire, there were two different measures of control (see the Appendix for the references for these scales). These were the Mastery Scale, which measures the degree to which people feel they have control over the events in their lives; and the Perceived Control of Internal States Scale (PCOISS), which measures the degree to which people feel they have control over their internal states (emotions, thoughts and physical reactions). In this example, I am interested in exploring how well the Mastery Scale and the PCOISS are able to predict scores on a measure of perceived stress.

It is a good idea to work through these examples on the computer using this data file. Hands-on practice is always better than just reading about it in a book. Feel free to play with the data file—substitute other variables for the ones that were used in the example. See what results you get, and practise interpreting them.

File name: **survey.sav**

Variables:
- Total perceived stress (tpstress): Total score on the Perceived Stress Scale. High scores indicate high levels of stress
- Total perceived control of internal states: Total score on the Perceived Control of Internal States Scale (tpcoiss). High scores indicate greater control over internal states
- Total mastery (tmast): Total score on the Mastery Scale. High scores indicate higher levels of perceived control over events and circumstances
- Total social desirability (tmarlow): Total scores on the Marlowe-Crowne Social Desirability Scale, which measures the degree to which people try to present themselves in a positive light
- Age: Age in years.

The examples included below cover the use of Standard Multiple Regression and Hierarchical Regression. Because of the criticism that has been levelled at the use of Stepwise Multiple Regression techniques, these approaches are not illustrated here.

Examples of research questions:
1. How well do the two measures of control (mastery, PCOISS) predict perceived stress? How much variance in perceived stress scores can be explained by scores on these two scales?
2. Which is the best predictor of perceived stress: control of external events (Mastery Scale) or control of internal states (PCOISS)?
3. If we control for the possible effect of age and socially desirable responding, is this set of variables still able to predict a significant amount of the variance in perceived stress?

What you need:
➤ one continuous, dependent variable (Total perceived stress)
➤ two or more continuous, independent variables (mastery, PCOISS). (You can also use dichotomous, independent variables—e.g. males = 1, females = 2.)

What it does: Multiple regression tells you how much of the variance in your dependent variable can be explained by your independent variables. It also gives you an indication of the relative contribution of each independent variable. Tests allow you to determine the statistical significance of the results, in terms of both the model itself and the individual independent variables.

Assumptions: The major assumptions for multiple regression are described in an earlier section of this chapter. Some of these assumptions can be checked as part of the multiple regression analysis (these are illustrated in the example that follows).

STANDARD MULTIPLE REGRESSION

In this example, two questions are addressed:

Question 1: How well do the two measures of control (mastery, PCOISS) predict perceived stress? This is addressed by finding out how much of the variance in perceived stress scores is explained by these two scales.

Question 2: Which is the best predictor of perceived stress: control of external events (Mastery Scale) or control of internal states (PCOISS)?

To address these questions, I use standard multiple regression. This involves all of the independent variables being entered into the model at once. The results indicate how well this set of variables is able to predict stress levels and tell us how much *unique* variance each of the independent variables (mastery, PCOISS) explains in the dependent variable *over and above* the other independent variables included in the set. For each of the procedures, I have included the syntax. For more information on the use of the **Syntax Editor** for recording and saving the commands, see Chapter 3.

Before you start the following procedure, choose **Edit** from the menu, select **Options**, and make sure there is a tick in the box **No scientific notation for small numbers in tables.**

Procedure for standard multiple regression

1. From the menu at the top of the screen, click on **Analyze**, then select **Regression**, then **Linear**.
2. Click on your continuous, dependent variable (e.g. Total perceived stress: tpstress) and move it into the **Dependent** box.
3. Click on your independent variables (Total Mastery: tmast, Total PCOISS: tpcoiss) and click on the arrow to move them into the **Independent(s)** box.
4. For **Method**, make sure **Enter** is selected. (This will give you standard multiple regression.)
5. Click on the **Statistics** button.
   ➤ Select the following: Estimates, Confidence Intervals, Model fit, Descriptives, Part and partial correlations and Collinearity diagnostics.
   ➤ In the Residuals section, select Casewise diagnostics and Outliers outside 3 standard deviations. Click on Continue.
6. Click on the **Options** button. In the **Missing Values** section, select **Exclude cases pairwise**. Click on **Continue**.
7. Click on the **Plots** button.
   ➤ Click on *ZRESID and the arrow button to move this into the Y box.
   ➤ Click on *ZPRED and the arrow button to move this into the X box.
   ➤ In the section headed Standardized Residual Plots, tick the Normal probability plot option. Click on Continue.
8. Click on the **Save** button.
   ➤ In the section labelled Distances, select Mahalanobis box and Cook's.
   ➤ Click on Continue and then OK (or on Paste to save to Syntax Editor).

The syntax generated from this procedure is:

```
REGRESSION
/DESCRIPTIVES MEAN STDDEV CORR SIG N
/MISSING PAIRWISE
/STATISTICS COEFF OUTS CI(95) R ANOVA COLLIN TOL ZPP
/CRITERIA=PIN(.05) POUT(.10)  /NOORIGIN
/DEPENDENT tpstress
/METHOD=ENTER tmast tpcoiss
/SCATTERPLOT=(*ZRESID ,*ZPRED )
/RESIDUALS NORMPROB (ZRESID)
/CASEWISE PLOT(ZRESID) OUTLIERS(3) /SAVE MAHAL COOK.
```

Selected output generated from this procedure is shown below.

Regression

Descriptive Statistics

	Mean	Std. Deviation	N
tpstress Total perceived stress	26.73	5.848	433
tmast Total Mastery	21.76	3.970	436
tpcoiss Total PCOISS	60.63	11.985	430

Correlations

		tpstress Total perceived stress	tmast Total Mastery	tpcoiss Total PCOISS
Pearson Correlation	tpstress Total perceived stress	1.000	-.612	-.581
	tmast Total Mastery	-.612	1.000	.521
	tpcoiss Total PCOISS	-.581	.521	1.000
Sig. (1-tailed)	tpstress Total perceived stress	.	.000	.000
	tmast Total Mastery	.000	.	.000
	tpcoiss Total PCOISS	.000	.000	.
N	tpstress Total perceived stress	433	433	426
	tmast Total Mastery	433	436	429
	tpcoiss Total PCOISS	426	429	430

Model Summary[b]

Model	R	R Square	Adjusted R Square	Std. Error of the Estimate
1	.684[a]	.468	.466	4.274

a. Predictors: (Constant), tpcoiss Total PCOISS, tmast Total Mastery

b. Dependent Variable: tpstress Total perceived stress

ANOVA[a]

Model		Sum of Squares	df	Mean Square	F	Sig.
1	Regression	6806.728	2	3403.364	186.341	.000[b]
	Residual	7725.756	423	18.264		
	Total	14532.484	425			

a. Dependent Variable: tpstress Total perceived stress

b. Predictors: (Constant), tpcoiss Total PCOISS, tmast Total Mastery

Coefficients[a]

Model		Unstandardized Coefficients		Standardized Coefficients	t	Sig.	95.0% Confidence Interval for B		Correlations			Collinearity Statistics	
		B	Std. Error	Beta			Lower Bound	Upper Bound	Zero-order	Partial	Part	Tolerance	VIF
1	(Constant)	50.97	1.273		40.035	.000	48.469	53.47					
	tmast Total Mastery	-.625	.061	-.424	-10.22	.000	-.745	-.505	-.612	-.445	-.4	.729	1.4
	tpcoiss Total PCOISS	-.175	.020	-.360	-8.660	.000	-.215	-.136	-.581	-.388	-.3	.729	1.4

a. Dependent Variable: tpstress Total perceived stress

Collinearity Diagnostics[a]

Model	Dimension	Eigenvalue	Condition Index	Variance Proportions		
				(Constant)	tmast Total Mastery	tpcoiss Total PCOISS
1	1	2.965	1.000	.00	.00	.00
	2	.019	12.502	.62	.01	.80
	3	.016	13.780	.38	.99	.20

a. Dependent Variable: tpstress Total perceived stress

Casewise Diagnostics[a]

Case Number	Std. Residual	tpstress Total perceived stress	Predicted Value	Residual
151	-3.475	14	28.85	-14.849

a. Dependent Variable: tpstress Total perceived stress

Residuals Statistics[a]

	Minimum	Maximum	Mean	Std. Deviation	N
Predicted Value	18.03	41.31	26.74	4.001	429
Std. Predicted Value	-2.174	3.644	.002	1.000	429
Standard Error of Predicted Value	.207	.800	.341	.111	429
Adjusted Predicted Value	18.04	41.39	26.75	4.009	426
Residual	-14.849	12.612	-.002	4.268	426
Std. Residual	-3.475	2.951	.000	.999	426
Stud. Residual	-3.514	2.969	.000	1.003	426
Deleted Residual	-15.190	12.765	-.001	4.306	426
Stud. Deleted Residual	-3.562	2.997	-.001	1.006	426
Mahal. Distance	.004	13.897	1.993	2.234	429
Cook's Distance	.000	.094	.003	.008	426
Centered Leverage Value	.000	.033	.005	.005	429

a. Dependent Variable: tpstress Total perceived stress

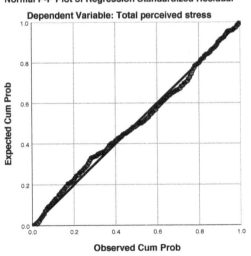

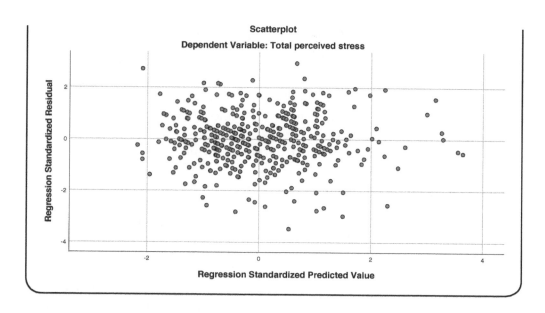

INTERPRETATION OF OUTPUT FROM STANDARD MULTIPLE
REGRESSION

There are lots of rather confusing numbers generated as output from regression. To
help you make sense of this, I take you on a guided tour of some of the output that
was obtained to answer Question 1.

Step 1: Check the assumptions
Multicollinearity
The correlations between the variables in your model are provided in the table labelled
Correlations. Check that the correlation between each of your independent (predictor) variables is not too high. You probably don't want to include two variables with
a bivariate correlation of .7 or more in the same analysis. If you find yourself in this
situation, you may need to consider omitting one of the highly correlated variables.
The collinearity diagnostics provided later in the regression output will help you with
this decision. In the example presented here the correlation is .52, so there is not likely
to be a problem.

IBM SPSS Statistics performs collinearity diagnostics on your variables as part of
the multiple regression procedure. This can pick up problems with multicollinearity that may not be evident in the correlation matrix which focuses on correlations
between pairs of variables. The results are presented in the table labelled **Coefficients**.
Two values are given: **Tolerance** and **VIF**. Tolerance is an indicator of how much of

the variability of the specified independent is not explained by the other independent variables in the model and is calculated using the formula $1 - R$ squared for each variable. If this value is very small (less than .10) it indicates that the multiple correlation with other variables is high, suggesting the possibility of multicollinearity. The other value given is the *VIF* (variance inflation factor), which is just the inverse of the Tolerance value (1 divided by Tolerance). *VIF* values above 10 would be a concern here, indicating multicollinearity.

I have quoted commonly used cut-off points for determining the presence of multicollinearity (tolerance value of less than .10, or *VIF* value of above 10). These values, however, still allow for quite high correlations between independent variables (above .9), so you should take them only as a warning sign and check the correlation matrix. In this example the tolerance value for each independent variable is .729, which is not less than .10; therefore, we have not violated the multicollinearity assumption. This is also supported by the *VIF* value, which is 1.372, well below the cut-off of 10. These results are not surprising, given that the Pearson correlation coefficient between these two independent variables was only .52 (see **Correlations** table). If you exceed the recommended values in your own results, you may need to consider removing one of the highly intercorrelated independent variables from the model, as this may result in potentially important variables being found to be non-significant in the model.

Outliers, normality, linearity, homoscedasticity, independence of residuals

One of the ways that these assumptions can be checked is by inspecting the **Normal Probability Plot (P-P) of the Regression Standardised Residual** and the **Scatterplot** that were requested as part of the analysis. These are presented at the end of the output. In the **Normal P-P Plot**, you are hoping that your points lie in a reasonably straight diagonal line from bottom left to top right. This would suggest no major deviations from normality. In the **Scatterplot** of the standardised residuals (the second plot displayed) you are hoping that the residuals are roughly rectangularly distributed, with most of the scores concentrated in the centre (along the 0 point). What you don't want to see is a clear or systematic pattern to your residuals (e.g. curvilinear, or higher on one side than the other). Deviations from a centralised rectangle suggest some violation of the assumptions. If you find this to be the case with your data, I suggest you see Tabachnick and Fidell (2013, p. 125) for a full description of how to interpret a residuals plot and how to assess the impact that violations may have on your analysis.

The presence of outliers can also be detected from the **Scatterplot**. Tabachnick and Fidell (2013) define outliers as cases that have a standardised residual (displayed in the scatterplot) of more than 3.3 or less than –3.3. With large samples, it is not uncommon to find outlying residuals. If you find only a few, it may not be necessary to take any action.

Outliers can also be checked by inspecting the **Mahalanobis distances** that are produced by the multiple regression program. These do not appear in the output but instead are presented at the end of your data file as an extra variable (Mah_1). To identify which cases are outliers, you will need to determine the critical chi-square value using the number of independent variables as the degrees of freedom. A full list of these values can be obtained from any statistics text (see Tabachnick & Fidell 2013, Table C.4). Tabachnick and Fidell (2013) suggest using an alpha level of .001. Using Tabachnick and Fidell's guidelines, I have summarised some of the key values for you in Table 13.1. To use this table, you need to:

➢ determine how many independent variables will be included in your multiple regression analysis
➢ find this value in one of the shaded columns
➢ read across to the adjacent column to identify the appropriate critical value.

In this example, I have two independent variables; therefore, the critical value is 13.82. To find out if any of the cases have a Mahalanobis distance value exceeding this value, go to the **Residuals Statistics** table, go to the row **Mahal. Distance** and across to the **Maximum** column. The maximum value in my data file is 13.89, which just slightly exceeds the critical value.

To find which case has this value, go back to your **Data Editor** window, select **Data** and then **Sort Cases** from the menu. Sort by the new variable at the bottom of your data file (Mahalanobis Distance, MAH-1) in **Descending** order. In the **Data View** window, the case with the largest Mahal Distance value will now be at the top of the data file. Given the size of the data file it is usual to find about 5 per cent of outliers, so in this case I am not worried too much about this one case, which is only very slightly outside the critical value. If you find cases with much larger values in your data, you may need to consider removing these cases from this analysis.

The other information in the output concerning unusual cases is in the table titled **Casewise Diagnostics**. This presents information about cases that have standardised residual values above 3 or below −3. In a normally distributed sample, we would

Number of indep. variables	Critical value	Number of indep. variables	Critical value	Number of indep. variables	Critical value	Table 13.1
2	13.82	4	18.47	6	22.46	Critical values for evaluating Mahalanobis distance values
3	16.27	5	20.52	7	24.32	

Source: Extracted and adapted from a table in Tabachnick and Fidell (2013); originally from Pearson, E.S. & Hartley, H.O. (eds) (1958). *Biometrika tables for statisticians* (2nd edn, vol. 1). New York: Cambridge University Press.

expect only 1 per cent of cases to fall outside this range. In this sample, we have found one case with a residual value of –3.48. You can see from the **Casewise Diagnostics** table that this person recorded a Total perceived stress score of 14, but our model predicted a value of 28.85. Clearly, our model did not predict this person's score very well—they are less stressed than we expected.

To check whether this strange case is having any undue influence on the results for our model as a whole, we can check the value for **Cook's Distance** given towards the bottom of the **Residuals Statistics** table. According to Tabachnick and Fidell (2013, p. 75), cases with values larger than 1 are a potential problem. In our example, the **Maximum** value for **Cook's Distance** is .094, suggesting no major problems. In your own data, if you obtain a maximum value above 1 you will need to go back to your data file and sort cases by the new variable that IBM SPSS Statistics created at the end of your file (Cook's Distance COO_1). Check each of the cases with values above 1—you may need to consider removing the offending case(s).

Step 2: Evaluate the model

Find the **Model Summary** table in the output and check the value given under the heading **R Square**. This tells you how much of the variance in the dependent variable (perceived stress) is explained by the model (which includes the variables Total Mastery and Total PCOISS). In this case, the value is .468. Expressed as a percentage (multiply by 100 by shifting the decimal point two places to the right), this means that our model explains 46.8 per cent of the variance in perceived stress. This is quite a respectable result (particularly when you compare it to some of the results that are reported in the journals!).

You will notice an **Adjusted R square** value in the output. When a small sample is involved, the R square value in the sample tends to be a rather optimistic overestimation of the true value in the population (see Tabachnick & Fidell 2013). The **Adjusted R square** statistic corrects this value to provide a better estimate of the true population value. If you have a small sample you may wish to consider reporting this value, rather than the normal **R square** value. To assess the statistical significance of the result, it is necessary to check in the table labelled **ANOVA**. This tests the null hypothesis that multiple R in the population equals 0. The model in this example reaches statistical significance (Sig. = .000; this really means $p < .0005$).

Step 3: Evaluate each of the independent variables

The next thing we want to know is which of the variables included in the model contributed to the prediction of the dependent variable. For this we need to use the information provided in the output table labelled **Coefficients**. Scan down the **Sig.** column and check which variables show a value less than .05. This tells you whether each variable is making a statistically significant *unique* contribution to the equation.

This is changeable depending on which variables are included in the equation and how much overlap there is among the independent variables. If the **Sig.** value is less than .05 (.01, .0001 etc.), the variable is making a significant unique contribution to the prediction of the dependent variable. If greater than .05, you can conclude that the variable is not making a significant unique contribution to the prediction of your dependent variable. This may be due to overlap with other independent variables in the model. In this case, both Total mastery and Total PCOISS made a unique, and statistically significant, contribution to the prediction of perceived stress scores.

The other useful piece of information in the coefficients table is the **Part** correlation coefficients. You will often see these values referred to in the literature as 'semipartial correlation coefficients' (see Tabachnick & Fidell 2013, p. 145). If you square this value, you get an indication of the contribution of that variable to the total R square. It tells you how much of the total variance in the dependent variable is uniquely explained by that variable and how much R square would drop if it wasn't included. In this example, the Mastery Scale has a part correlation coefficient of −.4. If we square this (multiply it by itself) we get .16, indicating that Mastery uniquely explains 16 per cent of the variance in Total perceived stress scores. For the PCOISS the value is −.3, which when squared gives us .09, indicating a unique contribution of 9 per cent to the explanation of variance in perceived stress. In this example the Mastery Scale explains more of the variance in stress scores than the PCOISS, but both make a unique contribution to our understanding of stress.

Note that the total **R square** value shown in the **Model Summary** table (in this case .468, or 46.8 per cent explained variance) does not equal all the squared part correlation values added up (.16 + .09 = .25). This is because the part correlation values represent only the *unique* contribution of each variable, with any overlap or shared variance removed or partialled out. The total **R square** value, however, includes the unique variance explained by each variable and also the shared variance. In this case, the two independent variables are reasonably strongly correlated ($r = .52$, as shown in the **Correlations** table); therefore, there is a lot of shared variance that is statistically controlled for when both variables are included in the model.

Step 4 : Use the information obtained from the output

The results of the analyses presented above allow us to answer the two research questions posed at the beginning of this section. Our model, which includes control of external events (Mastery) and control of internal states (PCOISS), explains a statistically significant 46.8 per cent of the variance in perceived stress (Question 1). Of these two predictor variables, mastery makes the largest unique contribution (explaining 16 per cent of the variance in stress), although PCOISS also made a statistically significant contribution, explaining 9 per cent of the variance, over and above that explained by the Mastery Scale (Question 2).

The standardised beta values displayed in the **Coefficients** table indicate the number of standard deviations that scores in the dependent variable would change if there was a 1 standard deviation unit change in the predictor. In the current example, if we could increase Mastery scores by 1 standard deviation (which is 3.97, from the **Descriptive Statistics** table) the perceived stress scores would be likely to drop by .42 standard deviation units.

The **Coefficients** table also provides the unstandardised regression coefficients *B* and a **Constant** value. This information can be used to prepare a prediction equation that allows other researchers or clinicians to predict an outcome using their scores on the independent variables. The formula, using the variables from this example, is:

Predicted stress score = constant (51.0) + (–.625 × mastery score) + (–.175 × total PCOISS score)

See Chapter 5 in Tabachnick and Fidell (2013) for a more detailed explanation of this.

HIERARCHICAL MULTIPLE REGRESSION

To illustrate the use of hierarchical multiple regression, I address a question that follows on from that discussed in the previous example. This time I evaluate the ability of the model (which includes Total Mastery and Total PCOISS) to predict perceived stress scores, after controlling for a set of additional variables (age, social desirability). The question is as follows:

Question 3: If we control for the possible effect of age and socially desirable responding, is our set of variables (Mastery, PCOISS) still able to predict a significant amount of the variance in perceived stress?

To address this question, we use hierarchical multiple regression (also referred to as 'sequential regression'). This means that we enter our variables in steps or blocks in a predetermined order (not letting the computer decide, as would be the case for stepwise regression). In the first block, we force age and socially desirable responding into the analysis. This has the effect of statistically controlling for these variables.

In the second step we enter the other independent variables into the model as a block, just as we did in the previous example. The difference this time is that the possible effect of age and socially desirable responding has been removed, and we can then see whether our block of independent variables is still able to explain some of the remaining variance in our dependent variable.

Procedure for hierarchical multiple regression
1. From the menu at the top of the screen, click on **Analyze**, then select **Regression**, then **Linear**.
2. Choose your continuous, dependent variable (e.g. total perceived stress: tpstress) and move it into the **Dependent** box.
3. Move the variables you wish to control for into the **Independent(s)** box (e.g. age, total social desirability: tmarlow). This will be the first block of variables to be entered in the analysis (Block 1 of 1).
4. Click on the button marked **Next**. This will give you a second independent variables box to enter your second block of variables into (you should see Block 2 of 2).
5. Choose your next block of independent variables (e.g. Total Mastery: tmast, Total PCOISS: tpcoiss).
6. In the **Method** box, make sure that this is set to the default (**Enter**).
7. Click on the **Statistics** button. Select the following: **Estimates**, **Model fit**, **R squared change**, **Descriptives**, **Part and partial correlations** and **Collinearity diagnostics**. Click on **Continue**.
8. Click on the **Options** button. In the **Missing Values** section, click on **Exclude cases pairwise**. Click on **Continue**.
9. Click on the **Plots** button.
   ➤ Click on *ZRESID and the arrow button to move this into the Y box.
   ➤ Click on *ZPRED and the arrow button to move this into the X box.
   ➤ In the section headed Standardized Residual Plots, tick the Normal probability plot option. Click on Continue.
10. Click on the **Save** button. Click on **Mahalanobis** and **Cook's**. Click on **Continue** and then **OK** (or on **Paste** to save to **Syntax Editor**).

The syntax from this procedure is:

```
REGRESSION
 /DESCRIPTIVES MEAN STDDEV CORR SIG N
 /MISSING PAIRWISE
 /STATISTICS COEFF OUTS R ANOVA COLLIN TOL CHANGE ZPP
 /CRITERIA=PIN(.05) POUT(.10)
 /NCORIGIN
 /DEPENDENT tpstress
 /METHOD=ENTER tmarlow age
 /METHOD=ENTER tmast tpcoiss
```

```
/SCATTERPLOT=(*ZRESID ,*ZPRED)
/RESIDUALS NORMPROB (ZRESID)
/SAVE MAHAL COOK .
```

Some of the output generated from this procedure is shown below.

Model Summary[c]

Model	R	R Square	Adjusted R Square	Std. Error of the Estimate	Change Statistics				
					R Square Change	F Change	df1	df2	Sig. F Change
1	.238[a]	.057	.052	5.693	.057	12.711	2	423	.000
2	.688[b]	.474	.469	4.262	.417	166.87	2	421	.000

a. Predictors: (Constant), tmarlow Total social desirability, age

b. Predictors: (Constant), tmarlow Total social desirability, age, tmast Total Mastery, tpcoiss Total PCOISS

c. Dependent Variable: tpstress Total perceived stress

ANOVA[a]

Model		Sum of Squares	df	Mean Square	F	Sig.
1	Regression	823.865	2	411.932	12.711	.000[b]
	Residual	13708.620	423	32.408		
	Total	14532.484	425			
2	Regression	6885.760	4	1721.440	94.776	.000[c]
	Residual	7646.724	421	18.163		
	Total	14532.484	425			

a. Dependent Variable: tpstress Total perceived stress

b. Predictors: (Constant), tmarlow Total social desirability, age

c. Predictors: (Constant), tmarlow Total social desirability, age, tmast Total Mastery, tpcoiss Total PCOISS

Coefficients[a]

Model		Unstandardized Coefficients		Standardized Coefficients			Correlations			Collinearity Statistics	
		B	Std. Error	Beta	t	Sig.	Zero-order	Partial	Part	Tolerance	VIF
1	(Constant)	31.08	.983		31.605	.000					
	age	-.031	.022	-.070	-1.438	.151	-.127	-.070	-.068	.928	1.077
	tmarlow Total social desirability	-.599	.140	-.209	-4.271	.000	-.228	-.203	-.202	.928	1.077
2	(Constant)	51.92	1.366		38.008	.000					
	age	-.021	.017	-.047	-1.239	.216	-.127	-.060	-.044	.860	1.163
	tmarlow Total social desirability	-.149	.108	-.052	-1.373	.171	-.228	-.067	-.049	.871	1.148
	tmast Total Mastery	-.641	.062	-.435	-10.286	.000	-.612	-.448	-.364	.699	1.432
	tpcoiss Total PCOISS	-.160	.022	-.327	-7.373	.000	-.581	-.338	-.261	.635	1.574

a. Dependent Variable: tpstress Total perceived stress

INTERPRETATION OF OUTPUT FROM HIERARCHICAL MULTIPLE REGRESSION

The output generated from this analysis is similar to the previous output, but with some extra pieces of information. In the **Model Summary** table there are two models listed. **Model 1** refers to the first block of variables that were entered (Total social desirability and age), while **Model 2** includes all the variables that were entered in both blocks (Total social desirability, age, Total Mastery, Total PCOISS).

Step 1: Evaluate the model

Check the **R square** values in the first **Model summary** row. After the variables in Block 1 (social desirability and age) have been entered, the overall model explains 5.7 per cent of the variance (.057 × 100). After Block 2 variables (Total Mastery, Total PCOISS) have also been included, the model *as a whole* explains 47.4 per cent (.474 × 100). It is important to note that this second R square value includes all the variables from both blocks, not just those included in the second step.

To find out how much of this overall variance is explained by our variables of interest (mastery, PCOISS) after the effects of age and socially desirable responding are removed, you need to check the column labelled **R Square Change**. In the output presented above you will see, in the row marked **Model 2**, that the **R square change** value is .417. This means that Mastery and PCOISS explain an *additional* 41.7 per cent (.417 × 100) of the variance in perceived stress, even when the effects of age and socially desirable responding are statistically controlled for. This is a statistically significant contribution, as indicated by the **Sig. F change** value for this row (.000). The **ANOVA** table indicates that the model as a whole (which includes both blocks of variables) is significant, $F (4, 421) = 94.776, p < .001$.

Step 2: Evaluate each of the independent variables

To find out how well each of the variables contributes to the final equation, we need to look in the **Coefficients** table in the Model 2 row. This summarises the results, with *all* the variables entered into the equation. Scanning the **Sig.** column, there are only two variables (Total Mastery, Total PCOISS) that make a unique statistically significant contribution (less than .05). In order of contribution to the percentage of variance explained (according to their Part correlation coefficient) they are: Mastery (–.364) and Total PCOISS (–.261). Neither age nor social desirability made a unique contribution. Remember, these Part correlation values represent the unique contribution of each variable, when the overlapping effects of all other variables are statistically removed. In different equations, with a different set of independent variables or with a different sample, these values would change.

PRESENTING THE RESULTS FROM MULTIPLE REGRESSION

There are several different ways of presenting the results of multiple regression, depending on the type of analysis conducted and the nature of the research question. As a minimum, you should indicate what type of analysis was performed (standard or hierarchical), standardised (beta) values, unstandardised (*B*) coefficients (with their standard errors) and the significance value. If you performed a hierarchical multiple regression, you should also provide the *R* square change values for each step and associated probability values.

An example of how you might choose to present the results of the analyses conducted in this chapter is presented below, both as a descriptive paragraph and in table format (see Tabachnick & Fidell 2013 and Nicol & Pexman 2010b for other examples). If presenting these results in a thesis, additional material (e.g. table of correlations, descriptive statistics) may need to be included in your appendix—check with your supervisor. It would be a good idea to search for examples of the presentation of statistical analysis in the journals relevant to your topic area. Given the tight space limitations, different journals have different requirements and expectations.

Note: All statistics except *p* values are rounded to two decimal places. Significance values shown in IBM SPSS Statistics as .000 are presented as *p* < .001. Consistent with APA style the statistic (e.g. *p*) is in italics. The **Part** correlation is referred to as a 'semi-partial correlation coefficient'.

Hierarchical multiple regression was used to assess the ability of two control measures (Mastery Scale, Perceived Control of Internal States Scale: PCOISS) to predict levels of stress (Perceived Stress Scale) after controlling for the influence of social desirability and age. Preliminary analyses were conducted to ensure no violation of the assumptions of normality, linearity, multicollinearity and homoscedasticity. Age and social desirability were entered at Step 1, explaining 6% of the variance in perceived stress. After entry of the Mastery Scale and PCOISS at Step 2 the total variance explained by the model as a whole was 47%, $F (4, 421) = 94.78$, $p < .001$. The two control measures explained an additional 42% of the variance in stress after controlling for age and socially desirable responding, R squared change $= .42$, F change $(2, 421) = 166.87$, $p < .001$. In the final model, only the two control measures were statistically significant, with the Mastery Scale recording a higher semipartial correlation value ($sr = -.36$, $p < .001$) than the PCOISS Scale ($sr = -.26$, $p < .001$).

Table 1

Hierarchical Multiple Regression Analysis Summary Predicting Total Perceived Stress With Age, Social Desirability, Total Mastery and Total PCOISS

Step and predictor variable	B	SE B	Beta	sr	Change in R^2	R^2
Step 1					.06***	.06
Constant	31.08	.98				
Age	-.03	.02	-.07	-.07		
Social desirability	-.60	.14	-.21***	-.20		
Step 2					.42***	.47
Constant	51.92	1.37				
Age	-.02	.02	-.05	-.04		
Social desirability	-.15	.11	-.05	-.05		
Total mastery	-.64	.06	-.43***	-.36		
Total PCOISS	-.16	.02	-.33***	-.26		

Note. sr = semipartial correlation coefficient; PCOISS = Perceived Control of Internal States Scale.

*** $p < .001$.

ADDITIONAL EXERCISES

Health

Data file: **sleep.sav**. See Appendix for details of the data file.

1. Conduct a standard multiple regression to explore factors that impact on people's level of daytime sleepiness. For your dependent variable, use the Sleepiness and Associated Sensations Scale total score (*totSAS*). For independent variables, use *sex*, *age*, physical fitness rating (*fitrate*) and scores on the HADS Depression Scale (*depress*). Assess how much of the variance in total sleepiness scores is explained by the set of variables (check your R square value). Which of the variables make a unique significant contribution (check your beta values)?

2. Repeat the above analysis, but this time use a hierarchical multiple regression procedure entering sex and age in the first block of variables and physical fitness and depression scores in the second block. After controlling for the demographic variables of sex and age, do the other two predictor variables make a significant contribution to explaining variance in sleepiness scores? How much additional variance in sleepiness is explained by physical fitness and depression after controlling for sex and age?

14

Logistic regression

In Chapter 13, Multiple Regression, we explored a technique to assess the impact of a set of predictors on a dependent variable (perceived stress). In that example the dependent variable was measured as a continuous variable (with scores ranging from 10 to 50). There are many research situations, however, when the dependent variable of interest is categorical (e.g. win/lose, fail/pass, dead/alive). Unfortunately, multiple regression is not suitable when you have categorical, dependent variables. For multiple regression your dependent variable (the thing that you are trying to explain or predict) needs to be a continuous variable, with reasonably normally distributed scores.

Logistic regression allows you to test models to predict categorical outcomes with two or more categories. Your predictor (independent) variables can be either categorical or continuous, or a mix of both in the one model. There is a family of logistic regression techniques available in IBM SPSS Statistics that will allow you to explore the predictive ability of sets, or blocks, of variables, and to specify the entry of variables. The purpose of this example is to demonstrate just the basics of logistic regression. Therefore, I use a **Forced Entry Method**, which is the default procedure available in IBM SPSS Statistics. In this approach, all predictor variables are tested in one block to assess their predictive ability while controlling for the effects of other predictors in the model.

Stepwise procedures (e.g. forward and backward) are available in IBM SPSS Statistics that allow you to specify a large group of potential predictors and let IBM SPSS Statistics pick a subset that provides the best predictive power. These, however, are *not* recommended. These stepwise procedures have been criticised (in both logistic and multiple regression), because they can be heavily influenced by random variation in the data, with variables being included or removed from the model on purely statistical grounds (see discussion in Tabachnick & Fidell 2013, p. 456).

In this chapter, I demonstrate how to perform logistic regression with a dichotomous, dependent variable (i.e. with only two categories or values). Here we use the procedure labelled **Binary Logistic**. If your dependent variable has more than two categories, you will need to use the **Multinomial Logistic** set of procedures (not covered here, but available in IBM SPSS Statistics—see the **Help** menu). Logistic regression is a complex technique, and I would strongly recommend further reading if you intend to use it (see Hosmer & Lemeshow 2000; Peat 2001; Tabachnick & Fidell 2013; Wright 1995).

ASSUMPTIONS

Sample size

As with most statistical techniques, you need to consider the size and nature of your sample if you intend to use logistic regression. One of the issues concerns the number of cases you have in your sample and the number of predictors (independent variables) you wish to include in your model. If you have a small sample with a large number of predictors, you may have problems with the analysis (including the problem of the solution failing to converge). This is particularly a problem when you have categorical predictors with limited cases in each category. Always run **Descriptive Statistics** on each of your predictors, and consider collapsing or deleting categories if they have limited numbers.

Multicollinearity

As discussed in Chapter 13, you should always check for high intercorrelations among your predictor (independent) variables. Ideally, your predictor variables will be strongly related to your dependent variable but not strongly related to each other. Unfortunately, there is no formal way in the logistic regression procedure of IBM SPSS Statistics to test for multicollinearity, but you can use the procedure described in Chapter 13 to request **collinearity diagnostics** under the **Statistics** button. Ignore the rest of the output, but focus on the **Coefficients table** and the columns labelled **Collinearity Statistics**. Tolerance values that are very low (less than .1) indicate that the variable has high correlations with other variables in the model. You may need to reconsider the set of variables that you wish to include in the model and remove one of the highly intercorrelating variables.

Outliers

It is important to check for the presence of outliers or cases that are not well explained by your model. In logistic regression terms, a case may be strongly predicted by your model to be one category but in reality be classified in the other category. These outlying cases can be identified by inspecting the residuals, a particularly important step if you have problems with the goodness of fit of your model.

DETAILS OF EXAMPLE

To demonstrate the use of logistic regression, I use a real data file (**sleep.sav**) available from the website for this book (see p. ix). These data were obtained from a survey

I conducted on a sample of university staff to identify the prevalence of sleep-related problems and their impact (see Appendix). In the survey, respondents were asked whether they considered that they had a sleep-related problem (yes/no). This variable is used as the dependent variable in this analysis. The set of predictors (independent variables) includes sex, age, the number of hours of sleep the person gets per weeknight, whether they have trouble falling asleep and whether they have difficulty staying asleep.

Scores on each of the variables were recoded to ensure their suitability for this analysis. The categorical variables were recoded, from their original scoring, so that 0 = no and 1 = yes. See Chapter 8 for instructions on how to do this.

DATA PREPARATION: CODING OF RESPONSES

In order to make sense of the results of logistic regression, it is important that you set up the coding of responses to each of your variables carefully. For the dichotomous, dependent variable, you should code the responses as 0 and 1 (or recode existing values using the **Recode** procedure in IBM SPSS Statistics—see Chapter 8). The value of 0 should be assigned to whichever response indicates a lack or absence of the characteristic of interest. In this example, 0 is used to code the answer 'no' to the question 'Do you have a problem with your sleep?' The value of 1 is used to indicate a 'yes' answer. A similar approach is used when coding the independent variables. Here, we have coded the answer 'yes' as 1 for both of the categorical variables relating to difficulty getting to sleep and difficulty staying asleep. For continuous, independent variables (number of hours sleep per night), high values should indicate more of the characteristic of interest.

File name: **sleep.sav**

Variables:
➢ probsleeprec: Score recoded to 0 = no, 1 = yes
➢ sex: 0 = female, 1 = male
➢ age in years
➢ hrswknight: In hours
➢ fallsleeprec: Score recoded to: 0 = no, 1 = yes
➢ staysleeprec: Score recoded to: 0 = no, 1 = yes.

Example of research question: What factors predict the likelihood that respondents would report that they had a problem with their sleep?

What you need:
➢ one categorical (dichotomous), dependent variable (problem: no/yes, coded 0/1)
➢ two or more continuous or categorical, predictor (independent) variables. Code

dichotomous variables using 0 and 1 (e.g. sex, fallsleeprec, staysleeprec). Measure continuous variables so that high values indicate more of the characteristic of interest (e.g. age, hrsweeknight).

What it does: Logistic regression allows you to assess how well your set of predictor variables predicts, or explains, your categorical, dependent variable. It gives you an indication of the adequacy of your model (set of predictor variables) by assessing goodness of fit. It provides an indication of the relative importance of each predictor variable or the interaction among your predictor variables. It provides a summary of the accuracy of the classification of cases based on the model, allowing the calculation of the sensitivity and specificity of the model and the positive and negative predictive values.

Assumptions: Logistic regression does not make assumptions concerning the distribution of scores for the predictor variables; however, it is sensitive to high correlations among the predictor variables (multicollinearity). Outliers can also influence the results of logistic regression.

Before you start the following procedure, choose **Edit** from the menu, select **Options**, and make sure there is a tick in the box **No scientific notation for small numbers in tables**.

Procedure for logistic regression

1. From the menu at the top of the screen, click on **Analyze**, then click on **Regression** and then **Binary Logistic**.
2. Choose your categorical, dependent variable (e.g. probsleeprec) and move it into the **Dependent** box.
   - ➤ Click on your predictor variables (sex, age, fallsleeprec: staysleeprec, hrswknight) and move them into the box labelled Covariates.
   - ➤ For Method, make sure that Enter is displayed.
3. If you have any categorical predictors (nominal or ordinal measurement), you will need to click on the **Categorical** button. Highlight each of the categorical variables (sex, fallsleeprec, staysleeprec) and move them into the **Categorical covariates** box.
   - ➤ Highlight each of your categorical variables in turn and click on the button labelled First in the Change contrast section. Click on the Change button and you will see the word (first) appear after the variable name. This will set the group to be used as the reference as the first group listed. Repeat for all categorical variables. Click on Continue.
4. Click on the **Options** button. Select **Classification plots, Hosmer-Lemeshow goodness of fit, Casewise listing of residuals**, and **CI for Exp(B)**.
5. Click on **Continue** and then **OK** (or on **Paste** to save to **Syntax Editor**).

The syntax from this procedure is:

```
LOGISTIC REGRESSION VARIABLES probsleeprec
 /METHOD=ENTER sex age fallsleeprec staysleeprec hrswknight
 /CONTRAST (sex)=Indicator(1)
 /CONTRAST (fallsleeprec)=Indicator(1)
 /CONTRAST (staysleeprec)=Indicator(1)
 /CLASSPLOT
 /CASEWISE OUTLIER(2)
 /PRINT=GOODFIT CI(95)
 /CRITERIA=PIN(0.05) POUT(0.10) ITERATE(20) CUT(0.5).
```

Selected parts of the output generated from this procedure are shown below.

Case Processing Summary

Unweighted Cases[a]		N	Percent
Selected Cases	Included in Analysis	241	88.9
	Missing Cases	30	11.1
	Total	271	100.0
Unselected Cases		0	.0
Total		271	100.0

a. If weight is in effect, see classification table for the total number of cases.

Dependent Variable Encoding

Original Value	Internal Value
0 no	0
1 yes	1

Categorical Variables Codings

		Frequency	Parameter coding (1)
staysleeprec prob staying asleep rec	0 no	138	.000
	1 yes	103	1.000
fallsleeprec prob falling asleep rec	0 no	151	.000
	1 yes	90	1.000
sex sex	0 female	140	.000
	1 male	101	1.000

Block 0: Beginning Block

Classification Table[a,b]

			Predicted		
			probsleeprec prob sleep recode 01		Percentage Correct
Observed			0 no	1 yes	
Step 0	probsleeprec prob sleep recode 01	0 no	138	0	100.0
		1 yes	103	0	.0
	Overall Percentage				57.3

a. Constant is included in the model.

b. The cut value is .500

Block 1: Method = Enter

Omnibus Tests of Model Coefficients

		Chi-square	df	Sig.
Step 1	Step	76.020	5	.000
	Block	76.020	5	.000
	Model	76.020	5	.000

Model Summary

Step	-2 Log likelihood	Cox & Snell R Square	Nagelkerke R Square
1	252.976[a]	.271	.363

a. Estimation terminated at iteration number 5 because parameter estimates changed by less than .001.

Hosmer and Lemeshow Test

Step	Chi-square	df	Sig.
1	10.019	8	.264

Contingency Table for Hosmer and Lemeshow Test

		probsleeprec prob sleep recode 01 = 0 no		probsleeprec prob sleep recode 01 = 1 yes		
		Observed	Expected	Observed	Expected	Total
Step 1	1	21	21.424	3	2.576	24
	2	23	20.587	1	3.413	24
	3	22	19.627	2	4.373	24
	4	18	18.587	6	5.413	24
	5	15	17.735	10	7.265	25
	6	12	13.878	12	10.122	24
	7	8	10.165	16	13.835	24
	8	6	7.353	18	16.647	24
	9	9	5.534	16	19.466	25
	10	4	3.110	19	19.890	23

Classification Table[a]

			Predicted		
			probsleeprec prob sleep recode 01		Percentage Correct
	Observed		0 no	1 yes	
Step 1	probsleeprec prob sleep recode 01	0 no	110	28	79.7
		1 yes	32	71	68.9
	Overall Percentage				75.1

a. The cut value is .500

Variables in the Equation

		B	S.E.	Wald	df	Sig.	Exp(B)	95% C.I.for EXP(B) Lower	Upper
Step 1[a]	sex(1)	-.108	.315	.118	1	.731	.897	.484	1.663
	age	-.006	.014	.193	1	.660	.994	.968	1.021
	prob falling asleep rec(1)	.716	.339	4.464	1	.035	2.05	1.053	3.976
	prob staying asleep rec(1)	1.984	.325	37.31	1	.000	7.27	3.848	13.748
	hrs sleep week nights	-.448	.165	7.366	1	.007	.639	.462	.883
	Constant	1.953	1.45	1.812	1	.178	7.05		

a. Variable(s) entered on step 1: sex, age, prob falling asleep rec, prob staying asleep rec, hrs sleep week nights.

Casewise List[b]

Case	Selected Status[a]	Observed probsleeprec prob sleep recode 01	Predicted	Predicted Group	Resid	ZResid	SResid
42	S	n**	.870	y	-.870	-2.583	-2.036
224	S	y**	.126	n	.874	2.633	2.049
227	S	y**	.133	n	.867	2.554	2.021
235	S	y**	.119	n	.881	2.721	2.076
265	S	y**	.121	n	.879	2.697	2.073

a. S = Selected, U = Unselected cases, and ** = Misclassified cases.

b. Cases with studentized residuals greater than 2.000 are listed.

INTERPRETATION OF OUTPUT FROM LOGISTIC REGRESSION

As with most IBM SPSS Statistics output, there is an almost overwhelming amount of information provided from logistic regression. I highlight only the key aspects here and strongly recommend that you consult other texts (e.g. Tabachnick & Fidell 2013, Chapter 10) for more detailed descriptions and interpretations.

The first things to check are the details concerning sample size provided in the **Case Processing Summary** table. Make sure you have the number of cases that you expect. The next table, **Dependent Variable Encoding**, tells you how the program has dealt with the coding of your dependent variable (in this case, whether people consider they have a problem with their sleep). IBM SPSS Statistics needs the variables to be coded using 0 and 1, but it will do it for you if your own coding does not match this (e.g. if your values are 1 and 2). I wanted to make sure that our problem with sleep variable was coded so that 0 = no problem and 1 = problem, so I created a new variable (using the **Recode** procedure—see Chapter 8), recoding the original response of 1 = yes, 2 = no to the format preferred by IBM SPSS Statistics of 1 = yes, 0 = no. This coding of the existence of the problem as 1 and the lack of problem as 0 makes the interpretation of the output a little easier.

Check the coding of your independent (predictor) variables in the next table, labelled **Categorical Variables Codings**. Also check the number of cases you have in each category in the column headed **Frequency**. You don't really want groups with very small numbers.

The next section of the output, headed **Block 0**, is the results of the analysis without any of our independent variables used in the model. This will serve as a baseline later for comparing the model with our predictor variables included. In the

Classification Table, the overall percentage of correctly classified cases is 57.3. In this case, IBM SPSS Statistics classified (guessed) that all cases would not have a problem with their sleep (this is because there was a higher percentage of people answering 'no' to the question). We hope that later, when our set of predictor variables is entered, we will be able to improve the accuracy of these predictions.

Skip down to the next section, headed **Block 1**. This is where our model (set of predictor variables) is tested. The **Omnibus Tests of Model Coefficients** gives us an overall indication of how well the model performs, over and above the results obtained for Block 0, with none of the predictors entered into the model. This is referred to as a 'goodness of fit' test. For this set of results, we want a highly significant value (the **Sig**. value should be less than .05). In this case, the value is .000 (which really means $p < .0005$). Therefore, the model (with our set of variables used as predictors) is better than the program's original guess shown in Block 0, which assumed that everyone would report no problem with their sleep. The chi-square value, which we need to report in our results, is 76.02 with 5 degrees of freedom.

The results shown in the table headed **Hosmer and Lemeshow Test** also support our model as being worthwhile. This test, which IBM SPSS Statistics states is the most reliable test of model fit available, is interpreted very differently from the omnibus test discussed above. For the **Hosmer-Lemeshow Goodness of Fit Test** poor fit is indicated by a significance value less than .05, so to support our model we actually want a value *greater* than .05. In our example, the chi-square value for the Hosmer-Lemeshow test is 10.019 with a significance level of .264. This value is larger than .05, therefore indicating support for the model.

The table headed **Model Summary** gives us another piece of information about the usefulness of the model. The **Cox & Snell *R* Square** and the **Nagelkerke *R* Square** values are described as 'pseudo' *R* square statistics, rather than the true *R* square values that you see provided in the multiple regression output. The Nagelkerke *R* Square value will always be higher, as it adjusts Cox and Snell's formula so that the maximum value is 1 (see Tabachnick & Fidell 2013, Chapter 10, for a more detailed description). Unlike the *R* square values in multiple regression they do not provide information about the amount of variance explained by the model. They can, however, be used to compare multiple models, predicting the same outcome in a data file, identifying which model better predicts the outcome.

The next table in the output to consider is the **Classification Table**. This provides us with an indication of how well the model is able to predict the correct category (sleep problem/no sleep problem) for each case. We can compare this with the **Classification Table** shown for Block 0 to see how much improvement there is when the predictor variables are included in the model. The model correctly classified 75.1 per cent of cases overall (sometimes referred to as the 'percentage accuracy in classification', or PAC), an improvement over the 57.3 per cent in Block 0. The results displayed in this table can also be used to calculate the additional statistics that you often see reported in the medical literature.

The *sensitivity* of the model is the percentage of the group with the characteristic of interest (e.g. sleep problem) that has been accurately identified by the model (the true positives). In this example, we were able to correctly classify 68.9 per cent of the people who did have a sleep problem. The *specificity* of the model is the percentage of the group without the characteristic of interest (no sleep problem) that is correctly identified (true negatives). In this example, the specificity is 79.7 per cent (people without a sleep problem correctly predicted not to have a sleep problem by the model).

The *positive predictive value* is the percentage of cases that the model classifies as having the characteristic that is actually observed in this group. To calculate this for the current example, you need to divide the number of cases in the predicted = yes, observed = yes cell (71) by the total number in the predicted = yes cells (28 + 71 = 99) and multiply by 100 to give a percentage. This gives us 71 divided by 99 × 100 = 71.7%. Therefore, the positive predictive value is 71.7 per cent, indicating that of the people predicted to have a sleep problem our model accurately picked 71.7 per cent of them. The *negative predictive value* is the percentage of cases predicted by the model not to have the characteristic that is actually observed not to have the characteristic. In the current example, the necessary values from the classification table are 110 divided by (110 + 32) × 100 = 77.5%. For further information on the use of classification tables see Wright (1995, p. 229), or for a simple worked example, see Peat (2001, p. 237).

The **Variables in the Equation** table gives us information about the contribution or importance of each of our predictor variables. The test that is used here is known as the Wald test, and you can see the value of the statistic for each predictor in the column labelled **Wald**. Scan down the column labelled **Sig.** looking for values less than .05. These are the variables that contribute significantly to the predictive ability of the model. In this case, we have three significant variables (staysleeprec $p = .000$, fallsleeprec $p = .035$, hrswknight $p = .007$). In this example, the major factors influencing whether a person reports having a sleep problem are difficulty getting to sleep, trouble staying asleep and the number of hours sleep per weeknight. Gender and age did not contribute significantly to the model.

The *B* values provided in the second column are equivalent to the *B* values obtained in a multiple regression analysis. These are the values that you would use in an equation to calculate the probability of a case falling into a specific category. You should check whether your *B* values are positive or negative. This tells you about the direction of the relationship (which factors increase the likelihood of a 'yes' answer and which factors decrease it). If you have coded all your dependent and independent, categorical variables correctly (with 0 = no, or lack of the characteristic; 1 = yes, or the presence of the characteristic), negative *B* values indicate that an increase in the independent variable score will result in a decreased probability of the case recording a score of 1 in the dependent variable (indicating the presence of sleep problems in this case). In this example, the variable measuring the number of hours slept each week-night showed a negative B value (−.448). This suggests that the more hours a person sleeps per night, the less likely they are to report having a sleep problem. For the two other significant categorical variables (trouble getting to sleep, trouble staying asleep), the B values are positive. This suggests that people saying they have difficulty getting to sleep or staying asleep are more likely to answer 'yes' to the question of whether they consider they have a sleep problem.

The other useful piece of information in the **Variables in the Equation** table is provided in the *Exp(B)* column. These values are the odds ratios (*OR*) for each of your independent variables. According to Tabachnick and Fidell (2013), the odds ratio represents 'the change in odds of being in one of the categories of outcome when the value of a predictor increases by one unit' (p. 461). In our example, the odds of a person answering 'yes', they have a sleep problem, is 7.27 times higher for someone who reports having problems staying asleep than for a person who does not have difficulty staying asleep, all other factors being equal.

The hours of sleep a person gets is also a significant predictor, according to the **Sig**. value ($p = .007$). The odds ratio for this variable, however, is .639, a value less than 1. This indicates that the more sleep a person gets per night, the less likely they are to report a sleep problem. For every extra hour of sleep a person gets, the odds of them reporting a sleep problem decrease by a factor of .639, all other factors being equal.

Note here that we have a continuous variable as our predictor; therefore, we report the increase (or decrease if less than 1) of the odds for each unit increase (in this case, a year) in the predictor variable. For categorical, predictor variables, we are comparing the odds for the two categories. For categorical variables with more than two categories, each category is compared with the reference group (usually the group coded with the lowest value if you have specified **First** in the **Contrast** section of the **Define Categorical Variables** dialogue box).

For odds ratios of less than 1, we can choose to invert these (1 divided by the value) when we report them, to aid interpretation. For example, in this case 1 divided by .639 equals 1.56. This suggests that for each hour less of sleep per night a person gets the odds of reporting a sleep problem increase by a factor of 1.56. If you do decide to invert, you will also need to invert the confidence intervals that you report (see next paragraph).

For each of the odds ratios, *Exp(B)*, shown in the **Variables in the Equation** table, there is a 95 per cent confidence interval (95.0% CI for *Exp(B)* displayed, giving a lower value and an upper value. These need to be reported in your results. In simple terms, this is the range of values that we can be 95 per cent confident encompasses the true value of the odds ratio. Remember, the value specified as the odds ratio is only a point estimate, or guess, at the true value, based on the sample data. The confidence that we have in this being an accurate representation of the true value (from the entire population) is dependent on the size of our sample. Small samples will result in very wide confidence intervals around the estimated odds ratio. Much smaller intervals will occur if we have large samples.

In this example, the confidence interval for our variable trouble staying asleep (staysleeprec OR = 7.27) ranges from 3.85 to 13.75. So, although we quote the calculated OR as 7.27, we can be 95 per cent confident that the actual value of OR in the population lies somewhere between 3.85 and 13.75, quite a wide range of values. The confidence interval in this case does not contain the value of 1; therefore, this result is statistically significant at $p < .05$. If the confidence interval had contained the value of 1, the odds ratio would not be statistically significant—we could not rule out the possibility that the true odds ratio was 1, indicating equal probability of the two responses ('yes'/'no').

The last table in the output, **Casewise List**, gives you information about cases in your sample for which the model does not fit well. Cases with **ZResid** values above 2 are shown in the table (in this example, showing case numbers 42, 224, 227, 235, 265). Cases with values above 2.5 (or less than –2.5) should be examined more closely, as these are clear outliers (given that 99% of cases will have values between –2.5 and +2.5). You can see from the other information in the casewise list that one of the cases (42) was predicted to be in the yes (sleep problem) category but in reality (in the **Observed** column) was found to answer the question with a 'no'. The remainder of the outliers were all predicted to answer 'no', but instead answered 'yes'. For all these cases (and certainly for **ZResid** values over 2.5), it would be a good idea to check the information entered and to find out more about them. You may find that there are certain groups of cases for which the model does not work well (e.g. those people on shiftwork). You may need to consider removing cases with very large **ZResid** values from the data file and repeating the analysis.

PRESENTING THE RESULTS FROM LOGISTIC REGRESSION

The results of this procedure could be presented as follows:

> Direct logistic regression was performed to assess the impact of a set of predictor variables on the odds that respondents would report that they had a problem with their sleep. The model contained five independent variables (sex, age, problems getting to sleep, problems staying asleep and hours of sleep per weeknight). The full model containing all predictors was statistically significant, χ^2 (5, N = 241) = 76.02, $p < .001$, indicating that the model was able to distinguish between respondents who reported versus did not report a sleep problem. The model as a whole correctly classified 75.1% of cases. As shown

in Table 1, only three of the independent variables made a unique statistically significant contribution to the model (hours sleep per night, problems getting to sleep and problems staying asleep). The strongest predictor of reporting a sleep problem was difficulty staying asleep, recording an odds ratio of 7.27. This indicated that the odds are 7.27 times greater that respondents who had difficulty staying asleep would report a sleep problem than those who did not have difficulty staying asleep, controlling for all other factors in the model. The odds ratio of .64 for hours sleep per night was less than 1, indicating that for every additional hour of sleep per night the odds were .64 times lower that respondents would report having a sleep problem, controlling for other factors in the model.

Table 1

Logistic Regression Predicting Likelihood of Reporting a Sleep Problem

	B	SE	Wald	df	p	Odds Ratio	95% CI for Odds Ratio Lower	Upper
Sex	−.11	.31	.12	1	.73	.90	.48	1.66
Age	−.01	.01	.19	1	.66	.99	.97	1.02
Getting to sleep	.72	.34	4.46	1	.03	2.05	1.05	3.98
Staying asleep	1.98	.32	37.31	1	.00	7.27	3.85	13.75
Hours sleep per night	−.45	.17	7.37	1	.01	.64	.46	.88
Constant	1.95	1.45	1.81		.18	7.05		

For other examples of how to present the results of logistic regression see Chapter 18 in Nicol and Pexman (2010b).

15

Factor analysis

Factor analysis is different from many of the other techniques presented in this book. It is included in IBM SPSS Statistics as a data reduction technique. It takes a large set of variables and identifies a way the data may be reduced, or summarised, using a smaller set of factors or components. It does this by scanning for clumps, or groups, among the intercorrelations of a set of variables. This is an almost impossible task to do by eye with anything more than a small number of variables.

Factor analytic techniques are used extensively by researchers involved in the development and evaluation of tests and scales. Typically, scale developers start with a large number of individual scale items and, by using factor analytic techniques, they can refine and reduce these items to form a smaller number of coherent subscales. Factor analysis can also be used to reduce a large number of related variables to a more manageable number, prior to using them in other analyses such as multiple regression or multivariate analysis of variance.

There are two main approaches to factor analysis that you will see described in the literature—exploratory and confirmatory. *Exploratory factor analysis* is often used in the early stages of research to explore the interrelationships among a set of variables. *Confirmatory factor analysis*, on the other hand, is a more complex set of techniques used later in the research process to confirm specific hypotheses concerning the structure underlying a set of variables.

The term 'factor analysis' encompasses a variety of different, although related, techniques. One of the main distinctions is between principal components analysis (PCA) and factor analysis (FA). These two sets of techniques are similar in many ways and are often used interchangeably by researchers. Both attempt to produce a smaller number of linear combinations of the original variables in a way that captures (or accounts for) most of the variability in the pattern of correlations. They do differ in a variety of ways, however. In principal components analysis the original variables are transformed into a smaller set of linear combinations, with all of the variance in the variables being used. In factor analysis, however, factors are estimated using a mathematical model whereby only the shared variance is analysed (see Tabachnick & Fidell 2013, Chapter 13, for more information on this).

Although both approaches (PCA and FA) often produce similar results, books on the topic often differ in terms of which approach they recommend. Stevens (1996, pp. 362–363) admits a preference for principal components analysis and gives reasons for this. He suggests that it is psychometrically sound and simpler mathematically, and it avoids some of the potential problems with 'factor indeterminacy' associated with factor analysis. Tabachnick and Fidell (2013), in their review of PCA and FA, conclude: 'If you are interested in a theoretical solution uncontaminated by unique and error variability . . . FA is your choice. If, on the other hand, you simply want an empirical summary of the data set, PCA is the better choice' (p. 640). I have chosen to demonstrate principal components analysis in this chapter. If you would like to explore the other approaches further, see Tabachnick and Fidell (2013).

Although PCA technically yields components, many authors use the term 'factor' to refer to the output of both PCA and FA. Don't assume, if you see the term 'factor' when you are reading journal articles, that the author has used FA. 'Factor analysis' is used as a general term to refer to the entire family of techniques.

Another potential area of confusion involving the use of the word 'factor' is that it has different meanings and uses in different types of statistical analyses. In factor analysis, it refers to the group, or clump, of related variables; in analysis of variance techniques, it refers to the independent variable. These are very different things, despite having the same name, so keep the distinction clear in your mind when you are performing the different analyses.

STEPS INVOLVED IN FACTOR ANALYSIS

There are three main steps in conducting factor analysis (I am using the term in a general sense to indicate any of this family of techniques, including principal components analysis).

Step 1: Assess the suitability of the data for factor analysis

There are two main issues to consider in determining whether a particular data set is suitable for factor analysis: sample size and the strength of the relationship among the variables (or items). While there is little agreement among authors concerning how large a sample should be, the recommendation generally is the larger, the better. In small samples, the correlation coefficients among the variables are less reliable, tending to vary from sample to sample. Factors obtained from small data sets do not generalise as well as those derived from larger samples. Tabachnick and Fidell (2013) review this issue and suggest that 'it is comforting to have at least 300 cases for factor analysis' (p. 613). However, they do concede that a smaller sample size (e.g. 150 cases) should be sufficient if solutions have several high loading marker variables (above .80). Stevens (1996, p. 372) suggests that the sample size requirements advocated by researchers have been reducing over the years as more research has been done on the topic. He makes several recommendations concerning the reliability of factor structures and the sample size requirements (see Stevens 1996, Chapter 11).

Some authors suggest that it is not the overall sample size that is of concern but the ratio of participants to items. Nunnally (1978) recommends a 10 to 1 ratio—that is, 10 cases for each item to be factor analysed. Others suggest that five cases for each item are adequate in most situations (see discussion in Tabachnick & Fidell 2013). I would recommend that you do more reading on the topic, particularly if you have a small sample (smaller than 150) or lots of variables. Check in your own literature area for examples of published articles describing factor analysis—see what is considered acceptable (and publishable!).

The second issue to be addressed concerns the strength of the intercorrelations among the items. Tabachnick and Fidell (2013) recommend an inspection of the correlation matrix for evidence of coefficients greater than .3. If few correlations above this level are found, factor analysis may not be appropriate. Two statistical measures are also generated by IBM SPSS Statistics to help assess the factorability of the data: Bartlett's Test of Sphericity (Bartlett 1954) and the Kaiser-Meyer-Olkin (KMO) Measure of Sampling Adequacy (Kaiser 1970, 1974). Bartlett's Test of Sphericity should be significant ($p < .05$) for the factor analysis to be considered appropriate. The KMO index ranges from 0 to 1, with .6 suggested as the minimum value for a good factor analysis (Tabachnick & Fidell 2013).

Step 2: Extract the factors

Factor extraction involves determining the smallest number of factors that can be used to best represent the interrelationships among the set of variables. There are different approaches that can be used to identify (extract) the number of underlying factors or dimensions. Some of the most commonly available extraction techniques (this always conjures up the image for me of a dentist pulling teeth!) are principal components, principal factors, image factoring, maximum likelihood factoring, alpha factoring, unweighted least squares, and generalised least squares.

The most commonly used approach is principal components analysis. This is demonstrated in the example given later in this chapter. It is up to the researcher to determine the number of factors that they consider best describes the underlying relationship among the variables. This involves balancing two conflicting needs: the need to find a simple solution with as few factors as possible and the need to explain as much of the variance in the original data set as possible. Tabachnick and Fidell (2013) recommend that researchers adopt an exploratory approach, experimenting with different numbers of factors until a satisfactory solution is found.

There are several different techniques that can be used to assist in the decision concerning the number of factors to retain: Kaiser's criterion, scree test and parallel analysis.

Kaiser's criterion

Perhaps the most widely used way of determining the number of factors is by the use of Kaiser's criterion, which is also known as the 'eigenvalues greater than one' rule. Using this rule, only factors with an eigenvalue of 1 or more are retained for further investigation (this will become clearer when you see the example presented later in this chapter). The eigenvalue of a factor represents the amount of the total variance explained by that factor. Kaiser's criterion has been criticised, however, as resulting in the retention of too many factors.

Scree test

Another approach that can be used is Catell's (1966) scree test. This involves plotting each of the eigenvalues of the factors (the program does this for you) and inspecting the plot to find a point at which the shape of the curve changes direction and becomes horizontal. Catell recommends retaining all factors above the elbow, or break in the plot, as these factors contribute the most to the explanation of the variance in the data set.

Parallel analysis

An additional technique gaining popularity, particularly in the social science literature (e.g. Choi, Fuqua & Griffin 2001; Stober 1998), is Horn's (1965) parallel analysis. Parallel analysis involves comparing the size of the eigenvalues with those obtained from a randomly generated data set of the same size. Only those eigenvalues that exceed the corresponding values from the random data set are retained. This approach to identifying the correct number of components to retain has been shown to be the most accurate, with both Kaiser's criterion and Catell's scree test tending to overestimate the number of components (Hubbard & Allen 1987; Zwick & Velicer 1986). If you intend to publish your results in a journal article in the psychology or education fields you will need to use, and report, the results of parallel analysis. Many journals (e.g. *Educational and Psychological Measurement, Journal of Personality Assessment*) are now making it a requirement before they will consider a manuscript for publication. These three techniques are demonstrated in the worked example presented later in this chapter.

Step 3: Rotate and interpret the factors

Once the number of factors has been determined, the next step is to try to interpret them. To assist in this process, the factors are rotated. This does not change the underlying solution; rather, it presents the pattern of loadings in a manner that is easier to interpret. The program does not label or interpret each of the factors for you. It just shows you which variables clump together. From your understanding of the content of the variables (and underlying theory and past research), it is up to you to propose possible interpretations.

There are two main approaches to rotation, resulting in either orthogonal (uncorrelated) or oblique (correlated) factor solutions. According to Tabachnick and Fidell (2013), orthogonal rotation results in solutions that are easier to interpret and to report; however, it does require the researcher to assume (usually incorrectly) that the underlying constructs are independent (not correlated). Oblique approaches allow for the factors to be correlated, but they are more difficult to interpret, describe and report (p. 642). In practice, the two approaches (orthogonal and oblique) often result in very similar solutions, particularly when the pattern of correlations among the items is clear (Tabachnick & Fidell 2013). I always recommend starting with an oblique rotation to check the degree of correlation between your factors.

Within the two broad categories of rotational approaches there are different techniques provided by IBM SPSS Statistics (orthogonal: Varimax, Quartimax, Equamax; oblique: Direct Oblimin, Promax). The most commonly used orthogonal approach is the Varimax method, which attempts to minimise the number of variables that have high loadings on each factor. The most commonly used oblique technique is Direct Oblimin. For a comparison of the characteristics of each of these approaches, see Tabachnick and Fidell (2013, p. 643). In the example presented in this chapter, Oblimin rotation is demonstrated.

Following rotation, you are hoping for what Thurstone (1947) refers to as 'simple structure'. This involves each of the variables loading strongly on only one component, and each component being represented by several strongly loading variables. This will help you interpret the nature of your factors by checking the variables that load strongly on each of them.

Additional resources

In this chapter only a very brief overview of factor analysis is provided. Although I have attempted to simplify it here, factor analysis is a sophisticated and complex family of techniques. If you are intending to use factor analysis with your own data, I suggest that you read up on the technique in more depth. For a thorough, but easy-to-follow, book on the topic I recommend Pett, Lackey and Sullivan (2003). For a more complex coverage, see Tabachnick and Fidell (2013).

DETAILS OF EXAMPLE

To demonstrate the use of factor analysis, I explore the underlying structure of one of the scales included in the **survey.sav** data file provided on the website accompanying this book (see p. ix and p. 337 for details): the Positive and Negative Affect

Scale (PANAS; Watson, Clark & Tellegen 1988; see Figure 15.1). This scale consists of 20 adjectives describing different mood states: 10 positive (e.g. proud, active, determined) and 10 negative (e.g. nervous, irritable, upset). The authors of the scale suggest that the PANAS consists of two underlying dimensions (or factors): positive affect and negative affect. To explore this structure with the current community sample the items of the scale are subjected to principal components analysis (PCA), a form of factor analysis that is commonly used by researchers interested in scale development and evaluation.

This scale consists of a number of words that describe different feelings and emotions. For each item indicate to what extent you have felt this way during the past few weeks. Write a number from 1 to 5 on the line next to each item.

Figure 15.1

Positive and
Negative Affect
Scale (PANAS)

very slightly or not at all	a little	moderately	quite a bit	extremely
1	2	3	4	5

1. interested_____	8. distressed_____	15. excited_____
2. upset_____	9. strong_____	16. guilty_____
3. scared_____	10. hostile_____	17. enthusiastic_____
4. proud_____	11. irritable_____	18. alert_____
5. ashamed_____	12. inspired_____	19. nervous_____
6. determined_____	13. attentive_____	20. jittery_____
7. active_____	14. afraid_____	

If you wish to follow along with the steps described in this chapter, you should start IBM SPSS Statistics and open the file labelled **survey.sav** (download from the website that accompanies this book). The variables that are used in this analysis are labelled pn1 to pn20. The scale used in the survey is presented in Figure 15.1. You will need to refer to these individual items when attempting to interpret the factors obtained. For full details and references for the scale, see the Appendix.

Example of research question: What is the underlying factor structure of the Positive and Negative Affect Scale? Past research suggests a two-factor structure (positive affect/negative affect).

What you need: A set of correlated continuous variables.

What it does: Factor analysis attempts to identify a small set of factors that represents the underlying relationships among a group of related variables.

Assumptions:
1. *Sample size:* Ideally, the overall sample size should be 150+ and there should be a ratio of at least five cases for each of the variables (see discussion in Step 1 earlier in this chapter).

2. *Factorability of the correlation matrix:* To be considered suitable for factor analysis, the correlation matrix should show at least some correlations of $r = .3$ or greater. Bartlett's Test of Sphericity should be statistically significant at $p < .05$ and the Kaiser-Meyer-Olkin value should be .6 or above. These values are presented as part of the output from factor analysis.

3. *Linearity:* Because factor analysis is based on correlation, it is assumed that the relationship between the variables is linear. It is certainly not practical to check scatterplots of all variables with all other variables. Tabachnick and Fidell (2013) suggest a spot check of some combination of variables. Unless there is clear evidence of a curvilinear relationship, you are probably safe to proceed, provided you have an adequate sample size and ratio of cases to variables (see Assumption 1).

4. *Outliers among cases:* Factor analysis can be sensitive to outliers, so as part of your initial data screening process (see Chapter 5) you should check for these and either remove or recode to a less extreme value.

PROCEDURE FOR FACTOR ANALYSIS: PART 1

Before you start the following procedure, choose **Edit** from the menu, select **Options**, then select the **General** tab and make sure there is a tick in the box **No scientific notation for small numbers in tables**.

Procedure (Part 1)

1. From the menu at the top of the screen, click on **Analyze**, then select **Dimension Reduction**, and then **Factor**.

2. Select all the required variables (or items on the scale). In this case, I would select the items that make up the PANAS (pn1 to pn20). Move them into the **Variables** box.

3. Click on the **Descriptives** button.
    ➤ In the Statistics section, make sure that Initial Solution is ticked.
    ➤ In the section marked Correlation Matrix, select the options Coefficients and KMO and Bartlett's test of sphericity. Click on Continue.

4. Click on the **Extraction** button.
    ➤ In the Method section, make sure Principal components is shown, or choose one of the other factor extraction techniques (e.g. Maximum likelihood).
    ➤ In the Analyze section, make sure the Correlation matrix option is selected. In the Display section, select Screeplot and make sure the Unrotated factor solution option is also selected.

> In the Extract section, select Based on Eigenvalue or, if you want to force a specific number of factors, click on Fixed number of factors and type in the number. Click on Continue.

5. Click on the **Rotation** button. Choose **Direct Oblimin** and press **Continue**.
6. Click on the **Options** button.
> In the Missing Values section, click on Exclude cases pairwise.
> In the Coefficient Display Format section, click on Sorted by size and Suppress small coefficients. Type the value of .3 in the box next to Absolute value below. This means that only loadings above .3 will be displayed, making the output easier to interpret.
7. Click on **Continue** and then **OK** (or on **Paste** to save to **Syntax Editor**).

The syntax from this procedure is:

```
FACTOR
/VARIABLES pn1 pn2 pn3 pn4 pn5 pn6 pn7 pn8 pn9 pn10 pn11 pn12 pn13 pn14
pn15 pn16 pn17 pn18 pn19 pn20
/MISSING PAIRWISE
/ANALYSIS pn1 pn2 pn3 pn4 pn5 pn6 pn7 pn8 pn9 pn10 pn11 pn12 pn13 pn14
pn15 pn16 pn17 pn18 pn19 pn20
/PRINT INITIAL CORRELATION KMO EXTRACTION ROTATION
/FORMAT SORT BLANK(.3)
/PLOT EIGEN
/CRITERIA MINEIGEN(1) ITERATE(25)
/EXTRACTION PC
/CRITERIA ITERATE(25) DELTA(0)
/ROTATION OBLIMIN
/METHOD=CORRELATION.
```

Selected output generated from this procedure is shown below.

KMO and Bartlett's Test

Kaiser-Meyer-Olkin Measure of Sampling Adequacy.		.874
Bartlett's Test of Sphericity	Approx. Chi-Square	3966.539
	df	190
	Sig.	.000

Total Variance Explained

Component	Initial Eigenvalues			Extraction Sums of Squared Loadings			Rotation Sums of Squared Loadings[a]
	Total	% of Variance	Cumulative %	Total	% of Variance	Cumulative %	Total
1	6.250	31.249	31.249	6.250	31.249	31.249	5.254
2	3.396	16.979	48.228	3.396	16.979	48.228	4.410
3	1.223	6.113	54.341	1.223	6.113	54.341	2.639
4	1.158	5.788	60.130	1.158	5.788	60.130	2.428
5	.898	4.490	64.619				
6	.785	3.926	68.546				
7	.731	3.655	72.201				
8	.655	3.275	75.476				
9	.650	3.248	78.724				
10	.601	3.004	81.728				
11	.586	2.928	84.656				
12	.499	2.495	87.151				
13	.491	2.456	89.607				
14	.393	1.964	91.571				
15	.375	1.875	93.446				
16	.331	1.653	95.100				
17	.299	1.496	96.595				
18	.283	1.414	98.010				
19	.223	1.117	99.126				
20	.175	.874	100.000				

Extraction Method: Principal Component Analysis.

a. When components are correlated, sums of squared loadings cannot be added to obtain a total variance.

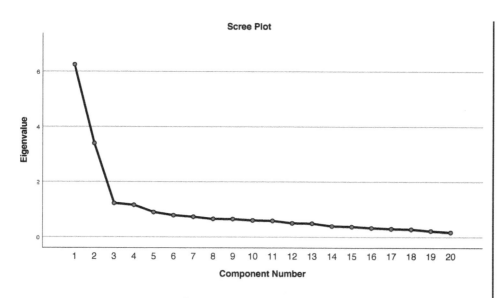

Scree Plot

Component Matrix[a]

	Component			
	1	2	3	4
pn17	.679	.474		
pn18	.639	.404		
pn7	.621			
pn8	-.614	.420		
pn9	.609	.323		
pn13	.607	.413		
pn1	.600	.381		
pn2	-.591	.408		
pn3	-.584	.449	-.457	
pn14	-.583	.456	-.451	
pn12	.582	.497		
pn19	-.569	.545		
pn11	-.554	.366	.462	
pn20	-.545	.459		
pn4	.474			
pn15	.477	.483		
pn6	.432	.437		
pn10	-.416	.426	.563	
pn5	-.429			.649
pn16	-.474	.357		.566

Extraction Method: Principal Component Analysis.

a. 4 components extracted.

Pattern Matrix[a]

| | Component | | | |
	1	2	3	4
pn17	.836			
pn12	.795			
pn13	.735			
pn18	.732			
pn15	.721			
pn1	.708			
pn9	.638			
pn6	.604			
pn7	.578			
pn4	.531			
pn3		.909		
pn14		.888		
pn19		.799		
pn20		.677		
pn8		.477	.413	
pn10			.808	
pn11			.707	
pn2		.434	.473	
pn5				.830
pn16				.773

Extraction Method: Principal Component Analysis.
Rotation Method: Oblimin with Kaiser Normalization.

a. Rotation converged in 8 iterations.

Component Correlation Matrix

Component	1	2	3	4
1	1.000	-.231	-.096	-.178
2	-.231	1.000	.327	.353
3	-.096	.327	1.000	.118
4	-.178	.353	.118	1.000

Extraction Method: Principal Component Analysis.
Rotation Method: Oblimin with Kaiser Normalization.

INTERPRETATION OF OUTPUT FROM FACTOR ANALYSIS: PART 1

As with most IBM SPSS Statistics procedures, there is a lot of output generated. In this section, I take you through the key pieces of information that you need.

Step 1

To verify that your data set is suitable for factor analysis, check that the **Kaiser-Meyer-Olkin Measure of Sampling Adequacy** (KMO) value is .6 or above and that the **Bartlett's Test of Sphericity** value is significant (i.e. the Sig. value should be .05 or smaller). In this example the *KMO* value is .874 and Bartlett's test is significant ($p = .000$); therefore, factor analysis is appropriate. In the **Correlation Matrix** table (not shown here for space reasons), search for correlation coefficients of .3 and above (see Assumption 2). If you don't find many in your matrix, you should reconsider the use of factor analysis.

Step 2

To determine how many components (factors) to extract, we need to consider a few pieces of information provided in the output. Using Kaiser's criterion, we are interested only in components that have an eigenvalue of 1 or more. To determine how many components meet this criterion, we need to inspect the **Total Variance Explained** table. Scan down the values provided in the first set of columns, labelled **Initial Eigenvalues**. The eigenvalues for each component are listed. In this example, only the first four components recorded eigenvalues above 1 (6.250, 3.396, 1.223, 1.158). These four components explain a total of 60.13 per cent of the variance (see **Cumulative %** column).

Step 3

Often, using the Kaiser criterion, you will find that too many components are extracted, so it is important to also examine the **Screeplot**. What you check for is a change (or elbow) in the shape of the plot. Only components above this point are retained. In this example, there is quite a clear break between the second and third components. Components 1 and 2 explain or capture much more of the variance than the remaining components. From this plot, I would recommend retaining (extracting) only two components. There is also another little break after the fourth component. Depending on the research context, this might also be worth exploring. Remember, factor analysis is used as a data exploration technique, so the interpretation and the use you put it to are up to your judgment rather than any hard and fast statistical rules.

Step 4

The third way of determining the number of factors to retain is parallel analysis (see discussion earlier in this chapter). For this procedure, you need to use the list of eigenvalues provided in the **Total Variance Explained** table and some additional information that you must get from another little statistical program, developed by Marley Watkins (2000), that is available from the website for this book. Follow the links to the **Additional Material** site and download the zip file (**parallel analysis. zip**) onto your computer. Unzip this onto your hard drive and click on the file **MonteCarloPA.exe**.

A program will start that is called Monte Carlo PCA for Parallel Analysis. You will be asked for three pieces of information: the number of variables you are analysing (in this case, 20), the number of participants in your sample (in this case, 435—check your descriptive statistics for this) and the number of replications (specify 100). Click on **Calculate**. This program will generate 100 sets of random data of the same size as your real data file (20 variables × 435 cases). It will calculate the average eigenvalues for these 100 randomly generated samples and print these out for you (see Table 15.1). Your numbers will not necessarily match my values, as each of the samples are randomly generated so will vary each time you use the program.

Your job is to systematically compare the first eigenvalue you obtained in IBM SPSS Statistics output with the corresponding first value from the random results

Table 15.1

Output from parallel analysis

7/03/2004 11:58:37 AM		
Number of variables:	20	
Number of subjects:	435	
Number of replications:	100	
Eigenvalue	Random Eigenvalue	Standard Dev
1	1.3984	.0422
2	1.3277	.0282
3	1.2733	.0262
4	1.2233	.0236
5	1.1832	.0191
6	1.1433	.0206
7	1.1057	.0192
8	1.0679	.0193
9	1.0389	.0186
10	1.0033	.0153
11	0.9712	.0180
12	0.9380	.0175
13	0.9051	.0187
14	0.8733	.0179
15	0.8435	.0187
16	0.8107	.0185
17	0.7804	.0190
18	0.7449	.0194
19	0.7090	.0224
20	0.6587	.0242

7/03/2004   11:58:50 AM
MonteCarlo PCA for Parallel Analysis
Watkins, M. W. (2000). MonteCarlo PCA for parallel analysis [computer software]. State College, PA: Ed & Psych Associates.

generated by parallel analysis. If your value is larger than the criterion value from parallel analysis, you retain this factor; if it is less, you reject it. The results for this example are summarised in Table 15.2. The results of parallel analysis support our decision from the Screeplot to retain only two factors for further investigation.

Component number	Actual eigenvalue from PCA	Criterion value from parallel analysis	Decision
1	6,250	1,3984	accept
2	3,396	1.3277	accept
3	1,223	1.2733	reject
4	1,158	1.2233	reject
5	898	1.1832	reject

Table 15.2 Comparison of eigenvalues from PCA and criterion values from parallel analysis

Step 5

Moving back to our IBM SPSS Statistics output, the next table we need to examine is the **Component Matrix**. This shows the unrotated loadings of each of the items on the four components. IBM SPSS Statistics uses the Kaiser criterion (retain all components with eigenvalues above 1) as the default. You can see from this table that most of the items load quite strongly (above .4) on the first two components. Very few items load on Components 3 and 4. This suggests that a two-factor solution is likely to be more appropriate.

Step 6

Before we make a final decision concerning the number of factors, we should inspect the rotated four-factor solution that is shown in the **Pattern Matrix** table. This shows the items loadings on the four factors, with 10 items loading above .3 on Component 1, six items loading on Component 2, four items on Component 3 and only two items on Component 4. Ideally, we would like three or more items loading on each component, so this solution is not optimal, further supporting our decision to retain only two factors.

Using the default options in IBM SPSS Statistics, we obtained a four-factor solution. It is now necessary to go back and force a two-factor solution.

PROCEDURE FOR FACTOR ANALYSIS: PART 2

Procedure (Part 2)
1. Repeat all steps in Procedure (Part 1), but when you click on the **Extraction** button click on **Fixed number of factors**. In the box next to **Factors to extract** type in the number of factors you would like to extract (e.g. 2).
2. Click on **Continue** and then **OK**.

The syntax from this procedure is:

```
FACTOR
 /VARIABLES pn1 pn2 pn3 pn4 pn5 pn6 pn7 pn8 pn9 pn10 pn11 pn12 pn13 pn14
 pn15 pn16 pn17 pn18 pn19
  pn20
 /MISSING PAIRWISE
 /ANALYSIS pn1 pn2 pn3 pn4 pn5 pn6 pn7 pn8 pn9 pn10 pn11 pn12 pn13 pn14
 pn15 pn16 pn17 pn18 pn19
  pn20
 /PRINT INITIAL CORRELATION KMO EXTRACTION ROTATION
 /FORMAT SORT BLANK(.3)
 /PLOT EIGEN
 /CRITERIA FACTORS(2) ITERATE(25)
 /EXTRACTION PC
 /CRITERIA ITERATE(25) DELTA(0)
 /ROTATION OBLIMIN
 /METHOD=CORRELATION.
```

Some of the output generated is shown below.

Total Variance Explained

Component	Initial Eigenvalues			Extraction Sums of Squared Loadings			Rotation Sums of Squared Loadings[a]
	Total	% of Variance	Cumulative %	Total	% of Variance	Cumulative %	Total
1	6.250	31.249	31.249	6.250	31.249	31.249	5.277
2	3.396	16.979	48.228	3.396	16.979	48.228	5.157
3	1.223	6.113	54.341				
4	1.158	5.788	60.130				
5	.898	4.490	64.619				
6	.785	3.926	68.546				
7	.731	3.655	72.201				
8	.655	3.275	75.476				
9	.650	3.248	78.724				
10	.601	3.004	81.728				
11	.586	2.928	84.656				
12	.499	2.495	87.151				
13	.491	2.456	89.607				
14	.393	1.964	91.571				
15	.375	1.875	93.446				
16	.331	1.653	95.100				
17	.299	1.496	96.595				
18	.283	1.414	98.010				
19	.223	1.117	99.126				
20	.175	.874	100.000				

Extraction Method: Principal Component Analysis.

a. When components are correlated, sums of squared loadings cannot be added to obtain a total variance.

Some of the output generated is shown below.

Component Matrix[a]

	Component	
	1	2
pn17	.679	.474
pn18	.639	.404
pn7	.621	
pn8	-.614	.420
pn9	.609	.323
pn13	.607	.413
pn1	.600	.381
pn2	-.591	.408
pn3	-.584	.449
pn14	-.583	.456
pn12	.582	.497
pn19	-.569	.545
pn11	-.554	.366
pn20	-.545	.459
pn4	.474	
pn16	-.474	.357
pn5	-.429	
pn15	.477	.483
pn6	.432	.437
pn10	-.416	.426

Extraction Method: Principal
Component Analysis.

a. 2 components extracted.

Communalities

	Initial	Extraction
pn1	1.000	.518
pn2	1.000	.585
pn3	1.000	.758
pn4	1.000	.323
pn5	1.000	.714
pn6	1.000	.448
pn7	1.000	.501
pn8	1.000	.588
pn9	1.000	.512
pn10	1.000	.705
pn11	1.000	.670
pn12	1.000	.629
pn13	1.000	.548
pn14	1.000	.751
pn15	1.000	.523
pn16	1.000	.708
pn17	1.000	.704
pn18	1.000	.582
pn19	1.000	.697
pn20	1.000	.561

Extraction Method: Principal
Component Analysis.

Pattern Matrix[a]

	Component	
	1	2
pn17	.825	
pn12	.781	
pn18	.742	
pn13	.728	
pn15	.703	
pn1	.698	
pn9	.656	
pn6	.635	
pn7	.599	
pn4	.540	
pn19		.806
pn14		.739
pn3		.734
pn8		.728
pn20		.718
pn2		.704
pn11		.645
pn10		.613
pn16		.589
pn5		.490

Extraction Method: Principal Component Analysis.
Rotation Method: Oblimin with Kaiser Normalization.

a. Rotation converged in 6 iterations.

Structure Matrix

	Component	
	1	2
pn17	.828	
pn12	.763	
pn18	.755	
pn13	.733	
pn1	.710	
pn9	.683	
pn15	.670	
pn7	.646	-.338
pn6	.605	
pn4	.553	
pn19		.784
pn8		.742
pn14		.740
pn3		.737
pn2		.717
pn20		.712
pn11		.661
pn16		.593
pn10		.590
pn5		.505

Extraction Method: Principal Component Analysis.
Rotation Method: Oblimin with Kaiser Normalization.

Component Correlation Matrix

Component	1	2
1	1.000	-.277
2	-.277	1.000

Extraction Method: Principal Component Analysis.
Rotation Method: Oblimin with Kaiser Normalization.

INTERPRETATION OF OUTPUT FROM FACTOR ANALYSIS: PART 2

The first thing we need to check is the percentage of variance explained by this two-factor solution shown in the **Total Variance Explained** table (in Part 1). For the two-factor solution only 48.2 per cent of the variance is explained, compared with over 60 per cent explained by the four-factor solution. This drop is expected, as we have forced the items to load on only two components, thereby increasing the proportion of unexplained variance—48 per cent is still a very respectable percentage of explained variance.

After rotating the two-factor solution, there are three new tables at the end of the output you need to consider. First, inspect the **Component Correlation Matrix** (at the end of the output). This shows you the strength of the relationship between the two factors (in this case the value is quite low, at −.277). This gives us information to decide whether it was reasonable to assume that the two components were not related (the assumption underlying the use of Varimax rotation) or whether it is necessary to use, and report, the Oblimin rotation solution shown here.

In this case the correlation between the two components is quite low, so we would expect very similar solutions from the Varimax and Oblimin rotations. If, however, your components are more strongly correlated (e.g. above .3), you may find discrepancies between the results of the two approaches to rotation. If that is the case, you need to report the Oblimin rotation.

Oblimin rotation provides two tables of loadings. The **Pattern Matrix** shows the factor loadings of each of the variables. Search for the highest loading items on each component to identify and label the component. In this example, the main loadings on Component 1 are Items 17, 12, 18 and 13. If you refer back to the actual items themselves (presented earlier in this chapter), you can see that these are all positive affect items (enthusiastic, inspired, alert, attentive). The main items on Component 2 (19, 14, 3, 8) are negative affect items (nervous, afraid, scared, distressed). In this case, identification and labelling of the two components is easy. This is not always the case, however.

The **Structure Matrix** table, which is unique to the Oblimin output, provides information about the correlation between variables and factors. If you need to present the Oblimin rotated solution in your output, you must present both of these tables.

Earlier in the output a table labelled **Communalities** is presented. This gives information about how much of the variance in each item is explained. Low values (e.g. less than .3) could indicate that the item does not fit well with the other items in its component. For example, Item pn5 has the lowest communality value (.258) for this two-factor solution, and it also shows the lowest loading (.49) on Component 2 (see **Pattern Matrix**). If you are interested in improving or refining a scale, you could use this information to select items for removal from the scale. Removing items with low communality values will increase the total variance explained, but it will change the content of the scale. Communality values can change dramatically depending on how many factors are retained, so it is often better to interpret the communality values after you have chosen how many factors you should retain using the Screeplot and parallel analysis.

Warning: The output in this example is a very clean result. Each of the variables loaded strongly on only one component, and each component was represented by a number of strongly loading variables (an example of simple structure). For a discussion of this topic, see Tabachnick and Fidell (2013, p. 652). Unfortunately, with your own data you may not always have such a straightforward result. Often, you will find that variables load moderately on several different components, and some components will have only one or two variables loading on them. In cases such as this, you may need to consider rotating a different number of components (e.g. one more and one less) to see whether a more optimal solution can be found. If you find that some variables just do not load on the components obtained, you may also need to consider removing them and repeating the analysis. You should read as much as you can on the topic to help you make these decisions. An easy-to-follow book to get you started is Pett, Lackey and Sullivan (2003).

PRESENTING THE RESULTS FROM FACTOR ANALYSIS

The information you provide in your results section is dependent on your discipline area, the type of report you are preparing and where it will be presented. If you are publishing in the areas of psychology and education particularly there are quite strict requirements for what needs to be included in a journal article that involves the use of factor analysis. You should include details of the method of factor extraction used, the criteria used to determine the number of factors (this should include parallel analysis), the type of rotation technique used (e.g. Varimax, Oblimin), the total variance explained, the initial eigenvalues and the eigenvalues after rotation.

A table of loadings should be included showing all values (not just those above .3). For the Varimax rotated solution, the table should be labelled 'pattern/structure coefficients'. If Oblimin rotation was used, then both the Pattern Matrix and the Structure Matrix coefficients should be presented in full (these can be combined into one table, as shown below), along with information on the correlations among the factors.

The results of the output obtained in the example above could be presented as follows (note that for APA style the results are reported to two decimal places, and the statistic *r* is italicised):

The 20 items of the Positive and Negative Affect Scale (PANAS) were subjected to principal components analysis (PCA) using IBM SPSS Statistics version 26. Prior to performing PCA, the suitability of data for factor analysis was assessed. Inspection of the correlation matrix revealed the presence of many coefficients of .3 and above. The Kaiser-Meyer-Olkin value was .87, exceeding the recommended value of .6 (Kaiser 1970, 1974), and Bartlett's (1954) Test of Sphericity reached statistical significance, supporting the factorability of the correlation matrix.

Principal components analysis revealed the presence of four components with eigenvalues exceeding 1, explaining 31.2%, 17.0%, 6.1% and 5.8% of the variance respectively. An inspection of the screeplot revealed a clear break after the second component. Using Catell's (1966) scree test, it was decided to retain two components for further investigation. This was further supported by the results of parallel analysis, which showed only two components with eigenvalues exceeding the corresponding criterion values for a randomly generated data matrix of the same size (20 variables × 435 respondents).

The two-component solution explained a total of 48.2% of the variance, with Component 1 contributing 31.25% and Component 2 contributing 17.0%. To aid in the interpretation of these two components, oblimin rotation was performed. The rotated solution revealed the presence of simple structure (Thurstone 1947), with both components showing several strong loadings and all variables loading substantially on only one component. The interpretation of the two components was consistent with previous research on the PANAS, with positive affect items loading strongly on Component 1 and negative affect items loading strongly on Component 2. There was a weak negative correlation between the two factors ($r = -.28$). The results of this analysis support the use of the positive affect items and the negative affect items as separate scales, as suggested by the scale authors (Watson, Clark & Tellegen 1988).

You should include both the Pattern Matrix and Structure Matrix in your report, with all loadings showing. To get the full display of loadings, you will need to rerun the analysis that you chose as your final solution (in this case, a two-factor Oblimin rotation), but this time you will need to turn off the option to display only coefficients above .3 (see Part 1 Procedures section). Click on **Options**, and in the **Coefficient Display Format** section remove the tick from the box **Suppress small coefficients**.

If you are presenting the results of this analysis in your thesis (rather than a journal article), you may also need to provide the screeplot and the table of un-rotated loadings (from the **Component Matrix**) in the appendix. This would allow the examiner to see if they agree with your decision to retain only two components.

Presentation of results in a journal article tends to be much briefer, given space limitations. If you would like to see an example of a published article using factor analysis, go to www.hqlo.com/content/3/1/82 and select the pdf option on the right-hand side of the screen that appears.

For other examples of how to present the results of factor analysis see Chapter 16 in Nicol and Pexman (2010b).

ADDITIONAL EXERCISES

Business

Data file: **staffsurvey.sav**. See Appendix for details of the data file.

1. Follow the instructions throughout the chapter to conduct a principal components analysis with Oblimin rotation on the 10 agreement items that make up the Staff Satisfaction Survey (Q1a *to* Q10a). You will see that, although two factors record eigenvalues over 1, the screeplot indicates that only one component should be retained. Run Parallel Analysis using 523 as the number of cases and 10 as the number of items. The results indicate only one component has an eigenvalue that exceeds the equivalent value obtained from a random data set. This suggests that the items of the Staff Satisfaction Scale are assessing only one underlying dimension (factor).

Health

Data file: **sleep.sav**. See Appendix for details of the data file.

1. Use the procedures shown in this chapter to explore the structure underlying the set of questions designed to assess the impact of sleep problems on various aspects of people's lives. These items are labelled *impact1* to *impact7*. Run Parallel Analysis (using 121 as the number of cases and 7 as the number of items) to check how many factors should be retained.

PART FIVE
Statistical techniques to compare groups

In Part Five of this book, we explore some of the techniques available in IBM SPSS Statistics to assess differences between groups or conditions. The techniques used are quite complex, drawing on a lot of underlying theory and statistical principles. Before you start your analysis using IBM SPSS Statistics, it is important that you have at least a basic understanding of the statistical techniques that you intend to use. There are many good statistical texts available that can help you with this. (A list of some suitable books is provided in the Recommended Reading section at the end of the book.) It would be a good idea to review this material now. This will help you understand what the program is calculating for you, what it means and how to interpret the complex output generated. In the following chapters, I have assumed that you have a basic grounding in statistics and are familiar with the terminology used.

TECHNIQUES COVERED IN PART FIVE

There is a whole family of techniques that can be used to test for significant differences between groups. Although there are many different statistical techniques available in the IBM SPSS Statistics package, only the main techniques are covered here. I have included both parametric and non-parametric techniques in this section of the book.

Parametric techniques make several assumptions about the population from which the sample has been drawn (e.g. normally distributed scores) and the nature of the data (interval level scaling). Non-parametric techniques do not have such stringent assumptions and are often the more suitable techniques for smaller samples or when the data collected are measured only at the ordinal (ranked) level. A list of the techniques covered in this part is shown in the table below.

List of parametric techniques and their non-parametric techniques covered in Part Five

Parametric technique	Non-parametric technique
None	Chi-Square Test for Goodness of Fit
None	Chi-Square Test for Independence
None	McNemar's Test
None	Cochran's Q Test
None	Kappa Measure of Agreement
Independent-samples t-test	Mann-Whitney U Test
Paired-samples t-test	Wilcoxon Signed Rank Test
One-way between-groups ANOVA	Kruskal-Wallis Test
One-way repeated measures ANOVA	Friedman Test
Two-way analysis of variance (between groups)	None
Mixed between-within subjects ANOVA	None
Multivariate analysis of variance (MANOVA)	None
Analysis of covariance	None

In Chapter 10, you were guided through the process of deciding which statistical technique would suit your research question. This depends on the nature of your research question, the types of data you have and the number of variables and groups you have. (If you have not read through that chapter, you should do so before proceeding any further.) Some of the key points to remember when choosing which technique is the right one for you are as follows:

➤ T-tests are used when you have only *two* groups (e.g. males/females) or two time points (e.g. pre-intervention, post-intervention).
➤ Analysis of variance techniques are used when you have *two or more* groups or time points.
➤ Paired-samples, or repeated measures, techniques are used when you test the *same people* on more than one occasion or when you have matched pairs.
➤ Between-groups, or independent-samples, techniques are used when the participants in each group are *different people* (or independent).

➤ One-way analysis of variance is used when you have only one *independent* variable (e.g. gender).

➤ Two-way analysis of variance is used when you have two *independent* variables (gender, age group).

➤ Multivariate analysis of variance is used when you have more than one *dependent* variable (anxiety, depression).

➤ Analysis of covariance (ANCOVA) is used when you need to *control* for an additional variable that may be influencing the relationship between your independent and dependent variables.

Before we begin to explore some of the techniques available, there are several common issues that need to be considered. These topics are relevant to many of the chapters included in this part of the book, so you may need to refer back to this section as you work through each chapter.

ASSUMPTIONS

There are some general assumptions that apply to all of the parametric techniques discussed here (e.g. t-tests, analysis of variance) and additional assumptions associated with specific techniques. The general assumptions are presented in this section, and the more specific assumptions are presented in the following chapters, as appropriate. You should refer back to this section when using any of the techniques presented in Part Five. For information on the procedures used to check for violation of assumptions, see Tabachnick and Fidell (2013, Chapter 4).

Level of measurement
Each of the parametric approaches assumes that the dependent variable is measured at the interval or ratio level—that is, using a continuous scale rather than discrete categories. Wherever possible when designing your study, try to make use of continuous, rather than categorical, measures of your dependent variable. This gives you a wider range of possible techniques to use when analysing your data.

Random sampling
The parametric techniques covered in Part Five assume that the scores are obtained using a random sample from the population. This is often not the case in real-life research.

Independence of observations
The observations that make up your data must be independent of one another; that is, each observation or measurement must not be influenced by any other observation

or measurement. Violation of this assumption, according to Stevens (1996, p. 238), is very serious. There are various research situations that may violate this assumption of independence. Examples of some such studies are described below (these are drawn from Stevens 1996, p. 239; and Gravetter & Wallnau 2004, p. 251):

> *Studying the performance of students working in pairs or small groups:* The behaviour of each member of the group influences all other group members, thereby violating the assumption of independence.
> *Studying the TV-watching habits and preferences of children drawn from the same family:* The behaviour of one child in the family (e.g. watching Program A) is likely to influence all children in that family; therefore, the observations are not independent.
> *Studying teaching methods within a classroom and examining the impact on students' behaviour and performance:* In this situation, all students could be influenced by the presence of a small number of trouble-makers; therefore, individual behavioural or performance measurements are not independent.

Any situation where the observations or measurements are collected in a group setting, or participants are involved in some form of interaction with one another, may require more specialist techniques such as multilevel (or hierarchical) modelling. This approach is commonly being used now in studies involving children in classrooms, within schools, within cities; or with patients, within different medical specialists, within a practice, within a city or country. For more information, see Chapter 15 in Tabachnick and Fidell (2013).

Normal distribution

For parametric techniques, it is assumed that the populations from which the samples are taken have normally distributed scores on the continuous, dependent and independent variables. In a lot of research (particularly in the social sciences), scores on the dependent variable are not normally distributed. Fortunately, most of the techniques are reasonably robust, or tolerant of violations of this assumption. With large enough sample sizes (e.g. 30+), the violation of this assumption should not cause any major problems. The distribution of scores for each of your groups can be checked using histograms obtained as part of the **Graphs** menu of IBM SPSS Statistics (see Chapter 7). For a more detailed description of this process, see Chapter 4 in Tabachnick and Fidell (2013).

Homogeneity of variance

Parametric techniques in this section make the assumption that samples are obtained from populations of equal variances. This means that the variability of scores for each of the groups is similar. To test this, IBM SPSS Statistics performs Levene's Test for Equality of Variances as part of the t-test and analysis of variance procedures. The results are presented in the output of each of these techniques. Be careful in interpreting the results of this test; you are hoping to find that the test is *not* significant (i.e. a significance level of *greater* than .05). If you obtain a significance value of less than .05, this suggests that variances for the two groups are not equal and you have therefore violated the assumption of homogeneity of variance. Don't panic if you find this to be the case. Analysis of variance is reasonably robust to violations of this assumption, provided the sizes of your groups are reasonably similar (e.g. largest/smallest = 1.5; Stevens 1996, p. 249). For t-tests, you are provided with two sets of results, for situations where the assumption is not violated and is violated. In this case, you just consult whichever set of results is appropriate for your data.

TYPE 1 ERROR, TYPE 2 ERROR AND POWER

The purpose of t-tests and analysis of variance procedures is to test hypotheses. With this type of analysis there is always the possibility of reaching the wrong conclusion. There are two different errors that we can make. We may reject the null hypothesis when it is, in fact, true (this is referred to as a Type 1 error). This occurs when we think there is a difference between our groups, but there really isn't. We can minimise this possibility by selecting an appropriate alpha level (the two levels often used are .05 and .01).

The second type of error that we can make (Type 2 error) occurs when we fail to reject a null hypothesis when it is, in fact, false (i.e. believing that the groups do not differ when, in fact, they do). Unfortunately, these two errors are inversely related. As we try to control for a Type 1 error, we increase the likelihood that we will commit a Type 2 error.

Ideally, we would like the tests that we use to correctly identify whether in fact there is a difference between our groups. This is called the 'power' of a test. Tests vary in terms of their power (e.g. parametric tests such as t-tests, analysis of variance etc. are potentially more powerful than non-parametric tests, if the assumptions are met); however, there are other factors that can influence the power of a test in a given situation:

➤ sample size
➤ effect size (the strength of the difference between groups, or the influence of the independent variable)
➤ alpha level set by the researcher (e.g. $p < .05$).

The power of a test is very dependent on the size of the sample used in the study. According to Stevens (1996), when the sample size is large (e.g. 100 or more participants) 'power is not an issue' (p. 6). However, when you have a study where the group size is small (e.g. $n = 20$), you need to be aware of the possibility that a non-significant result may be due to insufficient power.

There are tables available (see Cohen 1988) that will tell you how large your sample size needs to be to achieve sufficient power, given the effect size you wish to detect. There is also a growing number of software programs that can do these calculations for you. One of the best I have found is G*Power, which is available from www.gpower.hhu.de/.

Some of the IBM SPSS Statistics procedures also provide an indication of the power of the test that was conducted, taking into account effect size and sample size. Ideally, you would want an 80 per cent chance of detecting a relationship (if in fact one did exist). If you obtain a non-significant result and are using quite a small sample size, you could check these power values. If the power of the test is less than .80 (80% chance of detecting a difference), you would need to interpret the reason for your non-significant result carefully. This may suggest insufficient power of the test, rather than no real difference between your groups. The power analysis gives an indication of how much confidence you should have in the results when you fail to reject the null hypothesis. The higher the power, the more confident you can be that there is no real difference between the groups.

PLANNED COMPARISONS/POST-HOC ANALYSES

When you conduct analysis of variance, you are determining whether there are significant differences among the various groups or conditions. Sometimes, you may be interested in knowing if, overall, the groups differ (that your independent variable in some way influences scores on your dependent variable). In other research contexts, however, you might be more focused and interested in testing the differences between specific groups, not between all the various groups. It is important that you distinguish which applies in your case, as different analyses are used for each of these purposes.

Planned comparisons (also known as 'a priori') are used when you wish to test specific hypotheses (usually drawn from theory or past research) concerning the differences between a subset of your groups (e.g. do Groups 1 and 3 differ significantly?). These comparisons need to be specified, or planned, before you analyse your data, not after fishing around in your results to see what looks interesting!

Some caution needs to be exercised with this approach if you intend to specify a lot of different comparisons. Planned comparisons do not control for the increased risks of Type 1 errors. A Type 1 error involves rejecting the null hypothesis (e.g. there are no differences among the groups) when it is actually true. In other words, there is an increased risk of thinking that you have found a significant result when in fact it could have occurred by chance. If there is a large number of differences that you wish to explore, it may be safer to use post-hoc comparisons, which are designed to protect against Type 1 errors.

The other alternative is to apply what is known as a Bonferroni adjustment to the alpha level (*p* value) that you use to judge statistical significance. This involves setting a more stringent alpha level for each comparison, to keep the alpha across all the tests at a reasonable level. To achieve this, you can divide your alpha level (usually .05) by the number of comparisons that you intend to make, and then use this new value as the required alpha level. For example, if you intend to make three comparisons the new alpha level would be .05 divided by 3, which equals .017. For a discussion on variations to this technique, see Tabachnick and Fidell (2013, p. 52).

Post-hoc comparisons (also known as 'a posteriori') are used when you want to conduct a whole set of comparisons, exploring the differences between each of the groups or conditions in your study. If you choose this approach, your analysis consists of two steps. First, an overall *F* ratio is calculated that tells you whether there are any significant differences among the groups in your design. If your overall *F* ratio is significant (indicating that there are differences among your groups), you can then go on and perform additional tests to identify where these differences occur (e.g. does Group 1 differ from Group 2 or Group 3? Do Group 2 and Group 3 differ?).

Post-hoc comparisons are designed to guard against the possibility of an increased Type 1 error due to the large number of different comparisons being made. This is done by setting more stringent criteria for significance, and therefore it is often harder to achieve significance. With small samples this can be a problem, as it can be very hard to find a significant result even when the apparent difference in scores between the groups is quite large.

There are different post-hoc tests that you can use, and these vary in terms of their nature and strictness. The assumptions underlying the post-hoc tests also differ. Some assume equal variances for the two groups (e.g. Tukey); others do not assume equal variance (e.g. Dunnett's *C* Test). Two of the most commonly used post-hoc tests are Tukey's Honestly Significant Difference test (HSD) and the Scheffe Test. Of the two, the Scheffe Test is the more cautious method for reducing the risk of a Type 1 error. However, the cost here is power. You may be less likely to detect a difference between your groups using this approach. Check in your literature area to see what is generally reported.

EFFECT SIZE

All of the techniques discussed in this section will give you an indication of whether the difference between your groups is statistically significant (i.e. not likely to have occurred by chance). It is typically a moment of great excitement for most researchers and students when they find their results are significant! However, there is much more to research than just obtaining statistical significance. What the probability values do not tell you is the degree to which the two variables are associated with one another. With large samples, even very small differences between groups can become statistically significant. This does not mean that the difference has any practical or theoretical significance.

There is a strong movement in some literature areas away from the traditional null-hypothesis significance testing procedure (NHSTP), which utilises the p value to determine statistical significance. For example, in 2015 the journal *Basic and Applied Social Psychology* (BASP) published an editorial declaring that the NHSTP approach 'is invalid', and that 'from now on BASP is banning the NHSTP'. It is important that you check with journals in your own literature area to find out the approach that is recommended.

One way that you can assess the importance of your finding is to calculate the effect size (also known as 'strength of association'). This is a set of statistics that indicates the relative magnitude of the differences between means, or the amount of the total variance in the dependent variable that is predictable from knowledge of the levels of the independent variable (Tabachnick & Fidell 2013, p. 54). In most literature areas it is compulsory that you report the effect size statistics applicable to any statistical analyses conducted.

There are several different effect size statistics. The most commonly used to compare groups are partial eta squared and Cohen's *d*. IBM SPSS Statistics calculates partial eta squared for you as part of the output from some techniques (e.g. analysis of variance). It does not provide effect size statistics for t-tests, but you can use the information provided in IBM SPSS Statistics to calculate whichever effect size statistic you need.

Partial eta squared effect size statistics indicate the proportion of variance of the dependent variable that is explained by the independent variable. Values can range from 0 to 1. *Cohen's* d, on the other hand, presents difference between groups in terms of standard deviation units. Be careful not to get the different effect size statistics confused when interpreting the strength of the association. To interpret the strength of the different effect size statistics, the following guidelines were proposed by Cohen (1988, p. 22) when assessing research involving the comparison of different groups. Although Cohen specified guidelines for eta squared, they can be used to interpret the strength of partial eta squared. Partial eta squared involves a slightly different formula, using a different denominator from eta squared. For further information, see Tabachnick and Fidell (2013, p. 55).

Size	Eta squared (% of variance explained)	Cohen's *d* (standard deviation units)
Small	.01 or 1%	.2
Medium	.06 or 6%	.5
Large	.138 or 13.8%	.8

Please note that Cohen gives different guidelines for correlational designs (these are covered previously, in Part Four). The values shown above are for group comparisons.

MISSING DATA

When you are doing research, particularly with human beings, it is very rare that you will obtain complete data from every case (unless of course you are using online surveys and require each item to be answered). It is important that you inspect your data file for missing data. Run **Descriptives** and find out what percentage of values is missing for each of your variables. If you find a variable with a lot of unexpected missing data, you need to ask yourself why. You should also consider whether your missing values are happening randomly or whether there is some systematic pattern (e.g. lots of women failing to answer the question about their age). IBM SPSS Statistics has a **Missing Value Analysis** procedure that may help find patterns in your missing values. For more information on dealing with missing data, see Tabachnick and Fidell (2013, Chapter 4). In their fourth chapter, Tabachnick and Fidell discuss the different types of missing data (MCAR: missing completely at random, MNAR: missing not at random). They also review different strategies that are available for dealing with missing data: comparing mean substitution, regression, expectation maximisation (EM) methods and multiple imputation (currently considered the 'most respectable method of dealing with missing data'; p. 72).

You also need to consider how you will deal with missing values when you come to do your specific statistical analyses. The **Options** button in many of the IBM SPSS Statistics statistical procedures offers you choices for how you want the program to deal with missing data. It is important that you choose carefully, as it can have dramatic effects on your results. This is particularly important if you are including a list of variables and repeating the same analysis for all variables (e.g. correlations among a group of variables, t-tests for a series of dependent variables). The options that are available are:

➢ The **Exclude cases listwise** option includes cases (persons) in the analysis only if it has full data on *all of the variables* listed in your **Variables** box for that case. A case will be totally excluded from all the analyses if it is missing even one piece of information. This can severely, and unnecessarily, limit your sample size.

➢ The **Exclude cases pairwise** (sometimes shown as **Exclude cases analysis by analysis**) option, however, excludes the cases (persons) only if they are missing the data required for the specific analysis. They will still be included in any of the analyses for which they have the necessary information.

➢ The **Replace with mean** option, which is available in some IBM SPSS Statistics procedures, calculates the mean value for the variable and gives every missing case this value. This option should not be used as it can severely distort the results of your analysis, particularly if you have a lot of missing values.

Always press the **Options** button for any statistical procedure you conduct and check which of these options is ticked (the default option varies across procedures). I would recommend that you use pairwise exclusion of missing data, unless you have a pressing reason to do otherwise. The only situation where you might need to use listwise exclusion is when you want to refer only to a subset of cases that provided a full set of results.

Strange-looking numbers

In your output, you may come across some strange-looking numbers that take the form '1.24E-02'. These are small values presented in scientific notation. To prevent this happening, choose **Edit** from the main menu bar, select **Options**, and make sure there is a tick in the box **No scientific notation for small numbers in tables** on the **General** tab.

16

Non-parametric statistics

In statistics books you will often see reference to two different types of statistical techniques: parametric and non-parametric. What is the difference between these two sets of techniques? Why is the distinction important? The word 'parametric' comes from 'parameter', or characteristic of a population. The parametric tests (e.g. t-tests, analysis of variance) make assumptions about the population from which the sample has been drawn. This often includes assumptions about the shape of the population distribution (e.g. normally distributed). Non-parametric techniques, on the other hand, do not have such stringent requirements and do not make assumptions about the underlying population distribution (which is why they are sometimes referred to as 'distribution-free tests').

Despite being less fussy, non-parametric statistics do have their disadvantages. They tend to be less sensitive than their more powerful parametric cousins and may therefore fail to detect differences between groups that actually exist. If you have the right sorts of data, it is always better to use a parametric technique if you can. So, under what circumstances might you want or need to use non-parametric techniques?

Non-parametric techniques are ideal for use when you have data that are measured on nominal (categorical) and ordinal (ranked) scales. They are also useful when you have very small samples and when your data do not meet the stringent assumptions of the parametric techniques. Although IBM SPSS Statistics provides a wide variety of non-parametric techniques, only the main ones are discussed in this chapter. The topics covered in this chapter are presented below, along with their parametric alternatives (covered in later chapters).

SUMMARY OF TECHNIQUES COVERED IN THIS CHAPTER

Non-parametric technique	Parametric alternative
Chi-Square Test for Goodness of Fit	None
Chi-Square Test for Independence	None
McNemar's Test	None
Cochran's Q Test	None
Kappa Measure of Agreement	None
Mann-Whitney U Test	Independent-samples t-test (Chapter 17)
Wilcoxon Signed Rank Test	Paired-samples t-test (Chapter 17)
Kruskal-Wallis Test	One-way between-groups ANOVA (Chapter 18)
Friedman Test	One-way repeated measures ANOVA (Chapter 18)

The techniques in this chapter are designed primarily for comparing groups. The non-parametric alternative for correlation (Spearman *rho*) is presented in Chapter 11.

ASSUMPTIONS

Although the non-parametric techniques have less stringent assumptions, there are two general assumptions that should be checked.

➤ *Random samples.*
➤ *Independent observations:* Each person or case can be counted only once, they cannot appear in more than one category or group, and the data from one subject cannot influence the data from another. The exception to this is the repeated measures techniques (McNemar's Test, Wilcoxon Signed Rank Test, Friedman Test), where the same participants are retested on different occasions or under different conditions.

Some of the techniques discussed in this chapter have additional assumptions that should be checked. These specific assumptions are discussed in the relevant sections.

Throughout this chapter, the various non-parametric techniques are illustrated using examples from a set of data files on the website that accompanies this book. Full details of these data files are provided in the Appendix. If you wish to follow along with the steps detailed in each of these examples, you will need to start IBM SPSS Statistics and open the appropriate data file. This chapter provides only a brief summary of non-parametric techniques. For further reading, see Daniel (1990), Gravetter and Wallnau (2012), Siegel and Castellan (1988) and Peat (2001).

CHI-SQUARE

There are several different tests based on the chi-square statistic, all of which involve categorical data. For a review of chi-square, see Gravetter and Wallnau (2012).

Chi-Square Test for Goodness of Fit

This test, which is also referred to as the 'one-sample chi-square', is used to compare the proportion of cases from a sample with hypothesised values or the proportion obtained previously from a comparison population. All that is needed in the data file is one categorical variable and a specific proportion against which you wish to test the observed frequencies. This may test that there is no difference in the proportion in each category (50/50%), or a specific proportion obtained from a previous study.

Example of research question: Is the number of smokers in the **survey.sav** data file different from that reported in the literature from a previous, larger nationwide study (20%)?

What you need:
➤ one categorical variable with two or more categories: smoker (yes/no)
➤ a hypothesised proportion (20% smokers, 80% non-smokers, or .2/.8).

Procedure for Chi-Square Test for Goodness of Fit

To follow along with this example, open the **survey.sav** data file.

1. From the menu at the top of the screen, click on **Analyze**, then select **Nonparametric Tests**, then **Legacy Dialogs** and then **Chi-Square**.
2. Click on the categorical variable (smoker) and click on the arrow to move it into the **Test Variable List** box. In the **Expected Values** section, click on the **Values** option. In the **Values** box, you need to type in two values.
   ➤ Type in the first value (.2), which corresponds with the expected proportion for the first coded value for the variable (1 = yes, smoker). Click on **Add**.
   ➤ Type in the second value (.8), which is the expected proportion for the second coded value (2 = no, non-smoker). Click on Add. If your variable has more than two possible values, you would need to type in as many proportions as appropriate.
3. Click on **OK** (or on **Paste** to save to **Syntax Editor**).

The syntax from this procedure is:

```
NPAR TESTS
  /CHISQUARE=smoke
  /EXPECTED=.2 .8
  /MISSING ANALYSIS.
```

The output generated from this procedure is shown below.

smoke smoker

	Observed N	Expected N	Residual
1 YES	85	87.2	-2.2
2 NO	351	348.8	2.2
Total	436		

Test Statistics

	smoke smoker
Chi-Square	.069[a]
df	1
Asymp. Sig.	.792

a. 0 cells (0.0%) have expected frequencies less than 5. The minimum expected cell frequency is 87.2.

Interpretation of output from Chi-Square Test for Goodness of Fit

In the first table the observed frequencies from the current data file are presented, showing that 85 out of the 436 (19.5%) were smokers. The expected N from the previously reported proportion specified (20%) is given. In this case, 87 cases were expected, while 85 were observed.

The **Test Statistics** table reports the results of the **Chi-Square Test**, which compares the expected and observed values. In this case, the discrepancy is very small and not statistically significant (**Asymp. Sig.** = .79).

Reporting the results

In the results you need to report the chi-square value, the degrees of freedom (shown as *df* in the output) and the *p* value (shown as **Asymp. Sig.**).

A Chi-Square Goodness of Fit test indicates there was no significant difference in the proportion of smokers identified in the current sample (19.5%) as compared with the value of 20% that was obtained in a previous nationwide study, χ^2 (1, n = 436) = .07, p = .79.

Chi-Square Test for Independence

This test is used when you wish to explore the relationship between *two* categorical variables. Each of these variables can have two or more categories. This test compares the observed frequencies or proportions of cases that occur in each of the categories with the values that would be expected if there was no association between the two variables being measured. It is based on a crosstabulation table, with cases classified according to the categories in each variable (e.g. male/female, smoker/non-smoker).

When a 2 × 2 table (two categories in each variable) is encountered by IBM SPSS Statistics, the output from chi-square includes an additional correction value (Yates' Correction for Continuity). This is designed to compensate for what some writers feel is an overestimate of the chi-square value when used with a 2 × 2 table.

In the following procedure, I demonstrate chi-square with a 2 × 2 design using the **survey.sav** data file. If your study involves variables with more than two categories (e.g. 2 × 3, 4 × 4), you will notice some slight differences in the output.

Examples of research questions: There are different ways questions can be phrased: Is there an association between gender and smoking behaviour? Are males more likely to be smokers than females? Is the proportion of males that smoke the same as the proportion of females?

What you need: Two categorical variables, with two or more categories in each (e.g. gender: male/female, smoker: yes/no).

Additional assumptions: The lowest expected frequency in any cell should be 5 or more. Some authors suggest less stringent criteria: at least 80 per cent of cells should have expected frequencies of 5 or more. If you have a 2 × 2 table, it is recommended that the expected frequency be at least 10. If you have a 2 × 2 table that violates this assumption, you should consider reporting Fisher's Exact Probability Test instead. This is generated automatically by IBM SPSS Statistics and is provided as part of the output from chi-square.

Procedure for Chi-Square Test for Independence

To follow along with this example, open the **survey.sav** data file.

1. From the menu at the top of the screen, click on **Analyze**, then **Descriptive Statistics**, and then **Crosstabs**.
2. Click on one of your variables (e.g. sex) to be your row variable and click on the arrow to move it into the box marked **Row(s)**.
3. Click on the other variable to be your column variable (e.g. smoker) and click on the arrow to move it into the box marked **Column(s)**.
4. Click on the **Statistics** button. Tick **Chi-square** and **Phi and Cramer's V**. Click on **Continue**.

5. Click on the **Cells** button.
    ➤ In the Counts box, make sure there is a tick for Observed.
    ➤ In the Percentage section, click on the Row box.
    ➤ In the Residuals section click on Adjusted standardized.
6. Click on **Continue** and then **OK** (or on **Paste** to save to **Syntax Editor**).

The syntax from this procedure is:

```
CROSSTABS
 /TABLES=sex BY smoke
 /FORMAT= AVALUE TABLES
 /STATISTICS=CHISQ PHI
 /CELLS= COUNT ROW ASRESID
 /COUNT ROUND CELL.
```

Selected output generated from this procedure for a 2 × 2 table is shown below. If your variables have more than two categories the printout will look a little different, but the key information that you need to identify in the output is still the same.

sex sex * smoke smoker Crosstabulation

| | | | smoke smoker | | |
			1 YES	2 NO	Total
sex sex	1 MALES	Count	33	151	184
		% within sex sex	17.9%	82.1%	100.0%
		Adjusted Residual	-.7	.7	
	2 FEMALES	Count	52	200	252
		% within sex sex	20.6%	79.4%	100.0%
		Adjusted Residual	.7	-.7	
Total		Count	85	351	436
		% within sex sex	19.5%	80.5%	100.0%

Chi-Square Tests

	Value	df	Asymptotic Significance (2-sided)	Exact Sig. (2-sided)	Exact Sig. (1-sided)
Pearson Chi-Square	.494[a]	1	.482		
Continuity Correction[b]	.337	1	.562		
Likelihood Ratio	.497	1	.481		
Fisher's Exact Test				.541	.282
Linear-by-Linear Asscciation	.493	1	.483		
N of Valid Cases	436				

a. 0 cells (0.0%) have expected count less than 5. The minimum expected count is 35.87.

b. Computed only for a 2x2 table

Symmetric Measures

		Value	Approximate Significance
Nominal by Nominal	Phi	-.034	.482
	Cramer's V	.034	.482
N of Valid Cases		436	

Interpretation of output from Chi-Square Test for Independence

Assumptions

The first thing you should check is whether you have violated one of the assumptions of chi-square concerning the minimum expected cell frequency, which should be 5 or greater (or at least 80% of cells with expected frequencies of 5 or more). This information is given in a table note below the **Chi-Square Tests** table. The table note in this example indicates that 0 cells (.0%) have an expected count less than 5. This means that we have not violated the assumption, as all our expected cell sizes are greater than 5 (in our case, greater than 35.87).

Crosstabulation

To find what percentage of each sex are smokers, you need to examine the summary information provided in the table labelled **sex*smoker Crosstabulation**. This table may appear a little confusing to start with, with a fair bit of information presented in each cell. To find out what percentage of males are smokers you need to read across the page in the first row, which refers to males. In this case, we check the values next to **% within sex**. For this example 17.9 per cent of males were smokers, while 82.1 per cent were non-smokers. For females, 20.6 per cent were smokers and 79.4 per cent non-smokers. To ensure that you are reading the correct values, make sure that the two percentages within each sex add up to 100 per cent.

If we wanted to know what percentage of the sample as a whole smoked we would move down to the total row, which summarises across both sexes. In this case, we would inspect the values next to **% Within Sex**. According to these results, 19.5 per cent of the sample smoked, with 80.5 per cent being non-smokers.

In two of the rows you can see an extra value labelled **Adjusted Residual**. This is not relevant in the current example, which involves a 2 × 2 table, but is useful in larger tables (e.g. 2 × 3 tables). In that situation values of more than 2 indicate that the number of cases in the cell is significantly larger than expected, and values less than −2 suggest the number of cases is less than expected. This acts like a post-hoc test, helping you to identify which groups are different from the others.

Chi-square tests

The main value that you are interested in from the output is the **Pearson Chi-Square** value, which is presented in the **Chi-Square Tests** table. If you have a 2 × 2 table (i.e. each variable has only two categories), however, you should use the value in the second row (**Continuity Correction**). This is Yates' Correction for Continuity (which compensates for the overestimate of the chi-square value when used with a 2 × 2 table). In the example presented above the corrected value is .337, with an associated significance level of .562—this is presented in the column labelled **Asymptotic Significance** (2-sided). To be significant, the Sig. value needs to be .05 or smaller. In this case the value of .56 is *larger* than the alpha value of .05, so we can conclude that our result is *not* significant. This means that the proportion of males who smoke is not significantly different from the proportion of females who smoke. There appears to be no association between smoking status and gender.

Effect size

There are several effect size statistics available in the **Crosstabs** procedure. For 2 × 2 tables the most commonly used one is the **phi coefficient**, which is a correlation coefficient and can range from 0 to 1, with higher values indicating a stronger association between the two variables. In this example the **phi coefficient** value (shown in the table **Symmetric Measures**) is −.034, which is considered a very small effect using Cohen's (1988) criteria of .1 for small effect, .3 for medium effect and .5 for large effect.

For tables larger than 2 × 2 the value to report is **Cramer's V**, which takes into account the degrees of freedom. Slightly different criteria are recommended for judging the size of the effect for larger tables. To determine which criteria to use, first subtract 1 from the number of categories in your row variable (R − 1), and then subtract 1 from the number of categories in your column variable (C − 1). Pick whichever of these values is smaller.

➤ For R − 1 or C − 1 equal to 1 (two categories): small = .01, medium = .30, large = .50
➤ For either R − 1 or C − 1 equal to 2 (three categories): small = .07, medium = .21, large = .35
➤ For either R − 1 or C − 1 equal to 3 (four categories): small = .06, medium = .17, large = .29.

For more information on the phi coefficient and Cramer's V, see Gravetter and Wallnau (2012).

The results of this analysis could be presented as follows:

A Chi-Square Test for Independence (with Yates' Continuity Correction) indicated no significant association between gender and smoking status, χ^2 (1, n = 436) = .34, p = .56, phi = −.03.

McNEMAR'S TEST

When you have paired or repeated measures designs (e.g. pre-test/post-test), you cannot use the usual chi-square test. Instead, you need to use McNemar's Test. You need two variables, the first recorded at Time 1 (e.g. prior to an intervention) and the second recorded at Time 2 (e.g. after an intervention). Both these variables are categorical (with only two response options—see the Note at the end of this section) and assess the same information. In the health and medical area this might be the presence or absence of some health condition (0 = absent, 1 = present), while in a political context it might be the intention to vote for a particular candidate (0 = no, 1 = yes), before and after a campaign speech.

In the following example, using the **experim.sav** data file I compare the proportion of people who are diagnosed with clinical depression prior to and following an intervention designed to help with statistics anxiety.

Example of research question: Is there a change in the proportion of the sample diagnosed with clinical depression prior to, and following, the intervention?

What you need: Two categorical variables measuring the same characteristic (e.g. presence or absence of the characteristic: 0 = no, 1 = yes) collected from each participant at different time points (e.g. prior to/following an intervention).

Before you start this procedure, go to the **Edit** menu at the top of your screen and click on **Options**. Select the **Output** tab, and in the **Output Display** section select **Pivot tables and charts**. This ensures that the results display correctly.

Procedure for McNemar's Test

To follow along with this example, open the **experim.sav** data file.

1. From the menu at the top of the screen click on **Analyze**, then **Nonparametric Tests** and then on **Related Samples**.
2. Click on **Customize analysis** in the section **What is your objective?**
3. Click on the **Fields** tab. Choose the two variables (Time 1 Clinical Depress, Time 2 Clinical Depress) and click on the arrow button to move them into the **Test Fields** box.
4. Click on the **Settings** tab and choose **Customize tests**.
5. Click on the box to select **McNemar's test (2 samples)**.
6. Click on the **Run** button (or on **Paste** to save to the **Syntax Editor**).

The syntax from this procedure is:

```
NPTESTS
  /RELATED TEST(DepT1gp2 DepT2Gp2) MCNEMAR(SUCCESS=FIRST)
  /MISSING SCOPE=ANALYSIS USERMISSING=EXCLUDE
  /CRITERIA ALPHA=0.05  CILEVEL=95.
```

Selected sections from the output of McNemar's Test are shown below.

Time 1 Clinical Depress, Time 2 Clinical Depress

Related-Samples McNemar Change Test Summary

Total N	30
Test Statistic	.250[a]
Degree Of Freedom	1
Asymptotic Sig.(2-sided test)	.617
Exact Sig.(2-sided test)	.625

a. The exact p-value is computed based on the binomial distribution because there are 25 or fewer records.

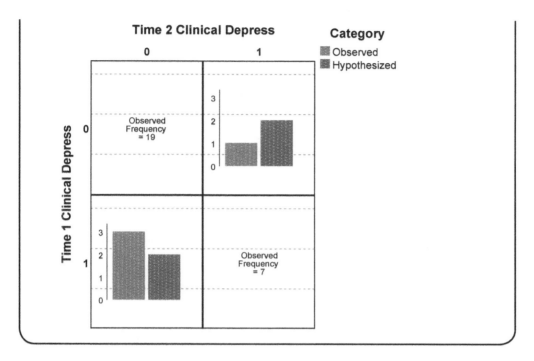

Interpretation of output from McNemar's Test

As you can see from the output the *p* value (shown as Sig.) is .625, which is not less than *p* < .05; therefore, we cannot reject the null hypothesis. This suggests that there is no significant change in the proportion of participants diagnosed as clinically depressed following the program when compared with the proportion prior to the program.

Note: The McNemar test described above is only applicable if you have two categories of response at each time point (e.g. absent/present, yes/no). However, you can still use this procedure if you have three or more categories (e.g. low/moderate/high). If IBM SPSS Statistics detects three or more categories in each variable then it automatically generates the results of the McNemar-Bowker Test of Symmetry.

COCHRAN'S *Q* TEST

McNemar's Test, described in the previous section, is suitable if you have only two time points. If you have three or more time points, you will need to use Cochran's *Q* Test.

Example of research question: Is there a change in the proportion of participants diagnosed with clinical depression across the three time points (a) prior to the program, (b) following the program and (c) 3 months post-program?

232 Statistical techniques to compare groups

What you need: Three categorical variables measuring the same characteristic (e.g. presence or absence of the characteristic: 0 = no, 1 = yes) collected from each participant at different time points.

Before you start this procedure, go to the **Edit** menu at the top of your screen and click on **Options.** Select the **Output** tab and in the **Output Display** section select **Pivot tables and charts.** This ensures that the results display correctly.

Procedure for Cochran's *Q* Test

To follow along with this example, open the **experim.sav** data file.

1. From the menu at the top of the screen click on **Analyze**, then **Nonparametric Tests** and then on **Related Samples**.
2. On the **Objective** tab click on **Customize analysis** in the section **What is your objective?**
3. Click on the **Fields** tab. Choose the three variables (Time 1 Clinical Depress, Time 2 Clinical Depress, Time 3 Clinical Depress) and click on the arrow button to move them into the **Test Fields** box.
4. Click on the **Settings** tab and choose **Customize tests**.
5. Click on the box **Cochran's Q (k samples)**. In the section **Multiple comparisons** make sure that **All pairwise** is selected. This will provide you with the post-hoc tests comparing each time point with all others.
6. Click on the **Run** button (or on **Paste** to save to the **Syntax Editor**).

The syntax from this procedure is:

```
NPTESTS
 /RELATED TEST(DepT1gp2 DepT2Gp2 DepT3gp2) COCHRAN(SUCCESS=FIRST
COMPARE=PAIRWISE)
 /MISSING SCOPE=ANALYSIS USERMISSING=EXCLUDE
 /CRITERIA ALPHA=0.05  CILEVEL=95.
```

The output is shown below.

Related-Samples Cochran's Q Test Summary

Total N	30
Test Statistic	8.000
Degree Of Freedom	2
Asymptotic Sig.(2-sided test)	.018

Pairwise Comparisons

Sample 1-Sample 2	Test Statistic	Std. Error	Std. Test Statistic	Sig.	Adj. Sig.[a]
DepT1gp2 Time 1 Clinical Depress-DepT2Gp2 Time 2 Clinical Depress	-.067	.072	-.926	.355	1.000
DepT1gp2 Time 1 Clinical Depress-DepT3gp2 Time 3 Clinical Depress	-.200	.072	-2.777	.005	.016
DepT2Gp2 Time 2 Clinical Depress-DepT3gp2 Time 3 Clinical Depress	-.133	.072	-1.852	.064	.192

Each row tests the null hypothesis that the Sample 1 and Sample 2 distributions are the same. Asymptotic significances (2-sided tests) are displayed. The significance level is .05.

a. Significance values have been adjusted by the Bonferroni correction for multiple tests.

Interpretation of output from Cochran's Q Test

To determine if there was a significant change in the proportion of participants who were diagnosed with clinical depression across the three time points you need to examine the value listed as **Asymptotic Sig** in the first table (2-Sided Test) **Related-Samples Cochran's Q Test Summary**. The value in this example is .018, which is less than the cut-point of $p < .05$; therefore, the result is statistically significant.

If you obtain a statistically significant result the next step is to check the **Pairwise Comparisons** shown in the second table. This is a comparison of each time point with the others. Scan down the column headed **Sig.** and see if any of the values are less than .05. In this example the only value to reach significance is between Time 1 and Time 3 ($p = .005$). The other two comparisons (Time 1 with Time 2, Time 2 with Time 3) were not significant.

KAPPA MEASURE OF AGREEMENT

One of the other statistics for categorical data available within the **Crosstabs** procedure is the Kappa Measure of Agreement. This is commonly used in the medical literature to assess inter-rater agreement (e.g. diagnosis from two different clinicians) or the consistency of two different diagnostic tests (newly developed test versus an established test or gold standard).

Kappa is an estimate of the proportion of agreement between the two raters (or instruments) that takes into account the amount of agreement that could have occurred by chance. Unfortunately, the value obtained for kappa is affected by the prevalence of the positive value (i.e. the presence of the characteristic of interest). This means that for studies where the event of interest is rare, the kappa statistic may be very low, despite high levels of agreement overall. If you find yourself in this situation you might want to read further. I suggest Viera and Garrett (2005), Feinstein and Cicchetti (1990) and Cicchetti and Feinstein (1990). These authors suggest that when there is a low prevalence of the characteristic of interest you consider reporting additional statistics (e.g. positive and negative agreement). There is a great (free!) spreadsheet that you can download that will do these calculations (and lots of others) for you at www.biostats.com.au/DAG_Stat.

Example of research question: How consistent are the diagnostic classifications of the Edinburgh Postnatal Depression Scale and the Depression scale of the Depression, Anxiety and Stress Scales (DASS)?

What you need: Two categorical variables with an equal number of categories (e.g. diagnostic classification from Rater 1 or Test 1: 0 = not depressed, 1 = depressed; and the diagnostic classification of the same person from Rater 2 or Test 2).

Assumptions: Assumes equal number of categories from Rater/Test 1 and Rater/Test 2.

Parametric alternative: None.

In the example below, we test the degree of agreement between two measures of depression in a sample of postnatal women. In the **depress.sav** file, each woman's scores on the Edinburgh Postnatal Depression Scale (EPDS; Cox, Holden & Sagovsky 1987) and the DASS Depression scale (DASS-Dep; Lovibond & Lovibond 1995) were classified according to the recommended cut-points for each scale. This resulted in two variables, with scores of 0 = not depressed and 1 = depressed. The aim here was to see if the women identified with depression on the EPDS were also classified as depressed on the DASS Depression Scale (DASS-Dep).

Procedure for Kappa Measure of Agreement

To follow along with this example, open the **depress.sav** data file.

1. From the menu at the top of the screen, click on **Analyze**, then **Descriptive Statistics**, and then **Crosstabs**.
2. Click on one of your variables (e.g. DASS Depress gps: DASSdepgp2) to be your row variable and click on the arrow to move it into the box marked **Row(s)**.
3. Click on the other variable (e.g. EPDS gps: EPDSgp2) to be your column variable and click on the arrow to move it into the box marked **Column(s)**.

4. Click on the **Statistics** button. Choose **Kappa**. Click on **Continue**.
5. Click on the **Cells** button.
6. In the **Counts** box, make sure that **Observed** is ticked.
7. In the **Percentage** section, click on **Column**. Click on **Continue** and then **OK** (or on **Paste** to save to **Syntax Editor**).

The syntax from this procedure is:

```
CROSSTABS
/TABLES=DASSdepgp2 BY EPDSgp2
/FORMAT= AVALUE TABLES
/STATISTICS=KAPPA
/CELLS= COUNT COLUMN
/COUNT ROUND CELL .
```

The output generated is shown below.

DASSdepgp2 DASS depress gps * EPDSgp2 EPDS gps Crosstabulation

| | | | EPDSgp2 EPDS gps | | |
			0 not depressed	1 likely depressed	Total
DASSdepgp2 DASS depress gps	0 not depressed	Count	225	34	259
		% within EPDSgp2 EPDS gps	94.1%	42.5%	81.2%
	1 mild to severe depression	Count	14	46	60
		% within EPDSgp2 EPDS gps	5.9%	57.5%	18.8%
Total		Count	239	80	319
		% within EPDSgp2 EPDS gps	100.0%	100.0%	100%

Symmetric Measures

		Value	Asymptotic Standard Error[a]	Approximate T[b]	Approximate Significance
Measure of Agreement	Kappa	.563	.055	10.231	.000
N of Valid Cases		319			

a. Not assuming the null hypothesis.
b. Using the asymptotic standard error assuming the null hypothesis.

Interpretation of output from Kappa Measure of Agreement

The main piece of information we are interested in is the table **Symmetric Measures**, which shows that the Kappa Measure of Agreement value is .56, with a significance of $p < .0005$. According to Peat (2001, p. 228), a value of .5 for Kappa represents moderate agreement, above .7 represents good agreement, and above .8 represents very good agreement. So, in this example the level of agreement between the classification of cases as depressed using the EPDS and the DASS-Dep is good.

Sensitivity and specificity

The frequencies and percentages provided in the **Crosstabulation** table can also be used to calculate the **sensitivity** and **specificity** of a measure or test. This is commonly used in the medical literature to assess the accuracy of a diagnostic test in detecting the presence or absence of disease or to assess the accuracy of a new test against some existing gold standard. **Sensitivity** reflects the proportion of cases with the disease or condition that were correctly diagnosed, while the **specificity** represents the proportion of cases without the condition that were correctly classified. In this example, we can test the consistency of the classification of the DASS-Dep against the commonly used screening test, the EPDS.

The **sensitivity** of the DASS-Dep can be determined by reading down the second column of the table. Out of the 80 cases identified as depressed by the EPDS (our acting gold standard), 46 were also classified depressed on the DASS-Dep. This represents a sensitivity value of 57.5 per cent (46/80).

The **specificity** is determined by reading down the first column of people who were classified as *not* depressed by the EPDS. The DASS-Dep correctly classified 225 out of the 239, representing a specificity rate of 94.1 per cent. The two scales are quite consistent in terms of the cases classified as not depressed; however, there is some inconsistency between the cases that each scale considers depressed. For further details of this study see the Appendix, and for a published article using this data go to www.biomedcentral.com/1471-244X/6/12. Click on pdf on the right-hand side to download the file.

MANN-WHITNEY *U* TEST

The Mann-Whitney *U* Test is used to test for differences between two independent groups on a continuous measure. For example, do males and females differ in terms of their self-esteem? This test is the non-parametric alternative to the t-test for independent samples. Instead of comparing means of the two groups, as in the case of the t-test, the Mann-Whitney *U* Test compares medians. It converts the scores on the continuous variable to ranks across the two groups. It then evaluates whether the ranks for the two groups differ significantly. As the scores are converted to ranks, the actual distribution of the scores does not matter.

Examples of research questions: Do males and females differ in terms of their levels of self-esteem? Do males have higher levels of self-esteem than females?

What you need:
➢ one categorical variable with two groups (e.g. sex)
➢ one continuous variable (e.g. total self-esteem).

Assumptions: See general assumptions for non-parametric techniques presented at the beginning of this chapter.

Parametric alternative: Independent-samples t-test.

Before you start this procedure, go to the **Edit** menu at the top of your screen and click on **Options**. Select the **Output** tab and in the **Output Display** section select **Pivot tables and charts**. This ensures that the results display correctly.

Procedure for Mann-Whitney *U* Test
To follow along with this example, open the **survey.sav** data file.
1. From the menu at the top of the screen click on **Analyze**, then **Nonparametric Tests** and then on **Independent Samples**.
2. In the **Objective** tab click on **Customize analysis** in the section **What is your objective?**
3. Click on the **Fields** tab.
4. Click on your categorical (independent) variable (e.g. sex) and move it into the **Groups** box.
5. Click on your continuous (dependent) variable (e.g. Total Self esteem: tslfest) and move it into the **Test Fields** box.
6. Click on the **Settings** tab and select **Customize tests**. Click on **Mann-Whitney U (2 samples)**.
7. Click on the **Run** button (or on **Paste** to save to the **Syntax Editor**).

The syntax from this procedure is:

```
NPTESTS
  /INDEPENDENT TEST (tslfest) GROUP (sex) MANN_WHITNEY
  /MISSING SCOPE=ANALYSIS USERMISSING=EXCLUDE
  /CRITERIA ALPHA=0.05  CILEVEL=95.
```

Selected output is shown below.

Hypothesis Test Summary

	Null Hypothesis	Test	Sig.	Decision
1	The distribution of tslfest Total Self esteem is the same across categories of sex sex.	Independent-Samples Mann-Whitney U Test	.220	Retain the null hypothesis.

Asymptotic significances are displayed. The significance level is .050.

Total Self esteem across sex

Independent-Samples Mann-Whitney U Test Summary

Total N	436
Mann-Whitney U	21594.000
Wilcoxon W	53472.000
Test Statistic	21594.000
Standard Error	1295.927
Standardized Test Statistic	-1.227
Asymptotic Sig.(2-sided test)	.220

Independent-Samples Mann-Whitney U Test

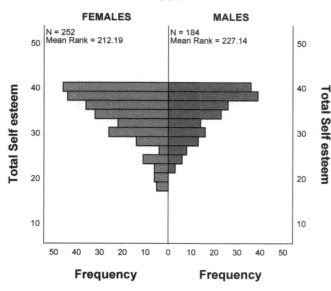

Interpretation of output from Mann-Whitney *U* Test

The first table (**Hypothesis Test Summary**) gives you a quick summary of the results of the test. In this case the **Sig**. value (which is our *p* value) is .220. This is not less than .05; therefore, the result is not significant. The statistics that you need to report in your results section are shown in the second table (**Independent-Samples Mann-Whitney *U* Test Summary**). The value reported varies across different disciplines; however, most report the **Mann-Whitney *U*** value (21594) and/or the **Standardized Test Statistic** (this is reported as a *z* score = -1.227).

If you find a statistically significant difference between your groups, you also need to describe the direction of the difference (which group is higher). You can determine this from the **Mean Rank** for each group, shown in the top corner of the bar graphs. When presenting your results, however, it would be better to report the median values for each group. Unfortunately, this is not available from this procedure—one more step is needed.

Procedure for obtaining median scores for each group

1. From the menu at the top of the screen, click on **Analyze**, then select **Compare means** and choose **Means**.
2. Click on your continuous variable (e.g. total self-esteem: tslfest) and move it into the **Dependent List** box.
3. Click on your categorical variable (e.g. sex) and move it into the **Independent List** box.
4. Click on the **Options** button. Click on **Median** in the **Statistics** section and move it into the **Cell Statistics** box. Click on **Mean** and **Standard Deviation** and remove them from the **Cell Statistics** box.
5. Click on **Continue**.
6. Click on OK (or on **Paste** to save to **Syntax Editor**).

The syntax from this procedure is:

```
MEANS TABLES=tslfest BY sex
  /CELLS=COUNT MEDIAN.
```

The output generated is shown below.

tslfest Total Self esteem

sex sex	N	Median
1 MALES	184	35.00
2 FEMALES	252	34.50
Total	436	35.00

Effect size

IBM SPSS Statistics does not provide an effect size statistic for the Mann-Whitney U Test; however, you can calculate an approximate value of r using the z value (shown as the **Standardized Test Statistic**) which is available in the **Test Summary** table: $r = z$ / square root of N (where N = total number of cases). In this example, $z = -1.23$ and $N = 436$; therefore, the r value is .06. This would be considered a very small effect size using Cohen (1988) criteria of .1 = small effect, .3 = medium effect, .5 = large effect.

The results of this analysis could be presented as:

A Mann-Whitney U Test revealed no significant difference in the self-esteem levels of males (Md = 35, n =184) and females (Md = 34.5, n = 252), U = 21594, z = –1.23, p = .22, r = .06.

WILCOXON SIGNED RANK TEST

The Wilcoxon Signed Rank Test (also referred to as the Wilcoxon Matched Pairs Signed Ranks Test) is designed for use with repeated measures—that is, when your participants are measured on two occasions, or under two different conditions. It is the non-parametric alternative to the repeated measures t-test, but, instead of comparing means, the Wilcoxon converts scores to ranks and compares them at Time 1 and at Time 2. The Wilcoxon can also be used in situations involving a matched subject design, where participants are matched on specific criteria.

To illustrate the use of this technique, I have used data from the **experim.sav** file included on the website accompanying this book (see p. ix and the Appendix for details of the study). In this example, I compare the scores on a Fear of Statistics Test administered before and after an intervention designed to help students cope with a statistics course.

Example of research question: Is there a change in the scores on the Fear of Statistics Test from Time 1 to Time 2?

What you need: One group of participants measured on the same continuous scale or measured on two different occasions. The variables involved are scores at Time 1 or Condition 1, and scores at Time 2 or Condition 2.

Assumptions: See general assumptions for non-parametric techniques presented at the beginning of this chapter.

Parametric alternative: Paired-samples t-test.

Before you start this procedure go to the **Edit** menu at the top of your screen and click on **Options**. Select the **Output** tab and in the **Output Display** section select **Pivot tables and charts**. This ensures that the results display correctly.

Procedure for Wilcoxon Signed Rank Test

To follow along with this example, open the **experim.sav** data file.

1. From the menu at the top of the screen, click on **Analyze**, then select **Nonparametric Tests**, and then **Related Samples**.
2. In the **Objective** tab click on **Customize analysis**.
3. Click on the **Fields** tab.
4. Select the variables that represent scores from Time 1 and Time 2 (e.g. fear of stats time1: fost1, fear of stats time2: fost2). Click on the arrow to move these into the **Test Fields** box.
6. Click on the **Settings** tab and select **Customize tests**. Click on **Wilcoxon matched-pair signed-rank (2 samples)**.
7. Click on the **Run** button (or on **Paste** to save to the **Syntax Editor**).

The syntax from this procedure is:

```
NPTESTS
 /RELATED TEST(fost1 fost2) WILCOXON
 /MISSING SCOPE=ANALYSIS USERMISSING=EXCLUDE
 /CRITERIA ALPHA=0.05  CILEVEL=95.
```

Selected output is displayed below.

Hypothesis Test Summary

	Null Hypothesis	Test	Sig.	Decision
1	The median of differences between fost1 fear of stats time1 and fost2 fear of stats time2 equals 0.	Related-Samples Wilcoxon Signed Rank Test	.000	Reject the null hypothesis.

Asymptotic significances are displayed. The significance level is .050.

Related-Samples Wilcoxon Signed Rank Test Summary

Total N	30
Test Statistic	26.000
Standard Error	45.811
Standardized Test Statistic	-4.180
Asymptotic Sig.(2-sided test)	.000

Interpretation of output from Wilcoxon Signed Rank Test

The first table (**Hypothesis Test Summary**) tells you that the *p* value (show in the output as **Sig.**) is .000 (which really means less than .0005). As this value is less than .05, we can conclude that there is a significant difference between scores on the Fear of Statistics Test at Time 1 and Time 2. The statistics you need to report are shown in the **Related-Samples Wilcoxon Signed Rank Test Summary table**. Typically, the **standardised test statistic** is reported as a *z*, which in this case is –4.18.

Effect size

The effect size for this test can be calculated using the same procedure as described for the Mann-Whitney *U* Test—that is, by dividing the *z* value by the square root of *N*. For this calculation you can ignore any negative sign out the front of the *z* value. In this situation, *N* is the number of observations over the two time points, not the number of cases. In this example, $z = 4.18$, $N = 60$ (cases × 2); therefore, $r = .54$, indicating a large effect size using Cohen (1988) criteria of .1 = small effect, .3 = medium effect, .5 = large effect.

In your write-up you should also report the median scores for both Time 1 and Time 2. These can be obtained by running **Frequencies**.

Procedure for obtaining median scores for each group

1. From the menu at the top of the screen click on **Analyze**, then select **Descriptive Statistics**, then slide across to select **Frequencies**.
2. Select the variables that represent scores from Time 1 and Time 2 (e.g. fear of stats time1: fost1, fear of stats time2: fost2). Click on the arrow to move these into the **Variable(s)** box.
3. Click on the box next to **Display frequency tables** to remove the tick.
4. Click on the **Statistics** button. Click on **Quartiles**.
5. Click on **Continue** and then **OK** (or on **Paste** to save to **Syntax Editor**).

```
FREQUENCIES VARIABLES=fost1 fost2
  /FORMAT=NOTABLE
  /NTILES=4
  /ORDER=ANALYSIS.
```

The output is displayed below.

Statistics

		fost1 fear of stats time1	fost2 fear of stats time2
N	Valid	30	30
	Missing	0	0
Percentiles	25	37.00	34.50
	50	40.00	38.00
	75	44.00	40.00

The results of this analysis could be presented as:

A Wilcoxon Signed Rank Test revealed a statistically significant reduction in fear of statistics following participation in the training program, $z = -4.18, n = 30, p < .001$, with a large effect size ($r = .54$). The median score on the Fear of Statistics Scale decreased from pre-program ($Md = 40$) to post-program ($Md = 38$).

KRUSKAL-WALLIS TEST

The Kruskal-Wallis Test (sometimes referred to as the Kruskal-Wallis H Test) is the non-parametric alternative to a one-way between-groups analysis of variance. It allows you to compare the scores on some continuous variable for *three or more groups*. It is similar in nature to the Mann-Whitney U Test presented *earlier in this chapter*, but it allows you to compare more than just two groups. Scores are converted to ranks and the mean rank for each group is compared. This is a between-groups analysis, so different people must be in each of the different groups.

Example of research question: Is there a difference in optimism levels across three age levels?

What you need:
➤ one categorical, independent variable with three or more categories (e.g. agegp3: 18–29, 30–44, 45+)
➤ one continuous, dependent variable (e.g. total optimism).

Assumptions: See general assumptions for non-parametric techniques presented at the beginning of this chapter.

Parametric alternative: One-way between-groups analysis of variance.

Before you start this procedure, go to the **Edit** menu at the top of your screen and click on **Options**. Select the **Output** tab, and in the **Output Display** section select **Pivot tables and charts**. This ensures that the results display correctly.

Procedure for Kruskal-Wallis Test

To follow along with this example, open the **survey.sav** data file.

1. From the menu at the top of the screen click on **Analyze**, select **Non-parametric Tests**. Select **Independent Samples**.
2. Select the **Customize analysis** option on the **Objective** tab screen.
3. Click on the **Fields** tab. Select your continuous, dependent variable (e.g. Total optimism) and move it into the **Test Fields** box.
4. Click on your categorical, independent variable (e.g. age 3 groups: agegp3) and move it into the **Groups** box.
5. Click on the **Settings** tab and select **Customize tests**.
6. Select the **Kruskal Wallis 1-way ANOVA** option. In the **Multiple comparisons** section make sure that **All pairwise** is selected.
7. Click on the **Run** button (or on **Paste** to save to **Syntax Editor**).

The syntax from this procedure is:

```
NPTESTS
  /INDEPENDENT TEST (toptim) GROUP (agegp3) KRUSKAL_
  WALLIS(COMPARE=PAIRWISE)
  /MISSING SCOPE=ANALYSIS USERMISSING=EXCLUDE
  /CRITERIA ALPHA=0.05  CILEVEL=95.
```

Selected output generated from this procedure is shown below.

Independent-Samples Kruskal-Wallis Test

Total Optimism across age 3 groups

Independent-Samples Kruskal-Wallis Test Summary

Total N	435
Test Statistic	8.573[a]
Degree Of Freedom	2
Asymptotic Sig.(2-sided test)	.014

a. The test statistic is adjusted for ties.

Pairwise Comparisons of agegp3 age 3 groups

Sample 1-Sample 2	Test Statistic	Std. Error	Std. Test Statistic	Sig.	Adj. Sig.[a]
1 18 - 29-2 30 - 44	-17.869	14.484	-1.234	.217	.652
1 18 - 29-3 45+	-43.623	14.949	-2.918	.004	.011
2 30 - 44-3 45+	-25.754	14.808	-1.739	.082	.246

Each row tests the null hypothesis that the Sample 1 and Sample 2 distributions are the same. Asymptotic significances (2-sided tests) are displayed. The significance level is .05.

a. Significance values have been adjusted by the Bonferroni correction for multiple tests.

You will also need to obtain the median optimism values for each age group.

Procedure for obtaining median scores for each group
1. From the menu at the top of the screen, click on **Analyze**, then select **Compare means** and choose **Means**.
2. Click on your continuous variable (e.g. total optimism: toptim) and move it into the **Dependent List** box.
3. Click on your categorical variable (e.g. agegp3) and move it into the **Independent List** box.
4. Click on the **Options** button. Click on **Median** in the **Statistics** section and move into the **Cell Statistics** box. Click on **Mean** and **Standard Deviation** and remove from the **Cell Statistics** box.
5. Click on **Continue**.
6. Click on **OK** (or on **Paste** to save to **Syntax Editor**).

The syntax for this is:

```
MEANS TABLES=toptim BY agegp3
    /CELLS=COUNT MEDIAN.
```

The output is shown below.

Report

toptim Total Optimism

agegp3 age 3 groups	N	Median
1 18 - 29	147	22.00
2 30 - 44	153	22.00
3 45+	135	23.00
Total	435	22.00

Interpretation of output from Kruskal-Wallis Test

The main pieces of information you need from this output are: Chi-Square (shown as **Test Statistic**) value, the degrees of freedom (**df**) and the significance level (presented as **Asymptotic. Sig.**). If this significance level is less than .05 (e.g. .04, .01, .001), you can conclude that there is a statistically significant difference in your continuous variable across the three groups. You can then inspect the **Mean Rank** for the three groups presented in your first output table. This will tell you which of the groups had the highest overall ranking that corresponds to the highest score on your continuous variable.

In the output presented above, the significance level was .01 (rounded). This is less than the alpha level of .05, so these results suggest that there is a difference in optimism levels across the different age groups. An inspection of the mean ranks for the groups suggests that the older group (45+) had the highest optimism scores, with the younger group reporting the lowest.

Post-hoc tests and effect size

If you obtain a significant result for your Kruskal-Wallis Test, you still don't know which of the groups are different from one another. This information is provided in the **Pairwise Comparisons of age 3 groups** table, where each group is compared with each of the other groups. Scan down the **Sig.** column (which reports the *p* value) and look for values less than .05. In this example there is one significant comparison: Group 1 (18–29) with Group 3 (45) *p* = .002.

The results of this analysis could be presented as:

> A Kruskal-Wallis Test revealed a statistically significant difference in optimism levels across three different age groups (Group 1, *n* = 147: 18–29 years; Group 2, *n* = 153: 30–44 years; Group 3, *n* = 135: 45+ years), χ^2 (2, *n* = 435) = 8.57, *p* = .014. The older age group (45+ years) recorded a significantly higher median score (*Md* = 23) than the youngest age group (18–29 years *p* = .004) which recorded a median value of 22.

FRIEDMAN TEST

The Friedman Test is the non-parametric alternative to the one-way repeated measures analysis of variance (see Chapter 18). It is used when you take the *same* sample of participants or cases and you measure them at *three or more* points in time, or under three different conditions.

Example of research question: Is there a change in Fear of Statistics Test scores across three time periods (pre-intervention, post-intervention and follow-up)?

What you need: One sample of participants, measured on the same scale, at three different time periods or under three different conditions.

Assumptions: See general assumptions for non-parametric techniques presented at the beginning of this chapter.

Parametric alternative: Repeated measures (within-subjects) analysis of variance.

Before you start this procedure, go to the **Edit** menu at the top of your screen and click on **Options**. Select the **Output** tab, and in the **Output Display** section select **Pivot tables and charts**. This ensures that the results display correctly.

Procedure for Friedman Test

To follow along with this example, open the **experim.sav** data file.

1. From the menu at the top of the screen, click on **Analyze**, select **Nonparametric Tests**, and then **Related Samples**.
2. In the **Objective** tab click on **Customize analysis**.
3. Click on the **Fields** tab.
4. Select the variables that represent scores from Time 1,Time 2 and Time 3 (e.g. fear of stats time1: fost1, fear of stats time2: fost2, fear of stats time3: fost3). Click on the arrow to move these into the **Test Fields** box.
6. Click on the **Settings** tab and select **Customize tests**. Click on **Friedman's 2-way ANOVA by ranks (k samples)** and make sure that **All pairwise** is selected for **Multiple comparisons**.
7. Click on the **Run** button (or on **Paste** to save to the **Syntax Editor**).

The syntax from this procedure is:

```
NPTESTS
  /RELATED TEST(fost1 fost2 fost3) FRIEDMAN(COMPARE=PAIRWISE)
  /MISSING SCOPE=ANALYSIS USERMISSING=EXCLUDE
  /CRITERIA ALPHA=0.05  CILEVEL=95.
```

The output is shown below.

Hypothesis Test Summary

	Null Hypothesis	Test	Sig.	Decision
1	The distributions of fost1 fear of stats time1, fost2 fear of stats time2 and fost3 fear of stats time3 are the same.	Related-Samples Friedman's Two-Way Analysis of Variance by Ranks	.000	Reject the null hypothesis.

Asymptotic significances are displayed. The significance level is .050.

Related-Samples Friedman's Two-Way Analysis of Variance by Ranks Summary

Total N	30
Test Statistic	41.568
Degree Of Freedom	2
Asymptotic Sig.(2-sided test)	.000

Related-Samples Friedman's Two-Way Analysis of Variance by Ranks

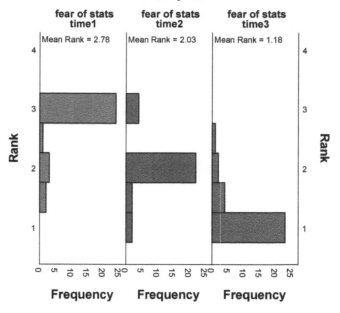

Pairwise Comparisons

Sample 1-Sample 2	Test Statistic	Std. Error	Std. Test Statistic	Sig.	Adj. Sig.[a]
fost3 fear of stats time3-fost2 fear of stats time2	.850	.258	3.292	.001	.003
fost3 fear of stats time3-fost1 fear of stats time1	1.600	.258	6.197	.000	.000
fost2 fear of stats time2-fost1 fear of stats time1	.750	.258	2.905	.004	.011

Each row tests the null hypothesis that the Sample 1 and Sample 2 distributions are the same.

Asymptotic significances (2-sided tests) are displayed. The significance level is .05.

a. Significance values have been adjusted by the Bonferroni correction for multiple tests.

Interpretation of output from Friedman Test

The results of this test suggest that there are significant differences in the Fear of Statistics Test scores across the three time periods. This is indicated by a **Sig.** level of .000 shown in the **Hypothesis Test Summary**. The bar graph shows a decrease in Fear of Statistics tests across the three points. Statistical comparison of the differences between each pair of time points is provided in the **Pairwise Comparisons** table.

In this example all comparisons reached statistical significance—this is shown in the **Adj. Sig.** column. These values represent the Bonferroni adjusted p values, designed to correct for the fact that multiple tests were undertaken (for more information on Bonferroni adjustment see the Planned Comparisons/Post-Hoc Analyses section presented in the Introduction to Part Five). Effect size statistics for these comparisons can be obtained using the same procedure as described in the earlier section on Wilcoxon Signed Rank Tests.

To report the results, you will also need to obtain the median scores on the Fear of Stats test for the three time points. Just follow the same instructions provided in the Wilcoxon Signed Rank Test procedures section of this chapter.

The results of this analysis could be presented as:

The results of the Friedman Test indicated that there was a statistically significant difference in Fear of Statistics Test scores across the three time points (pre-intervention, post-intervention, 3-month follow-up, χ^2 (2, $n = 30$) = 41.57, $p < .001$). Inspection of the median values showed a decrease in fear of statistics from pre-intervention ($Md = 40$) to post-intervention ($Md = 38$), and a further decrease at follow-up ($Md = 35.5$). Post-hoc tests (with Bonferroni correction for multiple tests) indicated that there were significant differences between each pair of time points (Time 1 – Time 2: $p = .011$, Time 1 – Time 3: $p < .001$, Time 2 – Time 3: $p = .003$).

ADDITIONAL EXERCISES

Business

Data file: **staffsurvey.sav**. See Appendix for details of the data file.

1. Use the Chi-Square Test for Independence to compare the proportions of permanent and casual staff (*employstatus*) who indicate they would recommend the organisation as a good place to work (*recommend*).
2. Use the Mann-Whitney *U* Test to compare the staff satisfaction scores (*totsatis*) for permanent and casual staff (*employstatus*).
3. Conduct a Kruskal-Wallis Test to compare staff satisfaction scores (*totsatis*) across each of the length of service categories (*servicegp3*).

Health

Data file: **sleep.sav**. See Appendix for details of the data file.

1. Use a Chi-Square Test for Independence to compare the proportions of males and females (*gender*) who indicate they have a sleep problem (*probsleeprec*).
2. Use the Mann-Whitney *U* Test to compare the mean sleepiness ratings (Sleepiness and Associated Sensations Scale total score: *totSAS*) for males and females (*gender*).
3. Conduct a Kruskal-Wallis Test to compare the mean sleepiness ratings (Sleepiness and Associated Sensations Scale total score: *totSAS*) for the three age groups defined by the variable *agegp3* (37 or under, 38–50, 51+).

17

T-tests

In this chapter two of the t-tests available in IBM SPSS Statistics are discussed:

➤ *independent-samples* t-*test:* Used when you want to compare the mean scores of two *different* groups of people or conditions
➤ *paired-samples* t-*test:* Used when you want to compare the mean scores for the *same* group of people on two different occasions, or when you have matched pairs.

In both cases, you are comparing the values on some continuous variable for *two* groups or on *two* occasions. If you have more than two groups or conditions, you will need to use analysis of variance instead.

For both of the t-tests discussed in this chapter there are a set of assumptions that you will need to check before conducting these analyses. The general assumptions common to both types of t-tests are presented in the introduction to Part Five. Before proceeding with the remainder of this chapter, you should read through the introduction to Part Five of this book.

INDEPENDENT-SAMPLES T-TEST

An independent-samples t-test is used when you want to compare the mean score on some *continuous* variable for *two* different groups of participants.

Details of example

To illustrate the use of this technique, the **survey.sav** data file is used. This example explores sex differences in self-esteem scores. The two variables used are sex (with males coded as 1, and females coded as 2) and Total self-esteem (tslfest), which is the total score that participants recorded on a 10-item Self-Esteem Scale (see the Appendix for more details on the study, the variables and the questionnaire that was used to collect the data). If you would like to follow along with the steps detailed below, you should start IBM SPSS Statistics and open the **survey.sav** file now.

Example of research question: Is there a significant difference in the mean self-esteem scores for males and females?

What you need:
➤ one categorical, independent variable (e.g. males/females)
➤ one continuous, dependent variable (e.g. self-esteem scores).

What it does: An independent-samples t-test will tell you whether there is a statistically significant difference in the mean scores for the two groups (i.e. whether males and females differ significantly in terms of their self-esteem levels). In statistical terms, you are testing the probability that the two sets of scores (for males and females) came from the same population.

Assumptions: The assumptions for this test are covered in the introduction to Part Five. You should read through that section before proceeding.

Non-parametric alternative: Mann-Whitney U Test (see Chapter 16).

Procedure for independent-samples t-test
1. From the menu at the top of the screen, click on **Analyze**, then select **Compare means**, then **Independent Samples T test**.
2. Move the dependent (continuous) variable (e.g. total self-esteem: tslfest) into the **Test variable** box.
3. Move the independent (categorical) variable (e.g. sex) into the section labelled **Grouping variable**.
4. Click on **Define groups** and type in the numbers used in the data set to code each group. In the current data file, 1 = males, 2 = females; therefore, in the **Group 1** box, type 1, and in the **Group 2** box, type 2. If you cannot remember the codes used, right click on the variable name and then choose **Variable Information** from the pop-up box that appears. This will list the codes and labels.
5. Click on **Continue** and then **OK** (or on **Paste** to save to **Syntax Editor**).

The syntax generated from this procedure is:

```
T-TEST GROUPS=sex(1 2)
    /MISSING=ANALYSIS
    /VARIABLES=tslfest
    /CRITERIA=CI(.95).
```

The output generated from this procedure is shown below.

Group Statistics

	sex sex	N	Mean	Std. Deviation	Std. Error Mean
tslfest Total Self esteem	1 MALES	184	34.02	4.911	.362
	2 FEMALES	252	33.17	5.705	.359

Independent Samples Test

		Levene's Test for Equality of Variances		t-test for Equality of Means					95% Confidence Interval of the Difference	
		F	Sig.	t	df	Sig. (2-tailed)	Mean Difference	Std. Error Difference	Lower	Upper
tslfest Total Self esteem	Equal variances assumed	3.506	.062	1.622	434	.105	.847	.522	-.179	1.873
	Equal variances not assumed			1.661	422.3	.098	.847	.510	-.156	1.850

Interpretation of output from independent-samples t-test
Step 1: Check the information about the groups
In the **Group Statistics** table, IBM SPSS Statistics gives you the mean and standard deviation for each of your groups (in this case, male/female). It also gives you the number of people in each group (*N*). Always check these values first. Are the *N* values for males and females correct? Or are there a lot of missing data? If so, find out why. Perhaps you have entered the wrong code for males and females (0 and 1, rather than 1 and 2). Check with your codebook.

Step 2: Check assumptions
The first section of the **Independent Samples Test** table gives you the results of Levene's Test for Equality of Variances. This tests whether the variance (variation) of scores for the two groups (males and females) is the same. The outcome of this test determines which of the *t* values that IBM SPSS Statistics provides is the correct one for you to use.

➢ If your Sig. value for Levene's test is larger than .05 (e.g. .07, .10) you should use the first row in the table, which refers to **Equal variances assumed**.

➢ If the significance level of Levene's test is $p = .05$ or less (e.g. .01, .001), this means that the variances for the two groups (males/females) are *not* the same. Therefore, your data violate the assumption of equal variance. Don't panic—IBM SPSS Statistics is very kind and provides you with an alternative t value which compensates for the fact that your variances are not the same. You should use the information in the *second* row of the t-test table, which refers to **Equal variances not assumed**.

In the example given in the output above, the significance level for Levene's test is .06. This is larger than the cut-off of .05. This means that the assumption of equal variances has not been violated; therefore, when you report your t value, you will use the one provided in the first row of the table.

Step 3: Assess differences between the groups

To find out whether there is a significant difference between your two groups, refer to the column labelled **Sig. (2-tailed)**, which appears under the section labelled t-**test for Equality of Means**. Two values are given, one for equal variance, the other for unequal variance. Choose whichever your Levene's test result says you should use (see Step 2 above).

➢ If the value in the **Sig. (2-tailed)** column is *equal to or less* than .05 (e.g. .03, .01, .001), there is a significant difference in the mean scores on your dependent variable for each of the two groups.

➢ If the value is *above* .05 (e.g. .06, .10), there is no significant difference between the two groups.

In the example presented in the output above, the **Sig. (2-tailed)** value is .105. As this value is *above* the required cut-off of .05, you conclude that there is *not* a statistically significant difference in the mean self-esteem scores for males and females. The **Mean Difference** between the two groups is also shown in this table, along with the **95% Confidence Interval of the Difference** showing the **Lower** value and the **Upper** value.

Calculating the effect size for independent-samples t-test

In the introduction to Part Five of this book, the issue of effect size was discussed. Effect size statistics provide an indication of the magnitude of the differences between your groups (not just whether the difference could have occurred by chance). There are several different effect size statistics, the most commonly used being eta squared and Cohen's *d*. Eta squared can range from 0 to 1 and represents the proportion of variance in the dependent variable that is explained by the independent (group) variable. Cohen's *d*, on the other hand, presents the difference between groups in terms of standard deviation units. Be careful not to get the different effect size statistics confused when interpreting the strength of the association.

IBM SPSS Statistics does not provide effect size statistics for t-tests in the output. There are, however, websites that allow you to calculate an effect size statistic using information provided in the output. If you do decide to use Cohen's *d* (often required for medical journals) please note that the criteria for interpreting the strength are different from those for eta squared in the current example. For Cohen's *d* .2 = small effect, .5 = medium effect, and .8 = large effect (Cohen 1988).

Eta squared can be calculated by hand using the information provided in the output.

The formula for eta squared is as follows:

$$\text{Eta squared} = \frac{t^2}{t^2 + (N1 + N2 - 2)}$$

Using the appropriate values from the example above:

$$\text{Eta squared} = \frac{1.62^2}{1.62^2 + (184 + 252 - 2)} = .006$$

The guidelines (proposed by Cohen 1988, pp. 284–287) for interpreting this value are: .01 = small effect, .06 = moderate effect, and .14 = large effect. For our current example, you can see that the effect size of .006 is very small. Expressed as a percentage (multiply your eta squared value by 100), only .6 per cent of the variance in self-esteem is explained by sex.

Presenting the results from independent-samples t-test

If you have conducted a t-test on only one variable you could present the results in a paragraph as follows:

> An independent-samples t-test was conducted to compare the self-esteem scores for males and females. There was no significant difference in scores for males ($M = 34.02$, $SD = 4.91$) and females ($M = 33.17$, $SD = 5.71$; $t(434) = 1.62$, $p = .11$, two-tailed). The magnitude of the differences in the means (mean difference = .85, 95% CI [–.18, 1.87]) was very small (eta squared = .006).

If you have conducted a series of t-tests you might want to present the results in a table. I have provided an example below, formatted in APA style (American Psychological Association 2019). For other examples, see Chapter 5 in Nicol and Pexman (2010b).

Presenting the results from a series of t-tests in a table

To provide the extra material for the table I conducted the t-test procedure detailed earlier in this chapter for both the Mastery and Optimism Scales (see output below). Both these measures recorded a significant result from Levene's Test for Equality of Variances. When presenting the results I therefore had to report the information provided in the second row of the Independent Samples Test (Equal Variances Not Assumed).

The output generated from this procedure is shown below.

Independent Samples Test

		Levene's Test for Equality of Variances		t-test for Equality of Means					95% Confidence Interval of the Difference	
		F	Sig.	t	df	Sig. (2-tailed)	Mean Difference	Std. Error Difference	Lower	Upper
tmast Total Mastery	Equal variances assumed	5.096	.024	2.423	434	.016	.927	.383	.175	1.679
	Equal variances not assumed			2.483	425.338	.013	.927	.373	.193	1.660
toptim Total Optimism	Equal variances assumed	4.491	.035	-.428	433	.669	-.184	.430	-1.030	.661
	Equal variances not assumed			-.440	424.751	.660	-.184	.419	-1.008	.639

The results of the analysis could be presented as follows:

Table X

Sex Differences in Measures of Self-Esteem, Mastery and Optimism

	Male			Female			Mean Difference	95% CI	df	t	p	Partial eta squared
	n	M	SD	n	M	SD						
Self-esteem	184	34.02	4.91	252	33.17	5.71	.85	-.18, 1.87	434	1.62	.10	.006
Mastery	185	22.3	3.57	251	21.37	4.20	.93	.19, 1.66	425.34	2.48	.013	.01
Optimism	184	22.01	3.98	251	22.20	4.73	-.18	-1.0, .64	424.75	-.44	.66	.000

PAIRED-SAMPLES T-TEST

A paired-samples t-test (also referred to as 'repeated measures') is used when you have only one group of people (or companies, machines etc.) and you collect data from them on two different occasions or under two different conditions. Pre-test and post-test experimental designs are examples of the type of situation where this technique is appropriate. You assess each person on some continuous measure at Time 1 and then again at Time 2 after exposing them to some experimental manipulation or intervention. This approach is also used when you have matched pairs of participants (i.e. each person is matched with another on specific criteria, such as age, sex). One of the pair is exposed to Intervention 1 and the other is exposed to Intervention 2. Scores on a continuous measure are then compared for each pair.

Paired-samples t-tests can also be used when you measure the same person in terms of their response to two different questions (e.g. asking them to rate the importance in terms of life satisfaction of two dimensions of life: health, financial security). In this case, both dimensions should be rated on the same scale (e.g. from 1 = not at all important to 10 = very important).

Details of example

To illustrate the use of the paired-samples t-test, I use the data from the file labelled **experim.sav** (included on the website accompanying this book). This is a manufactured data file—created and manipulated to illustrate different statistical techniques. Full details of the study design, the measures used and so on are provided in the Appendix.

For the example below, I explore the impact of an intervention designed to increase students' confidence in their ability to survive a compulsory statistics course. Students were asked to complete a Fear of Statistics Test (FOST) both before (Time 1) and after (Time 2) the intervention. The two variables from the data file that I use are fost1 (scores on the Fear of Statistics Test at Time 1) and fost2 (scores on the Fear of Statistics Test at Time 2). If you wish to follow along with the following steps, you should start IBM SPSS Statistics and open the file labelled **experim.sav**.

Examples of research questions: Is there a significant change in participants' Fear of Statistics Test scores following participation in an intervention designed to increase students' confidence in their ability to successfully complete a statistics course? Does the intervention have an impact on participants' Fear of Statistics Test scores?

What you need: One set of participants (or matched pairs). Each person (or pair) must provide both sets of scores. Two variables:

➤ one categorical, independent variable (in this case it is time, with two different levels: Time 1, Time 2)

> one continuous, dependent variable (e.g. Fear of Statistics Test scores) measured on two different occasions or under different conditions.

What it does: A paired-samples t-test will tell you whether there is a statistically significant difference in the mean scores for Time 1 and Time 2.

Assumptions: The basic assumptions for t-tests are covered in the introduction to Part Five. You should read through that section before proceeding.

Additional assumption: The difference between the two scores obtained for each subject should be normally distributed. With sample sizes of 30+, violation of this assumption is unlikely to cause any serious problems.

Non-parametric alternative: Wilcoxon Signed Rank Test (see Chapter 16).

Procedure for paired-samples t-test
1. From the menu at the top of the screen, click on **Analyze**, then select **Compare Means**, then **Paired Samples T test**.
2. Click on the two variables that you are interested in comparing for each subject (e.g. fear of stats time1 fost1, fear of stats time2 fost2) and move them into the box labelled **Paired Variables** by clicking on the arrow button. Click on **OK** (or on **Paste** to save to **Syntax Editor**).

The syntax for this is:

```
T-TEST PAIRS=fost1 WITH fost2 (PAIRED)
  /CRITERIA=CI(.9500)
  /MISSING=ANALYSIS.
```

The output generated from this procedure is shown below.

Paired Samples Statistics

		Mean	N	Std. Deviation	Std. Error Mean
Pair 1	fost1 fear of stats time1	40.17	30	5.160	.942
	fost2 fear of stats time2	37.50	30	5.151	.940

Paired Samples Correlations

		N	Correlation	Sig.
Pair 1	fost1 fear of stats time1 & fost2 fear of stats time2	30	.862	.000

Paired Samples Test

			Paired Differences						
					95% Confidence Interval of the Difference				
		Mean	Std. Deviation	Std. Error Mean	Lower	Upper	t	df	Sig. (2-tailed)
Pair 1	fost1 fear of stats time1 - fost2 fear of stats time2	2.667	2.708	.494	1.655	3.678	5.394	29	.000

Interpretation of output from paired-samples t-test

Step 1: Determine overall significance

In the table labelled **Paired Samples Test** you need to look in the final column, labelled **Sig. (2-tailed)**—this is your probability (p) value. If this value is less than .05 (e.g. .04, .01, .001), you can conclude that there is a significant difference between your two scores. In the example given above, the probability value is .000. This has been rounded down to three decimal places—it means that the actual probability value was less than .0005. This value is substantially smaller than our specified alpha value of .05. Therefore, we can conclude that there is a significant difference in the Fear of Statistics Test scores at Time 1 and at Time 2. Take note of the t value (in this case, 5.39) and the degrees of freedom ($df = 29$), as you will need these when you report your results. You should also note that the **Mean** difference in the two scores was 2.67, with a 95 per cent confidence interval stretching from a **Lower** bound of 1.66 to an **Upper** bound of 3.68.

Step 2: Compare mean values

Having established that there is a significant difference, the next step is to find out which set of scores is higher (Time 1 or Time 2). To do this, inspect the first printout table, labelled **Paired Samples Statistics**. This box gives you the **Mean** scores for each of the two sets of scores. In our case, the mean fear of statistics score at Time 1 was 40.17 and the mean score at Time 2 was 37.50. Therefore, we can conclude that there was a significant decrease in Fear of Statistics Test scores from Time 1 (prior to the intervention) to Time 2 (after the intervention).

Caution: Although we obtained a significant difference in the scores before and after the intervention, we cannot say that the intervention caused the drop in Fear of Statistics Test scores. Research is never that simple, unfortunately! There are many other factors that may have also influenced the decrease in fear scores. Just the passage of time (without any intervention) could have contributed. Any number of other events may also have occurred during this period that influenced students' attitudes to statistics. Perhaps the participants were exposed to previous statistics students who told them how great the instructor was and how easy it was to pass the course. Perhaps they were all given an illegal copy of the statistics exam (with all answers included!). There are many other possible confounding or contaminating factors. Wherever possible, the researcher should try to anticipate these confounding factors and either control for them or incorporate them into the research design. In the present case, the use of a control group that was not exposed to an intervention but was similar to the participants in all other ways would have improved the study. This would have helped to rule out the effects of time, other events and so on that may have influenced the results of the current study.

Calculating the effect size for paired-samples t-test

Although the results presented above tell us that the difference we obtained in the two sets of scores was unlikely to occur by chance, it does not tell us much about the magnitude of the intervention's effect. One way to discover this is to calculate an effect size statistic (see the introduction to Part Five for more on this topic).

IBM SPSS Statistics does not provide effect size statistics for t-tests in the output. There are, however, websites that will allow you to calculate an effect size statistic using information provided in the output. If you do decide to use Cohen's d (often required for medical journals) please note that the criteria for interpreting the strength are different from those for eta squared in the current example. For Cohen's d .2 = small effect, .5 = medium effect and .8 = large effect (Cohen 1988).

The procedure for calculating and interpreting eta squared (one of the most commonly used effect size statistics) by hand is presented below.

Eta squared can be obtained using the following formula:

$$\text{Eta squared} = \frac{t^2}{t^2 + (N-1)}$$

$$\text{Eta squared} = \frac{(5.39)^2}{5.39^2 + (30-1)}$$

$$= \frac{29.05}{29.05 + 30 - 1}$$

$$= .50$$

The guidelines (proposed by Cohen 1988, pp. 284–287) for interpreting this value are: .01 = small effect, .06 = moderate effect, .14 = large effect. Given our eta squared value of .50 we can conclude that there was a large effect, with a substantial difference in the Fear of Statistics Test scores obtained before and after the intervention.

Presenting the results from paired-samples t-test

The key details that need to be presented are the name of the test, the purpose of the test, the *t*-value, the degrees of freedom (*df*), the probability value and the means and standard deviations for each of the groups or administrations. Most journals now require an effect size statistic (e.g. eta squared) to be reported as well. If you conduct a t-test on only one variable you could present the results in a paragraph as shown below.

> A paired-samples t-test was conducted to evaluate the impact of the intervention on students' scores on the Fear of Statistics Test (FOST). There was a statistically significant decrease in FOST scores from Time 1 ($M = 40.17$, $SD = 5.16$) to Time 2 ($M = 37.5$, $SD = 5.15$), $t(29) = 5.39$, $p < .001$ (two-tailed). The mean decrease in FOST scores was 2.67, with a 95% confidence interval ranging from 1.66 to 3.68. The eta squared statistic (.50) indicated a large effect size.

If you conduct several t-tests using the same dependent variable, it would be more appropriate to present the results in a table (see the example provided for the independent t-test earlier in this chapter).

ADDITIONAL EXERCISES

Business
Data file: **staffsurvey.sav**. See Appendix for details of the data file.

1. Follow the procedures in the section on independent-samples t-tests to compare the mean staff satisfaction scores (*totsatis*) for permanent and casual staff (*employstatus*). Is there a significant difference in mean satisfaction scores?

Health
Data file: **sleep.sav**. See Appendix for details of the data file.

1. Follow the procedures in the section on independent-samples t-tests to compare the mean sleepiness ratings (Sleepiness and Associated Sensations Scale total score: *totSAS*) for males and females (*gender*). Is there a significant difference in mean sleepiness scores?

18

One-way analysis of variance

In the previous chapter, we used t-tests to compare the scores of two different groups or conditions. In many research situations, however, we are interested in comparing the mean scores of more than two groups. In this situation, we would use analysis of variance (ANOVA). One-way analysis of variance involves one independent variable (referred to as a 'factor') which has two or more different levels. These levels correspond to the different groups or conditions. For example, in comparing the effectiveness of three different teaching styles on students' mathematics scores, you would have one factor (teaching style) with three levels (e.g. whole class, small group activities, self-paced computer activities). The dependent variable is a continuous variable (in this case, scores on a mathematics test).

Analysis of variance is so called because it compares the variance (variability in scores) *between* the different groups (believed to be due to the independent variable) with the variance *within* each of the groups (believed to be due to chance). An F ratio is calculated, which represents the variance between the groups divided by the variance within the groups. A large F ratio indicates that there is more variability between the groups (caused by the independent variable) than there is within each group (referred to as the 'error term').

A significant F-test indicates that we can reject the null hypothesis, which states that the population means are equal. It does not, however, tell us which of the groups differ. For this we need to conduct post-hoc tests. The alternative to conducting post-hoc tests after obtaining a significant omnibus F-test is to plan your study to conduct only specific comparisons (referred to as 'planned comparisons'). A comparison of post-hoc with planned comparisons is presented in the introduction to Part Five of this book. There are advantages and disadvantages to each approach—you should consider your choice carefully before beginning your analysis. Post-hoc tests are designed to help protect against the likelihood of a Type 1 error, but this approach is stricter, making it more difficult to obtain statistically significant differences. Unless you have clear conceptual grounds for wishing only to compare specific groups, then it may be more appropriate to use post-hoc analysis.

In this chapter, two different types of one-way ANOVAs are discussed:

> *Between-groups ANOVA* is used when you have different participants or cases in each of your groups (this is referred to as an 'independent-groups design')
> *Repeated measures analysis of variance* is used when you are measuring the same participants under different conditions (or at different points in time; this is also referred to as a 'within-subjects design').

In the between-groups ANOVA section that follows, the use of both post-hoc tests and planned comparisons is illustrated.

ONE-WAY BETWEEN-GROUPS ANOVA WITH POST-HOC TESTS

One-way between-groups ANOVA is used when you have one independent (grouping) variable with three or more levels (groups) and one dependent, continuous variable. The 'one-way' part of the title indicates there is only one independent variable, and 'between-groups' means that you have different participants in each of the groups.

Details of example

To demonstrate the use of this technique, I use the **survey.sav** data file included on the website accompanying this book (see p. ix). The data come from a survey that was conducted to explore the factors that affect respondents' psychological adjustment, health and wellbeing. This is a real data file from actual research conducted by a group of my graduate diploma students. Full details of the study, the questionnaire and scales used are provided in the Appendix. If you wish to follow along with the steps described in this chapter, you should start IBM SPSS Statistics and open the file **survey.sav**.

Details of the variables used in this analysis are provided below.

File name: **survey.sav**

Variables:
> Total optimism (Toptim): Total score on the Optimism Scale. Scores can range from 6 to 30, with high scores indicating higher levels of optimism.
> age 3 group (agegp3): This variable is a recoded variable, dividing age into three equal groups (see instructions for how to do this in Chapter 8). Group 1: 18–29 = 1, Group 2: 30–44 = 2, Group 3: 45+ = 3.

Example of research question: Is there a difference in optimism scores for young, middle-aged and old participants?

What you need:

➤ one categorical, independent variable with three or more distinct categories. This can also be a continuous variable that has been recoded to give three equal groups (e.g. age group: participants divided into three age categories, 29 and younger, between 30 and 44, 45 or above)
➤ one continuous, dependent variable (e.g. optimism scores).

What it does: One-way ANOVA will tell you whether there are significant differences in the mean scores on the dependent variable across the three groups. Post-hoc tests can then be used to find out where these differences lie.

Assumptions: See discussion of the general ANOVA assumptions presented in the introduction to Part Five.

Non-parametric alternative: Kruskal-Wallis Test (see Chapter 16).

Procedure for one-way between-groups ANOVA with post-hoc tests

1. From the menu at the top of the screen, click on **Analyze**, then select **Compare Means**, then **One-way ANOVA**.
2. Click on your dependent (continuous) variable (e.g. Total optimism: toptim). Move this into the box marked **Dependent List** by clicking on the arrow button.
3. Click on your independent, categorical variable (e.g. age 3 groups: agegp3). Move this into the box labelled **Factor**.
4. Click the **Options** button and click on **Descriptive**, **Homogeneity of variance test**, **Brown-Forsythe**, **Welch** and **Means Plot**.
5. For **Missing values**, make sure there is a dot in the option marked **Exclude cases analysis by analysis**. Click on **Continue**.
6. Click on the button marked **Post Hoc**. Click on **Tukey**.
7. Click on **Continue** and then **OK** (or on **Paste** to save to **Syntax Editor**).

The syntax from this procedure is:

```
ONEWAY toptim BY agegp3
  /STATISTICS DESCRIPTIVES HOMOGENEITY BROWNFORSYTHE WELCH
  /PLOT MEANS
  /MISSING ANALYSIS
  /POSTHOC=TUKEY ALPHA(0.05).
```

The output generated from this procedure is shown below.

Descriptives

toptim Total Optimism

	N	Mean	Std. Deviation	Std. Error	95% Confidence Interval for Mean Lower Bound	Upper Bound	Minimum	Maximum
1 18 - 29	147	21.36	4.551	.375	20.62	22.10	7	30
2 30 - 44	153	22.10	4.147	.335	21.44	22.77	10	30
3 45+	135	22.96	4.485	.386	22.19	23.72	8	30
Total	435	22.12	4.429	.212	21.70	22.53	7	30

Test of Homogeneity of Variances

		Levene Statistic	df1	df2	Sig.
toptim Total Optimism	Based on Mean	.746	2	432	.475
	Based on Median	.715	2	432	.490
	Based on Median and with adjusted df	.715	2	417.368	.490
	Based on trimmed mean	.715	2	432	.490

ANOVA

toptim Total Optimism

	Sum of Squares	df	Mean Square	F	Sig.
Between Groups	179.069	2	89.535	4.641	.010
Within Groups	8333.951	432	19.292		
Total	8513.021	434			

Robust Tests of Equality of Means

toptim Total Optimism

	Statistic[a]	df1	df2	Sig.
Welch	4.380	2	284.508	.013
Brown-Forsythe	4.623	2	423.601	.010

a. Asymptotically F distributed.

Multiple Comparisons

Dependent Variable: toptim Total Optimism

Tukey HSD

(I) agegp3 age 3 groups	(J) agegp3 age 3 groups	Mean Difference (I-J)	Std. Error	Sig.	95% Confidence Interval	
					Lower Bound	Upper Bound
1 18 - 29	2 30 - 44	-.744	.507	.308	-1.94	.45
	3 45+	-1.595*	.524	.007	-2.83	-.36
2 30 - 44	1 18 - 29	.744	.507	.308	-.45	1.94
	3 45+	-.851	.519	.230	-2.07	.37
3 45+	1 18 - 29	1.595*	.524	.007	.36	2.83
	2 30 - 44	.851	.519	.230	-.37	2.07

*. The mean difference is significant at the 0.05 level.

Interpretation of output from one-way between-groups ANOVA with post-hoc tests

Descriptives

This table gives you information about each group (number in each group, means, standard deviation, minimum and maximum etc.). Always check this table first. Are the Ns for each group correct?

Test of homogeneity of variances

The homogeneity of variance option gives you **Levene's Test for Homogeneity of Variances**, which tests whether the variance in scores is the same for each of the three groups. Check the significance value (**Sig.**) for Levene's test. If this number is *greater* than .05 (e.g. .08, .28), you have *not* violated the assumption of homogeneity of variance. In this example, the **Sig**. value is .475. As this is greater than .05, we have not violated the homogeneity of variance assumption. If you have found that you violated this assumption, you will need to consult the table in the output headed **Robust Tests of Equality of Means**. The two tests shown there (**Welch** and **Brown-Forsythe**) are preferable when the assumption of the homogeneity of variance is violated.

ANOVA

This table gives both between-groups and within-groups sums of squares, degrees of freedom and so on. The main thing you are interested in is the column marked **Sig.** (this is the *p* value). If the **Sig**. value is less than or equal to .05 (e.g. .03, .001), there is a significant difference somewhere among the mean scores on your dependent variable for the three groups. This does not tell you which group is different from which other group. The statistical significance of the differences between each pair of groups is provided in the table labelled **Multiple Comparisons**, which gives the results of the post-hoc tests (described below). The means for each group are given in the **Descriptives** table. In this example the overall **Sig**. value is .01, which is less than .05, indicating a statistically significant result somewhere among the groups. Having received a statistically significant difference, we can now examine the results of the post-hoc tests that we requested.

Multiple comparisons

You should look at this table only if you found a significant difference in your overall ANOVA—that is, if the **Sig**. value was equal to or less than .05. The post-hoc tests in this table will tell you exactly where the differences among the groups occur. Scan down the column labelled **Mean Difference**. Identify any asterisks (*) next to the values listed. An asterisk means that the two groups being compared are significantly different from one another at the p < .05 level. The exact significance value is given in the column labelled **Sig**. In the results presented above, only Group 1 and Group 3 are statistically significantly different from one another. That is, the 18–29 years age group and the 45+ years age group differ significantly in terms of their optimism scores.

Means plots

This plot provides an easy way to compare the mean scores for the different groups. You can see from this plot that the 18–29 years age group recorded the lowest optimism scores, with the 45+ years age group recording the highest.

Warning: These plots can be misleading. Depending on the scale used on the Y axis (in this case, representing Optimism scores), even small differences can appear dramatic. In the above example, the actual difference in the mean scores between the groups is very small (21.36, 22.10, 22.96), while on the graph it appears substantial. The lesson here is: don't get too excited about your plots until you have compared the mean values (available in the **Descriptives** box) and the scale used in the plot.

Calculating effect size

Although IBM SPSS Statistics does not generate it for this analysis, it is possible to determine the effect size for this result (see the introduction to Part Five for a discussion on effect sizes). The information you need to calculate, **eta squared**, one of the most common effect size statistics, is provided in the **ANOVA** table (a calculator would be useful here). The formula is:

$$\text{Eta squared} = \frac{\text{Sum of squares between groups}}{\text{Total sum of squares}}$$

In this example, all you need to do is to divide the sum of squares for between groups (179.069) by the total sum of squares (8513.021). The resulting eta squared value is .02, which in Cohen's (1988, pp. 284–287) terms would be considered a small effect size. Cohen classifies .01 as a small effect, .06 as a medium effect and .14 as a large effect.

Warning: In this example we obtained a statistically significant result, but the actual difference in the mean scores of the groups was very small (21.36, 22.10, 22.96). This is evident in the small effect size obtained (eta squared = .02). With a large enough sample (in this case, $N = 435$) quite small differences can become statistically significant, even if the difference between the groups is of little practical importance. Always interpret your results carefully, considering all the information you have available. Don't rely too heavily on statistical significance—many other factors also need to be considered.

Presenting the results from one-way between-groups ANOVA with post-hoc tests

If you have conducted an ANOVA on only one variable you could present the results in a paragraph as follows:

A one-way between-groups analysis of variance was conducted to explore the impact of age on levels of optimism, as measured by the Life Orientation Test (LOT). Participants were divided into three groups according to their age (Group 1: 29yrs or less; Group 2: 30 to 44; Group 3: 45 and above). There was a statistically significant difference at the $p < .05$ level in LOT scores for the three age groups: $F (2, 432) = 4.64, p = .01$. Despite reaching statistical significance, the actual difference in mean scores between the groups was quite small. The effect size, calculated using eta squared, was .02. Post-hoc comparisons using the Tukey HSD test indicated that the mean score for Group 1 ($M = 21.36, SD = 4.55$) was significantly different from that of Group 3 ($M = 22.96, SD = 4.49$). Group 2 ($M = 22.10, SD = 4.15$) did not differ significantly from either Group 1 or Group 3.

If you have conducted analysis of variance on a series of variables it would be more appropriate to present the results in a table. I have provided an example below, formatted in APA style (American Psychological Association 2019). For other examples, see Chapter 9 in Nicol and Pexman (2010b).

Presenting the results from a series of one-way between-groups ANOVAs in a table

To provide the extra material for the table I conducted a one-way between-groups ANOVA following the procedure detailed earlier in this chapter using the Perceived Stress Scale.

The output generated from this procedure is shown below.

Descriptives

tpstress Total perceived stress

		N	Mean	Std. Deviation	Std. Error	95% Confidence ... Lower Bound
1 18 - 29		147	27.53	5.733	.473	26.60
2 30 - 44		152	26.54	5.851	.475	25.60
3 45+		134	26.06	5.909	.510	25.05
Total		433	26.73	5.848	.281	26.18
Model	Fixed Effects			5.829	.280	26.18
	Random Effects				.430	24.88

Descriptives

tpstress Total perceived stress

		95% Confidence Interval for Mean				Between-Component Variance
		Upper Bound	Minimum	Maximum		
1 18 - 29		28.47	12	46		
2 30 - 44		27.48	13	42		
3 45+		27.07	12	42		
Total		27.28	12	46		
Model	Fixed Effects	27.28				
	Random Effects	28.58				.319

ANOVA

tpstress Total perceived stress

	Sum of Squares	df	Mean Square	F	Sig.
Between Groups	159.945	2	79.973	2.353	.096
Within Groups	14611.898	430	33.981		
Total	14771.843	432			

Table X

One-Way Analysis of Variance Comparing Optimism and Perceived Stress Across Three Age Groups

	18–29 years			30–44 years			45+ years			df	F	p	Partial eta squared
Variable	n	M	SD	n	M	SD	n	M	SD				
Optimism	147	21.36	4.55	153	22.10	4.15	135	22.96	4.49	2,432	4.64	.01	.02
Perceived Stress	147	27.53	5.73	152	26.54	5.85	134	26.06	5.91	2,430	2.35	.10	.01

ONE-WAY BETWEEN-GROUPS ANOVA WITH PLANNED COMPARISONS

In the example provided above, we were interested in comparing optimism scores across each of the three groups. In some situations, however, researchers may be interested only in comparisons between specific groups. For example, in an experimental study with five different interventions we may want to know whether Intervention 1 is superior to each of the other interventions. In that situation, we may not be interested in comparing all the possible combinations of groups. If we are interested in only a subset of the possible comparisons it makes sense to use planned comparisons, rather than post-hoc tests, because of power issues (see discussion of power in the introduction to Part Five).

Planned comparisons are more sensitive in detecting differences. Post-hoc tests, on the other hand, set more stringent significance levels to reduce the risk of a Type 1 error, given the larger number of tests performed. The choice of whether to use planned comparisons or post-hoc tests must be made before you begin your analysis. It is not appropriate to try both and see which results you prefer! To illustrate planned comparisons I use the same data as those in the previous example. Normally, you would not conduct both analyses. In this case we will consider a slightly different question: 'Are participants in the older age group (45+) more optimistic than those in the two younger age groups (18–29, 30–44)?'

Specifying coefficient values

In the following procedure, you will be asked by IBM SPSS Statistics to indicate which groups you wish to compare. To do this, you need to specify coefficient values. Many students find this confusing initially, so I explain this process here.

First, you need to identify your groups based on the different values of the independent variable (agegp3):

➢ Group 1 (coded as 1): Age 18–29
➢ Group 2 (coded as 2): Age 30–44
➢ Group 3 (coded as 3): Age 45+

Next, you need to decide which of the groups you wish to compare and which you wish to ignore. I illustrate this process using a few examples.

Example 1

To compare Group 3 with the other two groups, the coefficients would be as follows:

➢ Group 1: –1
➢ Group 2: –1
➢ Group 3: 2

The values of the coefficients should add up to 0. Coefficients with different values are compared. If you wished to ignore one of the groups, you would give it a coefficient of 0. You would then need to adjust the other coefficient values so that they added up to 0.

Example 2

To compare Group 3 with Group 1 (ignoring Group 2), the coefficients would be as follows:

- Group 1: −1
- Group 2: 0
- Group 3: 1

This information on the coefficients for each of your groups are required in the **Contrasts** section of the procedure that follows.

Procedure for one-way between-groups ANOVA with planned comparisons

1. From the menu at the top of the screen, click on **Analyze**, then select **Compare Means**, then **One-way ANOVA**.
2. Click on your dependent (continuous) variable (e.g. total optimism: toptim). Click on the arrow to move this variable into the box marked **Dependent List**.
3. Click on your independent, categorical variable (e.g. agegp3). Move this into the box labelled **Factor**.
4. Click the **Options** button and click on **Descriptive**, **Homogeneity of variance test**, **Brown-Forsythe**, **Welch** and **Means Plot**.
5. For **Missing Values**, make sure there is a dot in the option marked **Exclude cases analysis by analysis**. Click on **Continue**.
6. Click on the **Contrasts** button.
   - In the Coefficients box, type the coefficient for the first group (from Example 1 above, this value would be −1). Click on Add.
   - Type in the coefficient for the second group (−1). Click on Add.
   - Type in the coefficient for the third group (2). Click on Add.
   - The Coefficient Total down the bottom of the table should be 0 if you have entered all the coefficients correctly.
7. Click on **Continue** and then **OK** (or on **Paste** to save to **Syntax Editor**).

The syntax from this procedure is:

```
ONEWAY toptim BY agegp3
 /CONTRAST=-1 -1 2
  /STATISTICS DESCRIPTIVES HOMOGENEITY BROWNFORSYTHE WELCH
  /PLOT MEANS
  /MISSING ANALYSIS
  /POSTHOC=TUKEY ALPHA(0.05).
```

Selected output generated from this procedure is shown below.

Contrast Coefficients

| Contrast | agegp3 age 3 groups | | |
	1 18 - 29	2 30 - 44	3 45+
1	-1	-1	2

Contrast Tests

		Contrast	Value of Contrast	Std. Error	t	df	Sig. (2-tailed)
toptim Total Optimism	Assume equal variances	1	2.45	.910	2.687	432	.007
	Does not assume equal variances	1	2.45	.922	2.654	251.32	.008

Interpretation of output from one-way between-groups ANOVA with planned comparisons

The **Descriptives** and **Test of homogeneity of variances** tables generated as part of this output are the same as obtained in the previous example for one-way ANOVA with post-hoc tests. Only the output relevant to planned comparisons is discussed here.

Step 1

In the table labelled **Contrast Coefficients**, the coefficients that you specified for each of your groups is provided. Check that this is what you intended.

Step 2

The main results that you are interested in are presented in the table labelled **Contrast Tests**. As we can assume equal variances (our Levene's test was not significant), we use the first row in this table. The **Sig.** level for the contrast that we specified is .007. This is less than .05, so we can conclude that there is a statistically significant difference between Group 3 (45+ age group) and the other two groups. Although statistically significant, the actual difference between the mean scores of these groups is very small (21.36, 22.10, 22.96). Refer to the previous section for further discussion on this point.

You will notice that the result of the planned comparisons analysis is expressed using a t statistic, rather than the usual F ratio associated with analysis of variance. To obtain the corresponding F value, all you need to do is to square the t value. In this example the t value is 2.687, which when squared equals 7.22. To report the results, you also need the degrees of freedom. The first value (for all planned comparisons) is 1; the second is given in the table next to the t value (in this example the value is 432). Therefore, the results would be expressed as $F (1, 432) = 7.22, p = .007$.

ONE-WAY REPEATED MEASURES ANOVA

In a one-way repeated measures ANOVA design, each subject is exposed to two or more different conditions or measured on the same continuous scale on three or more occasions. It can also be used to compare respondents' responses to two or more different questions or items. These questions, however, must be measured using the same scale (e.g. 1 = strongly disagree to 5 = strongly agree).

Details of example

To demonstrate the use of this technique, the data file labelled **experim.sav** (included on the website) is used. Details of this data file can be found in the Appendix. A group of students were invited to participate in an intervention designed to increase their confidence in their ability to do statistics. Their confidence levels (as measured by a self-report scale) were assessed before the intervention (Time 1), after the intervention (Time 2) and again 3 months later (Time 3).

If you wish to follow along with the procedure, you should start IBM SPSS Statistics and open the file labelled **experim.sav**. Details of the variable names and labels from the data file are provided below.

File name: **experim.sav**

Variables:

➤ confidence scores at Time 1 (confid1): Total scores on the Confidence in Coping with Statistics Test administered prior to the program. Scores range from 10 to 40. High scores indicate higher levels of confidence

➤ confidence scores at Time 2 (confid2): Total scores on the Confidence in Coping with Statistics Test administered after the program

➤ confidence scores at Time 3 (confid3): Total scores on the Confidence in Coping with Statistics Test administered 3 months later.

Example of research question: Is there a change in confidence scores over the three time periods?

What you need: One group of participants measured on the same scale on three different occasions or under three different conditions, *or* each person measured on three different questions or items (using the same response scale). This involves two variables:

➤ one independent (categorical) variable (e.g. Time 1/Time 2/Time 3)

➤ one dependent (continuous) variable (e.g. scores on the Confidence in Coping with Statistics Test). The scores on the test for each time point will appear in the data file in different columns.

What it does: This technique will tell you if there is a significant difference somewhere among the three sets of scores.

Assumptions: See discussion of the general ANOVA assumptions presented in the introduction to Part Five.

Non-parametric alternative: Friedman Test (see Chapter 16).

Procedure for one-way repeated measures ANOVA

1. From the menu at the top of the screen, click on **Analyze**, then **General Linear Model**, then **Repeated Measures**.
2. In the **Within Subject Factor Name** box, type in a name that represents your independent variable (e.g. time or condition). This is not an actual variable name, just a label you give your independent variable.
3. In the **Number of Levels** box, type the number of levels or groups (time periods) involved (in this example, it is 3).
4. Click **Add**.
5. Click on the **Define** button.
6. Select the three variables that represent your repeated measures variable (e.g. confidence time1: confid1, confidence time2: confid2, confidence time3: confid3). Click on the arrow button to move them into the **Within Subjects Variables** box.
7. Click on the **Options** box.
8. Tick the **Descriptive Statistics** and **Estimates of effect size** boxes. Click on **Continue**.
9. Click on the **EM Means** button. Select your independent variable name (e.g. Time) in the **Factor and Factor Interactions** section and move it into the **Display Means for** box. Tick **Compare main effects**. In the **Confidence interval adjustment** section, click on the down arrow and choose the second option, **Bonferroni**.
10. Click on **Continue** and then **OK** (or on **Paste** to save to **Syntax Editor**).

The syntax generated from this procedure is:

```
GLM confid1 confid2 confid3
  /WSFACTOR=Time 3 Polynomial
  /METHOD=SSTYPE(3)
  /EMMEANS=TABLES(Time) COMPARE ADJ(BONFERRONI)
  /PRINT=DESCRIPTIVE ETASQ
  /CRITERIA=ALPHA(.05)
  /WSDESIGN=Time.
```

Some of the output generated from this procedure is shown below.

Descriptive Statistics

	Mean	Std. Deviation	N
confid1 confidence time1	19.00	5.369	30
confid2 confidence time2	21.87	5.594	30
confid3 confidence time3	25.03	5.203	30

Multivariate Tests[a]

Effect		Value	F	Hypothesis df	Error df	Sig.	Partial Eta Squared
Time	Pillai's Trace	.749	41.711[b]	2.000	28.000	.000	.749
	Wilks' Lambda	.251	41.711[b]	2.000	28.000	.000	.749
	Hotelling's Trace	2.979	41.711[b]	2.000	28.000	.000	.749
	Roy's Largest Root	2.979	41.711[b]	2.000	28.000	.000	.749

a. Design: Intercept
   Within Subjects Design: Time

b. Exact statistic

Mauchly's Test of Sphericity[a]

Measure: MEASURE_1

Within Subjects Effect	Mauchly's W	Approx. Chi-Square	df	Sig.	Epsilon[b] Greenhouse-Geisser	Epsilon[b] Huynh-Feldt	Epsilon[b] Lower-bound
Time	.592	14.660	2	.001	.710	.737	.500

Tests the null hypothesis that the error covariance matrix of the orthonormalized transformed dependent variables is proportional to an identity matrix.

a. Design: Intercept
   Within Subjects Design: Time

b. May be used to adjust the degrees of freedom for the averaged tests of significance. Corrected tests are displayed in the Tests of Within-Subjects Effects table.

Pairwise Comparisons

Measure: MEASURE_1

(I) Time	(J) Time	Mean Difference (I-J)	Std. Error	Sig.[b]	95% Confidence Interval for Difference[b]	
					Lower Bound	Upper Bound
1	2	-2.867*	.868	.008	-5.072	-.661
	3	-6.033*	.833	.000	-8.149	-3.918
2	1	2.867*	.868	.008	.661	5.072
	3	-3.167*	.447	.000	-4.304	-2.030
3	1	6.033*	.833	.000	3.918	8.149
	2	3.167*	.447	.000	2.030	4.304

Based on estimated marginal means

*. The mean difference is significant at the .05 level.

b. Adjustment for multiple comparisons: Bonferroni.

Interpretation of output from one-way repeated measures ANOVA

You will notice that this technique generates a lot of complex-looking output. This includes tests for the assumption of sphericity, and both univariate and multivariate ANOVA results. Full discussion of the difference between the univariate and multivariate results is beyond the scope of this book; in this chapter, only the multivariate results are discussed (see Stevens 1996, pp. 466–469, for more information). The reason for interpreting the multivariate statistics provided by IBM SPSS Statistics is that the univariate statistics make the assumption of sphericity. The sphericity assumption requires that the variance of the population difference scores for any two conditions are the same as the variance of the population difference scores for any other two conditions (an assumption that is commonly violated). This is assessed by IBM SPSS Statistics using Mauchly's Test of Sphericity.

The multivariate statistics, however, do not require sphericity. You can see in our example that we have violated the assumption of sphericity, as indicated by the **Sig**. value of .001 in the table labelled **Mauchly's Test of Sphericity**. Although there are ways to compensate for this assumption violation, it is safer to inspect the multivariate statistics provided in the output.

Let's explore the key values in the output.

Descriptive statistics

In the first output table, you are provided with the descriptive statistics for your three sets of scores (**Mean, Standard deviation, N**). It is a good idea to check that these make sense. Is there the right number of people in each group? Do the mean values make sense given the scale that was used? In the example above, you can see that the lowest mean confidence score was for Time 1 (before the intervention) and the highest for Time 3 (after the statistics course was completed).

Multivariate tests

In this table, the value that you are interested in is **Wilks' Lambda** and the associated probability value given in the column labelled **Sig.** All of the multivariate tests yield the same result, but the most commonly reported statistic is Wilks' Lambda. In this example the value for Wilks' Lambda is .25, with a probability value of .000 (which really means $p < .0005$). The p value is less than .05; therefore, we can conclude that there is a statistically significant effect for time. This suggests that there was a change in confidence scores across the three different time periods.

Effect size

Although we have found a statistically significant difference between the three sets of scores, we also need to assess the effect size of this result (see discussion on effect sizes in the introduction to Part Five of this book). The value you are interested in is **Partial Eta Squared**, given in the **Multivariate Tests** output table. The value obtained in this study is .749. Using the commonly used guidelines proposed by Cohen (1988, pp. 284–287); .01 = small effect, .06 = moderate effect, .14 = large effect), this result suggests a very large effect size.

Pairwise comparisons

If you obtain a statistically significant result from the above analyses, this suggests that there is a difference somewhere among your groups. It does not tell you which groups or set of scores (in this case, Time 1, Time 2, Time 3) differ from one another. This information is provided in the **Pairwise Comparisons** table, which compares each pair of time points and indicates whether the difference between them is significant (see **Sig.** column). In this example, each of the differences is significant (all **Sig.** values are less than .05).

Presenting the results from one-way repeated measures ANOVA

The results of one-way repeated measures ANOVA could be presented as follows:

A one-way repeated measures ANOVA was conducted to compare scores on the Confidence in Coping with Statistics Test at Time 1 (prior to the intervention), Time 2 (following the intervention) and Time 3 (3-month follow-up). The means and standard deviations are presented in Table 1. There was a significant effect for time, Wilks' Lambda = .25, $F (2, 28) = 41.17, p < .001$, multivariate partial eta squared = .75.

Table 1
Descriptive Statistics for Confidence in Coping with Statistics Test Scores for Time 1, Time 2 and Time 3

Time Period	N	Mean	Standard deviation
1 (Pre-intervention)	30	19.00	5.37
2 (Post-intervention)	30	21.87	5.59
3 (3-month follow-up)	30	25.03	5.20

Presenting the results from a series of one-way repeated measures ANOVAs in a table

If you have conducted analysis of variance on a series of variables it would be more appropriate to present the results in a table. I have provided an example below, formatted in APA style (American Psychological Association 2019). For other examples see Chapter 9 in Nicol and Pexman (2010b). To provide the extra material for the table I conducted a one-way repeated measures ANOVA procedure (as detailed earlier in this chapter) using the Fear of Statistics Test.

The output generated from this procedure is shown below.

Descriptive Statistics

	Mean	Std. Deviation	N
fost1 fear of stats time1	40.17	5.160	30
fost2 fear of stats time2	37.50	5.151	30
fost3 fear of stats time3	35.23	6.015	30

Multivariate Tests[a]

Effect		Value	F	Hypothesis df	Error df	Sig.	Partial Eta Squared
time	Pillai's Trace	.635	24.356[b]	2.000	28.000	.000	.635
	Wilks' Lambda	.365	24.356[b]	2.000	28.000	.000	.635
	Hotelling's Trace	1.740	24.356[b]	2.000	28.000	.000	.635
	Roy's Largest Root	1.740	24.356[b]	2.000	28.000	.000	.635

a. Design: Intercept
   Within Subjects Design: time
b. Exact statistic

Table X
One-Way Repeated Measures Analysis of Variance Comparing Confidence and Fear of Statistics Scores Across Three Time Points

	Time 1		Time 2		Time 3					
Variable	M	SD	M	SD	M	SD	df	F	p	Partial eta squared
Confidence	19.0	5.37	21.87	5.59	25.03	5.20	2, 28	41.17	< .001	.75
Fear of Statistics	40.17	5.16	37.50	5.15	35.23	6.01	2, 28	24.36	< .001	.63

Note. N = 30 for each timepoint.

ADDITIONAL EXERCISES

Business

Data file: **staffsurvey.sav**. See Appendix for details of the data file.

1. Conduct a one-way ANOVA with post-hoc tests (if appropriate) to compare staff satisfaction scores (*totsatis*) across each of the length of service categories (*servicegp3*).

Health

Data file: **sleep.sav**. See Appendix for details of the data file.

1. Conduct a one-way ANOVA with post-hoc tests (if appropriate) to compare the mean sleepiness ratings (Sleepiness and Associated Sensations Scale total score: *totSAS*) for the three age groups defined by the variable *agegp3* (37 or under, 38–50, 51+).

19

Two-way between-groups ANOVA

In this chapter, we explore two-way between-groups analysis of variance. 'Two-way' means that there are two independent variables, and 'between-groups' indicates that different people are in each of the groups. This technique allows us to assess the individual and joint effects of two independent variables on one dependent variable. In Chapter 18, we used one-way between-groups ANOVA to compare the optimism scores for three age groups (18–29, 30–44, 45+). We found a significant difference between the groups, with post-hoc tests indicating that the major difference was between the youngest and oldest groups. Older people reported higher levels of optimism.

The next question we can ask is: 'Is this the case for both males and females?' One-way ANOVA cannot answer this question—the analysis was conducted on the sample as a whole, with males and females combined. In this chapter I take the investigation a step further and consider the impact of gender on this finding. I therefore have two independent variables (age group and sex) and one dependent variable (optimism).

The advantage of using a two-way design is that we can test the main effect for each independent variable and also explore the possibility of an interaction effect. An interaction effect occurs when the effect of one independent variable on the dependent variable depends on the level of a second independent variable. For example, in this case we may find that the influence of age on optimism is different for males and females. For males optimism may increase with age, while for females it may decrease. If that were the case, we would say that there is an interaction effect. In order to describe the impact of age, we must specify which group (males/females) we are referring to.

If you are not clear on main effects and interaction effects, I suggest you review this material in any good statistics text (see Gravetter & Wallnau 2012; Harris 1994; Runyon, Coleman & Pittenger 2000; Tabachnick & Fidell 2013). Before proceeding I would also recommend that you read through the introduction to Part Five of this book, where I discuss a range of topics relevant to analysis of variance techniques.

DETAILS OF EXAMPLE

To demonstrate the use of this technique, I use the **survey.sav** data file included on the website accompanying this book (see p. ix). The data come from a survey that was conducted to explore the factors that affect respondents' psychological adjustment, health and wellbeing. This is a real data file from actual research conducted by a group of my graduate diploma students. Full details of the study, the questionnaire and scales used are provided in the Appendix. If you wish to follow along with the steps described in this chapter, you should start IBM SPSS Statistics and open the file labelled **survey.sav**. Details of the variables used in this analysis are provided below.

File name: **survey.sav**

Variables:
➤ total optimism (Toptim): Total score on the Optimism Scale. Scores can range from 6 to 30, with high scores indicating higher levels of optimism
➤ age group (agegp3): This variable is a recoded variable, dividing age into three equal groups. Group 1: 18–29 = 1; Group 2: 30–44 = 2; Group 3: 45+ = 3 (see instructions for how to do this in Chapter 8)
➤ sex: Males = 1, females = 2.

Examples of research questions: What is the impact of age and gender on optimism? Does gender moderate the relationship between age and optimism?

What you need:
➤ two categorical, independent variables (e.g. sex: males/females, age group: young, middle, old)
➤ one continuous, dependent variable (e.g. total optimism).

What it does: Two-way ANOVA allows you to simultaneously test for the effect of each of your independent variables on the dependent variable and also identifies any interaction effect. For example, it allows you to test for sex differences in optimism; differences in optimism for young, middle and old participants; and the interaction of these two variables—is there a difference in the effect of age on optimism for males and females?

Assumptions: See the introduction to Part Five for a discussion of the assumptions underlying ANOVA.

Non-parametric alternative: None.

Procedure for two-way ANOVA

1. From the menu at the top of the screen, click on **Analyze**, then select **General Linear Model**, then **Univariate**.
2. Click on your dependent, continuous variable (e.g. Total optimism: toptim) and click on the arrow to move it into the box labelled **Dependent Variable**.
3. Click on your two independent, categorical variables (agegp3, sex) and move these into the box labelled **Fixed Factors**.
4. Click on the **Options** button.
   - Click on Descriptive Statistics, Estimates of effect size and Homogeneity tests.
   - Click on Continue.
5. Click on the **Post Hoc** button.
   - From the Factors listed on the left-hand side, choose all the independent variables you are interested in (this variable should have three or more levels or groups—e.g. agegp3).
   - Click on the arrow button to move it into the Post Hoc Tests for section.
   - Choose the test you wish to use (in this case, Tukey).
   - Click on Continue.
6. Click on the **Plots** button.
   - In the Horizontal Axis box, put the independent variable that has the most groups (e.g. agegp3).
   - In the box labelled Separate Lines, put the other independent variable (e.g. sex).
   - Click on Add.
   - In the section labelled Plots, you should now see your two variables listed (e.g. agegp3*sex).
7. Click on **Continue** and then **OK** (or on **Paste** to save to **Syntax Editor**).

The syntax from this procedure is:

```
UNIANOVA toptim BY agegp3 sex
 /METHOD=SSTYPE(3)
 /INTERCEPT=INCLUDE
 /POSTHOC=agegp3(TUKEY)
 /PLOT=PROFILE(agegp3*sex) TYPE=LINE ERRORBAR=NO
MEANREFERENCE=NO YAXIS=AUTO
 /PRINT ETASQ DESCRIPTIVE HOMOGENEITY
 /CRITERIA=ALPHA(.05)
 /DESIGN=agegp3 sex agegp3*sex.
```

Selected output generated from this procedure is shown below. The graph has been modified to be easier to read in black and white.

Descriptive Statistics

Dependent Variable: toptim Total Optimism

agegp3 age 3 groups	sex sex	Mean	Std. Deviation	N
1 18 - 29	1 MALES	21.38	4.330	60
	2 FEMALES	21.34	4.722	87
	Total	21.36	4.551	147
2 30 - 44	1 MALES	22.38	3.549	68
	2 FEMALES	21.88	4.578	85
	Total	22.10	4.147	153
3 45+	1 MALES	22.23	4.090	56
	2 FEMALES	23.47	4.704	79
	Total	22.96	4.485	135
Total	1 MALES	22.01	3.985	184
	2 FEMALES	22.20	4.734	251
	Total	22.12	4.429	435

Levene's Test of Equality of Error Variances[a,b]

		Levene Statistic	df1	df2	Sig.
toptim Total Optimism	Based on Mean	1.083	5	429	.369
	Based on Median	.996	5	429	.420
	Based on Median and with adjusted df	.996	5	400.454	.420
	Based on trimmed mean	1.029	5	429	.400

Tests the null hypothesis that the error variance of the dependent variable is equal across groups.

a. Dependent variable: toptim Total Optimism

b. Design: Intercept + agegp3 + sex + agegp3 * sex

Tests of Between-Subjects Effects

Dependent Variable: toptim Total Optimism

Source	Type III Sum of Squares	df	Mean Square	F	Sig.	Partial Eta Squared
Corrected Model	238.647[a]	5	47.729	2.475	.032	.028
Intercept	206790.069	1	206790.069	10721.408	.000	.962
agegp3	150.863	2	75.431	3.911	.021	.018
sex	5.717	1	5.717	.296	.586	.001
agegp3 * sex	55.709	2	27.855	1.444	.237	.007
Error	8274.374	429	19.288			
Total	221303.000	435				
Corrected Total	8513.021	434				

a. R Squared = .028 (Adjusted R Squared = .017)

Multiple Comparisons

Dependent Variable: toptim Total Optimism

Tukey HSD

(I) age 3 groups	(J) age 3 groups	Mean Difference (I-J)	Std. Error	Sig.	95% Confidence Interval	
					Lower Bound	Upper Bound
1 18 - 29	2 30 - 44	-.74	.507	.308	-1.94	.45
	3 45+	-1.60*	.524	.007	-2.83	-.36
2 30 - 44	1 18 - 29	.74	.507	.308	-.45	1.94
	3 45+	-.85	.519	.230	-2.07	.37
3 45+	1 18 - 29	1.60*	.524	.007	.36	2.83
	2 30 - 44	.85	.519	.230	-.37	2.07

toptim Total Optimism

Tukey HSD[a,b,c]

age 3 groups	N	Subset 1	Subset 2
1 18 - 29	147	21.36	
2 30 - 44	153	22.10	22.10
3 45+	135		22.96
Sig.		.321	.227

Means for groups in homogeneous subsets are displayed.
Based on observed means.
The error term is Mean Square(Error) = 19.288.

a. Uses Harmonic Mean Sample Size = 144.606.

b. The group sizes are unequal. The harmonic mean of the group sizes is used. Type I error levels are not guaranteed.

c. Alpha = .05.

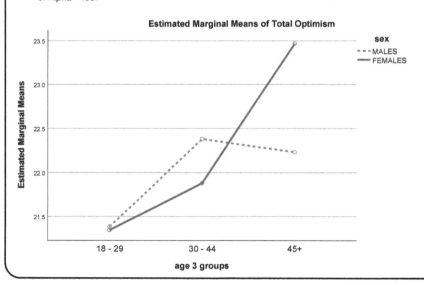

Estimated Marginal Means of Total Optimism

INTERPRETATION OF OUTPUT FROM TWO-WAY ANOVA

Descriptive statistics

These provide the **Mean** scores, **Std deviations** and *N* for each subgroup. Check that these values are correct. Inspecting the pattern of these values can also give you an indication of the impact of your independent variables.

Levene's Test of Equality of Error Variances

This tests one of the assumptions underlying analysis of variance. The value you are most interested in is the **Sig.** level. You want this to be *greater* than .05 and therefore *not* significant. A significant result (**Sig.** value less than .05) suggests that the variance of your dependent variable across the groups is not equal. If you find this to be the case in your study, it is recommended that you set a more stringent significance level (e.g. .01) for evaluating the results of your two-way ANOVA. That is, you consider the main effects and interaction effects significant only if the Sig. value is greater than .01. In the example displayed above, the **Sig.** level is .369. As this is larger than .05, we can conclude that we have not violated the homogeneity of variances assumption.

The main output from two-way ANOVA is a table labelled **Tests of Between-Subjects Effects**. This gives you several pieces of information, not necessarily in the order in which you need to check them.

Interaction effects

The first thing you need to do is to check for the possibility of an interaction effect (e.g. that the influence of age on optimism levels depends on whether you are male or female). If you find a significant interaction effect, you cannot easily and simply interpret the main effects. This is because in order to describe the influence of one of the independent variables you need to specify the level of the other independent variable. In the output, the row we need to focus on is labelled **agegp3*sex**. To find out whether the interaction is significant, check the **Sig.** column for that row. If the value is less than or equal to .05 (e.g. .03, .01, .001), there is a significant interaction effect. In our example, the interaction effect is not significant (agegp3*sex: Sig. = .237). This indicates that there is no significant difference in the effect of age on optimism for males and females.

Warning: When checking significance levels in this output, make sure you read the correct column (the one labelled **Sig.**—a lot of students make the mistake of reading the **Partial Eta Squared** column, with dangerous consequences!).

Main effects

We did not have a significant interaction effect; therefore, we can safely interpret the main effects. These are the simple effect of one independent variable (e.g. the effect of sex with all age groups collapsed). In the left-hand column, find the variable you are interested in (e.g. agegp3). To determine whether there is a main effect for each independent variable, check in the column marked **Sig.** If the value is less than or equal to .05 (e.g. .03, .001), there is a significant main effect for that independent variable. In the example shown above, there is a significant main effect for age group (agegp3: Sig. = .021) but no significant main effect for sex (sex: Sig. = .586). This means that males and females do not differ in terms of their optimism scores, but there is a difference in scores for young, middle-aged and old participants.

Effect size

The effect size for the agegp3 variable is provided in the column labelled **Partial Eta Squared** (.018). Using Cohen's (1988) criterion, this can be classified as small (see introduction to Part Five). So, although this effect reaches statistical significance, the actual difference in the mean values is very small. From the **Descriptive Statistics** table we can see that the mean scores for the three age groups (collapsed for sex) are 21.36, 22.10 and 22.96. The difference between the groups appears to be of little practical significance.

Post-hoc tests

Although we know that our age groups differ, we do not know where these differences occur: is Group 1 different from Group 2, is Group 2 different from Group 3, is Group 1 different from Group 3? To investigate these questions, we need to conduct post-hoc tests (see description of these in the introduction to Part Five). Post-hoc tests are relevant only if you have more than two levels (groups) to your independent variable. These tests systematically compare each of your pairs of groups and indicate whether there is a significant difference in the means of each. These post-hoc tests are provided as part of the ANOVA output. You are, however, not supposed to look at them until you find a significant main effect or interaction effect in the overall (omnibus) analysis of variance test. In this example, we obtained a significant main effect for Group 3 in our ANOVA; therefore, we are entitled to dig further using the post-hoc tests for age group.

Multiple comparisons

The results of the post-hoc tests are provided in the table labelled **Multiple Comparisons**. We have requested the Tukey Honestly Significant Difference (**HSD**) test, as this is one of the more commonly used tests. Scan down the column labelled **Sig.** for any values less than .05. Significant results are also indicated by an asterisk in the column labelled **Mean Difference**. In the above example, only Group 1 (18–29) and Group 3 (45+) differ significantly from one another.

Plots

You can see at the end of the output a plot of the optimism scores for males and females, across the three age groups. This plot is very useful for allowing you to visually inspect the relationships, among your variables. This is often easier than trying to decipher a large table of numbers. Although presented last, the plots are often useful to inspect first to help you better understand the impact of your two independent variables.

Warning: When interpreting these plots, remember to consider the scale used to plot your dependent variable. Sometimes, what appears to be an enormous difference on the plot may involve only a few points of difference. You can see this in the current example. In the plot, there appears to be quite a large difference in male and female scores for the older age group (45+). If you read across to the scale, however, the difference is only small (22.2 as compared with 23.5).

PRESENTING THE RESULTS FROM TWO-WAY ANOVA

The results of the analysis conducted above could be presented as follows:

A two-way between-groups analysis of variance was conducted to explore the impact of sex and age on levels of optimism, as measured by the Life Orientation Test (LOT). Participants were divided into three groups according to their age (Group 1: 18–29 years, Group 2: 30–44 years, Group 3: 45 years and above). The interaction effect between sex and age group was not statistically significant, $F (2, 429) = 1.44$, $p = .24$. There was a statistically significant main effect for age, $F (2, 429) = 3.91$, $p = .02$; however, the effect size was small (partial eta squared $= .02$). Post-hoc comparisons using the Tukey HSD test indicated that the mean score for the 18–29 years age group ($M = 21.36$, $SD = 4.55$) was significantly different from the 45+ years age group ($M = 22.96$, $SD = 4.49$). The 30–44 years age group ($M = 22.10$, $SD = 4.15$) did not differ significantly from either of the other groups. The main effect for sex, $F (1, 429) = .30$, $p = .59$, did not reach statistical significance.

For other examples of how to present the results of analysis of variance see Chapter 9 in Nicol and Pexman (2010b).

ADDITIONAL ANALYSES IF YOU OBTAIN A SIGNIFICANT INTERACTION EFFECT

If you obtain a significant result for your interaction effect, you may wish to conduct follow-up tests to explore this relationship further (this applies only if one of your variables has three or more levels). One way that you can do this is to conduct an analysis of simple effects. This means that you consider the results for each of the subgroups separately. This involves splitting the sample into groups according to one of your independent variables and running separate one-way ANOVAs to explore the effect of the other variable. If we had obtained a significant interaction effect in the above example, we might choose to split the file by sex and assess the effect of age on optimism separately for males and females. To split the sample and repeat analyses for each group, you need to use the **Split File** option. This option allows you to split your sample according to one categorical variable and to repeat analyses separately for each group.

Procedure for splitting the sample

1. From the menu at the top of the screen, click on **Data**, then click on **Split File**.
2. Click on **Organize output by groups**.
3. Move the grouping variable (sex) into the box marked **Groups based on**.
4. This splits the sample by sex and repeats any analyses that follow for these two groups separately.
5. Click on **OK**.

After splitting the file, you then perform a one-way ANOVA (see Chapter 18), comparing optimism levels for the three age groups. With the **Split File** in operation, you obtain separate results for males and females.

Important: Once you have completed the analysis remember to turn off the **Split File** option; otherwise, all subsequent analyses will be split for the two groups. To turn it off, choose **Data** from the menu and select **Split File**. Tick the first option, **Analyze all cases, do not create groups**, and then click on **OK**.

ADDITIONAL EXERCISES

Business
Data file: **staffsurvey.sav**. See Appendix for details of the data file.

1. Conduct a two-way ANOVA with post-hoc tests (if appropriate) to compare staff satisfaction scores (*totsatis*) across each of the length of service categories (*servicegp3*) for permanent and casual staff (*employstatus*).

Health
Data file: **sleep.sav**. See Appendix for details of the data file.

1. Conduct a two-way ANOVA with post-hoc tests (if appropriate) to compare male and female (*gender*) mean sleepiness ratings (Sleepiness and Associated Sensations Scale total score: *totSAS*) for the three age groups defined by the variable *agegp3* (37 or under, 38–50, 51+).

20

Mixed between–within subjects analysis of variance

In the previous analysis of variance chapters, we have explored the use of both between-subjects designs (comparing two or more different groups) and within-subjects, or repeated measures, designs (one group of participants exposed to two or more conditions). Up until now, we have treated these approaches separately. There may be situations, however, where you want to combine the two approaches in the one study, with one independent variable being between-subjects and the other within-subjects. For example, you may want to investigate the impact of an intervention on clients' anxiety levels (using a pre-test/post-test design), but you would also like to know whether the impact is different for males and females. In this case, you have two independent variables: one is a between-subjects variable (gender: males/females); the other is a within-subjects variable (time). In this case, you would expose a group of both males and females to the intervention and measure their anxiety levels at Time 1 (pre-intervention) and again at Time 2 (after the intervention).

IBM SPSS Statistics allows you to combine between-subjects and within-subjects variables in the one analysis. You may see this analysis referred to in some texts as a 'split-plot ANOVA', (SPANOVA) design. I have chosen to use Tabachnick and Fidell's (2013) term, 'mixed between-within subjects ANOVA' because I feel this best describes what is involved. This technique is an extension to the repeated measures design discussed in Chapter 18. It would be a good idea to review that chapter before proceeding further.

This chapter is intended as a very brief overview of mixed between-within subjects ANOVA. If you intend to use this technique in your own research, read more broadly (e.g. Harris 1994; Keppel & Zedeck 2004; Stevens 1996; Tabachnick & Fidell 2013).

DETAILS OF EXAMPLE

To illustrate the use of mixed between-within subjects ANOVA, I use the **experim.sav** data file included on the website that accompanies this book (see p. ix). These data refer to a fictitious study that involves testing the impact of two different types of interventions in helping students cope with their anxiety concerning a forthcoming statistics course (see the Appendix for full details of the study). Students were divided into two equal groups and asked to complete a Fear of Statistics Test. One group was given a series of sessions designed to improve their mathematical skills; the second group participated in a program designed to build their confidence. After the program, they were again asked to complete the same test they had done before the program. They were also followed up 3 months later. If you wish to follow the procedures detailed below, you will need to start IBM SPSS Statistics and open the **experim.sav** file.

In this example, I compare the impact of the maths skills class (Group 1) and the confidence-building class (Group 2) on participants' scores on the Fear of Statistics Test across the three time periods. Details of the variable names and labels from the data file are provided below.

File name: **experim.sav**

Variables:
➢ type of class (group): 1 = maths skills, 2 = confidence building
➢ fear of Statistics Test scores at Time 1 (fost1): Administered before the program. Scores range from 20 to 60. High scores indicate greater fear of statistics
➢ fear of Statistics Test scores at Time 2 (fost2): Administered at the end of the program
➢ fear of Statistics Test scores at Time 3 (fost3): Administered 3 months after the program was complete.

Examples of research questions: Which intervention is more effective in reducing participants' Fear of Statistics Test scores across the three time periods (pre-intervention, post-intervention, 3-month follow-up)? Is there a change in participants' Fear of Statistics Test scores across the three time periods?

What you need: At least three variables are involved:
➢ one categorical, independent, between-subjects variable with two or more levels (Group 1/Group 2)
➢ one categorical, independent, within-subjects variable with two or more levels (Time 1/Time 2/Time 3)
➢ one continuous, dependent variable (scores on the Fear of Statistics Test measured at each time period).

What it does: This analysis tests whether there are main effects for each of the independent variables and whether the interaction between them is significant. In this example, it tells us whether there is a change in Fear of Statistics Test scores over the three time periods (main effect for time). It compares the two interventions (maths skills/confidence building) in terms of their effectiveness in reducing fear of statistics (main effect for group). Finally, it tells us whether the change in Fear of Statistics Test scores over time is different for the two groups (interaction effect).

Assumptions: See the introduction to Part Five for a discussion of the general assumptions underlying ANOVA.

Additional assumption: Homogeneity of intercorrelations. For each of the levels of the between-subjects variable, the pattern of intercorrelations among the levels of the within-subjects variable should be the same. This assumption is tested as part of the analysis, using Box's M statistic. Because this statistic is very sensitive, a more conservative alpha level of .001 should be used. You are hoping that the statistic is not significant (i.e. the probability level should be greater than .001).

Non-parametric alternative: None.

Procedure for mixed between-within ANOVA
1. From the menu at the top of the screen, click on **Analyze**, then select **General Linear Model**, then **Repeated measures**.
2. In the box labelled **Within-Subject Factor Name**, type a name that describes the within-subjects factor (e.g. time). This is not an actual variable name but a descriptive term that you choose.
3. In the **Number of Levels** box, type the number of levels that this factor has (in this case there are three time periods; therefore, you would type 3).
4. Click on the **Add** button. Click on the **Define** button.
5. Click on the variables that represent the within-subjects factor (e.g. fear of stats scores from Time 1, Time 2 and Time 3).
6. Click on the arrow to move these into the **Within-Subjects Variables** box. You will see them listed (using only the short variable names: fost1, fost2, fost3).
7. Click on your between-subjects variable (e.g. type of class: group). Click on the arrow to move this variable into the **Between-Subjects Factors** box.
8. Click on the **Options** button.
   ➤ Select Descriptive statistics, Estimates of effect size, Homogeneity tests.
   ➤ Click on Continue.
9. Click on the **Plots** button.
   ➤ Click on the within-groups factor (e.g. time) and move it into the box labelled Horizontal Axis.

➢ Click on the between-groups variable (e.g. group) and move it into the Separate Lines box.
10. Click on **Add**. In the **Plots** box, you should see your variables listed (e.g. time*group).
11. Click on **Continue** and then **OK** (or on **Paste** to save to **Syntax Editor**).

The syntax from this procedure is:

```
GLM fost1 fost2 fost3 BY group
  /WSFACTOR=time 3 Polynomial
  /METHOD=SSTYPE(3)
  /PLOT=PROFILE(time*group) TYPE=LINE ERRORBAR=NO
  MEANREFERENCE=NO YAXIS=AUTO
  /PRINT=DESCRIPTIVE ETASQ HOMOGENEITY
  /CRITERIA=ALPHA(.05)
  /WSDESIGN=time
  /DESIGN=group.
```

Selected output generated from this procedure is shown below.

Descriptive Statistics

	group type of class	Mean	Std. Deviation	N
fost1 fear of stats time1	1 maths skills	39.87	4.596	15
	2 confidence building	40.47	5.817	15
	Total	40.17	5.160	30
fost2 fear of stats time2	1 maths skills	37.67	4.515	15
	2 confidence building	37.33	5.876	15
	Total	37.50	5.151	30
fost3 fear of stats time3	1 maths skills	36.07	5.431	15
	2 confidence building	34.40	6.631	15
	Total	35.23	6.015	30

Box's Test of Equality of Covariance Matrices[a]

Box's M	1.520
F	.224
df1	6
df2	5680.302
Sig.	.969

Tests the null hypothesis that the observed covariance matrices of the dependent variables are equal across groups.

a. Design: Intercept + group
   Within Subjects Design: time

Multivariate Tests[a]

Effect		Value	F	Hypothesis df	Error df	Sig.	Partial Eta Squared
time	Pillai's Trace	.663	26.593[b]	2.000	27.000	.000	.663
	Wilks' Lambda	.337	26.593[b]	2.000	27.000	.000	.663
	Hotelling's Trace	1.970	26.593[b]	2.000	27.000	.000	.663
	Roy's Largest Root	1.970	26.593[b]	2.000	27.000	.000	.663
time * group	Pillai's Trace	.131	2.034[b]	2.000	27.000	.150	.131
	Wilks' Lambda	.869	2.034[b]	2.000	27.000	.150	.131
	Hotelling's Trace	.151	2.034[b]	2.000	27.000	.150	.131
	Roy's Largest Root	.151	2.034[b]	2.000	27.000	.150	.131

Mauchly's Test of Sphericity[a]

Measure: MEASURE_1

Within Subjects Effect	Mauchly's W	Approx. Chi-Square	df	Sig.	Epsilon[b] Greenhouse-Geisser	Epsilon[b] Huynh-Feldt	Lower-bound
time	.348	28.517	2	.000	.605	.640	.500

Tests the null hypothesis that the error covariance matrix of the orthonormalized transformed dependent variables is proportional to an identity matrix.

a. Design: Intercept + group
   Within Subjects Design: time

b. May be used to adjust the degrees of freedom for the averaged tests of significance. Corrected tests are displayed in the Tests of Within-Subjects Effects table.

Levene's Test of Equality of Error Variances[a]

		Levene Statistic	df1	df2	Sig.
fost1 fear of stats time1	Based on Mean	.893	1	28	.353
	Based on Median	.855	1	28	.363
	Based on Median and with adjusted df	.855	1	27.441	.363
	Based on trimmed mean	.897	1	28	.352
fost2 fear of stats time2	Based on Mean	.767	1	28	.389
	Based on Median	.815	1	28	.374
	Based on Median and with adjusted df	.815	1	27.589	.375
	Based on trimmed mean	.789	1	28	.382
fost3 fear of stats time3	Based on Mean	.770	1	28	.388
	Based on Median	.652	1	28	.426
	Based on Median and with adjusted df	.652	1	27.565	.426
	Based on trimmed mean	.736	1	28	.398

Tests of Between-Subjects Effects

Measure: MEASURE_1

Transformed Variable: Average

Source	Type III Sum of Squares	df	Mean Square	F	Sig.	Partial Eta Squared
Intercept	127464.100	1	127464.100	1531.757	.000	.982
group	4.900	1	4.900	.059	.810	.002
Error	2330.000	28	83.214			

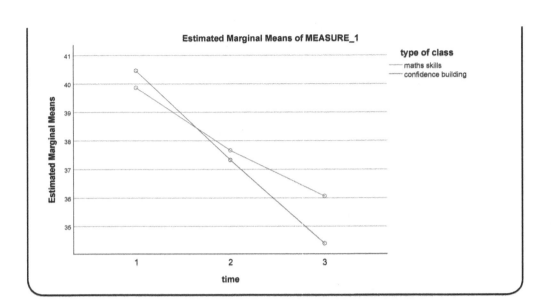

INTERPRETATION OF OUTPUT FROM MIXED BETWEEN-WITHIN SUBJECTS ANOVA

You will notice (once again) that this technique generates a good deal of rather complex-looking output. If you have worked your way through the previous chapters, you will recognise some of the output from other analysis of variance procedures. This output provides tests for the assumptions of sphericity, univariate ANOVA results and multivariate ANOVA results. Full discussion of the difference between the univariate and multivariate results is beyond the scope of this book; in this chapter, only the multivariate results are discussed (for more information see Stevens 1996, pp. 466–469). The reason for interpreting the multivariate statistics is that the univariate statistics make the assumption of sphericity. The sphericity assumption requires that the variance of the population difference scores for any two conditions are the same as the variance of the population difference scores for any other two conditions (an assumption that is commonly violated). This is assessed using Mauchly's Test of Sphericity. The multivariate statistics do not require sphericity. You can see in our example that we have violated the assumption of sphericity, as indicated by the Sig. value of .000 in the table labelled **Mauchly's Test of Sphericity**. Although there are ways to compensate for this assumption violation, it is safer to inspect the multivariate statistics provided in the output.

Let's explore the key values in the output.

Descriptive statistics

In the first output table, you are provided with the descriptive statistics for your three sets of scores (**Mean, Std Deviation, N**). It is a good idea to check that these make sense. Are there the right numbers of people in each group? Do the **Mean** values make sense given the scale that was used? In the example above, you can see that the highest Fear of Statistics Test scores are at Time 1 (39.87 and 40.47), that they drop at Time 2 (37.67 and 37.33) and drop even further at Time 3 (36.07 and 34.40). What we don't know, however, is whether these differences are large enough to be considered statistically significant.

Assumptions

Check the **Levene's Test of Equality of Error Variances** table to see if you have violated the assumption of homogeneity of variances. We want the **Sig.** value to be non-significant (bigger than .05). In this case, the value for each variable is greater than .05 (.35, .39, .39); therefore, we are safe and can proceed.

The next thing to check is **Box's Test of Equality of Covariance Matrices**. We want a **Sig.** value that is bigger than .001. In this example the value is .97; therefore, we have not violated this assumption.

Interaction effect

Before we can investigate the main effects, we first need to assess the interaction effect. Is there the same change in scores over time for the two different groups (maths skills/confidence building)? This is indicated in the second set of rows in the **Multivariate Tests** table (**time*group**). The value that you are interested in is **Wilks' Lambda** and the associated probability value given in the column labelled **Sig.** All of the multivariate tests yield the same result; however, the most commonly reported statistic is Wilks' Lambda. In this case, the interaction effect is not statistically significant (the **Sig.** level for Wilks' Lambda is .15, which is greater than our alpha level of .05).

Main effects

Because we have shown that the interaction effect is *not* significant, we can now move on and assess the main effects for each of our independent variables. If the interaction effect was significant, we would have to be very careful in interpreting the main effects. This is because a significant interaction means that the impact of one variable is influenced by the level of the second variable; therefore, general conclusions (as in main effects) are usually not appropriate. If you get a significant interaction, always check your plot to guide your interpretation.

In this example, the value for **Wilks' Lambda** for time is .337, with a **Sig.** value of .000 (which really means $p < .0005$). Because our p value is less than .05, we can conclude that there is a statistically significant effect for time. This suggests that there was a change in Fear of Statistics Test scores across the three different time periods. The main effect for time was significant.

Although we have found a statistically significant difference among the time periods, we also need to assess the effect size of this result (see discussion on effect sizes in the introduction to Part Five). The value you are interested in is **Partial Eta Squared**, given in the **Multivariate Tests** output table. The value obtained for time in this study is .663. Using the commonly used guidelines proposed by Cohen (1988, pp. 284–287): .01 = small effect, .06 = moderate effect, .14 = large effect, this result suggests a very large effect size.

Between-subjects effect

Now that we have explored the within-subjects effects, we need to consider the main effect of our between-subjects variable (type of class: maths skills/confidence building).

The results that we need to consider are in the table labelled **Tests of Between-Subjects Effects**. Read across the row labelled **Group** (this is the shortened IBM SPSS Statistics variable name for the type of class). The **Sig**. value is .81. This is not less than our alpha level of .05, so we conclude that the main effect for group is not significant. There was no significant difference in the Fear of Statistics Test scores for the two groups (those who received maths skills training and those who received the confidence-building intervention).

The effect size of the between-subjects effect is also given in the **Tests of Between-Subjects Effects** table. The **Partial Eta Squared** value for **group** in this case is .002. This is very small. It is therefore not surprising that it did not reach statistical significance.

PRESENTING THE RESULTS FROM MIXED BETWEEN-WITHIN ANOVA

The method of presenting the results for this technique is a combination of that used for a between-groups ANOVA (see Chapter 19) and a repeated measures ANOVA (see Chapter 18). Always report the interaction effect first, as this will impact on your ability to interpret the main effects for each independent variable. Note that for APA style the statistics are italicised.

A mixed between-within subjects analysis of variance was conducted to assess the impact of two different interventions (maths skills, confidence building) on participants' scores on the Fear of Statistics Test across three time periods (pre-intervention, post-intervention and 3-month follow-up). There was no significant interaction between program type and time, Wilks' Lambda = .87, $F(2, 27) = 2.03$, $p = .15$, partial eta squared = .13. There was a substantial main effect for time, Wilks' Lambda = .34, $F(2, 27) = 26.59$, $p < .001$, partial eta squared = .66, with both groups showing a reduction in Fear of Statistics Test scores across the three time periods (see Table 1). The main effect comparing the two types of interventions was not significant, $F(1, 28) = .059$, $p = .81$, partial eta squared = .002, suggesting no difference in the effectiveness of the two teaching approaches.

Table 1

Fear of Statistics Test Scores for the Maths Skills and Confidence-Building Programs Across Three Time Periods

Time period	Maths Skills			Confidence Building		
	n	M	SD	n	M	SD
Pre-intervention	15	39.87	4.60	15	40.47	5.82
Post-intervention	15	37.67	4.51	15	37.33	5.88
3-month follow-up	15	36.07	5.43	15	34.40	6.63

For other examples of how to present the results of analysis of variance see Chapter 9 in Nicol and Pexman (2010b).

21

Multivariate analysis of variance

In previous chapters, we explored the use of analysis of variance to compare groups on a *single* dependent variable. In many research situations, however, we are interested in comparing groups on a range of different characteristics. This is quite common in clinical research, where the focus is on the evaluation of the impact of an intervention on a variety of outcome measures (e.g. anxiety, depression).

Multivariate analysis of variance (MANOVA) is an extension of analysis of variance for use when you have *more than one dependent* variable. These dependent variables should be related in some way, or there should be some conceptual reason for considering them together. MANOVA compares the groups and tells you whether the mean differences between the groups on the combination of dependent variables are likely to have occurred by chance. To do this, MANOVA creates a new summary dependent variable, which is a linear combination of each of your original dependent variables. It then performs an analysis of variance using this new combined dependent variable. MANOVA will tell you if there is a significant difference between your groups on this composite dependent variable; it also provides the univariate results for each of your dependent variables separately.

Some of you might be thinking: 'Why not just conduct a series of ANOVAs separately for each dependent variable?' This is in fact what many researchers do. Unfortunately, by conducting a whole series of analyses you run the risk of an inflated Type 1 error. (See the introduction to Part Five for a discussion of Type 1 and Type 2 errors.) Put simply, this means that the more analyses you run the more likely you are to find a significant result, even if, in reality, there are no differences between your groups. The advantage of using MANOVA is that it controls or adjusts, for this increased risk of a Type 1 error; however, this comes at a cost. MANOVA is a much more complex set of procedures, and it has a set of additional assumptions that must be met.

If you decide that MANOVA is a bit out of your depth just yet, all is not lost. You can still perform a series of ANOVAs separately for each of your dependent variables. If you choose to do this, you might like to reduce the risk of a Type 1 error by setting a more stringent alpha value. One way to control for the Type 1 error across multiple tests is to use a Bonferroni adjustment. To do this, you divide your normal alpha value (typically .05) by the number of tests that you intend to perform. If there are three dependent variables, you would divide .05 by 3 (which equals .017 after rounding) and you would use this new value as your cut-off. Differences between your groups would need a probability value of less than .017 before you could consider them statistically significant.

MANOVA can be used in one-way, two-way and higher-order factorial designs (with multiple independent variables) and when using analysis of covariance (controlling for an additional variable). In the example provided in this chapter, a simple one-way MANOVA is demonstrated. Coverage of more complex designs is beyond the scope of this book. If you intend to use MANOVA in your own research, I strongly recommend that you read up on it and make sure you understand it fully. Suggested reading includes Tabachnick and Fidell (2013); Hair, Black, Babin, Anderson and Tatham (2009); and Stevens (1996).

DETAILS OF EXAMPLE

To demonstrate MANOVA, I have used the data file **survey.sav** on the website that accompanies this book. For a full description of this study, please see the Appendix. In this example, the difference between males and females on a set of measures of well-being is explored. These include measures of negative mood (Negative Affect Scale), positive mood (Positive Affect Scale) and perceived stress (Total Perceived Stress Scale). If you wish to follow along with the procedures described below, you should start IBM SPSS Statistics and open the file labelled **survey.sav**.

Examples of research questions: Do males and females differ in terms of overall well-being? Are males better adjusted than females in terms of their positive and negative mood states and levels of perceived stress?

What you need: One-way MANOVA:
➤ one categorical, independent variable (e.g. sex)
➤ two or more continuous, dependent variables that are related (e.g. negative affect, positive affect, perceived stress).

MANOVA can also be extended to two-way and higher-order designs involving two or more categorical, independent variables.

What it does: Compares two or more groups in terms of their means on a group of dependent variables. Tests the null hypothesis that the population means on a set of dependent variables do not vary across different levels of a factor or grouping variable.

Assumptions: MANOVA has a set of assumptions. These are discussed in more detail in the next section. You should also review the material on assumptions in the introduction to Part Five of this book.

Non-parametric alternative: None.

ASSUMPTIONS TESTING

Before proceeding with the main MANOVA analysis, we test whether our data conform to the assumptions. Some of these tests are not strictly necessary given our large sample size, but I demonstrate them so that you can see the steps involved.

1. Sample size
You need to have more cases in each cell than you have dependent variables. Ideally, you should have more than this, but this is the absolute minimum. Having a larger sample can also help you get away with violations of some of the other assumptions (e.g. normality). The minimum required number of cases in each cell in this example is three (the number of dependent variables). We have a total of six cells (two levels of our independent variable, male/female, and three dependent variables for each). The number of cases in each cell is provided as part of the MANOVA output. In our case, we have many more than the required number of cases per cell (see the **Descriptive statistics** table in the **Output**).

2. Normality
Although the significance tests of MANOVA are based on the multivariate normal distribution, in practice it is reasonably robust to modest violations of normality (except where the violations are due to outliers). According to Tabachnick and Fidell (2013, p. 253), a sample size of at least 20 in each cell should ensure robustness. You need to check both univariate normality (see Chapter 6) and multivariate normality (using Mahalanobis distances). The procedures used to check for normality can also help you identify any outliers (see Assumption 3).

3. Outliers
MANOVA is quite sensitive to outliers (i.e. data points or scores that are different from the remainder of the scores). You need to check for univariate outliers (for each of the dependent variables separately) and multivariate outliers. Multivariate outliers are participants with a strange combination of scores on the various dependent vari-

ables (e.g. very high on one variable, but very low on another). Check for univariate outliers by using **Explore** (see Chapter 6). The procedure to check for multivariate outliers and multivariate normality is demonstrated below.

Checking multivariate normality

To test for multivariate normality, we ask IBM SPSS Statistics to calculate Mahalanobis distances using the **Regression** menu. *Mahalanobis distance* is the distance of a particular case from the centroid of the remaining cases, where the centroid is the point created by the means of all the variables (Tabachnick & Fidell 2013). This analysis will pick up on any cases that have a strange pattern of scores *across* the three dependent variables.

The procedure detailed below will create a new variable in your data file (labelled 'mah_1'). Each person or subject receives a value on this variable that indicates the degree to which their pattern of scores differs from the remainder of the sample. To decide whether a case is an outlier, you need to compare the Mahalanobis distance value against a critical value (this is obtained using a chi-square critical value table). If an individual's mah_1 score exceeds this value, it is considered an outlier. MANOVA can tolerate a few outliers, particularly if their scores are not too extreme and you have a reasonable size data file. With too many outliers, or very extreme scores, you may need to consider deleting the cases or, alternatively, transforming the variables involved (see Tabachnick & Fidell 2013, p. 72).

Procedure for obtaining Mahalanobis distances
1. From the menu at the top of the screen, click on **Analyze**, then select **Regression**, then **Linear**.
2. Click on the variable in your data file that uniquely identifies each of your cases (in this case, it is ID). Move this variable into the **Dependent** box.
3. In the **Independent** box, put the continuous, dependent variables that you will be using in your MANOVA analysis (e.g. Total Negative Affect: tnegaff, total positive affect: tposaff, total perceived stress: tpstress).
4. Click on the **Save** button. In the section marked **Distances**, click on **Mahalanobis**.
5. Click on **Continue** and then **OK** (or on **Paste** to save to **Syntax Editor**).

The syntax from this procedure is:

```
REGRESSION
  /MISSING LISTWISE
  /STATISTICS COEFF OUTS R ANOVA
  /CRITERIA=PIN(.05) POUT(.10)
  /NOORIGIN
  /DEPENDENT id
  /METHOD=ENTER tposaff tnegaff tpstress
  /SAVE MAHAL .
```

Some of the output generated from this procedure is shown below.

Residuals Statistics[a]

	Minimum	Maximum	Mean	Std. Deviation	N
Predicted Value	239.04	317.73	276.25	13.576	432
Std. Predicted Value	-2.741	3.056	.000	1.000	432
Standard Error of Predicted Value	8.344	34.955	15.220	4.870	432
Adjusted Predicted Value	233.16	316.81	276.23	13.654	432
Residual	-297.100	448.062	.000	165.473	432
Std. Residual	-1.789	2.698	.000	.997	432
Stud. Residual	-1.805	2.711	.000	1.001	432
Deleted Residual	-302.419	452.382	.012	167.023	432
Stud. Deleted Residual	-1.810	2.732	.000	1.002	432
Mahal. Distance	.090	18.101	2.993	2.793	432
Cook's Distance	.000	.025	.002	.003	432
Centred Leverage Value	.000	.042	.007	.006	432

a. Dependent Variable: id

Towards the bottom of this table, you can see a row labelled **Mahal. Distance**. Check across to the column marked **Maximum**. Take note of this value (in this example, it is 18.1). You will be comparing this number to a critical value. This critical value is determined by using a chi-square table, with the number of dependent variables that you have as your degrees of freedom (*df*) value. The alpha value that you use is .001. To simplify this whole process I have summarised the key values for you in Table 21.1, for studies up to 10 dependent variables.

Find the column with the number of dependent variables that you have in your study (in this example, it is 3). Read across to find the critical value (in this case, it is 16.27). Compare the maximum value you obtained from your output (e.g. 18.1) with

Numbere of dependent variables	Critical value	Number of dependent variables	Critical value	Number of dependent variables	Critical value	Table 21.1
2	13.82	5	20.52	8	26.13	Critical values for evaluating
3	16.27	6	22.46	9	27.88	Mahalanobis
4	18.47	7	24.32	10	29.59	distance values

Source: extracted and adapted from a table in Tabachnick and Fidell (1996); originally from Pearson, E.S. and Hartley, HO. (Eds) (1958). *Biometrika tables for statisticians* (vol. 1, 2nd edn). New York: Cambridge University Press.

this critical value. If your number of dependent variables is larger than the critical value, you have multivariate outliers in your data file. In my example at least one of my cases exceeded the critical value of 16.27, suggesting the presence of multivariate outliers. I need to do further investigation to find out how many cases are involved and just how different they are from the remaining cases. If the maximum value for Mahalanobis distance was less than the critical value, I could safely have assumed that there were no substantial multivariate outliers and proceeded to check other assumptions.

The easiest way to find out more about these outliers is to follow the instructions in Chapter 5 to sort the cases (descending) by the new variable that appears in your data file (MAH_1). It is labelled MAH_2 in my data file because I already had a MAH_1 from the earlier chapter on multiple regression. In the **Data View** window the cases are listed in order from largest to smallest MAH_2, with the largest value of 18.1 at the top of the MAH_2 column.

In our example, only one person had a score that exceeded the critical value. This was the person with ID = 415 and a score of 18.1. Because we only have one person and their score is not too high, I decide to leave this person in the data file. If there had been a lot of outlying cases, I might have needed to consider transforming this group of variables (see Chapter 8) or removing the cases from the data file. If you find yourself in this situation, make sure you read in more detail about these options before deciding to take either of these courses of action (Tabachnick & Fidell 2013, p. 72).

4. Linearity
This assumption refers to the presence of a straight-line relationship between each pair of your dependent variables. This can be assessed in a variety of ways, the most straightforward of which is to generate a matrix of scatterplots between each pair of your variables. The instructions for how to do this, and the output obtained, are provided in Chapter 7. The plots in the example do not show any obvious evidence of non-linearity; therefore, our assumption of linearity is satisfied.

5. Homogeneity of regression

This assumption is important only if you are intending to perform a stepdown analysis. This approach is used when you have some theoretical or conceptual reason for ordering your dependent variables. It is quite a complex procedure and is beyond the scope of this book. If you are interested in finding out more, see Tabachnick and Fidell (2013, p. 254).

6. Multicollinearity and singularity

MANOVA works best when the dependent variables are moderately correlated. With low correlations, you should consider running separate univariate analysis of variance for your various dependent variables. When the dependent variables are highly correlated, this is referred to as 'multicollinearity'. This can occur when one of your variables is a combination of other variables (e.g. the total scores of a scale that is made up of subscales that are also included as dependent variables). This is referred to as 'singularity', and can be avoided by knowing what your variables are and how the scores are obtained.

While there are quite sophisticated ways of checking for multicollinearity, the simplest way is to run **Correlation** and to check the strength of the correlations among your dependent variables (see Chapter 11). Correlations up around .8 or .9 are reason for concern. If you find any of these, you may need to consider removing one variable in any pair of strongly correlated dependent variables.

7. Homogeneity of variance-covariance matrices

The test of this assumption is generated as part of your MANOVA output: **Box's *M* Test of Equality of Covariance Matrices**. This is discussed in more detail in the interpretation of the output presented below.

PERFORMING MANOVA

The procedure for performing a one-way multivariate analysis of variance to explore sex differences in our set of dependent variables (Total Negative Affect, Total Positive Affect, Total perceived stress) is described below. This technique can be extended to perform a two-way or higher-order factorial MANOVA by adding additional independent variables. It can also be extended to include covariates (see Chapter 22).

Procedure for MANOVA

1. From the menu at the top of the screen, click on **Analyze**, then select **General Linear Model**, then **Multivariate**.
2. In the **Dependent Variables** box, enter each of your dependent variables (e.g. Total Positive Affect, Total Negative Affect, Total perceived stress).

3. In the **Fixed Factors** box, enter your independent variable (e.g. sex).
4. Click on the **Model** button. Make sure that the **Full factorial** button is selected in the **Specify Model** box.
5. Down the bottom in the **Sum of squares** box, **Type III** should be displayed. This is the default method of calculating sums of squares. Click on **Continue**.
6. Click on the **Options** button. Select **Descriptive Statistics**, **Estimates of effect size** and **Homogeneity tests**. Click on **Continue**.
7. Click on the **EM Means** button. In the section labelled **Factor and Factor interactions** click on your independent variable (e.g. sex). Move it into the box marked **Display Means for**.
8. Click on **Continue** and then **OK** (or on **Paste** to save to **Syntax Editor**).

The syntax generated from this procedure is:

```
GLM
  tposaff tnegaff tpstress BY sex
  /METHOD = SSTYPE(3)
  /INTERCEPT = INCLUDE
  /EMMEANS = TABLES(sex)
  /PRINT = DESCRIPTIVE ETASQ HOMOGENEITY
  /CRITERIA = ALPHA(.05)
  /DESIGN = sex .
```

Selected output generated from this procedure is shown below.

Descriptive Statistics

	sex sex	Mean	Std. Deviation	N
tposaff Total positive affect	1 MALES	33.63	6.985	184
	2 FEMALES	33.69	7.439	248
	Total	33.66	7.241	432
tnegaff Total negative affect	1 MALES	18.71	6.901	184
	2 FEMALES	19.98	7.178	248
	Total	19.44	7.082	432
tpstress Total perceived stress	1 MALES	25.79	5.414	184
	2 FEMALES	27.42	6.078	248
	Total	26.72	5.854	432

Box's Test of Equality of Covariance Matrices[a]

Box's M	6.942
F	1.148
df1	6
df2	1074771.869
Sig.	.331

Tests the null hypothesis that the observed covariance matrices of the dependent variables are equal across groups.

a. Design: Intercept + sex

Multivariate Tests[a]

Effect		Value	F	Hypothesis df	Error df	Sig.	Partial Eta Squared
Intercept	Pillai's Trace	.987	10841.625[b]	3.000	428.000	.000	.987
	Wilks' Lambda	.013	10841.625[b]	3.000	428.000	.000	.987
	Hotelling's Trace	75.993	10841.625[b]	3.000	428.000	.000	.987
	Roy's Largest Root	75.993	10841.625[b]	3.000	428.000	.000	.987
sex	Pillai's Trace	.024	3.569[b]	3.000	428.000	.014	.024
	Wilks' Lambda	.976	3.569[b]	3.000	428.000	.014	.024
	Hotelling's Trace	.025	3.569[b]	3.000	428.000	.014	.024
	Roy's Largest Root	.025	3.569[b]	3.000	428.000	.014	.024

a. Design: Intercept + sex

b. Exact statistic

Levene's Test of Equality of Error Variances[a]

		Levene Statistic	df1	df2	Sig.
tposaff Total positive affect	Based on Mean	1.065	1	430	.303
	Based on Median	1.036	1	430	.309
	Based on Median and with adjusted df	1.036	1	429.355	.309
	Based on trimmed mean	1.029	1	430	.311
tnegaff Total negative affect	Based on Mean	1.251	1	430	.264
	Based on Median	1.467	1	430	.226
	Based on Median and with adjusted df	1.467	1	428.196	.226
	Based on trimmed mean	1.374	1	430	.242
tpstress Total perceived stress	Based on Mean	2.074	1	430	.151
	Based on Median	2.056	1	430	.152
	Based on Median and with adjusted df	2.056	1	425.730	.152
	Based on trimmed mean	2.057	1	430	.152

Tests the null hypothesis that the error variance of the dependent variable is equal across groups.

a. Design: Intercept + sex

Tests of Between-Subjects Effects

Source	Dependent Variable	Type III Sum of Squares	df	Mean Square	F	Sig.	Partial Eta Squared
Corrected Model	tposaff Total positive affect	.440[a]	1	.440	.008	.927	.000
	tnegaff Total negative affect	172.348[b]	1	172.348	3.456	.064	.008
	tpstress Total perceived stress	281.099[c]	1	281.099	8.342	.004	.019
Intercept	tposaff Total positive affect	478633.634	1	478633.634	9108.270	.000	.955
	tnegaff Total negative affect	158121.903	1	158121.903	3170.979	.000	.881
	tpstress Total perceived stress	299040.358	1	299040.358	8874.752	.000	.954
sex	tposaff Total positive affect	.440	1	.440	.008	.927	.000
	tnegaff Total negative affect	172.348	1	172.348	3.456	.064	.008
	tpstress Total perceived stress	281.099	1	281.099	8.342	.004	.019
Error	tposaff Total positive affect	22596.218	430	52.549			
	tnegaff Total negative affect	21442.088	430	49.865			
	tpstress Total perceived stress	14489.121	430	33.696			
Total	tposaff Total positive affect	512110.000	432				
	tnegaff Total negative affect	184870.000	432				
	tpstress Total perceived stress	323305.000	432				
Corrected Total	tposaff Total positive affect	22596.657	431				
	tnegaff Total negative affect	21614.435	431				
	tpstress Total perceived stress	14770.220	431				

a. R Squared = .000 (Adjusted R Squared = -.002)

b. R Squared = .008 (Adjusted R Squared = .006)

c. R Squared = .019 (Adjusted R Squared = .017)

Estimated Marginal Means

sex

Dependent Variable	sex	Mean	Std. Error	95% Confidence Interval	
				Lower Bound	Upper Bound
tposaff Total positive affect	1 MALES	33.625	.534	32.575	34.675
	2 FEMALES	33.690	.460	32.785	34.594
tnegaff Total negative affect	1 MALES	18.707	.521	17.683	19.730
	2 FEMALES	19.984	.448	19.103	20.865
tpstress Total perceived stress	1 MALES	25.788	.428	24.947	26.629
	2 FEMALES	27.419	.369	26.695	28.144

INTERPRETATION OF OUTPUT FROM MANOVA

The key aspects of the output generated by MANOVA are presented below.

Descriptive statistics

Check that the information is correct. In particular, check that the N values correspond to what you know about your sample. These N values are your cell sizes (see Assumption 1 earlier in this chapter). Make sure that you have more cases in each cell than the number of dependent variables. If you have over 30, then any violations of normality or equality of variance that may exist are not going to matter too much.

Box's Test of Equality of Covariance Matrices

The output table labelled **Box's Test of Equality of Covariance Matrices** tells you whether your data violate the assumption of homogeneity of variance-covariance matrices. If the Sig. value is *larger* than .001, you have *not* violated the assumption. Tabachnick and Fidell (2013, p. 254) warn that Box's M can tend to be too strict when you have a large sample size and equal group sizes. Fortunately, in our example the Box's M Sig. value is .33; therefore, we have not violated this assumption.

Levene's Test of Equality of Error Variances

The next table to inspect is **Levene's Test of Equality of Error Variances**. In the **Sig.** column, scan for any values that are *less* than .05. These would indicate that you have violated the assumption of equality of variance for that variable. In the current example, none of the variables recorded a significant value; therefore, we can assume equal variances. If you do violate this assumption of equality of variances, you may need to consider setting a more conservative alpha level for determining significance for that variable in the univariate F-test. Tabachnick and Fidell (2013) suggest an alpha of .025 or .01 rather than the conventional .05 level.

Multivariate tests

This set of multivariate tests of significance indicates whether there are statistically significant differences among the groups on a linear combination of the dependent variables. There are several different statistics to choose from (Wilks' Lambda, Hotelling's Trace, Pillai's Trace). One of the most commonly reported statistics is **Wilks' Lambda**. Tabachnick and Fidell (2013) recommend Wilks' Lambda for general use; however, if your data have problems (small sample size, unequal *N* values, violation of assumptions), then Pillai's Trace is more robust (see comparison of statistics in Tabachnick & Fidell 2013, p. 271). In situations where you have only two groups, the *F*-tests for Wilks' Lambda, Hotelling's Trace and Pillai's Trace are identical.

Wilks' Lambda

You can find the value you are looking for in the *second* section of the **Multivariate Tests** table, in the row labelled with the name of your independent, or grouping, variable (in this case, Sex). Don't make the mistake of using the first set of figures, which refers to the intercept. Find the value of **Wilks' Lambda** and its associated significance level (**Sig.**). If the significance level is *less* than .05, then you can conclude that there is a difference among your groups. Here, we obtained a **Wilks' Lambda** value of .976, with a significance value of .014. This is less than .05; therefore, there is a statistically significant difference between males and females in terms of their overall wellbeing.

Between-subjects effects

If you obtain a significant result on this multivariate test of significance, this gives you permission to investigate further in relation to each of your dependent variables. Do males and females differ on all of the dependent measures, or just some? This information is provided in the **Tests of Between-Subjects Effects** output table. Because you are performing several separate analyses here, it is suggested that you set a higher alpha level to reduce the chance of a Type 1 error (i.e. finding a significant result when there isn't really one). The most common way of doing this is to apply a Bonferroni adjustment. In its simplest form, this involves dividing your original alpha level of .05 by the number of analyses that you intend to do (see Tabachnick & Fidell 2013, p. 272, for more sophisticated versions of this formula). In this case, we have three dependent variables to investigate; therefore, we would divide .05 by 3, giving a new alpha level of .017. We consider our results significant only if the probability value (**Sig.**) is less than .017.

In the **Tests of Between-Subjects Effects** box, move down to the third set of values, the row labelled with your independent variable (in this case, Sex). You can see each of your dependent variables listed, with their associated univariate *F*, *df* and **Sig.** values. You interpret these in the same way as you would a normal one-way analysis of variance. In the **Sig.** column, scan for any values that are less than .017 (our new adjusted alpha level). In our example, only one of the dependent variables (total perceived stress) recorded a significance value less than our cut-off (with a **Sig.** value of .004). In this study, the only significant difference between males and females was on their perceived stress scores.

Effect size

The importance of the impact of sex on perceived stress can be evaluated using the effect size statistic provided in the final column. **Partial Eta Squared** represents the proportion of the variance in the dependent variable (perceived stress scores) that can be explained by the independent variable (sex). The value in this case is .019, which, according to generally accepted criteria (Cohen 1988, pp. 284–287), is considered quite a small effect (see the introduction to Part Five for a discussion of effect size). This represents only 1.9 per cent of the variance in perceived stress scores explained by sex.

Comparing group means

Although we know that males and females differed in terms of perceived stress, we do not know who had the higher scores. To find this out, we refer to the output table provided in the section labelled **Estimated Marginal Means**. For Total perceived stress, the mean score for males was 25.79 and for females 27.42. Although statistically significant, the actual difference in the two mean scores was very small: fewer than 2 scale points.

Follow-up analyses

In the example shown above, there were only two levels to the independent variable (males, females). When you have independent variables with three or more levels, it is necessary to conduct follow-up univariate analyses to identify where the significant differences lie (compare Group 1 with Group 2, and compare Group 2 with Group 3 etc.). One way to do this would be to use one-way ANOVA on the dependent variables that were significant in the MANOVA (e.g. perceived stress). Within the one-way ANOVA procedure (see Chapter 18), you could request post-hoc tests for your variable with three or more levels. Remember to make the necessary adjustments to your alpha level using the Bonferroni adjustment if you run multiple analyses.

PRESENTING THE RESULTS FROM MANOVA

The results of this multivariate analysis of variance could be presented as follows:

A one-way between-groups multivariate analysis of variance was performed to investigate sex differences in psychological wellbeing. Three dependent variables were used: positive affect, negative affect and perceived stress. The independent variable was gender. Preliminary assumption testing was conducted to check for normality, linearity, univariate and multivariate outliers, homogeneity of variance-covariance matrices, and multicollinearity, with no serious violations noted. There was a statistically significant difference between males and females on the combined dependent variables, $F(3, 428)$ = 3.57, p = .014, Wilks' Lambda = .98, partial eta squared = .02. When the results for the dependent variables were considered separately, the only difference to reach statistical significance, using a Bonferroni adjusted alpha level of .017, was perceived stress, $F(1, 430)$ = 8.34, p = .004, partial eta squared = .02. An inspection of the mean scores indicated that females reported slightly higher levels of perceived stress (M = 27.42, SD = 6.08) than males (M = 25.79, SD = 5.41).

For other examples of how to present the results of multivariate analysis of variance see Chapter 10 in Nicol and Pexman (2010b).

ADDITIONAL EXERCISE

Health
Data file: **sleep.sav**. See Appendix for details of the data file.

1. Conduct a one-way MANOVA to see if there are gender differences in each of the individual items that make up the Sleepiness and Associated Sensations Scale. The variables you need as dependent variables are *fatigue*, *lethargy*, *tired*, *sleepy* and *energy*.

22

Analysis of covariance

Analysis of covariance is an extension of analysis of variance (discussed in Chapter 18) that allows you to explore differences between groups while statistically controlling for an additional (continuous) variable. This additional variable (called a 'covariate') is a variable that you suspect may be influencing scores on the dependent variable. IBM SPSS Statistics uses regression procedures to remove the variation in the dependent variable that is due to any covariates and then performs the normal analysis of variance techniques on the corrected or adjusted scores. By removing the influence of these additional variables, ANCOVA can increase the power or sensitivity of the F-test. That is, it may increase the likelihood that you will be able to detect differences between your groups.

Analysis of covariance can be used as part of one-way, two-way and multivariate ANOVA techniques. In this chapter, IBM SPSS Statistics procedures are discussed for analysis of covariance associated with the following designs:

➤ one-way between-groups ANOVA (one independent variable, one dependent variable)
➤ two-way between-groups ANOVA (two independent variables, one dependent variable).

In the following sections, I provide some background on the technique and assumptions that need to be tested, followed by some worked examples. Before running the analyses, I suggest you read the introductory sections in this chapter and revise the appropriate ANOVA chapters (Chapters 18 and 19). Multivariate ANCOVA is not illustrated in this chapter. If you are interested in this technique, I suggest you read Tabachnick and Fidell (2013).

USES OF ANCOVA

ANCOVA can be used when you have a two-group pre-test/post-test design (e.g. comparing the impact of two different interventions, taking before and after measures for each group). The scores on the pre-test are treated as a covariate to control for pre-existing differences between the groups. This makes ANCOVA very useful in situations when you have quite small sample sizes and only small or medium effect sizes (see discussion on effect sizes in the introduction to Part Five). Under these circumstances (which are very common in social science research), Stevens (1996) recommends the use of two or three carefully chosen covariates to reduce the error variance and increase your chances of detecting a significant difference between your groups.

ANCOVA is also handy when you have been unable to randomly assign your participants to the different groups and instead have had to use existing groups (e.g. classes of students). As these groups may differ across a variety of attributes, not just the one you are interested in, ANCOVA can be used to reduce some of these differences. The use of well-chosen covariates can help address the confounding influence of group differences. This is certainly not an ideal situation, as it is not possible to control for all possible differences; however, it does help reduce this systematic bias. The use of ANCOVA with intact or existing groups is a contentious issue among writers in the field. It would be a good idea to read more widely if you find yourself in this situation. Some of these issues are summarised in Stevens (1996, pp. 324–327).

Choosing appropriate covariates

ANCOVA can be used to control for one or more covariates at the same time. These covariates need to be chosen carefully, however (see Stevens 1996, p. 320; Tabachnick & Fidell 2013, p. 205). In identifying possible covariates, you should ensure you have a good understanding of the theory and previous research that has been conducted in your topic area. The variables that you choose as your covariates should be continuous variables, measured reliably (see Chapter 9), and should correlate significantly with the dependent variable. Ideally, you should choose a small set of covariates that are only moderately correlated with one another, so that each contributes uniquely to the variance explained. The covariate must be measured before the treatment or experimental manipulation is performed. This is to prevent scores on the covariate from also being influenced by the treatment.

Alternatives to ANCOVA

There are a number of assumptions or limitations associated with ANCOVA. Sometimes, you will find that your research design or your data are not suitable. Both Tabachnick and Fidell (2013, p. 223) and Stevens (1996, p. 327) suggest alternative approaches to ANCOVA. It would be a good idea to explore these alternatives and to evaluate the best course of action given your particular circumstances.

ASSUMPTIONS

In this chapter, only the key assumptions for ANCOVA are discussed. I suggest that you read further on this topic if you intend to use this approach in your own research. Tabachnick and Fidell (2013, p. 203) give a good, detailed coverage of this topic, including the issues of unequal sample sizes, outliers, multicollinearity, normality, homogeneity of variance, linearity, homogeneity of regression and reliability of covariates (what an impressive and awe-inspiring list of statistical jargon!).

1. Influence of treatment on covariate measurement
In designing your study, you should ensure that the covariate is measured *prior to* the treatment or experimental manipulation. This is to avoid scores on the covariate also being influenced by the treatment. If the covariate is affected by the treatment condition, this change will be correlated with the change that occurs in your dependent variable. When ANCOVA removes (controls for) the covariate it will also remove some of the treatment effect, thereby reducing the likelihood of obtaining a significant result.

2. Reliability of covariates
ANCOVA assumes that covariates are measured without error, which is a rather unrealistic assumption in the majority of social science research. Some variables that you may wish to control, such as age, can be measured reasonably reliably; others that rely on a scale may not meet this assumption. There are several things you can do to improve the reliability of your measurement tools:

➤ Search for good, well-validated scales and questionnaires. Make sure they measure what you think they measure (don't just rely on the title—check the manual and inspect the items) and that they are suitable for your sample.
➤ Check the internal consistency (a form of reliability) of your scale by calculating Cronbach alpha (see Chapter 9). Values should be above .7 (preferably above .8) to be considered reliable.
➤ If you have had to write the questions yourself, make sure they are clear, appropriate and unambiguous. Make sure the questions and response scales are appropriate for all of your groups. Always pilot-test your questions before conducting the full study.
➤ If you are using any form of equipment or measuring instrumentation, make sure that it is functioning properly and calibrated appropriately. Make sure the person operating the equipment is competent and trained in its use.

> ➤ If your study involves using other people to observe or rate behaviour, make sure they are trained and that each observer uses the same criteria. Preliminary pilot-testing to check inter-rater consistency would be useful here.

3. Correlations among covariates

There should not be strong correlations among the variables you choose for your covariates. Ideally, you want a group of covariates that correlate substantially with the dependent variable but not with one another. To choose appropriate covariates, you should use the existing theory and research to guide you. Run some preliminary correlation to explore the strength of the relationship among your proposed covariates. If you find that the covariates you intend to use correlate strongly (e.g. $r = .80$), you should consider removing one or more of them (see Stevens 1996, p. 320). Each of the covariates you choose should pull its own weight—overlapping covariates do not contribute to a reduction in error variance.

4. Linear relationship between dependent variable and covariate

ANCOVA assumes that the relationship between the dependent variable and each of your covariates is linear (straight-line). If you are using more than one covariate, it also assumes a linear relationship between each of the pairs of your covariates. Violations of this assumption are likely to reduce the power (sensitivity) of your test. Remember, one of the reasons for including covariates was to increase the power of your analysis of variance test.

Scatterplots can be used to test for linearity, but these need to be checked separately for each of your groups (i.e. the different levels of your independent variable). If you discover any curvilinear relationships, these may be corrected by transforming your variable (see Chapter 8), or, alternatively, you may wish to drop the offending covariate from the analysis. Disposing of covariates that misbehave is often easier, given the difficulty in interpreting transformed variables.

5. Homogeneity of regression slopes

This impressive-sounding assumption requires that the relationship between the covariate and dependent variable for each of your groups is the same. This is indicated by similar slopes on the regression line for each group. Unequal slopes would indicate that there is an interaction between the covariate and the treatment. If there is an interaction then the results of ANCOVA are misleading, and therefore it should not be conducted (see Stevens 1996, pp. 323, 331; Tabachnick & Fidell 2013, p. 205). The procedure for checking this assumption is provided in the examples presented later in this chapter.

ONE-WAY ANCOVA

In this section, I take you step by step through the process of performing a one-way analysis of covariance. One-way ANCOVA involves one independent, categorical variable (with two or more levels or conditions), one dependent, continuous variable, and one or more continuous covariates. This technique is often used when evaluating the impact of an intervention or experimental manipulation while controlling for pre-test scores.

Details of example

To illustrate the use of one-way ANCOVA, I use the **experim.sav** data file included on the website that accompanies this book (see p. ix). These data refer to a fictitious study that involves testing the impact of two different types of interventions in helping students cope with their anxiety concerning a forthcoming statistics course (see the Appendix for full details of the study). Students were divided into two equal groups and asked to complete a set of scales (including one that measures fear of statistics). One group was given sessions designed to improve their mathematical skills; the second group participated in a program designed to build their confidence. After the program, they were again asked to complete the same scales they completed before the program. If you wish to follow the procedures detailed below, you will need to start IBM SPSS Statistics and open the data file **experim.sav**.

In this example, I explore the impact of the maths skills class (Group 1) and the confidence-building class (Group 2) on participants' scores on the Fear of Statistics Test while controlling for the scores on this test administered before the program. Details of the variable names and labels from the data file are provided below.

File name: **experim.sav**

Variables:
- type of class (group) 1 = maths skills, 2 = confidence building
- fear of Statistics Test scores at Time 1 (fost1): Administered prior to the program. Scores range from 20 to 60. High scores indicate greater fear of statistics
- fear of Statistics Test scores at Time 2 (fost2): Administered after the program
- fear of Statistics Test scores at Time 3 (fost3): Administered 3 months after the program.

Example of research question: Is there a significant difference in the Fear of Statistics Test scores for the maths skills group (Group 1) and the confidence-building group (Group 2) while controlling for their pre-test scores on this test?

What you need: At least three variables are involved:

➢ one categorical, independent variable with two or more levels (Group 1/Group 2)
➢ one continuous, dependent variable (scores on the Fear of Statistics Test at Time 2)
➢ one or more continuous covariates (scores on the Fear of Statistics Test at Time 1).

What it does: ANCOVA will tell us if the mean Fear of Statistics Test scores at Time 2 for the two groups are significantly different after the initial pre-test scores are controlled for.

Assumptions: All normal one-way ANOVA assumptions apply (see the introduction to Part Five). These should be checked first. Additional ANCOVA assumptions (see description of these presented earlier in this chapter):

1. Covariate is measured prior to the intervention or experimental manipulation
2. Covariate is measured without error (or as reliably as possible)
3. Covariates are not strongly correlated with one another
4. Linear relationship between the dependent variable and the covariate for all groups (linearity)
5. The relationship between the covariate and dependent variable is the same for each of the groups (homogeneity of regression slopes).

Non-parametric alternative: None.

Testing assumptions

Before you can begin testing the specific assumptions associated with ANCOVA, check the assumptions for a normal one-way analysis of variance (normality, homogeneity of variance). You should review the introduction to Part Five and Chapter 18 before going any further here. To save space, I do not repeat that material here; I focus on the additional ANCOVA assumptions listed in the summary above.

1. Measurement of the covariate

This assumption specifies that the covariate should be measured before the treatment or experimental manipulation begins. This is not tested statistically but instead forms part of your research design and procedures. This is why it is important to plan your study with a good understanding of the statistical techniques that you intend to use.

2. Reliability of the covariate

This assumption concerning the reliability of the covariate is also part of your research design and involves choosing the most reliable measuring tools available. If you have used a psychometric scale or measure, you can check the internal consistency reliability by calculating Cronbach alpha using the **Reliability** procedures (see Chapter 9). Given that I have manufactured the data to illustrate this technique, I cannot test the reliability of the Fear of Statistics Test. If they were real data, I would check that the Cronbach alpha value was at least .70 (preferably .80).

3. Correlations among the covariates

If you are using more than one covariate, you should check to see that they are not too strongly correlated with one another ($r = .8$ and above). To do this, you need to use the **Correlation** procedure (this is described in detail in Chapter 11). As I have only one covariate, I do not need to do this here.

4. Linearity

There is a range of different ways you can check the assumption of a linear relationship between the dependent variable and the covariates for all your groups. In the procedure section below, I show you a quick way.

Procedure for checking linearity for each group

To follow along with this example, open the **experim.sav** file.

Step 1

1. From the menu at the top of the screen, click on **Graphs**, then **Chart Builder**, and then **OK**.
2. Click on the **Gallery** tab and select **Scatter/Dot**. Click on the third graph (**Grouped Scatter**) and drag this to the **Chart Preview** area by holding your left mouse button down.
3. Choose your categorical, independent variable (e.g. group) and drag to the **Set Colour** box.
4. Click and drag your covariate (fear of stats time1: fost1) to the **X-Axis**, and click and drag your dependent variable (fear of stats time2: fost2) to the **Y-Axis**.
5. Click on **OK** (or on **Paste** to save to **Syntax Editor**).

The syntax from this procedure is:

```
GGRAPH
 /GRAPHDATASET NAME="graphdataset" VARIABLES=fost1 fost2 group
 MISSING=LISTWISE REPORTMISSING=NO
 /GRAPHSPEC SOURCE=INLINE
 /FITLINE TOTAL=NO SUBGROUP=NO.
BEGIN GPL
 SOURCE: s=userSource(id("graphdataset"))
```

```
DATA: fost1=col(source(s), name("fost1"))
DATA: fost2=col(source(s), name("fost2"))
DATA: group=col(source(s), name("group"), unit.category())
GUIDE: axis(dim(1), label("fear of stats time1"))
GUIDE: axis(dim(2), label("fear of stats time2"))
GUIDE: legend(aesthetic(aesthetic.color.interior), label("type of class"))
GUIDE: text.title(label("Grouped Scatter of fear of stats time2 by fear of stats time1
by type ",
  "of class"))
SCALE: cat(aesthetic(aesthetic.color.interior), include("1", "2"))
ELEMENT: point(position(fost1*fost2), color.interior(group))
END GPL.
```

Step 2
1. Once you have the scatterplot displayed, double-click on it to open the **Chart Editor** window.
2. From the menu, click on **Elements** and select **Fit line at Subgroups**. Two lines will appear on the graph representing line of best fit for each group. The equation for each line will also appear superimposed on the lines.
3. Click on **File** and then **Close**.

The output from this procedure is shown below.

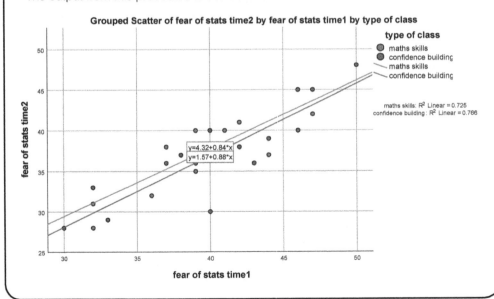

Grouped Scatter of fear of stats time2 by fear of stats time1 by type of class

Check the general distribution of scores for each of your groups. Does there appear to be a linear (straight-line) relationship for each group? What you don't want to see is an indication of a curvilinear relationship. In the above example the relationship is clearly linear, so we have not violated the assumption of a linear relationship. If you find a curvilinear relationship you may want to reconsider the use of this covariate, or, alternatively, you could try transforming the variable (see Chapter 8) and repeating the scatterplot to see whether there is an improvement.

5. Homogeneity of regression slopes

This final assumption concerns the relationship between the covariate and the dependent variable for each of your groups. What you are checking is that there is no interaction between the covariate and the treatment or experimental manipulation. There are several different ways to evaluate this assumption.

Graphically, you can inspect the scatterplot between the dependent variable and the covariate obtained when testing for Assumption 4 (see above). Are the two lines (corresponding to the two groups in this study) similar in their slopes? In the above example the two lines are very similar, so it does not appear that we have violated this assumption. If the lines had been noticeably different in their orientation, this might suggest that there is an interaction between the covariate and the treatment (as shown by the different groups). This would mean a violation of this assumption.

This assumption can also be assessed statistically, rather than graphically. This involves checking to see whether there is a statistically significant interaction between the treatment and the covariate. If the interaction is significant at an alpha level of .05, then we have violated the assumption. The procedure to check this is described next.

Procedure to check for homogeneity of regression slopes
1. From the menu at the top of the screen, click on **Analyze**, then select **General Linear Model**, then **Univariate**.
2. In the **Dependent Variables** box put your dependent variable (e.g. fear of stats time2: fost2).
3. In the **Fixed Factor** box put your independent, or grouping, variable (e.g. type of class: group).
4. In the **Covariate** box put your covariate (e.g. fear of stats time1: fost1).
5. Click on the **Model** button. Click on **Build Terms**.
6. Check that the **Interaction** option is showing in the **Build Terms** box.
7. Click on your independent variable (group) and then the arrow button to move it into the **Model** box.
8. Click on your covariate (fost1) and then the arrow button to move it into the **Model** box.

9. Go back and click on your independent variable (group) again on the left-hand side (in the **Factors and Covariates** section). While this is highlighted, hold down the Ctrl key, and then click on your covariate variable (fost1). Click on the arrow button to move this into the right-hand side box labelled **Model**.
10. In the **Model** box, you should now have listed your independent variable (group), your covariate (fost1) and an extra line of the form: covariate * independent variable (fost1*group). The final term is the interaction that we are checking for.
11. Click on **Continue** and then **OK** (or on **Paste** to save to **Syntax Editor**).

The syntax from this procedure is:

```
UNIANOVA fost2 BY group WITH fost1
  /METHOD = SSTYPE(3)
  /INTERCEPT = INCLUDE
  /CRITERIA = ALPHA(.05)
  /DESIGN = group fost1 fost1*group .
```

Selected output generated by this procedure is shown below.

Tests of Between-Subjects Effects

Dependent Variable: fost2 fear of stats time2

Source	Type III Sum of Squares	df	Mean Square	F	Sig.
Corrected Model	577.689[a]	3	192.563	26.102	.000
Intercept	3.877	1	3.877	.525	.475
group	.846	1	.846	.115	.738
fost1	538.706	1	538.706	73.022	.000
group * fost1	.409	1	.409	.055	.816
Error	191.811	26	7.377		
Total	42957.000	30			
Corrected Total	769.500	29			

a. R Squared = .751 (Adjusted R Squared = .722)

In the output obtained from this procedure, the only value that you are interested in is the significance level of the interaction term (shown above as **Group*Fost1**). You can ignore the rest of the output. If the **Sig.** level for the interaction is less than or equal to .05 your interaction is statistically significant, indicating that you have violated the assumption. In this situation, we do *not* want a significant result. We want a **Sig.** value of *greater* than .05. In the above example the **Sig.** or probability value is .816, safely above the cut-off. We have not violated the assumption of homogeneity of regression slopes. This supports the earlier conclusion gained from an inspection of the scatterplots for each group.

Now that we have finished checking the assumptions, we can proceed with the ANCOVA analysis to explore the differences between our treatment groups.

Procedure for one-way ANCOVA

1. From the menu at the top of the screen, click on **Analyze**, then select **General Linear Model**, then **Univariate**.
2. In the **Dependent Variables** box put your dependent variable (e.g. fear of stats time2: fost2).
3. In the **Fixed Factor** box put your independent, or grouping, variable (e.g. type of class: group).
4. In the **Covariate** box put your covariate (e.g. fear of stats time1: fost1).
5. Click on the **Model** button. Click on **Full Factorial**. Click on **Continue**.
6. Click on the **Options** button. Tick **Descriptive statistics**, **Estimates of effect size** and **Homogeneity tests**. Click on **Continue**.
7. Click on the **EM Means** button. Click on your independent variable (group) and move it into the **Display Means for** box.
8. Click on **Continue** and then **OK** (or on **Paste** to save to **Syntax Editor**).

The syntax generated from this procedure is:

```
UNIANOVA fost2 BY group WITH fost1
 /METHOD=SSTYPE(3)
 /INTERCEPT=INCLUDE
 /EMMEANS=TABLES(group) WITH(fost1=MEAN)
 /PRINT ETASQ DESCRIPTIVE HOMOGENEITY
 /CRITERIA=ALPHA(.05)
 /DESIGN=fost1 group.
```

The output generated from this procedure is shown below.

Descriptive Statistics

Dependent Variable: fost2 fear of stats time2

group type of class	Mean	Std. Deviation	N
1 maths skills	37.67	4.515	15
2 confidence building	37.33	5.876	15
Total	37.50	5.151	30

Levene's Test of Equality of Error Variances[a]

Dependent Variable: fost2 fear of stats time2

F	df1	df2	Sig.
.141	1	28	.710

Tests the null hypothesis that the error variance
of the dependent variable is equal across
groups.

a. Design: Intercept + fost1 + group

Tests of Between-Subjects Effects

Dependent Variable: fost2 fear of stats time2

Source	Type III Sum of Squares	df	Mean Square	F	Sig.	Partial Eta Squared
Corrected Model	577.279[a]	2	288.640	40.543	.000	.750
Intercept	3.510	1	3.510	.493	.489	.018
fost1	576.446	1	576.446	80.970	.000	.750
group	5.434	1	5.434	.763	.390	.027
Error	192.221	27	7.119			
Total	42957.000	30				
Corrected Total	769.500	29				

a. R Squared = .750 (Adjusted R Squared = .732)

Estimated Marginal Means

type of class

Dependent Variable: fost2 fear of stats time2

type of class	Mean	Std. Error	95% Confidence Interval Lower Bound	Upper Bound
1 maths skills	37.926[a]	.690	36.512	39.341
2 confidence building	37.074[a]	.690	35.659	38.488

a. Covariates appearing in the model are evaluated at the following values: fost1 fear of stats time1 = 40.17.

Interpretation of output from one-way ANCOVA

➤ Check that the details in the **Descriptive Statistics** table are correct.

➤ Check the **Levene's Test of Equality of Error Variances** table to see if you violated the assumption of equality of variance. You want the **Sig.** value to be *greater* than .05. If this value is smaller than .05 (and therefore significant), this means that your variances are not equal and that you have violated the assumption. In this case we have not violated the assumption, because our **Sig.** value is .71, which is much larger than our cut-off of .05.

➤ The main ANCOVA results are presented in the next table, labelled **Test of Between-Subjects Effects**. We want to know whether our groups are significantly different in terms of their scores on the dependent variable (e.g. fear of statistics Time 2). Find the row corresponding to your independent variable (group) and read across to the column labelled **Sig.** If the value in this column is *less* than .05 (or an alternative alpha level you have set), your groups differ significantly. In this example our value is .39, which is greater than .05; therefore, our result is *not* significant. There is not a significant difference in the Fear of Statistics Test scores for participants in the maths skills group and the confidence-building group after controlling for scores on the Fear of Statistics Test administered prior to the intervention.

➤ You should also consider the effect size, as indicated by the corresponding **Partial Eta Squared** value (see the introduction to Part Five for a description of what an effect size is). The value in this case is only .027 (a small effect size according to Cohen's [1988] guidelines). This value also indicates how much of the variance in the dependent variable is explained by the independent variable. Convert the partial eta squared value to a percentage by multiplying by 100 (shift the decimal point two places to the right). In this example, we are able to explain only 2.7 per cent of the variance.

➤ The other piece of information that we can gain from the Test of Between-Subjects Effects table concerns the influence of our covariate. Find the row in the table that corresponds to the covariate (e.g. fost1: Fear of Statistics at Time 1). Read across to the **Sig.** level. This indicates whether there is a significant relationship between the covariate and the dependent variable while controlling for the independent variable (group). In the row corresponding to fost1 (our covariate), you can see that the Sig. value is .000 (which actually means less than .0005). This is less than .05, so our covariate is significant. In fact, it explained 75 per cent of the variance in the dependent variable (partial eta squared of .75 multiplied by 100).

➤ The final table in the ANCOVA output (**Estimated Marginal Means**) provides us with the adjusted means on the dependent variable for each of our groups. 'Adjusted' refers to the fact that the effect of the covariate has been statistically removed.

Presenting the results from one-way ANCOVA

The results of this one-way analysis of covariance could be presented as follows (note that for APA style the statistics are italicised):

A one-way between-groups analysis of covariance was conducted to compare the effectiveness of two different interventions designed to reduce participants' fear of statistics. The independent variable was the type of intervention (maths skills, confidence building), and the dependent variable consisted of scores on the Fear of Statistics Test administered after the intervention was completed. Participants' scores on the pre-intervention administration of the Fear of Statistics Test were used as the covariate in this analysis.

Preliminary checks were conducted to ensure that there was no violation of the assumptions of normality, linearity, homogeneity of variances, homogeneity of regression slopes or reliable measurement of the covariate. After adjusting for pre-intervention scores, there was no significant difference between the two intervention groups on post-intervention scores on the Fear of Statistics Test, $F (1, 27) = .76$, $p = .39$, partial eta squared $= .03$. There was a strong relationship between the pre-intervention and post-intervention scores on the Fear of Statistics Test, as indicated by a partial eta squared value of .75.

In presenting the results of this analysis, you would also provide a table of means for each of the groups. If the same scale is used to measure the dependent variable (Time 2) and the covariate (Time 1), you should include the means at Time 1 and Time 2. You can get these by running **Descriptives** (see Chapter 6).

If a different scale is used to measure the covariate, you will provide the unadjusted mean (and standard deviation) and the adjusted mean (and standard error) for the two groups. The unadjusted mean is available from the **Descriptive Statistics** table. The adjusted mean (controlling for the covariate) is provided in the **Estimated Marginal Means** table. It is also a good idea to include the number of cases in each of your groups.

For other examples of how to present the results of analysis of covariance see Chapter 11 in Nicol and Pexman (2010b).

TWO-WAY ANCOVA

In this section, I take you step by step through the process of performing a two-way analysis of covariance. Two-way ANCOVA involves two independent, categorical variables (with two or more levels or conditions), one dependent, continuous variable and one or more continuous covariates. It is important that you have a good understanding of the standard two-way analysis of variance procedure and assumptions before proceeding further here. Refer to Chapter 19 in this book.

The example that I use here is an extension of that presented in the one-way ANCOVA section above. In that analysis, I was interested in determining which intervention (maths skills or confidence building) was more effective in reducing students' fear of statistics. I found no significant difference between the groups.

Suppose that in reading further in the literature on the topic I found some research that suggested there might be a difference in how males and females respond to different interventions. You may see this additional variable (e.g. sex) described in the literature as a 'moderator'. That is, it moderates or influences the effect of the other independent variable. Often, these moderator variables are individual difference variables, characteristics of individuals that influence the way in which they respond to an experimental manipulation or treatment condition.

It is important if you obtain a non-significant result for your one-way ANCOVA that you consider the possibility of moderator variables. Some of the most interesting research occurs when a researcher stumbles across (or systematically investigates) moderator variables that help to explain why some researchers obtain statistically significant results while others do not. In your own research always consider factors such as gender and age, as these can play an important part in influencing the results. Studies conducted on young university students don't necessarily generalise to broader (and older) community samples. Research on males sometimes yields quite different results when repeated using female samples. The message here is to consider the possibility of moderator variables in your research design and, where appropriate, include them in your study.

Details of example

In the example presented below I use the same data that were used in the previous section, but I add an additional independent variable (gender: 1 = male, 2 = female). This allows me to broaden my analysis to see whether gender is acting as a moderator variable in influencing the effectiveness of the two programs. I am interested in the possibility of a significant interaction effect between sex and intervention group. Males might benefit most from the maths skills intervention, while females might benefit more from the confidence-building program.

Warning: The sample size used to illustrate this example is very small, particularly when you break the sample down by the categories of the independent variables (gender and group). If using this technique with your own research you should really try to have a much larger data file overall, with a good number in each of the categories of your independent variables.

If you wish to follow along with the steps detailed below, you need to start IBM SPSS Statistics and open the data file labelled **experim.sav** provided on the website accompanying this book.

Examples of research questions: Does gender influence the effectiveness of two programs designed to reduce participants' fear of statistics? Is there a difference, shown in post-intervention Fear of Statistics Test scores, between males and females in their response to a maths skills program and a confidence-building program?

What you need: At least four variables are involved:
- ➤ two categorical, independent variables with two or more levels (sex: male/female; group: maths skills/confidence building)
- ➤ one continuous, dependent variable (Fear of Statistics Test scores at Time 2)
- ➤ one or more continuous covariates (Fear of Statistics Test scores at Time 1).

What it does: ANCOVA will control for scores on your covariate(s) and then perform a normal two-way ANOVA. This can tell you if there is a:
- ➤ significant main effect for your first independent variable (group)
- ➤ main effect for your second independent variable (sex)
- ➤ significant interaction between the two.

Assumptions: All normal two-way ANOVA assumptions apply (e.g. normality, homogeneity of variance). These should be checked first (see the introduction to Part Five).

Additional ANCOVA assumptions: See discussion of these assumptions, and the procedures to test them, in the one-way ANCOVA section presented earlier in this chapter.

Non-parametric alternative: None.

Procedure for two-way ANCOVA

1. From the menu at the top of the screen, click on **Analyze**, then select **General Linear Model**, then **Univariate**.
2. Click on your dependent variable (e.g. fear of stats time2: fost2) and move it into the **Dependent Variables** box.
3. Click on your two independent, or grouping, variables (e.g. group, sex). Move these into the **Fixed Factor** box.
4. In the **Covariate** box put all of your covariates (e.g. fear of stats time1: fost1).
5. Click on the **Model** button. Make sure **Full Factorial** is ticked. Click on **Continue**.
6. Click on the **Options** button. Tick **Descriptive statistics**, **Estimates of effect size** and **Homogeneity tests**. Click on **Continue**.
7. Click on the **EM Means** button. Click on your two independent variables (group, sex) and move them into the **Display Means for** box.
8. Click on the extra interaction term (e.g. group*sex). Move this into the box. This will provide you with the mean scores on your dependent variable split for each group and adjusted for the influence of the covariate. Click on **Continue**.

9. Click on the **Plots** button.
   - Highlight your first independent variable (e.g. group) and move this into the **Horizontal** box. This variable will appear across the bottom of your graph.
   - Click on your second independent variable (e.g. sex) and move this into the **Separate Lines** box. This variable will be represented by different lines for each group.
   - Click on **Add**.
10. Click on **Continue** and then **OK** (or on **Paste** to save to **Syntax Editor**).

The syntax generated from this procedure is:

```
UNIANOVA fost2 BY group sex WITH fost1
 /METHOD=SSTYPE(3)
 /INTERCEPT=INCLUDE
 /PLOT=PROFILE(group*sex) TYPE=LINE ERRORBAR=NO
 MEANREFERENCE=NO YAXIS=AUTO
 /EMMEANS=TABLES(group) WITH(fost1=MEAN)
 /EMMEANS=TABLES(sex) WITH(fost1=MEAN)
 /EMMEANS=TABLES(group*sex) WITH(fost1=MEAN)
 /PRINT ETASQ DESCRIPTIVE HOMOGENEITY
 /CRITERIA=ALPHA(.05)
 /DESIGN=fost1 group sex group*sex.
```

The output generated from this procedure is shown below.

Descriptive Statistics

Dependent Variable: fost2 fear of stats time2

group type of class	sex	Mean	Std. Deviation	N
1 maths skills	1 male	37.25	5.497	8
	2 female	38.14	3.436	7
	Total	37.67	4.515	15
2 confidence building	1 male	40.57	5.563	7
	2 female	34.50	4.781	8
	Total	37.33	5.876	15
Total	1 male	38.80	5.596	15
	2 female	36.20	4.475	15
	Total	37.50	5.151	30

Levene's Test of Equality of Error Variances[a]

Dependent Variable: fost2 fear of stats time2

F	df1	df2	Sig.
2.204	3	26	.112

Tests the null hypothesis that the error variance of the dependent variable is equal across groups.

a. Design: Intercept + fost1 + group + sex + group * sex

Tests of Between-Subjects Effects

Dependent Variable: fost2 fear of stats time2

Source	Type III Sum of Squares	df	Mean Square	F	Sig.	Partial Eta Squared
Corrected Model	686.728[a]	4	171.682	51.854	.000	.892
Intercept	4.137	1	4.137	1.250	.274	.048
fost1	545.299	1	545.299	164.698	.000	.868
group	4.739	1	4.739	1.431	.243	.054
sex	4.202	1	4.202	1.269	.271	.048
group * sex	104.966	1	104.966	31.703	.000	.559
Error	82.772	25	3.311			
Total	42957.000	30				
Corrected Total	769.500	29				

a. R Squared = .892 (Adjusted R Squared = .875)

Estimated Marginal Means

1. type of class

Dependent Variable: fost2 fear of stats time2

type of class	Mean	Std. Error	95% Confidence Interval Lower Bound	Upper Bound
1 maths skills	38.024[a]	.472	37.053	38.996
2 confidence building	37.226[a]	.471	36.255	38.197

a. Covariates appearing in the model are evaluated at the following values: fost1 fear of stats time1 = 40.17.

2. sex

Dependent Variable: fost2 fear of stats time2

sex	Mean	Std. Error	95% Confidence Interval	
			Lower Bound	Upper Bound
1 male	38.009[a]	.476	37.028	38.989
2 female	37.242[a]	.476	36.261	38.222

a. Covariates appearing in the model are evaluated at the following values: fost1 fear of stats time1 = 40.17.

3. type of class * sex

Dependent Variable: fost2 fear of stats time2

type of class	sex	Mean	Std. Error	95% Confidence Interval	
				Lower Bound	Upper Bound
1 maths skills	1 male	36.532[a]	.646	35.202	37.862
	2 female	39.517[a]	.696	38.083	40.950
2 confidence building	1 male	39.485[a]	.693	38.058	40.912
	2 female	34.966[a]	.644	33.639	36.294

a. Covariates appearing in the model are evaluated at the following values: fost1 fear of stats time1 = 40.17.

Profile Plots

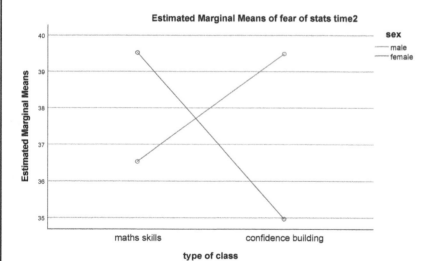

Interpretation of output from two-way ANCOVA

There are a set of steps in interpreting the output from a two-way ANCOVA.

> In the table labelled **Descriptive Statistics**, check that the details are correct (e.g. number in each group, mean scores).

> The details in the **Levene's Test of Equality of Error Variances** table allow you to check that you have not violated the assumption of equality of variance. You want the **Sig.** value to be *greater* than .05. If this value is smaller than .05 (and therefore significant), this means that your variances are not equal and that you have violated the assumption. In this case we have not violated the assumption, because our **Sig.** value is .11, which is much larger than our cut-off of .05.

> The main ANCOVA results are presented in the next table, labelled **Test of Between-Subjects Effects**. We want to know whether there is a significant main effect for any of our independent variables (group or sex) and whether the interaction between these two variables is significant. Of most interest is the interaction, so we check this first. If the interaction is significant the two main effects are not important, because the effect of one independent variable is dependent on the level of the other independent variable. Find the row corresponding to the interaction effect (group * sex in this case). Read across to the column labelled **Sig.** If the value in this column is *less* than .05 (or an alternative alpha level you have set), the interaction is significant. In this case our **Sig.** (or probability) value is .000 (read this as less than .0005), which is less than .05; therefore, our result is significant. This significant interaction effect suggests that males and females respond differently to the two programs. The main effects for **group** and for **sex** are not statistically significant (group: $p = .24$, sex: $p = .27$). We cannot say that one intervention is better than the other, because we must consider whether we are referring to males or females. We cannot say that males benefit more than females, because we must consider which intervention was involved.

> You should also consider the effect size, as indicated by the corresponding partial eta squared value (see the introduction to Part Five for a description of what an effect size is). The value in this case is .56 (a large effect size according to Cohen's [1988] guidelines). This value also indicates how much of the variance in the dependent variable is explained by the independent variable. Convert the partial eta squared value to a percentage by multiplying by 100 (shift the decimal point two places to the right). In this example, we are able to explain 56 per cent of the variance.

> The other piece of information that we can gain from Tests of Between-Subject Effects concerns the influence of our covariate. Find the row in the table that corresponds to the covariate (e.g. fost1: Fear of Statistics at Time 1). Read across to the **Sig.** level. This indicates whether there is a significant relationship between the covariate and the dependent variable, while controlling for the independent

variable (group). In the row corresponding to fost1 (our covariate), you can see that the **Sig.** value is .000 (which actually means less than .0005). This is less than .05; therefore, our covariate was significant. In fact, it explained 87 per cent of the variance in the dependent variable (partial eta squared of .87 multiplied by 100).

➤ The final set of tables in the ANCOVA output (**Estimated Marginal Means**) provides us with the adjusted means on the dependent variable for each of our groups, split according to each of our independent variables separately and then jointly. Adjusted refers to the fact that the effect of the covariate has been statistically removed. Given that the interaction effect was significant, our main focus is the final table, labelled **type of class * sex**.

➤ As an optional extra, I requested a plot of the adjusted means for the Fear of Statistics Test, split for males and females and for the two interventions. It is clear to see from this plot that there is an interaction between the two independent variables. For males, Fear of Statistics Test scores were lowest (the aim of the program) in the maths skills intervention. For females, however, the lowest scores occurred in the confidence-building intervention. This clearly suggests that males and females respond differently to the programs and that in designing interventions you must consider the gender of the participants.

Caution: Don't let yourself get too excited when you get a significant result. You must keep in mind what the analysis was all about. For example, the results here do not indicate that all males benefited from the maths skills program or that all females preferred the confidence-building approach. Remember, we are comparing the mean score for each group. By summarising across each group, we inevitably lose some information about individuals. In evaluating programs, you may wish to consider additional analyses to explore how many people benefited versus how many people got worse.

While one hopes that interventions designed to help people do no harm, sometimes this does happen. In the field of stress management, there have been studies that have shown an unexpected increase in participants' levels of anxiety after some types of treatments (e.g. relaxation training). The goal in this situation is to find out why this is the case for some people and to identify what the additional moderator variables are.

Presenting the results from two-way ANCOVA
The results of this analysis could be presented as follows:

A 2 × 2 between-groups analysis of covariance was conducted to assess the effectiveness of two programs in reducing fear of statistics for male and female participants. The independent variables were the type of program (maths skills, confidence building) and gender. The dependent variable was scores on the Fear of Statistics Test (FOST), administered following completion of the intervention programs (Time 2). Scores on the

FOST administered prior to the commencement of the programs (Time 1) were used as a covariate to control for individual differences.

Preliminary checks were conducted to ensure that there was no violation of the assumptions of normality, linearity, homogeneity of variances, homogeneity of regression slopes or reliable measurement of the covariate. After adjusting for FOST scores at Time 1, there was a significant interaction effect. $F_{(1, 25)} = 31.7$, $p < .001$, with a large effect size (partial eta squared = .56). Neither of the main effects was statistically significant, program: $F_{(1, 25)} = 1.43$, $p = .24$; gender: $F_{(1, 25)} = 1.27$, $p = .27$. These results suggest that males and females respond differently to the two types of interventions. Males showed a more substantial decrease in fear of statistics after participation in the maths skills program. Females, on the other hand, appeared to benefit more from the confidence-building program.

In presenting the results of this analysis, you would also provide a table of means for each of the groups. If the same scale is used to measure the dependent variable (Time 2) and the covariate (Time 1), you would include the means at Time 1 and Time 2. You can get these easily by running **Descriptives** (see Chapter 6). If a different scale is used to measure the covariate, you would provide the unadjusted mean (and standard deviation) and the adjusted mean (and standard error) for the two groups. The unadjusted mean is available from the **Descriptive Statistics** table. The adjusted mean (controlling for the covariate) is provided in the **Estimated Marginal Means** tables. It is also a good idea to include the number of cases in each of your groups.

For more details and examples of how to present the results of analysis of covariance you might want to consult Chapter 11 of Nicol and Pexman (2010b).

Appendix:
Details of data files

This appendix contains information about the data files that are included on the website accompanying this book (for details see p. ix). The files are provided for you to follow along with the procedures and exercises described in the different chapters of this book. To use the data files, you need to go to the website and download each file to your hard drive or to a memory stick by following the instructions on screen. You should start IBM SPSS Statistics and open the data file you wish to use. These files can only be opened in this program. For each file, information is provided in this Appendix concerning the variables and associated coding instructions.

SURVEY.SAV DATAFILE

Description
The **survey.sav** file is a real data file, condensed from a study that was conducted by my Graduate Diploma in Educational Psychology students. The study was designed to explore the factors that impact on respondents' psychological adjustment and well-being. The survey contained a variety of validated scales measuring constructs that the extensive literature on stress and coping suggests influence people's experience of stress. The scales measured self-esteem, optimism, perceptions of control, perceived stress, positive and negative affect and life satisfaction. A scale was also included that measured people's tendency to present themselves in a favourable or socially desirable manner. The survey was distributed to members of the general public in Melbourne, Australia and surrounding districts. The final sample size was 439, consisting of 42 per cent males and 58 per cent females, with ages ranging from 18 to 82 years (mean = 37.4).

Details of scales
The scales are listed in the order in which they appear in the survey.

Scale	Reference
Life Orientation Test (Optimism) (6 items)	Scheier, M.F. & Carver, C.S. (1985). Optimism, coping and health: An assessment and implications of generalized outcome expectancies. Health Psychology, 4, 219–247. Scheier, M.F., Carver, C.S. & Bridges, M.W. (1994). Distinguishing optimism from neuroticism (and trait anxiety, self-mastery and self-esteem): A re-evaluation of the Life Orientation Test. Journal of Personality and Social Psychology, 67(6), 1063–1078.
Mastery Scale (7 items)	Pearlin, L. & Schooler, C. (1978). The structure of coping. Journal of Health and Social Behavior, 19, 2–21.
Positive and Negative Affect Scale (20 items)	Watson, D., Clark, L.A. & Tellegen, A. (1988). Development and validation of brief measures of positive and negative affect: The PANAS scales. Journal of Personality and Social Psychology, 54, 1063–1070.
Satisfaction with Life Scale (5 items)	Diener, E., Emmons, R.A., Larson, R.J. & Griffin, S. (1985). The Satisfaction with Life Scale. Journal of Personality Assessment, 49, 71–76.
Perceived Stress Scale (10 items)	Cohen, S., Kamarck, T. & Mermelstein, R. (1983). A global measure of perceived stress. Journal of Health and Social Behavior, 24, 385–396.
Self-esteem Scale (10 items)	Rosenberg, M. (1965). Society and the adolescent self image. Princeton, NJ: Princeton University Press.
Social Desirability Scale (10 items)	Crowne, D.P. & Marlowe, P. (1960). A new scale of social desirability independent of psychopathology. Journal of Consulting Psychology, 24, 349–354. Strahan, R. & Gerbasi, K. (1972). Short, homogeneous version of the Marlowe-Crowne Social Desirability Scale. Journal of Clinical Psychology, 28, 191–193.
Perceived Control of Internal States Scale (PCOISS) (18 items)	Pallant, J. (2000). Development and validation of a scale to measure perceived control of internal states. Journal of Personality Assessment, 75(2), 308–337.

Codebook

SPSS variable name	Full variable name	Coding instructions	Measurement level
id	Identification number	Identification number	scale
sex	Sex	1=males, 2=females	nominal
age	Age	in years	scale
marital	Marital status	1=single, 2=steady relationship, 3=living with a partner, 4=married for the first time, 5=remarried, 6=separated, 7=divorced, 8=widowed	nominal
child	Children	1=yes, 2=no	nominal
educ	Highest level of education	1=primary, 2=some secondary, 3=completed high school, 4=some additional training, 5=completed undergraduate, 6=completed postgraduate	ordinal
source	Major source of stress	1=work, 2=spouse or partner, 3=relationships, 4=children, 5=family, 6=health/illness, 7=life in general, 8=finances, 9=time (lack of, too much to do)	nominal
smoke	Do you smoke?	1=yes, 2=no	nominal
smokenum	Cigarettes smoked per week	Number of cigarettes smoked per week	scale
op1 to op6	Optimism Scale	1=strongly disagree, 5=strongly agree	scale
mast1 to mast7	Mastery Scale	1=strongly disagree, 4=strongly agree	scale
pn1 to pn20	PANAS	1=very slightly, 5=extremely	scale
lifsat1 to lifsat5	Life Satisfaction Scale	1 =strongly disagree, 7=strongly agree	scale
pss1 to pss10	Perceived Stress Scale	1=never, 5=very often	scale
sest1 to sest10	Self-Esteem Scale	1=strongly disagree, 4=strongly agree	scale
m1 to m10	Marlowe-Crowne Social Desirability Scale	1=true, 2=false	nominal
pc1 to pc18	Perceived Control of Internal States Scale (PCOISS)	1=strongly disagree, 5=strongly agree	scale

Total scale scores

Full variable name	SPSS variable name	Coding instructions
Total Optimism	toptim	reverse items op2, op4, op6 add all scores op1 to op6 range 6 to 30
Total Mastery	tmast	reverse items mast1, mast3, mast4, mast6, mast7 add all items mast1 to mast7 range 7 to 28
Total Positive Affect	tposaff	add items pn1, pn4, pn6, pn7, pn9, pn12, pn13, pn15, pn17, pn18 range 10 to 50
Total Negative Affect	tnegaff	add items pn2, pn3, pn5, pn8, pn10, pn11, pn14, pn16, pn19, pn20 range 10 to 50
Total Life Satisfaction	tlifesat	add all items lifsat1 to lifsat5 range 5 to 35
Total Perceived Stress	tpstress	reverse items pss4, pss5, pss7, pss8 add all items pss1 to pss10 range 10 to 50
Total Self-esteem	tslfest	reverse items sest3, sest5, sest7, sest9, sest10 add all items sest1 to sest10 range 10 to 40
Total Social Desirability	tmarlow	reverse items m6 to m10 (recode true=1, false=0) add all items m1 to m10 range 0 to 10
Total Perceived Control of Internal States	tpcoiss	reverse items pc1, pc2, pc7, pc11, pc15, pc16 add all items pc1 to pc18 range 18 to 90
New Education categories	educ2	recoded the categories primary, some secondary into one group because of small numbers in each group: 1=primary/some secondary; 2=completed secondary; 3=some additional training; 4=completed undergraduate university; 5=completed postgraduate university
Age group 3 categories	agegp3	1=18–29yrs, 2=30–44yrs, 3=45+yrs
Age group 5 categories	agegp5	1=18–24yrs, 2=25–32yrs, 3=33–40yrs, 4=41–49yrs, 5=50+yrs

Questionnaire

I have included a portion of the questionnaire used to collect the data included in the **survey.sav** file. The complete questionnaire is available from the website associated with this book. Go to **www.mheducation.co.uk/SPSS** and select the link to the 7th edition.

If you do use this questionnaire or any of the scales included in it for a research project or thesis make sure you acknowledge the authors of each of the scales appropriately (see references earlier in this Appendix).

On the pages that follow, I have included a portion of the actual questionnaire used to collect the data included in the survey.sav file. The first page includes the demographic questions, followed by the Life Orientation Test (6 items) and the Positive and Negative Affect Scale (20 items). Full reference details of each scale included in the questionnaire are provided in the list given earlier in this appendix.

Sample questionnaire

1. Sex: ❐ male
                 ❐ female   *(please tick whichever applies)*

2. Age: _____ (in years)

3. What is your marital status? *(please tick whichever applies)*
   - ❐ 1. single
   - ❐ 2. in a steady relationship
   - ❐ 3. living with partner
   - ❐ 4. married for first time
   - ❐ 5. remarried
   - ❐ 6. separated
   - ❐ 7. divorced
   - ❐ 8. widowed

4. Do you have any children currently living at home with you?
   - ❐ yes
   - ❐ no   *(please tick)*

5. What is the **highest** level of education that you have completed? *(please tick the **highest level** you have completed)*
   - ❐ 1. primary school
   - ❐ 2. some secondary school
   - ❐ 3. completed secondary school
   - ❐ 4. some additional training (apprenticeship, trade courses)
   - ❐ 5. undergraduate university
   - ❐ 6. postgraduate university

ERROR.SAV DATAFILE

The data in the **error.sav** file has been modified from the **survey.sav** file to incorporate some deliberate errors to be identified using the procedures covered in Chapter 5. For information on the variables and so on, see details on **survey.sav**.

EXPERIM.SAV DATAFILE

Description

The **experim.sav** file is a manufactured (fake) data set that was created to provide suitable data for the demonstration of statistical techniques such as t-test for repeated measures and one-way ANOVA for repeated measures. This data set refers to a fictitious study that involves testing the impact of two different types of interventions in helping students cope with their anxiety concerning a forthcoming statistics course. Students were divided into two equal groups and asked to complete a set of scales (Time 1). These included a Fear of Statistics Test, Confidence in Coping with Statistics Scale and Depression Scale. One group (Group 1) was given several sessions designed to improve mathematical skills; the second group (Group 2) was subjected to a program designed to build confidence in the ability to cope with statistics. After the program (Time 2), they were asked to complete the same scales that they completed before the program. They were also followed up 3 months later (Time 3). Their performance on a statistics exam was also measured.

Codebook

Full variable name	SPSS variable name	SPSS variable label	Coding instructions
Identification number	id	id	Identification number
Sex	sex	sex	1=males, 2=females
Age	age	age	in years
Group	group	type of class	1=maths skills, 2=confidence building
Fear of Statistics test at Time 1	fost1	fear of stats time1	Fear of Statistics test score at Time 1. Possible range 20–60. High scores indicate high levels of fear.
Confidence in Coping with Statistics Time 1	conf1	confidence time1	Confidence in Coping with Statistics Test score at Time 1. Possible range 10–40. High scores indicate higher levels of confidence.
Depression Time 1	depress1	depression time1	Depression scale scores at Time 1. Possible range 20–60. High scores indicate high levels of depression.
Fear of Statistics test at Time 2	fost2	fear of stats time2	Fear of Statistics test score at Time 2. Possible range 20–60. High scores indicate high levels of fear.
Confidence in Coping with Statistics Time 2	confid2	confidence time2	Confidence in Coping with Statistics test score at Time 2. Possible range 10–40. High scores indicate high levels of confidence.
Depression Time 2	depress2	depression time2	Depression scale scores at Time 2. Possible range 20–60. High scores indicate high levels of depression.
Fear of Statistics test at Time 3	fost3	fear of stats time3	Fear of Statistics test score at Time 3. Possible range 20–60. High scores indicate high levels of fear.
Confidence in Coping with Statistics Time 3	conf3	confidence time3	Confidence in Coping with Statistics test score at Time 3. Possible range 10–40. High scores indicate high levels of confidence.
Depression Time 3	depress3	depression time3	Depression scale scores at Time 3. Possible range 20–60. High scores indicate high levels of depression.
Statistics Exam scores	exam	exam	Scores on the statistics exam. Possible range 0–100.

MANIPULATE.SAV DATAFILE

Description

The **manipulate.sav** file was included to provide the opportunity to practise some of the procedures discussed in Chapter 8, Manipulating the Data. It contains data that have been entered as text (males, females) and need to be converted to numeric data for statistical analyses. It also contains dates which can be manipulated using the **Date and Time Wizard**. The data have been extracted from a hospital database containing patients' admission and discharge details and converted to IBM SPSS Statistics.

Codebook

Description of variable	SPSS Variable name	Type of variable	Coding instructions
Identification number	ID	Numeric	Patient ID
Sex	Sex	String	M=male, F=female
Funding code	FundCode	String	HOS, TAC, DVA, PRIV, WCA, OTH
Arrival date to hospital	ArrivalDate	Date	Date format dd-mmm-yyyy
Arrival in emergency	EmergDate	Date	Date format dd-mmm-yyyy
Discharge date from hospital	DischargeDate	Date	Date format dd-mmm-yyyy
Length of stay in hospital	LengthofStay	Numeric	Calculated using Date Wizard from ArrivalDate and DischargeDate

DEPRESS.SAV DATAFILE

Description

The data provided in **depress.sav** are a small part of a real data file that includes each woman's scores on the Edinburgh Postnatal Depression Scale (EPDS; Cox, Holden & Sagovsky 1987) and the Depression Scale (DASS-Dep) of the Depression, Anxiety and Stress Scales (DASS; Lovibond & Lovibond 1995). This file has been included to allow the demonstration of some specific techniques in Chapter 16 (see Kappa Measure of Agreement).

In Chapter 16 I show how to test the level of agreement between two measures of depression in a sample of postnatal women using the **depress.sav** file. The aim was to see if the women identified with depression on the EPDS were also classified as depressed on the DASS-Dep. Scores were categorized according to the recommended cut-points for each scale. This resulted in two variables (DASSdepgp2, EPDSgp2) with scores of 0 (not depressed) and 1 (depressed).

SLEEP.SAV DATAFILE

Description

The **sleep.sav** datafile is real data extracted from a study conducted to explore the prevalence and impact of sleep problems on various aspects of people's lives. Staff from a university in Melbourne, Australia, were invited to complete a questionnaire containing questions about their sleep behaviour (e.g. hours slept per night), sleep problems (e.g. difficulty getting to sleep) and the impact that these problems have on aspects of their lives (work, driving, relationships). The sample consisted of 271 respondents (55% female, 45% male) ranging in age from 18 to 84 years (mean = 44 years).

Codebook

Description of variable	SPSS variable name	Coding instructions
Identification number	id	
Sex	sex	0=female, 1=male
Age	age	
Marital status	marital	1=single, 2=married/defacto, 3=divorced, 4=widowed
Highest education level achieved	edlevel	1=primary, 2=secondary, 3=trade, 4=undergrad, 5=postgrad
Weight (kg)	weight	
Height (cm)	height	
Rate general health	healthrate	1=very poor, 10=very good
Rate physical fitness	fitrate	1=very poor, 10=very good
Rate current weight	weightrate	1=very underweight, 10=very overweight
Do you smoke?	smoke	1=yes, 2=no
How many cigarettes per day?	smokenum	Cigs per day
How many alcoholic drinks per day?	alcohol	Drinks per day
How many caffeine drinks per day?	caffeine	Drinks per day
Hours sleep/weekends	hourwend	Hrs sleep on average each weekend night
How many hours sleep needed?	hourneed	Hrs of sleep needed to not feel sleepy

Description of variable	SPSS variable name	Coding instructions
Trouble falling asleep	trubslep	1=yes, 2=no
Trouble staying asleep?	trubstay	1=yes, 2=no
Wake up during night?	wakenite	1=yes, 2=no
Work night shift?	niteshft	1=yes, 2=no
Light sleeper?	liteslp	1=yes, 2=no
Wake up feeling refreshed weekdays?	refreshd	1=yes, 2=no
Satisfaction with amount of sleep?	satsleep	1=very dissatisfied, 10=to a great extent
Rate quality of sleep	qualslp	1=very poor, 2=poor, 3=fair, 4=good, 5=very good, 6=excellent
Rating of stress over last month	stressmonth	1=not at all, 10=extremely
Medication to help you sleep?	medhelp	1=yes, 2=no
Do you have a problem with your sleep?	problem	1=yes, 2=no
Rate impact of sleep problem on mood	impact1	1=not at all, 10=to a great extent
Rate impact of sleep problem on energy level	impact2	1=not at all, 10=to a great extent
Rate impact of sleep problem on concentration	impact3	1=not at all, 10=to a great extent
Rate impact of sleep problem on memory	impact4	1=not at all, 10=to a great extent
Rate impact of sleep problem on life satisfaction	impact5	1=not at all, 10=to a great extent
Rate impact of sleep problem on overall wellbeing	impact6	1=not at all, 10=to a great extent
Rate impact of sleep problem on relationships	impact7	1=not at all, 10=to a great extent
Stop breathing during your sleep?	stopb	1=yes, 2=no
Restless sleeper?	restlss	1=yes, 2=no

Description of variable	SPSS variable name	Coding instructions
Ever fallen asleep while driving?	drivevsleep	1=yes, 2=no
Drvsleep recoded 0 1	drvsleeprec	0=no 1=yes
Epworth Sleepiness Scale	ess	Total ESS score (range from 0=low to 24=high daytime sleepiness)
HADS Anxiety	anxiety	Total HADS Anxiety score (range from 0=no anxiety to 21=severe anxiety)
HADS Depression	depress	Total HADS Depression score (range from 0=no depression to 21=severe depression)
Rate level of fatigue over last week	fatigue	1=not at all, 10=to a great extent
Rate level of lethargy over last week	lethargy	1=not at all, 10=to a great extent
Rate how tired over last week	tired	1=not at all, 10=to a great extent
Rate how sleepy over last week	sleepy	1=not at all, 10=to a great extent
Rate lack of energy over the last week	energy	1=not at all, 10=to a great extent
Quality of sleep recoded into 4 groups	qualsleeprec	1=very poor, poor; 2=fair; 3=good; 4=very good, excellent
Number of cigs per day recoded into 3 groups	cigsgp3	1=<=5, 2=6–15, 3=16+
Age recoded into 3 groups	agegp3	1=<=37yrs, 2=38–50yrs, 3=51+yrs
Sleepiness and Associated Sensations Scale	totsas	Total Sleepiness and Associated Sensations Scale score (5=low, 50=extreme sleepiness)
Problem with sleep recoded into 0/1	probsleeprec	0=no, 1=yes
Hours sleep/weeknight	hourwnit	Hrs sleep on average each weeknight
Problem getting to sleep recoded	getsleeprec	0=no, 1=yes
Problem staying asleep recoded	staysleeprec	0=no, 1=yes

STAFFSURVEY.SAV DATAFILE

Description

The **staffsurvey.sav** file is a real data file condensed from a study conducted to assess the satisfaction levels of staff from an educational institution with branches across Australia. Staff were asked to complete a short, anonymous questionnaire containing questions about their opinions of various aspects of the organisation and the treatment they have received as employees.

Staff survey (selected items)

Age: ☐ under 20
☐ 21 to 30
☐ 31 to 40
☐ 41 to 50
☐ over 50 yrs

Length of service with the organisation (in years): _____

Employment status: ☐ permanent ☐ casual

For each of the aspects shown below please rate your level of agreement and importance using the following scales:

Agreement: 1=not at all, 2=slight extent, 3=moderate extent, 4=great extent, 5=very great extent

Importance: 1=not at all, 2=slightly important, 3=moderately important, 4=very important, 5=extremely important

	Agreement	Importance
1. Is it clear what is expected of you at work?	1 2 3 4 5	1 2 3 4 5
2. At work have you been provided with all the equipment and materials required for you to do your work efficiently?	1 2 3 4 5	1 2 3 4 5
3. Does the organisation keep you up to date with information concerning development and changes?	1 2 3 4 5	1 2 3 4 5
4. Do you receive recognition from the organisation for doing good work?	1 2 3 4 5	1 2 3 4 5
5. Does your manager or supervisor encourage your development at work?	1 2 3 4 5	1 2 3 4 5
6. Do you feel that your opinions seem to count to the organisation?	1 2 3 4 5	1 2 3 4 5
7. Does the organisation make you feel that your job is important?	1 2 3 4 5	1 2 3 4 5
8. Do you feel that your fellow workers are committed to doing good quality work?	1 2 3 4 5	1 2 3 4 5
9. Has your performance been assessed or discussed in the last six months?	1 2 3 4 5	1 2 3 4 5
10. Have you had the opportunity over the last year at work to improve your skills?	1 2 3 4 5	1 2 3 4 5

Would you recommend this organisation as a good place to work?   ☐ Yes   ☐ No

Recommended reading

Some of the articles, books and websites I have found most useful for my own research and my teaching are listed here. Keep an eye out for new editions of these titles; many are updated every few years. I have classified these according to different headings, but many cover a variety of topics. The titles that I highly recommend have an asterisk next to them.

Research design

Bowling, A. (2014). *Research methods in health: Investigating health and health services* (4th edn). Buckingham: Open University Press.

*Boyce, J. (2004). *Marketing research* (2nd edn). Boston: McGraw-Hill.

*Cone, J. & Foster, S. (2006). *Dissertations and theses from start to finish* (2nd edn). Washington: American Psychological Association.

Goodwin, C.J. (2012). *Research in psychology: Methods and design* (7th edn). New York: John Wiley.

Harris, P. (2008). *Designing and reporting experiments in psychology* (3rd edn). Maidenhead: Open University Press.

Polgar, S. & Thomas, S.A. (2013). *Introduction to research in the health sciences* (6th edn). Edinburgh: Churchill Livingstone.

Stangor, C. (2006). *Research methods for the behavioral sciences* (3rd edn). Belmont, CA: Wadsworth.

*Tharenou, P., Donohue, R. & Cooper, B. (2007). *Management research methods*. Cambridge: Cambridge University Press.

Questionnaire design

*De Vaus, D.A. (2014). *Surveys in social research* (6th edn). Sydney: Allen & Unwin.

Scale selection and construction

Dawis, R.V. (1987). Scale construction. *Journal of Counseling Psychology, 34,* 481–489.

*DeVellis, R.F. (2012). *Scale development: Theory and applications* (3rd edn). Thousand Oaks, CA: Sage.

Gable, R.K. & Wolf, M.B. (1993). *Instrument development in the affective domain:*

Measuring attitudes and values in corporate and school settings. Boston: Kluwer Academic.

Kline, P. (1986). *A handbook of test construction.* New York: Methuen.

Kline, T.J.B. (2005). *Psychological testing: A practical approach to design and evaluation.* Thousand Oaks, CA: Sage.

Robinson, J.P., Shaver, P.R. & Wrightsman, L.S. (eds) (1991). *Measures of personality and social psychological attitudes.* Hillsdale, NJ: Academic Press.

*Streiner, D.L. & Norman, G.R. (2015). *Health measurement scales: A practical guide to their development and use* (5th edn). Oxford: Oxford University Press.

Basic statistics

*Barton, B. & Peat, J. (2014). *Medical statistics: A guide to data analysis and critical appraisal.* Oxford: John Wiley and Sons.

Cooper, D.R. & Schindler, P.S. (2013). *Business research methods* (12th edn). Boston: McGraw-Hill.

*Gravetter, F.J. & Wallnau, L.B. (2012). *Statistics for the behavioral sciences* (9th edn). Belmont, CA: Wadsworth.

Motulsky, H. (2013). *Intuitive biostatistics: A nonmathematical guide to statistical thinking* (3rd edn). New York: Oxford University Press.

Norman, G.R. & Streiner, D.L. (2014). *Biostatistics: The bare essentials* (4th edn). Shelton, CT: People's Medical Publishing House—USA.

Pagano, R.R. (2013). *Understanding statistics in the behavioral sciences* (10th edn). Belmont, CA: Wadsworth.

*Peat, J. (2001). *Health science research: A handbook of quantitative methods.* Sydney: Allen & Unwin.

Advanced statistics

Hair, J.F., Black, W.C., Babin, B.J., Anderson, R.E. & Tatham, R.L. (2009). *Multivariate data analysis* (7th edn). Upper Saddle River, NJ: Pearson Education.

Pett, M.A., Lackey, N.R. & Sullivan, J.J. (2003). *Making sense of factor analysis: The use of factor analysis for instrument development in health care research.* Thousand Oaks, CA: Sage.

Stevens, J. (2009). *Applied multivariate statistics for the social sciences* (5th edn). Mahwah, NJ: Lawrence Erlbaum.

*Tabachnick, B.G. & Fidell, L.S. (2013). *Using multivariate statistics* (6th edn). Boston: Pearson Education.

Preparing your report

American Psychological Association (2019). *Publication manual of the American Psychological Association* (7th edn). Washington: American Psychological Association.

Belcher, W.L. (2009). *Writing your journal article in 12 weeks: A guide to academic publishing success.* Thousand Oaks, CA: Sage.

McInerney, D.M. (2001). *Publishing your psychology research.* Sydney: Allen & Unwin.

Nicol, A.A.M. & Pexman, P.M. (2010a). *Displaying your findings: A practical guide for creating figures, posters, and presentations* (6th edn). Washington: American Psychological Association.

—— (2010b). *Presenting your findings: A practical guide to creating tables* (6th edn). Washington: American Psychological Association.

*Peacock, J. & Kerry, S. (2007). *Presenting medical statistics from proposal to publication: A step-by-step guide.* Oxford: Oxford University Press.

Useful websites

http://vassarstats.net

This is a link to the VassarStats website, which provides a range of tools for performing statistical computation. There is a companion online textbook that goes with this site available from http://vassarstats.net/textbook/

www.gpower.hhu.de/

From this site you can download G*Power, a very powerful program that allows you to conduct power analysis to determine the numbers of cases you need to obtain for your study. This issue of power is discussed in the introductory section to Part Five.

www.biostats.com.au/DAG_Stat

DAG_Stat provides a comprehensive range of statistics calculable from 2 × 2 tables that are useful in evaluating diagnostic tests and inter-rater agreement (this is discussed in Chapter 16 in the section on Kappa Measure of Agreement).

http://edpsychassociates.com/Watkins3.html

This site contains free downloads of a wide variety of statistics tools and calculators. It provides a parallel analysis program which is discussed in Chapter 15, Factor Analysis.

References

Aiken, L.S. & West, S.G. (1991). *Multiple regression: Testing and interpreting interactions.* Newbury Park, CA: Sage.

American Psychological Association (2019). *Publication manual of the American Psychological Association* (7th edn). Washington: American Psychological Association.

Antonakis, J. & Dietz, J. (2011). Looking for validity or testing it? The perils of stepwise regression, extreme-scores analysis, heteroscedasticity, and measurement error. *Personality and Individual Differences, 50*(3), 409–415.

Bartlett, M.S. (1954). A note on the multiplying factors for various chi square approximations. *Journal of the Royal Statistical Society, 16* (Series B), 296–298.

Berry, W.D. (1993). *Understanding regression assumptions.* Newbury Park, CA: Sage.

Bowling, A. (1997). *Research methods in health: Investigating health and health services.* Buckingham: Open University Press.

—— (2001). *Measuring disease* (2nd edn). Buckingham: Open University Press.

—— (2004). *Measuring health: A review of quality of life measurement scales.* Buckingham: Open University Press.

Boyce, J. (2003). *Market research in practice.* Boston: McGraw-Hill.

Briggs, S.R. & Cheek, J.M. (1986). The role of factor analysis in the development and evaluation of personality scales. *Journal of Personality, 54*, 106–148.

Catell, R.B. (1966). The scree test for number of factors. *Multivariate Behavioral Research, 1*, 245–276.

Choi, N., Fuqua, D.R. & Griffin, B.W. (2001). Exploratory analysis of the structure of scores from the multidimensional scales of perceived self efficacy. *Educational and Psychological Measurement, 61*, 475–489.

Cicchetti, D.V. & Feinstein, A.R. (1990). High agreement but low kappa: II. Resolving the paradoxes. *Journal of Clinical Epidemiology, 43*, 551–558.

Cohen, J. & Cohen, P. (1983). *Applied multiple regression/correlation analysis for the behavioral sciences* (2nd edn). New York: Erlbaum.

Cohen, J.W. (1988). *Statistical power analysis for the behavioral sciences* (2nd edn). Hillsdale, NJ: Lawrence Erlbaum Associates.

Cohen, S., Kamarck, T. & Mermelstein, R. (1983). A global measure of perceived stress. *Journal of Health and Social Behavior, 24*, 385–396.

Cone, J. & Foster, S. (2006). *Dissertations and theses from start to finish* (2nd edn). Washington: American Psychological Association.

Cooper, D.R. & Schindler, P.S. (2013). *Business research methods* (12th edn). Boston: McGraw-Hill.

Cox, J.L., Holden, J.M. & Sagovsky, R. (1987). Detection of postnatal depression: Development of the 10-item Edinburgh Postnatal Depression Scale. *British Journal of Psychiatry, 150,* 782–786.

Crowne, D.P. & Marlowe, D. (1960). A new scale of social desirability independent of psychopathology. *Journal of Consulting Psychology, 24,* 349–354.

Daniel, W. (1990). *Applied nonparametric statistics* (2nd edn). Boston: PWS-Kent.

Dawis, R.V. (1987). Scale construction. *Journal of Counseling Psychology, 34,* 481–489.

De Vaus, D.A. (2014). *Surveys in social research* (6th edn). Sydney: Allen & Unwin.

DeVellis, R.F. (2012). *Scale development: Theory and applications* (3rd edn). Thousand Oaks, CA: Sage.

Diener, E., Emmons, R.A., Larson, R.J. & Griffin, S. (1985). The Satisfaction with Life Scale. *Journal of Personality Assessment, 49,* 71–76.

Edwards, A.L. (1967). *Statistical methods* (2nd edn). New York: Holt.

Everitt, B.S. (1996). *Making sense of statistics in psychology: A second level course.* Oxford: Oxford University Press.

Feinstein, A.R. & Cicchetti, D.V. (1990). High agreement but low kappa: I. The problems of two paradoxes. *Journal of Clinical Epidemiology, 43,* 543–549.

Fox, J. (1991). *Regression diagnostics.* Newbury Park, CA: Sage.

Gable, R.K. & Wolf, M.B. (1993). *Instrument development in the affective domain: Measuring attitudes and values in corporate and school settings.* Boston: Kluwer Academic.

Glass, G.V., Peckham, P.D. & Sanders, J.R. (1972). Consequences of failure to meet the assumptions underlying the use of analysis of variance and covariance. *Review of Educational Research, 42,* 237–288.

Goodwin, C.J. (2007). *Research in psychology: Methods and design* (5th edn). New York: John Wiley.

Gorsuch, R.L. (1983). *Factor analysis.* Hillsdale, NJ: Erlbaum.

Gravetter, F.J. & Wallnau, L.B. (2004). *Statistics for the behavioral sciences* (6th edn). Belmont, CA: Wadsworth.

—— (2012) *Statistics for the behavioural sciences* (9th edn). Belmont, CA: Wadsworth.

Greene, J. & d'Oliveira, M. (1999). *Learning to use statistical tests in psychology* (2nd edn). Buckingham: Open University Press.

Hair, J.F., Black, W.C., Babin, B.J., Anderson, R.E. & Tatham, R.L. (2009). *Multivariate data analysis* (7th edn). Upper Saddle River, NJ: Pearson Education.

Harrell, F.E. Jr. (2001). *Regression modeling strategies.* New York: Springer.

Harris, R.J. (1994). *ANOVA: An analysis of variance primer.* Itasca, IL: Peacock.

Hayes, N. (2000). *Doing psychological research: Gathering and analysing data.* Buckingham: Open University Press.

Horn, J.L. (1965). A rationale and test for the number of factors in factor analysis. *Psychometrika, 30,* 179–185.

Hosmer, D.W. & Lemeshow, S. (2000). *Applied logistic regression.* New York: Wiley.

Hubbard, R. & Allen, S.J. (1987). An empirical comparison of alternative methods for principal component extraction. *Journal of Business Research, 15,* 173–190.

Kaiser, H. (1970). A second generation Little Jiffy. *Psychometrika, 35,* 401–415.

—— (1974). An index of factorial simplicity. *Psychometrika, 39,* 31–36.

Keppel, G. & Zedeck, S. (1989). *Data analysis for research designs: Analysis of variance and multiple regression/correlation approaches.* New York: Freeman.

—— (2004). *Design and analysis: A researcher's handbook* (4th edn). New York: Prentice Hall.

Kline, P. (1986). *A handbook of test construction.* New York: Methuen.

Kline, T.J.B. (2005). *Psychological testing: A practical approach to design and evaluation.* Thousand Oaks, CA: Sage.

Lovibond, S.H. & Lovibond, P.F. (1995). *Manual for the Depression Anxiety Stress Scales* (2nd edn). Sydney: Psychology Foundation of Australia.

McCall, R.B. (1990). *Fundamental statistics for behavioral sciences* (5th edn). Fort Worth: Harcourt Brace Jovanovich College Publishers.

Nicol, A.A.M. & Pexman, P.M. (2010a). *Displaying your findings: A practical guide for creating figures, posters, and presentations* (6th edn). Washington: American Psychological Association.

—— (2010b). *Presenting your findings: A practical guide to creating tables* (6th edn). Washington: American Psychological Association.

Norman, G.R. & Streiner, D.L. (2014). *Biostatistics: The bare essentials* (4th edn). Shelton, CT: People's Medical Publishing House—USA.

Nunnally, J.O. (1978). *Psychometric theory.* New York: McGraw-Hill.

Pagano, R.R. (1998). *Understanding statistics in the behavioral sciences* (5th edn). Pacific Grove, CA: Brooks/Cole.

Pallant, J. (2000). Development and validation of a scale to measure perceived control of internal states. *Journal of Personality Assessment, 75*(2), 308–337.

Pavot, W., Diener, E., Colvin, C.R. & Sandvik, E. (1991). Further validation of the Satisfaction with Life Scale: Evidence for the cross method convergence of well-being measures. *Journal of Personality Assessment, 57,* 149–161.

Pearlin, L. & Schooler, C. (1978). The structure of coping. *Journal of Health and Social Behavior, 19,* 2–21.

Peat, J. (2001). *Health science research: A handbook of quantitative methods.* Sydney: Allen & Unwin.

Pett, M.A., Lackey, N.R. & Sullivan, J.J. (2003). *Making sense of factor analysis: The use of factor analysis for instrument development in health care research.* Thousand Oaks, CA: Sage.

Raymondo, J.C. (1999). *Statistical analysis in the behavioral sciences.* Boston: McGraw-Hill College.

Robinson, J.P., Shaver, P.R. & Wrightsman, L.S. (eds). *Measures of personality and social psychological attitudes.* Hillsdale, NJ: Academic Press.

Rosenberg, M. (1965). *Society and the adolescent self-image.* Princeton, NJ: Princeton University Press.

Runyon, R.P., Coleman, K.A. & Pittenger, D.J. (2000). *Fundamentals of behavioral statistics* (9th edn). Boston: McGraw-Hill.

Scheier, M.F. & Carver, C.S. (1985). Optimism, coping and health: An assessment and implications of generalized outcome expectancies. *Health Psychology, 4,* 219–247.

Scheier, M.F., Carver, C.S. & Bridges, M.W. (1994). Distinguishing optimism from neuroticism (and trait anxiety, self-mastery, and self-esteem): A re-evaluation of the Life Orientation Test. *Journal of Personality and Social Psychology, 67*(6), 1063–1078.

Siegel, S. & Castellan, N. (1988). *Nonparametric statistics for the behavioral sciences* (2nd edn). New York: McGraw-Hill.

Smithson, M. (2000). *Statistics with confidence.* London: Sage.

Stangor, C. (2006). *Research methods for the behavioral sciences* (3rd edn). Boston: Houghton Mifflin.

Stevens, J. (1996). *Applied multivariate statistics for the social sciences* (3rd edn). Mahwah, NJ: Lawrence Erlbaum.

Stober, J. (1998). The Frost multidimensional perfectionism scale revisited: More perfect with four (instead of six) dimensions. *Personality and Individual Differences, 24,* 481–491.

Strahan, R. & Gerbasi, K. (1972). Short, homogeneous version of the Marlowe-Crowne Social Desirability Scale. *Journal of Clinical Psychology, 28,* 191–193.

Streiner, D.L. & Norman, G.R. (2015). *Health measurement scales: A practical guide to their development and use* (5th edn). Oxford: Oxford University Press.

Tabachnick, B.G. & Fidell, L.S. (2013). *Using multivariate statistics* (6th edn). Boston: Pearson Education.

Thompson, B. (1989). Why won't stepwise methods die? *Measurement and Evaluation in Counseling and Development, 21*(4), 146–148.

—— (1995). Stepwise regression and stepwise discriminant analysis need not apply here: A guidelines editorial. *Educational and Psychological Measurement, 55*(4), 525–534.

—— (2001). Significance, effect sizes, stepwise methods and other issues: Strong arguments move the field. *The Journal of Experimental Education, 70*(1), 80–93.

Thurstone, L.L. (1947). *Multiple factor analysis.* Chicago: University of Chicago Press.

Viera, A.J. & Garrett, J.M. (2005). Understanding interobserver agreement: the kappa statistic. *Family Medicine, 37,* 360–363.

Watkins, M.W. (2000). *Monte Carlo PCA for parallel analysis* [computer software]. State College, PA: Ed & Psych Associates.

Watson, D., Clark, L.A. & Tellegen, A. (1988). Development and validation of brief measures of positive and negative affect: The PANAS scales. *Journal of Personality and Social Psychology, 54,* 1063–1070.

Wright, R.E. (1995). Logistic regression. In L.G. Grimm & P.R. Yarnold (eds). *Reading and understanding multivariate statistics* (Chapter 7). Washington, DC: American Psychological Association.

Zwick, W.R. & Velicer, W.F. (1986). Comparison of five rules for determining the number of components to retain. *Psychological Bulletin, 99,* 432–442.

Index

Terms in bold indicate a specific SPSS procedure

variable type 32
Variable View 32
Varimax rotation 192, 206–207
Viewer window 17–19
Visual Binning 91–92

website xi
Wilcoxon Signed Rank Test 120, 124, 212, 222,
    240–243, 258
Wilks' Lambda 276, 278, 297, 312

Zero order correlation 135